Wilson H. Bain has taught at Glasgow High School, Moray House College of Education and The University of Edinburgh.

He can remember listening to wireless reports direct from the Melbourne Olympics, shortly after watching his first football match.

He now works as a volunteer for the RNIB and its Insight Radio station in Glasgow. In 2011 he was honoured as a 'Local hero' by the Scottish Parliament.

GOALD!
OLYMPIC FOOTBALL:
the road from 1900 to 2012

Wilson H. Bain

Copyright © 2013 Wilson H. Bain

The moral right of the author has been asserted.

Apart from any fair dealing for the purposes of research or private study, or criticism or review, as permitted under the Copyright, Designs and Patents Act 1988, this publication may only be reproduced, stored or transmitted, in any form or by any means, with the prior permission in writing of the publishers, or in the case of reprographic reproduction in accordance with the terms of licences issued by the Copyright Licensing Agency. Enquiries concerning reproduction outside those terms should be sent to the publishers.

Matador
9 Priory Business Park,
Wistow Road, Kibworth Beauchamp,
Leicestershire. LE8 0RX
Tel: (+44) 116 279 2299
Fax: (+44) 116 279 2277
Email: books@troubador.co.uk
Web: www.troubador.co.uk/matador

ISBN 9781 780884 196

British Library Cataloguing in Publication Data.
A catalogue record for this book is available from the British Library.

Typeset by Troubador Publishing Ltd, Leicester, UK

Matador is an imprint of Troubador Publishing Ltd

This book is for my brother
James David Bain
and remembers our parents
Jean Dysart Harvey Bain
and James Bain

'One thing I do ... I press on
toward the goal for the prize'

(St Paul's letter to the church at Philippi in Greece, chapter 3.
Revised Standard Version)

Contents

Foreword: by Bill Slater, Peter Buchanan and Millar Hay	ix
Acknowledgements	xi
1. Olympic football: 'the problem and the charm'	1
2. 1900: Under Paris skies	4
3. 1904: Meet me in St Louis	8
4. 1908: Welcome to White City	12
5. 1912: North by North East	18
6. 1920: A new dawn	27
7. 1924: The Uruguayan comet	37
8. 1928: Return of the comet	49
9. 1936: A tournament like no other	61
10. 1948: Matt Busby's Britain	71
11. 1952: The magnificent Magyars	84
12. 1956: Beneath the Southern Cross	99
13. 1960: All roads lead to Rome	109
14. 1964: Tokyo melody	130
15. 1968: South of the Border	149
16. 1972: Football in perspective	169
17. 1976: Maple leaf matches	198
18. 1980: Boycotting the Bear	218
19. 1984: California, here I come	241
20. 1988: The last Eastern victory	268
21. 1992: Gaudi weeks	300
22. 1996: Georgia on my mind	330
23. Women's football: towards a level playing field	369
24. 2000: Tropic of Capricorn	401
25. 2004: Back home to Greece	441
26. 2008: Blue and white tango	478
27. Paralympic tournaments, 1984-2008	514
28. 2012: London pride	520
29. Olympic footballers and lifelong memories	526
Bibliography, and a note on the 1906 tournament	530

Foreword

By Olympic footballers Bill Slater, Peter Buchanan, and Millar Hay.

'I was hugely impressed by the Hungarian team which won the (1952) competition, and I was not surprised when later Hungary defeated the full England team.

There are problems about the selection of a representative British football team, because of the separate governing bodies of football in England, Scotland, Wales and Northern Ireland. But I hope it will be possible for a well-prepared British team to compete in the 2012 Olympic Games.'

Bill Slater CBE OBE (Great Britain, 1952, and England)

'Earlier in my playing days with Queen's Park FC at Hampden Park in Glasgow, I had the honour of being selected to play for the Scottish Amateur football team in the Home Internationals, and in the Scottish side that won the European Amateur Championship in 1963.

To have achieved these honours, I felt, meant that I had reached the pinnacle of my amateur football career – I was on top of the world.

However, in 1964 I received notification from The Football Association in London that I had been selected to represent Great Britain, in the qualifying stages of the Olympic Games (later) held in Tokyo. No greater honour could have been bestowed upon me: I felt on a real high that I had been considered to be among the top amateur footballers throughout Great Britain.

It is a feeling of pride that will remain with me for the rest of my life.'

Peter Buchanan (Great Britain, 1964, and Scotland)

'I regularly travelled to London to train with the Olympic team. We trained morning and afternoon, and on several occasions I stayed on to play practice matches.

Those games were against top opposition and included a victory over a strong Chelsea team, a draw with Arsenal, and wins against Watford. These were essential for developing team plays and set-piece moves, and I relished the chance to play against quality opposition.

When we went to Spain in 1968 for the final qualifying match, we had a comprehensive programme of training sessions, rest periods, tactics meetings, before training in the ground at the same time we were due to play the following night.

In the match I received a hairline fracture, and played in the return two weeks later, thinking it was only bad bruising. My memories were of frustration at being only 1-0 down and seeing many good chances not taken. The game was played at London's White City with two massive clocks, one at each end. You could see time running out in the 0-0 draw.'

Millar Hay (Great Britain, 1968, and Scotland)

Acknowledgements

My warm thanks go to everyone who has encouraged me as I was writing this book.

Bill Slater, Peter Buchanan and Millar Hay contributed to the Foreword, and told me about their individual experience of Olympic football.

Hazel Martin typed the book, a span of 100,000 words and 112 years, with skill and good humour.

They and other friends believed in the project and ensured I did complete it. Thank you –

Hollie Miller, Robin Dunlop, Stevie Marshall, David and Margo Kidd, Sandra Murray, Maureen Smith, Peter Hill, Nina Lenton, Iain McGillivray, Pauline Brown, Irene Munro, Sheila Gemmell, Nimmo and Mattie Davidson, Grace McKinnon, Richard and Fiona Garwood, Tommy MacKay, Jim Mackie and the Ulph family, Andrew Reid, Anne Dunnett, Christine Graham, Christine Vickery, Ann MacPhail.

Staff at The British Olympic Library, University of East London; The National Library of Scotland, Edinburgh; The Mitchell Library, Glasgow; The University of Glasgow Library; and lending libraries throughout the West of Scotland.

Friends at Moray House College Staff Association; The University of Edinburgh; Newton Mearns Parish Church of Scotland and The Choir at the Cross; The RNIB's Transcription Centre and Insight Radio station, Glasgow.

All of you deserve gold medals.

1. Olympic football: 'The problem and the charm'

The last football team to qualify for London 2012 were Senegal, who defeated Oman 2-0 at the City of Coventry Stadium, before 11,000 spectators.

For Paul Kelso, Chief Olympics correspondent at 'The Daily Telegraph', that match encapsulated 'the problem and the charm of Olympic football' (24 April 2012). A small crowd, limited media coverage, few household names – there lies the 'problem'; the 'charm' comes with a genial atmosphere, and that bright aspiration to be part of the Olympic dream in your sport.

In his 'Autobiography' (2009), Sir Chris Hoy focussed on the problem. A keen footballer as a boy, he looked up to the Olympics as the pinnacle of any sport. Football's peak is the World Cup, and it should part company with the Olympians.

Such an argument, from the great British cyclist, must carry weight, but other views can be considered.

Many do associate the Games with athletics, swimming, and cycling, but it is less clear how the public regards minority sports and their various championships. Do their 'world' titles outrank 'Olympic'? Boxing – the last amateur Olympic sport – cannot outweigh an individual world title with a gold medal, but Dick McTaggart, Muhammad Ali, and many more have added lustre to the Olympiads.

Olympic tennis also raises a similar problem. Would Steffi Graf prize her grand slam titles and trophies more highly than a gold? The medal, for representing her country and available far less often, is distinct and distinctive.

Football retains a potency, a 'charm', for over 100 nations who enter the qualifying event for their continent, drawn by a compound of the world's most popular sport and Olympian prestige. Some nations' medal hopes may rest on football, notably Uruguay with their two golds, in 1924 and 1928.

Tradition is central to the Games, and football has played its part at every Olympics except 1896 and 1932. One of its supporters was Baron Pierre de Coubertin, founding father of the modern Olympics, who was so impressed by British team sports.

The most watched, and the biggest earner, of Olympic sports today is football. At the 2012 Games there are 2.5 million seats available for 56 matches. Although not every match or stadium will sell out, the likelihood is that up to 2 million spectators will experience these Games through football, outpacing the other sports.

Not only that, but football helps to solve a conundrum. The IOC (International Olympic Committee) always invites bids from cities, not countries, to host the Games. Yet a whole nation should embrace the Olympics and their significance. The 2012 torch relay began at Land's End on May 19 and traversed 8,000 miles over 70 days. Football also carries a metaphorical baton. For many years it has been the engine for extending the Games across a country.

This year Glasgow, Cardiff, Coventry, Newcastle, Manchester as well as London host football matches. In 2011, Sir Chris Hoy also recognised that this matters. In his foreword to the Bank of Scotland guide, 'Get involved in London 2012', he describes the Olympics' coming to Scotland with the torch relay, and football at Hampden Park. The article is entitled 'It's your London 2012'.

In May 2012 David Seaman, the England goalkeeper, recognised that Olympic football retains an appeal, but he would restore its 'amateur' status, before it became professional in 1984.

Others would welcome a journey back to the age of smaller, simpler Olympics, but there are difficulties in constructing the transport for this. Where would nations discover so many talented amateur players? More fundamentally, what is an amateur – and when was the last genuinely amateur tournament at the Games?

As long ago as 1924 there were problems in defining 'amateur'. Should players be paid for 'broken time', wages they lost when training or competing in matches? The four British home nations, supported by the Scandinavian F.A.s were adamant that such payments were not compatible with amateur status. Other countries took the opposite view.

More fundamental was the divide between 'State-sponsored amateurs', especially in Soviet countries, and Olympians from other nations. In football, that sponsorship tilted the advantage towards Eastern Europe between 1952 and 1984, when professionals could officially enter most Olympic sports.

Another intermittent problem is the tension between IOC and FIFA, which organises the football tournament for the Committee. Disagreement between the two contributed to football's absence from the 1932 Games, and more recently there have been uneasy compromises over the sport.

In 1984, professionals became eligible for the Olympic tournament unless they had played for European or South American teams in the World Cup. Then, in 1992, only players aged under 23 could take part – and four years later three squad members could be older. That is the present situation, unlike the unrestricted nature of most Olympic sports, where ability is the key to entry.

To recast Olympic football as an amateur event, however we define the term, or to restrict it even further, would close doors to many remarkable footballers from every continent.

Open the doors to past Olympiads, and we find players, teams, contests to remember and celebrate.

And the story begins 112 years ago, under Paris skies.

2. Paris, 1900

Under Paris Skies

The second Games included the first Olympic football matches. De Coubertin was determined to include the sport, one of those British inventions he admired, but few countries were interested, in the last year of the nineteenth century. Originally Switzerland and Germany intended to take part in this new football event, but then withdrew.

No national teams took part, nor did several outstanding clubs who were asked, such as Havre Athletic Club from France or Belgium's Racing Club de Bruxelles. Eventually three teams played just two matches.

Upton Park, an amateur club from London, represented Great Britain. By 1900 the Football authorities in England and Scotland had reluctantly accepted professionalism, and most leading players were paid wages to take part. Why Upton Park were chosen is unclear, although they were used to crossing the Channel to play friendly matches in Jersey and Guernsey, where a trophy still bears the London club's name.

In France, where there was still no football association to oversee the sport, the USFSA (Union des Societes Francaises des Sports Athletiques) invited Club Francais de Paris to take part. The club had finished second in the French League that year, and now represented France, with three guests from Racing Club de Paris. The team wore white jerseys with the five Olympic rings on this occasion.

Belgium's FA inserted newspaper adverts to find players, and those who accepted were mostly students, some from The University of Brussels, as well as a Dutch and an English player.

20 September	Great Britain	4-0	France		Velodrome Municipal de Vincennes
	Nicholas (2 goals)				
	Haslam				
	Zealley				
23 September	France	6-2	Belgium		Velodrome Municipal de Vincennes
	Lambert		Spannoghe		
	Peltier (2 goals)		Van Heuckelum		
	(3 goals' scorers unknown)				

The status of the first Olympic tournament remains disputed. The IOC retrospectively awarded medals to the three teams, although the players did not realise the significance of their involvement. Mallon regards it as a proper Olympic event – open to amateurs and with international teams – and Wallechinsky includes the 1900 medallists. However, no national football association now describes these as full international matches. The IFFHS calls them friendlies, and other writers call them 'exhibition' or 'demonstration' games, although no such concept existed in 1900.

The two matches took place at the cycle track in the Bois de Vincennes, part of a young Olympics which played second fiddle to the lavish Exposition Universelle in Central Paris.

This Exhibition was enormously successful, visited by 50 million people during six months, and was one of a sequence in Paris and other great cities ever since the Great Exhibition in Hyde Park in 1851. The sensations were not sporting contests – but wonders of the age – cinema, escalators, the newly built Grand and Petit Palais, and a Ferris Wheel similar to the Viennese version featured in the film 'The Third man'.

The British footballers were certainly the best of these three teams. Their finest defenders were Alfred Chalk, right half, and the right back Claude Buckenham, also a cricketer for Essex and England. The goalkeeper and secretary, J.H. Jones, asked William Gosling to join the Olympic side; at 31, he played for Chelmsford and had served in The Scots Guards.

Unlike later Great Britain sides, they turned out in their club colours, scarlet and black. Against France, Nicholas at centre forward had a successful first half with two goals, but had to leave the field after spraining his ankle. Long before the era of substitutes, the 10 men were still too strong for their opponents and won the match 4-0.

Their compatriot, Eric Thornton, turned out for Belgium, at a time when Olympic rules were still relaxed about multi-national sides. Modern audiences may regard such a small-scale event as haphazard and less than truly Olympian – or view it as a friendly, genuinely amateur occasion when football and other sports were still finding their feet, encouraged by the modern Olympics.

The medal winners

Gold: Great Britain (Upton Park FC)

Jones	Turner
Buckenham	Spackman
Gosling	Nicholas
Chalk	Zealley
Barridge	Haslam (captain)
Quash	

Silver: France (USFSA)

Huteau	Fraysse (captain)/Duparc Peltier
Bach	Garnier
Allamane	Lambert
Gaillard	Grandjean
Bloch	Canelle
Macaire	

Bronze: Belgium (including players from The Universities of Brussels, Liege, Louvain and other clubs)

Leboutte	Thornton	
Kelecom	Delbeuque	
De Melon	Span(n)oghe	
Renier	Van Heuckelum	
Pelgrims (captain)		Londot
Van Hoorden		Neets

Referees

M. Maignard (France): GB v France
J. Wood (GB): France v Belgium

3. St Louis, 1904

Meet me in St Louis

Three American cities have hosted the Olympics – St Louis, Los Angeles (twice), and Atlanta. Not one of them is in the North, despite the ambition of New York and Chicago, which was the original choice, in 1904.

However, the IOC and Chicago's organising committee disagreed over the plans for the Third Olympiad. President Theodore Roosevelt then negotiated for the Games to be held in another city celebrating its centenary with a World's Fair – St Louis.

When MGM made the nostalgic musical, 'Meet me in St Louis' (1944), the story referred to the 1904 World's Fair and even offered a two minute tour of what it looked like. There was not a word about the Olympics, which were once again dwarfed by the exhibition, as in Paris four years earlier.

Athletes from only eight countries travelled to compete in the range of events in St Louis, although four other nations were represented by men living in the US. Amateur competitors needed weeks off work, without pay, to cross the Atlantic and take the train to Missouri. Not surprisingly, the USA won 67 golds and no other country won more than four. Football matches were scheduled for 16th and 17th November, when most clubs were immersed in League fixtures. As in Paris, only three teams could be found to take part. Two local sides agreed, St Rose Parish and Christian Brothers' College, while a much stronger team, Galt FC travelled from Ontario.

Galt, 60 miles from Toronto, had won the Ontario Cup in 1901-3 and later the unofficial Canadian championship. Five other Canadian teams, such as the University of Ontario, entered but then could not afford the travel expenses and time – or did not expect to win the gold.

Galt did not lack experience or confidence as they headed South, with 50 supporters and red and white flags festooning The Grand Trunk Railway.

| 16 November | Canada (Galt FC) | 7-0 | USA (Christian Brothers College) (4-0) | Olympic Stadium, Washington University, St Louis (Francis Field) |

Hall (3 goals)

Steep

McDonald (2 goals)

Taylor

| 17 November | Canada (Galt FC) | 4-0 | USA (St Rose Parish) (0-0) | Olympic Stadium |

Taylor (2 goals)

Henderson

one o.g.

| 18 November | USA (Christian Brothers College) | 0-0 | USA (St Rose Parish) | Olympic Stadium |

| 23 November | USA (Christian Brothers College) | 2-0 | USA (St Rose Parish) | Olympic Stadium |

Scorers unknown

Football in St Louis is sometimes seen as even less Olympian than in 1900. The matches lasted only one hour, except for the goalless draw on 18 November (with extra time of another 30 minutes). Just two nations took part and the US teams were College sides.

A rare voice in praise of the tournament was that of Galt's Mayor, Mark Munday, who thanked the World's Fair Department of Physical Culture for its 'excellent management'. (In 1908 the Department's head, James E. Sullivan, was to become world famous).

As with 1900, much later the IOC awarded the teams full Olympic status, and the Canadians each received gold medals immediately after their second victory. Mayor Munday was delighted to present them.

Three Galt men were born in Britain – George Ducker, Albert Linton, and Alexander Hall, from Peterhead, who went on to win the Scottish Cup with Dundee in 1910, play for Newcastle United and manage Dunfermline Athletic. Hall's career shows the calibre of this Canadian team, in which he was not even regarded as the best player. That was 'Tom' Taylor, born in Galt, and the best right winger in the country, very fast and with an accurate shot, as his three goals in St Louis indicated.

The two U.S. sides could not match that quality, and their amateur league only included four teams. It was founded by Joseph Lydon, a welterweight boxer who won a bronze in St Louis as well as the silver with Christian Brothers College.

The CBC team included three brothers – John, Thomas and Charles January. St Rose Parish also chose brothers – George and Thomas Cook, the young inside left who unfortunately broke his leg in the match against Galt.

This is the only Olympic men's football tournament at which North American teams have won medals. However, in the women's event the picture is very different, and the USA have won 3 golds and one silver since 1996.

The medal winners

Gold: Canada (Galt F.C.)

Linton	Taylor	Christman
Ducker	Steep	
Gourlay (captain)		Hall
Lane	McDonald	
Johnston	Twaits	
Fraser	Henderson	

Silver: USA (Christian Brothers College)

Menges	Brittingham
Lydon	Cudmore
January (Thomas)	Bartliff
January (John)	Brockmeyer
January (Charles)	Lawlor
Ratican	

Bronze: USA (St Rose Parish)

Frost   Cosgrove
Cook (George)   O'Connell
Jameson (Henry)   Jameson (Claude)
Brady   Tate
Dooling   Cook (Thomas)
Dierkes   Johnson

Referee

P. McQueeney (USA): Canada v USA (both games)
Other referees: not known.

4. London, 1908

Welcome to White City

The 1908 Olympics featured the first football tournament which both FIFA and IOC recognise as official, and it can be regarded as the world's first international competition for the sport – 22 years before FIFA's inaugural World Cup.

Bohemia and Hungary intended to take part in the football matches but neither was regarded by FIFA as independent – they remained part of the Austro-Hungarian Empire for another decade – and withdrew. So six teams contested the medal places.

They were the hosts, Great Britain, Denmark, The Netherlands, Sweden and two teams representing France. Their matches took place in October, long after the track and field athletes had packed up and left in July.

As in 1900 and 1904, the Olympics took place beside a grand Exhibition, which marked the Entente Cordiale and was named the Franco-British. For the first time, an Exhibition's success and spectacular if temporary buildings called 'White City' encouraged big crowds to attend athletic events.

Track and field contests, swimming and football took place in the brand new permanent stadium which formed part of the Exhibition in Shepherd's Bush, North West London. Soon 'The Stadium' became known as White City.

Visitors and journalists, such as Arthur Conan Doyle – an enthusiast for the Olympics – took a keen interest in athletics, especially in one event, the marathon.

The single incident which galvanised worldwide attention and publicised those early Olympics, above all others, was Dorando Pietri's gallant failure to complete the marathon unaided.

The Italian baker, whose fragile health after 26 miles so concerned everyone, was helped over the line and awarded gold – but only for a few hours. (Then the next runner, America's Jim Hayes, was adjudged the winner.) Even so, his valiant effort and the special cup he received from Queen Alexandra became a big news story of 1908.

Crowds were much smaller for the football matches in October, but the atmosphere was friendly and sportsmanlike. There were none of the disagreements between the US athletics team (managed by James E.

Sullivan) and British officials, which marred the summer harmony and produced a whole series of American protests over the tug-of-war, the 400 metres and the marathon.

By the close of the Olympics in October, those specific disagreements had ebbed away. The celebratory dinner in London, for all the nations' leading officials, toasted the Games and praised their efficient organisation in a mood of camaraderie.

Round One

19 October　　　　　Denmark 9-0 France 'B' (4-0)　White City Stadium, London

N. Middelboe
(2 goals)

Wolfhagen
(4 goals)

Bohr (2 goals)

S. Nielsen

20 October　　　　　Great Britain 12-1 Sweden (7-0)　White City

Stapley 2　　Bergstrom 65
(first goal: 15")

Purnell 4

Woodward 2

Hawkes 2

Berry

Chapman

Semi-Finals

22 October			Great Britain 4-0 Netherlands (1-0) White City
			Stapley 37, 60, 64, 75

22 October			Denmark 17-1 France 'A' (6-1) White City
			S. Nielsen 3, 4, 6, 39, 46,	Sartorius 16
			    48, 52, 64, 66, 76
			Lindgren 18, 37
			Wolfhagen 60, 72, 82, 89
			N. Middelboe 68

Bronze Medal Match

23 October		Netherlands 2-0 Sweden (1-0) White City
			Reeman 6
			Snethlage 58

Final

24 October		Great Britain 2-0 Denmark (1-0) White City
			Chapman 20
			Woodward 46

Great Britain's players were England's amateur team. Scotland, Ireland and Wales decided not to send football teams, for reasons which are not clear – all four competed separately in the hockey event in London.

The opening match saw Denmark, who won the 1906 football honours, face France's 'B' team. There was a considerable gap between the Danish national team, led by the outstanding Middelboe brothers, and the two teams from France, selected from 41 enthusiasts just before the Olympics. Nils Middelboe represented his country in 1908, 1912 and 1920 Olympic tournaments and was called 'The Great Dane' when he played for Chelsea. Four goals of the nine in Denmark's stroll to victory came from Wolfhagen, two from Middelboe, two from Bohr – not the renowned physicist Niels but his brother Harald, and one from Sofus Nielsen, whose zenith arrived later.

Britain's first opponents were Sweden, soon to host the 1912 games.

The best feature of the match for Sweden was that only 2,000 people saw them lose 12-1; for British supporters paying 6d or more it was a bargain.

Henry Stapley, the home centre-forward, took 15 minutes to score, but afterwards it was a procession towards Oskar Bengtsson in the Swedish goal. Vivian Woodward, captaining Britain with his usual style and authority at inside-right, was outstanding.

Four forwards and two half-backs hit the net, Clyde Purnell taking the honours with four goals. Even Sweden's consolation goal went in off centre-half Frederick Chapman.

The British press were hard to please, blaming poor Swedish clearances rather than praising the torrent of goals.

Sweden's right-winger Almkvist hit the bar right at the start but later his colleagues tended to shoot from a distance instead of passing to better placed forwards. The British team were faster and switched positions unpredictably.

In their semi-final, Britain found The Netherlands much more difficult opponents. They won 4-0, but only because of three goals in the last half-hour. Once again, Stapley put his side ahead, near the interval, and ended with all four goals. His ability to run straight at goal and shrug off defenders' tackles led to two of those goals and he headed the fourth from Hardman's left-wing cross.

Of the 6,000 spectators, only a thousand stayed on to watch Denmark play France 'A'. The Danes, who had already defeated France's 'B' team 9-0, now produced a record scoreline never likely to be equalled at the Olympics, winning 17-1.

Sofus Nielsen alone, at the heart of Denmark's forward line, hit ten goals, including a hat-trick in the opening six minutes. The 13th goal came from his captain and left-half Nils Middelboe. France's early reply by Sartorius, making it 3-1, was a rare excursion anywhere near the Danish keeper Drescher. Any suggestion that Denmark might ease up was put aside – they scored their 17th goal in the last minute.

Britain and Denmark therefore reached the Final, but before that the bronze medal place was to be decided by a four-team contest. France 'A' and 'B' were due to play each other, but after losing 26 goals, one can hardly blame them for withdrawing.

The Netherlands took third place by overcoming Sweden 2-0, a highly creditable performance from the Swedes who played well despite losing an early goal.

On 24 October at 3.30 pm (the kick-off delayed to allow the lacrosse Final to end), Britain and Denmark took the field at the White City stadium before a crowd of 8,000.

After an even episode of play, Chapman gave Britain the lead by moving out of defence and snapping up a chance when Drescher, in goal, dropped the ball. Unlike other teams, however, Denmark were not overawed by the Olympic atmosphere. They had scored an enormous number of goals on this pitch and their success in 1906 was a matter of pride.

The Middelboe brothers, Christian and Nils, marked dangerous forwards such as Stapley, Purnell and Woodward out of the game for long spells. Horace Bailey, Britain's keeper, found the muddy ball hard to handle. The Danes made chances but this time failed to convert them, and it was Woodward who turned the match, soon after half-time. Escaping his marker, he hit a shot hard and true to make the score 2-0.

The world's finest football nations had produced a match of high quality and 100% commitment, and the two teams received their medals that October evening from The Lord Mayor of London.

Although only six teams took part, the 1908 tournament showed that football deserved to play an important role in the modern Olympics. As more countries founded football associations, the sport's potential to create interest and draw crowds to the Games could only increase.

There is a unique personal link between these first London Games and the second in 1948. Britain's gold medallist Harold Hardman, their left-winger, went on to become a director of Manchester United. He was a member of the Board when the club chose Matt Busby as their manager in 1945. So successful was he in that post that three years later the British Olympic Association asked Sir Matt to manage Great Britain's footballers in London.

The Medal Winners

Gold: Great Britain

Bailey	Berry
Corbett	Woodward
Smith	Stapley
Hunt	Purnell
Chapman (captain)	Hardman
Hawkes	

Silver: Denmark

Drescher	O. Nielsen
Von Buchwald	Lindgren
Hansen	S. Nielsen
Bohr	Wolfhagen

C. Middelboe (captain) Rasmussen
N. Middelboe Andersen
Gandil

Bronze: Netherlands

Beevwkes Weicker
Heijting E. Snethlage
Otten Reeman
Sol J. Snethlage
de Korver (co-captain) Thomee
Mundt (co-captain) Kops
Kok

Goal Scorers

S. Nielsen (Denmark): 11
Wolfhagen (Denmark): 8
Stapley (Great Britain): 6.

Referees

(All from Great Britain)
J. T. Ibbotson: Denmark v France 'B'; Great Britain v Sweden
J. T. Howcroft: Great Britain v Netherlands
T. P. Campbell: Denmark v France 'A'
J. H. Pearson: Netherlands v Sweden
J. Lewis: Great Britain v Denmark
T. Kyle: Denmark v France 'B'

5. Stockholm, 1912

North by North East

Sweden's organisation of the fifth Olympics built on the success and improved organisation of 1908. In Stockholm there was no Fair or Exhibition to overshadow the Games, which had to stand on their own two feet.

At one time, football was not certain to feature in 1912, since the Swedish Olympic committee debated whether the sport worldwide was significant enough. Once again, the IOC, led by de Coubertin, argued that there should be a football tournament – and won the day.

This was a more complex event than in London, with twice the number of entrants and two tournaments staged. Eleven nations took part after France, Belgium and Bohemia withdrew. Great Britain, as in 1908, were represented by English players after Scotland, Ireland and Wales decided not to enter, although those four countries were allowed to send a team by the IOC.

All the matches were held in the Stockholm area, at three recently built stadia. Temperatures in June and July were unusually high, and the powerful heat played a part in some high-scoring games. The organisers helpfully provided water on the touchlines – in buckets rather than bottles, and even sitting down on the scorching ground was no relief for the players.

Round One

29 June   Netherlands 4-3 Sweden (2-1)   Olympic Stadium Stockholm
           (after extra time)
       Bouvy 28, 52   Svensson 3, 80
       Vos 43, 91   E. Borjesson
                            (p) 62

29 June   Austria 5-1 Germany (0-1) Idrottsplats, Rasunda
       Studnicka 58   Jager 35
       Neubauer 62
       Merz 75, 81
       Cimera 89

29 June   Finland 3-2 Italy (2-2)   Sportplats, Traneberg
           (after extra time)
           Ohman 2   Bontadini 10
           E. Soinio 40   Sardi 25
           Wiberg 105

Round One

The home team opened the event against The Netherlands, before a crowd of 14,000, who were disappointed to watch Sweden lose a close match by the odd goal in seven.

After an outstanding start in their new Olympic Stadium, when Svensson scored in three minutes, Sweden let the Dutch back into the game. Their left-wing partnership Bouvy and Vos put them into a 2-1 lead at half-time.

Although Sweden soon went two goals behind, they responded to their supporters' cheers and equalised through the centre-forward Borjesson and inside-right Svensson. Into extra time, when The Netherlands came fastest out of the blocks and scored immediately to take the match.

Two other preliminary games, held in smaller stadia on the capital's outskirts, produced fine performances in those energy-sapping conditions.

Germany's captain Jager gave them the lead over their neighbours Austria and they held on for nearly an hour. Once Studnicka equalised, however, the Austrians ran away with the match, their left-sided forwards and left half scoring another four in the 5-1 victory.

Finland, one of four Scandinavian teams competing, had recently lost 7-1 to a Swedish reserve side, and seemed to have little chance against Italy. But the result was a surprise. They scored in just two minutes, came back from being 2-1 down to level the match, and won the day half way through extra-time. Yet the most significant figure in the stadium was the referee, Hugo Meisl, who later fashioned the Austrian 'wonder team' of the next two decades, along with England's Jimmy Hogan.

Quarter-Finals

30 June	Finland 2-1 Russia (1-0)		Traneberg
	Wiberg 30 Butusov 72		
	Ohman 80		
30 June	Great Britain 7-0 Hungary (3-0)		Rasunda
	Walden 21, 23, 49, 55, 85		
	Woodward 45, 53		
30 June	Denmark 7-0 Norway (3-0)		Rasunda
	A. Olsen 4, 70, 88		
	Wolfhagen 25		
	N. Middelboe 37		
	S. Nielsen 60, 85		
30 June	Netherlands 3-1 Austria (3-1)		Rasunda
	Bouvy 8 A. Muller 41		
	ten Cate 12		
	Vos 30		

Quarter-Finals

All four quarter-finals were played the next day, three of them in Rasunda. Austria again proved to be slow starters, and against the Dutch they could not overturn a lead as they had against Germany. The Netherlands effectively won in the first half hour, with their reliable forwards Bouvy, Vos and centre-forward ten Cate all finding the net. Muller's goal did not spark a revival.

Finland continued their excellent form, the 2-1 defeat of Russia based on goals from Wiberg and Ohman, both scorers against Italy. The crowd was only 200, surprisingly small for a match between countries whose rivalry extended beyond sport. Their defeat meant that Russia were eligible to play in the Consolation Tournament, which proved to be quite another story.

The biggest attendance of this round, 12,000, turned up to watch Great Britain play their first match, against Hungary. The British players had limited training to an hour each day to conserve their energy. Their key forward was Harold Walden, who finished the tournament as top scorer. Here he hit either five or six goals (sources disagree) in the 7-0 win. Certainly he scored both goals in the first half and was one of several players to be hurt. Indeed Hanney could not continue after the interval, Britain reorganised their defence and Ivan Sharpe was the lone forward on the left side of their attack. Hungary were a skilful team but their forwards were nervous and did not take chances they made. Their form did improve in the Consolation event, however, and they went on to win it.

Denmark had shown their power in 1906 and 1908, and here they outplayed Norway. Olsen, at centre-forward, collected a hat-trick after his goal in four minutes, Nils Middelboe – formidable centre-half – also scored, while Sofus Nielsen added two more in the 7-0 win.

Semi-Finals

2 July   Denmark 4-1 Netherlands (3-0)   Olympic Stadium
                Jorgensen 7   H. Hansen o.g. 85
            A. Olsen 14, 87
             P. Nielsen 37

2 July   Great Britain 4-0 Finland (2-0)   Olympic Stadium
               Walden 1, 7, 75
            (and his fourth goal
              was scored after
                75 minutes)

Bronze Medal match

4 July   Netherlands 9-0 Finland (4-0)   Rasunda
            van der Sluis 24, 57
              de Groot 28, 86
           Vos 29, 43, 46, 74, 78

Semi-Finals

Denmark and Great Britain, as in London, were the strongest teams and they proved it in the semi-finals.

Both matches were held in the Olympic Stadium, and Britain defeated the giant-killers Finland 4-0. It is clear that they were two up in the first six or seven minutes, and that Walden scored at least twice in the game.

Mallon states that the first minute goal was scored into his own net by the Finnish right-back Holopainen, but Reyes and Menary award it to Walden. The late, fourth goal is credited to either Walden or his captain Woodward.

Heavy rain affected this match, and Woodward's team held the ball rather than building on their very early lead. Knight also missed a penalty, possibly because the British team thought the award was unjust. As rain abated, Finland played better but could not break through the well organised British defence, and in the final 15 minutes Britain doubled their score.

Denmark's victory over The Netherlands was equally convincing. Jorgensen came into the Danish side at centre-half, allowing Middelboe to move to right-back and scoring in only seven minutes. P. Nielsen, another new player in the event, hit the third goal and even Hansen's own goal did not turn the match around, Olsen scoring twice for Denmark.

The Bronze medal contest was one match too many for the Finns, who lost comprehensively to The Netherlands, after containing the Dutch forwards for 24 minutes. The prolific inside-left Vos added five to his personal account as his team collected another Bronze after their medals in 1908.

Final

4 July   Great Britain   4-2   Denmark (4-1)   Olympic Stadium
         Walden 10   A. Olsen 27, 81
         Hoare 22, 41
         Berry 43

The Final

Denmark v Great Britain was a re-run, on neutral ground, of the London Games Final

Arthur Berry's ankle had healed sufficiently for him to return at outside-right, replacing Wright, his appropriately named colleague who had played against Finland.

The contest was end-to-end entertainment before a crowd as large as the Sweden v Netherlands opening match attendance. Walden quickly found the net in ten minutes, Gordon Hoare doubled the lead, but Anton Olsen swiftly reduced it to 2-1.

Then came an important incident, when Charles von Buchwald broke his arm after 40 minutes and was taken off the field. Immediately, Britain added two goals – Hoare headed in and Berry scored with a fine solo effort.

In the second half, Denmark's ten men dominated the match and attacked for long periods – Olsen's second goal was poor recompense. Late in the day, as the Danes tired, Woodward had clear opportunities to score but Hansen saved Denmark time and again.

Consolation Tournament

Round One

1 July   Germany 16-0 Russia (8-0)   Rasunda

Fuchs 2, 9, 21, 28, 34, 46, 51, 55, 65, 69

Forderer 6, 27, 53, 66

Burger 30

Oberle 58

1 July   Italy 1-0 Sweden (1-0)   Rasunda

Bontadini 15

1 July   Austria 1-0 Norway (1-0)   Traneberg

Grundwald 2

Bye - Hungary

Semi-Finals

3 July　　　　　　Hungary　3-1　Germany (2-0)　Rasunda

　　　Schlosser 3, 39, 82　　　Forderer 56

3 July　　　　　　　Austria　5-1　Italy (2-0)　　Traneberg

　　　　　A. Muller 30　　　　Berardo 81

　　　Grundwald 40, 89

　　　　　　Hussak 49

　　　　　Studnicka 65

Consolation Final

5 July　　　　　　Hungary　3-0　Austria (1-0)　Rasunda

　　　　　Schlosser 32

　　　　　　Pataki 60

　　　　　　Bodnar 76

The first Consolation Tournament in Olympic football history offered the seven teams losing in Round One or the Quarter-finals a second chance of a medal. The Swedish FA awarded silver medals as first prize, taken by Hungary, and bronze medals for the runners-up, Austria. Both nations had bright futures in international football, Austria between the two World Wars, Hungary in the 1950's and 1960's.

The most extraordinary match finished Germany 16, Russia 0, with Gottfried Fuchs, the German centre-forward, scoring ten between the second minute and the 69th; there were no more goals in the last 20 minutes. After losing to Finland the day before, Russia had made several changes, and the fortunate defenders were those who did not play in the second match. Fuchs's tally equalled Sofus Nielsen's for Denmark against France 'A' four years earlier.

Although attendances varied, the size of crowds enabled the Swedish FA to use a healthy profit and take over what had been a privately run League competition in their country.

Overall, there was a general sense of satisfaction with the Stockholm tournament – well run, plenty of goals, improving standards of play, matches contested in an atmosphere of good sportsmanship.

The Medal Winners

Gold. Great Britain (who also won the challenge trophy donated by the FA)

Brebner	Berry	Stamper
Burn	Woodward (Captain)	Wright
Knight	Walden	
McWhirter	Hoare	
Littlewort	Sharpe	
Dines	Hanney	

Silver. Denmark

S. Hansen	O. Nielsen	P. Nielsen	
N. Middelboe (captain)		Thufason	Lykke
H. Hansen	A. Olsen	Petersen	
Buchwald	S. Nielsen	Christoffersen	
Jorgensen	Wolfagen		
Berth			

Bronze. Netherlands

Gobel	Kolff	Bouman
Wijnveldt	de Groot	Fortgens
Feith	van der Sluis	ten Cate
de Wolf	Vos	de Korver
Lotsy (captain)		Bouvy
Boutmy		

Goalscorers (Main tournament)

Walden (Great Britain): 10 (or 11) (sources vary on the number of goals)
Vos (Netherlands): 8
A. Olsen (Denmark): 7

Referees

G. W. Simmons (Great Britain) — Netherlands v Sweden
H. J. Willing (Netherlands) — Austria v Germany
H. Meisl (Austria) — Italy v Finland
D. Philip (Great Britian) — Netherlands v Austria
R. Gelbord (Sweden) — Denmark v Norway
Great Britain v Finland (Semi-Final)
P. Sjoblom (Sweden) — Finland v Russia
Netherlands v Finland (Bronze medal)
C. J. Groothoff (Netherlands) — Great Britain v Hungary
Great Britain v Denmark (Final)
E. Herezog (Hungary) — Denmark v Netherlands (Semi-Final)

Consolation Tournament Referees

J. Groothoff (Netherlands) — Germany v Russia
Hungary v Germany
H. J. Willing (Netherlands) — Italy v Sweden
Austria v Italy
Hungary v Austria
P. Sjoblom (Sweden) — Austria v Norway

6. Antwerp, 1920

A New Dawn

The 1920 Olympics came eight years after Stockholm's, momentous years darkened by the first global war. Olympism was set aside for the duration, and with it the Berlin Games set for 1916.

But even during the conflicts on land and sea – and now in the air – de Coubertin and the IOC looked to post-war Olympics. The 'clock' of four-year Olympiads does not stop, and 1920 was therefore the VIIth.

In 1914 three cities wanted to host the 1920 Games – Budapest, Amsterdam and Antwerp. By the Armistice in November 1918, Hungary's capital was no longer considered. The nations seen as aggressors, Germany, Austria, Hungary, Bulgaria and Turkey, would not even be allowed to send athletes in 1920.

Amsterdam stepped aside to support the valiant people of Antwerp, which had suffered so much and now should be the host city. In 1928 the Dutch city had its own Olympics.

There were also preliminary bids from across the Atlantic – Havana, Cleveland, Philadelphia, and Atlanta were the ambitious candidates, but all quickly withdrew their bids.

So Antwerp was the IOC's choice in 1919, but the war had understandably depleted its citizens' enthusiasm for such a demanding enterprise. The Belgian Prime Minister and local leaders had to intercede to rekindle the dream of holding the Olympics.

The scale of the Antwerp Games was the largest yet, with more nations and competitors than ever, and 154 events, compared with the London Olympics' peak of 109. De Coubertin opposed barring the five enemy nations from taking part, but he had to accept the situation for the time being.

In 1920, some events were held in cities other than the host's, such as Brussels and Ghent.

In 1908 there had been sailing contests on England's South coast and in Glasgow, but the 1920 dispersal was more extensive.

The football tournament was contested by fourteen nations, after Switzerland's late withdrawal for financial reasons. Had they been allowed to compete, Austria, Hungary and Germany would almost certainly have wanted to take part.

The sport was now being played across the world, and, although no

South American team came to Belgium, there was one from Africa – Egypt. New nations had been created at the Treaty of Versailles, and one way to assert their pride was to form national football teams.

The 1920 Olympics saw a genuinely international football event, with crowds of ten, twenty and forty thousand dwarfing those of 1908 and 1912, and showing the importance of football to the post-war Games and their supporters.

In the main tournament, there was a straightforward knockout system from Round One to the Final. Complexities only arose in deciding the silver and bronze medal winners, especially after the most controversial Final in Olympic history.

Round One

28 August	Czechoslovakia	7-0	Yugoslavia (3-0)	Stade Royal Antwerp FC, Antwerp
	Vanik 20, 46, 79 (p)			
	Janda 34, 50, 75			
	Sedlacek 43			
28 August	Spain	1-0	Denmark (0-0)	Stade d'Union, St Gilloise, Brussels
	Arabolaza 54			
28 August	Italy	2-1	Egypt (1-1)	Stade de AA, La Gantoise, Ghent
	Baloncieri 25		Z. Osman 30	
	Brezzi 57			
28 August	Norway	3-1	Great Britain (1-1)	Olympic (Beerschot) Stadium, Antwerp
	Gundersen 13, 51		Nicholas 25	
	Wilhelms 63			
28 August	Netherlands	3-0	Luxembourg (1-0)	Stade d'Union, Brussels
	J. Bulder 30			
	Groosjohan 47, 85			

28 August   Sweden 9-0 Greece (6-0)   Olympic Stadium,
                                            Antwerp
            Olsson 4, 79
            Karlsson 15, 20,
                21, 51, 85
            Wicksell 25
            Dahl 31

Byes – Belgium
       France (who were drawn to play Switzerland, but the Swiss withdrew).

Round One

The first tournament for eight years – and what momentous years they had been – got underway with a match between two new nations. Czechoslovakia and Yugoslavia had been within two Empires that ended in 1918 – respectively the Austro-Hungarian and the Ottoman.

The Czechs won a unique tournament for servicemen on the Allied side, within The Inter-Allied Games of 1919, and were a highly talented team. Against Yugoslavia, they were never under pressure once Jan Vanik scored in 20 minutes. The inside-left collected a hat-trick, while Janda, the other inside forward, also added three and Sedlacek yet another. Theirs was the highest scoring side in the 1920 Olympics, with 15 goals.

Spain, new to the event, surprised Denmark, still featuring the Great Dane, Nils Middelboe, at right back. The single goal, early in the second half, was scored by Arabolaza, and it ended the fine Danish record of reaching every Final since 1906.

Italy found Africa's only representative, Egypt, a hard team to overcome, but Brezzi won the tie in 57 minutes after goals by Baloncieri for Italy and Osman for Egypt, in the evenly contested first half.

The Netherlands, bronze medallists in 1908 and 1912, played their neighbours Luxembourg and won 3-0 without being entirely convincing. The prolific Groosjohan scored two goals after the interval, early and late, to make the difference, when Jaap Bulder's goal on the half hour might not have sufficed.

Sweden had the easiest victory of the whole event. They played Greece, back after the unfortunate final of 1906. The Swedish team of 1908 had lost comprehensively to Britain and then, as hosts in 1912, improved but still disappointed their supporters.

Here they did not delay. In four minutes Albert Olsson put them ahead, Herbert Karlsson raced to a hat-trick within 6 minutes and added two more later on. Their team were six ahead at half-time and eventually stopped at nine.

Only the host country, Belgium, were officially given a bye in the First Round when the draw was made. However, France did not have to play Switzerland, who decided not to take part 'for financial reasons' in this tournament. They did take part in 1924, when they enjoyed their best ever Olympic football results.

But the big story on the evening of 28 August 1920 was that the reigning champions, Great Britain, lost to Norway.

Britain's original choice of captain, Max Woosnam, was an all-round sportsman, who opted to play tennis in these Olympics and won a gold and silver in the men's and mixed doubles.

His role was taken by Arthur Knight, a gold medallist in 1912, but the British team found it difficult to contain the younger Norwegian side. Norway won the toss and had wind and sun at their backs when Einar Gundersen took his chance in 13 minutes, benefiting from fine inter-passing between Andersen and Wilhelms.

Back came Britain, and Frederick Nicholas equalised within 12 minutes. However, injuries hampered his colleagues Herbert Prince and Richard Sloley, and even against the wind Norway's forwards and their right-half Adolph Wold kept attacking. Gundersen hit his second after Per Holm, the outside-left, made the opportunity. Just on the hour, Holm again passed shrewdly to Wilhelms who made it 3-1.

Writing in 1948, Sir Stanley Rous, then Secretary of the F.A. in England, described the defeat as a check to Great Britain's supremacy. The war had affected so many facets of people's lives, and outstanding players had been lost. Amateur footballers had to find jobs after four years in the services, and had less time for sport than before 1914.

He also spoke with appreciation of the immense improvement in other countries' footballing standards, often led by British coaches and former players working with clubs and national teams.

Quarter-Finals

29 August   Netherlands 5-4 Sweden (2-3)   Olympic Stadium
(after extra time)
Groosjohan 10, 57   Karlsson 16, 32
J. Bulder 44, 88 (p)   Olsson 20
de Natris 115   Dahl 72

29 August   France 3-1 Italy (2-1)   Olympic Stadium
Bard 10, 54   Brezzi 33 (p)
Boyer 14

29 August   Czechoslovakia 4-0 Norway (2-0)   Stade d'Union, Brussels
Vanik 8
Janda 17, 66, 77

29 August   Belgium 3-1 Spain (1-0)   Olympic Stadium
Coppee 11, 52, 55   Arrate 62 (p)

Quarter-Finals

The quarter-finals were played the day after Round One, and included the best match of the tournament, a nine-goal feast between The Netherlands and Sweden.

    The Dutch team took the lead in ten minutes, but were rocked back on their heels when Karlsson and Olsson continued their excellent form and put Sweden 3-1 ahead in barely 30 minutes.

    Jaap Bulder got one back just on half-time, and Groosjohan took his second chance, to level the match before an hour had passed. 3-3. Dahl, the Swedish inside-left, made it 4-3, and it stayed like that until The Netherlands were offered a penalty lifeline seconds before the whistle. Bulder stepped up to score. Four goals apiece, extra time, and de Natris hit the winner after almost two hours. 5-4, and one of the most exciting of matches was over.

France, with no match the day before, had an excellent start against Italy, with two goals in 14 minutes from their inside forwards, and did not allow Brezzi's penalty to knock them out of their stride. They won 3-1, a very different result from the two huge defeats by Denmark in 1908.

The Czechs were too strong for Norway's giant-killers and Vanik quickly put them ahead. Janda then collected his second hat-trick in 24 hours to ensure his team progressed.

To support the home team, Belgians flocked to Antwerp's Olympic Stadium and saw Spain lose to three goals from Robert Coppee at inside-right, their new hero, with a penalty from Arrate the Spanish response. Both teams soon took home medals in the tournament.

Semi-Finals

31 August	Czechoslovakia 4-1	France (1-0)	Olympic Stadium
	Mazal 18, 75, 87	Boyer 79	
	Steiner 70		

31 August	Belgium 3-0	Netherlands (0-0)	Olympic Stadium
	Larnoe 46		
	Van Hege 55		
	Bragard 85		

Semi-Finals

Now Czechoslovakia extended their fine run of high-scoring victories by defeating France 4-1. Otaker Mazal put them ahead in 18 minutes, but the revitalized French still had a chance until the last twenty minutes, when Steiner doubled the lead and Mazal ended with a hat-trick, the Czechs' third so far. Boyer's late goal was France's last contribution to the tournament.

Anticipation was high for the derby match between Belgium and The Netherlands, and this was a tight contest until Larnoe put the host nation ahead immediately after the interval. Ten minutes later, Van Hege scored their second, and Bragard ensured the win near the end. The British referee, John Lewis, had a much more taxing job in the Final.

Final

2 September   Belgium 2-0 Czechoslovakia (2-0) Olympic Stadium

Coppee 6 (p)
Larnoe 30

(The match ended after 40 minutes, and was awarded to Belgium; Czechoslovakia's team were disqualified, after they refused to play on, and they were not included in the subsidiary tournament to decide second and third places).

Final

For Belgium v Czechoslovakia the Olympic (Beerschot) Stadium in Antwerp was full and the official attendance, 40,000, was an understatement. Stewards and soldiers found it hard to stop the crowd from encroaching on the pitch, something quite new in Olympic football.

What spectators came to see was a match between two teams new to the event; the hosts with a proud and partisan support in their own stadium, the Czechs the best team so far with three clear victories and 15 goals behind them.

What spectators actually saw was barely 40 minutes of football, dominated by two Belgian goals and the Czechs' disagreement with John Lewis's decisions as referee.

Robert Coppee scored from a penalty in only six minutes, and Larnoe made it 2-0 in 30 minutes. The referee then sent off the Czech left-back, Karel Steiner, for a foul on Coppee. Czechoslovakia's players first made their views clear to Mr Lewis and then left the field en masse, refusing to continue the match.

The tournament organisers decided to disqualify the Czech side and award the gold medals to Belgium. They later turned down Czech protests about the upholding of both Belgian goals by the referee, and the conduct of local soldiers present at the match.

So ended this most notorious and unfortunate Olympic Final, out of character with an enjoyable and exciting series of matches.

Matches to decide second and third places

Round One

31 August   Italy 2-1 Norway (0-1)   Olympic Stadium
(after extra time)
Sardi 46   A. Andersen 41
Badini 96

1 September   Spain 2-1 Sweden (0-1)   Olympic Stadium
Belauste 51   Dahl 28
Gomez-Acedo 53

Semi-Finals

2 September   Spain 2-0 Italy (1-0) Olympic Stadium
Sesumaga 43, 72

Netherlands v France: France withdrew, Netherlands went through to the Final

Final

5 September   Spain 3-1 Netherlands   Olympic Stadium
Sesumaga 7, 35   Groosjohan 68
'Pichichi' 72

Match to decide 8th place

30 August   Egypt 4-2 Yugoslavia (2-1) Olympic Stadium
Abaza (2 goals)   Dubravcic
Allouba   Ruzic
Hegazi

Times of goals: not known

Instead of requiring the defeated semi-finalists (France and The Netherlands) to play off for the bronze medals, as became standard practice from 1936, the organisers chose a much more complex system. This was a modified version of the Bergvall System, and required teams losing their Quarter-Final to play in a Consolation Tournament, similar to the one in 1912.

All agreed to do so, except for France – most of her players had gone home.

In the event, all the matches were closely contested. Italy beat Norway after extra time, and Spain overturned an early Swedish goal to progress from Round One before defeating Italy.

The Netherlands, with a bye and a walkover against France, reached the Final without a match. They faced a resurgent Spanish team who improved with each day and ended as silver medallists. Sesumaga, Spain's centre-forward, emerged as the star of this extra event with four goals.

There was even a match to decide eighth place, in which Egypt defeated Yugoslavia 4-2, the first win by any African team in this event, long before the golden years of 1996 and 2000.

The Medal Winners

(Gold) Belgium

de Bie	van Hege	Nisot
Swartenbroeks	Larnoe	Hebdin
Verbeeck	Bragard	
Musch	Coppee	
Hanse	Bastin	
Fierens	Balyu	

(Silver) Spain

Zamora	Equizabal	Pagazaurtundua
Vallana	Sesumaga	Otero
Arrate	Arabolaza	Vazquez-Gonzalez
Samitier	'Pichichi' Moreno	'Moncho' Fegueiros
Belauste	Gomez-Acedo	Bilbao
Sancho	Artola	Izaguirre

(Bronze) Netherlands

MacNeill	van Rappard	E. Bulder

Denis   van Dort   Bieshaar
Verweij   Groosjohan
Bosschart   van Heijden
Kuipers   J. Bulder
Steeman   de Natris

Referees

R. L. Van Praag (Netherlands)   Czechoslovakia v Yugoslavia
D. J. Mutters (Netherlands)   Norway v Great Britain
                                       Belgium v Spain
                                       Czechoslavakia v France
P. Putz (Belgium)   Italy v Egypt
                                       Italy v Spain
                                       Spain v Netherlands
G. Hubrecht (Belgium)   Netherlands v Luxembourg
C. Barette (Belgium)   Sweden v Greece
                                     Czechoslovakia v Norway
W. Eymers (Netherlands)   Spain v Denmark
H. Christophe (Belgium)   France v Italy
                                     Egypt v Yugoslavia
J. Fanta (Czechoslovakia)   Netherlands v Sweden
J. Lewis (Great Britain)   Belgium v Netherlands
                                   Belgium v Czechoslovakia (Final)
L. Fourgous (France)   Netherlands v Italy
G. Mauro (Italy)   Spain v Sweden

Goal scorers in the main tournament

Karlsson (Sweden): 7
Janda (Czechoslovakia): 6
Coppee (Belgium): 4
Vanik (Czechoslovakia): 4
Groosjohan (Netherlands): 4

7. Paris, 1924

The Uruguayan Comet

The Official Report on the 1924 Olympics did not suffer from false modesty, describing the Paris football tournament as a triumph without precedent.

That claim was justified by the number of teams, the size of crowds, and the standards of play; all set new benchmarks.

The presence of 22 teams made it the biggest event till the 1982 World Cup, and more nations could have taken part. Portugal withdrew at the last minute, while Denmark and Great Britain did not enter. Both the Danish FA and all four home nations in the UK rejected FIFA's definition of the key word 'amateur'.

FIFA allowed national associations to pay amateur footballers for 'broken time' off work, wages they lost while training, travelling, or playing matches. Meeting FIFA representatives in 1923, the British were adamant that if a man received pay (or other 'consideration') for playing, he was a professional. Only necessary travel and hotel expenses could be refunded to an amateur.

The disagreement was central to Great Britain sitting out the 1924 and 1928 Olympic football events; the home nations also left FIFA from 1928 to 1946. Denmark held a similar view on 'amateurism' and did not compete again until 1948.

The Official Report called Britain's absence 'the most notable abstention' – she was, after all, the 'cradle of football', although those remarks are more evocative in the original French.

Still, 1924 benefited from new nations. From Western Europe came Ireland; from Central Europe Poland, Romania, Hungary and Bulgaria; there were three Baltic countries in Latvia, Estonia and Lithuania; and Turkey was the first from Asia.

Above all, the South Americans arrived with Uruguay, holders of the Copa America, their continent's premier achievement. The Report became lyrical when looking back at the energy, ball skills, and perfection of Uruguay's approach. With their short-passing game, they played this team sport as a team, and had no obvious weaknesses in defence, midfield or attack. If any opponents did create chances, an agile keeper would foil them.

Other sides, especially medal winners, received praise from the Report. Switzerland were solid in defence and fast moving, while Sweden were another powerful team. The Swiss had the disadvantage of playing three hard matches in six days before reaching the Final.

And what of the reigning champions and their hosts? While Belgium did not match other sides' technique, their 8-1 defeat by Sweden remains an extraordinary upset. France gave a very good account of themselves, and were unlucky to be drawn against Uruguay in the quarter-finals.

So successful was the 1924 tournament – not least in bringing healthy income to the Paris Olympics – that FIFA, led by Frenchmen Jules Rimet and Henri Delaunay, determined to arrange their own international competition, unhindered by Olympian amateur rules.

Uruguay, the bright comet visible at only two Olympic tournaments (1924 and 1928) had proved they were the best in the world, and went on to host the first World Cup in 1930, and win that too.

Round One

25 May Switzerland 9-0 Lithuania (4-0) Stade Pershing, Paris
Sturzenegger 2, 43, 68, 85
Dietrich 14
Abbeglen 41, 50, 58
Ramseyer 63 (p)

25 May USA 1-0 Estonia (1-0) Stade Pershing
Stradan 15 (p)

25 May Czechoslovakia 5-2 Turkey (3-0) Stade Bergeyre, Paris
Stapl 21   Bekir 63, 82
Sedlacek 28, 37
J. Novak 64
Capek 74

25 May Italy 1-0 Spain (0-0) Stade Olympique de Colombes, Paris
Vallana o.g. 84

26 May   Uruguay 7-0 Yugoslavia (3-0)   Stade Olympique de
                                                          Colombes
              Vidal 20
              Scarone 23
              Petrone 35, 61
              Cea 50, 80
              Romano 58

26 May   Hungary 5-0 Poland (1-0)   Stade Bergeyre
              Eisenhoffer 14
              Hirzer 51, 58
              Opata 70, 87

Round One

Lithuania v Switzerland opened the Paris tournament in the Stade Pershing, named after the American general in the recent Great War and the setting for Inter-Allied Games in 1919.

The new Baltic nation could find no way through a powerful Swiss defence. Nor did Swiss forwards offer Lithuania any respite, scoring in two minutes and 4-0 up at the interval. Max Abegglen, inside-left, was first to a hat-trick but Sturzenegger went one better, in the most comprehensive victory of the whole event.

The USA met another Baltic team, Estonia, but this match provided only one goal. It was a penalty in 15 minutes, which the American captain and centre-forward Stradan netted. Kaljot could have equalised for Estonia in 68 minutes, but his penalty missed the mark, even when retaken.

At the same time in Stade Bergeyre, Czechoslovakia returned to the Olympics after their unhappy Antwerp final against Belgium. Now they faced Turkey, the first Asian team to take part and one barred from the 1920 event.

In a one-sided first half, the Czech captain Stapl opened the scoring in 21 minutes, and his outside-right Sedlacek added two more. After the interval, Turkey found better form with Bekir's double, balancing goals by Novak and Capek, but the Czechs won comfortably.

Italy (one of the favourites to win gold) and Spain drew 20,000 to the Olympic Stadium. This was not the goal feast for which the crowd hoped – even the one goal scored was put into his own net by Spain's captain, the unfortunate Vallana. By then the Spanish were hampered by the loss of Larraza, sent off in 55 minutes, which deprived them of their centre-half.

Much smaller attendances turned up next day and enjoyed two matches full of goals.

Only a thousand saw Uruguay's debut, against Yugoslavia. Though 20 minutes passed before Vidal, the Uruguayan centre-half, scored, his team's high quality was already apparent. Their forwards Scarone, Cea, Romano and 18 year old Pedro Petrone, brought the score to 7-0. Yugoslavia lost as heavily as they did in 1920; they were not the only team to be outplayed by the South Americans.

Hungary, who had not been allowed to compete in 1908, 1912 or 1920, made up for lost time in the 5-0 win over Poland. This was not as straightforward as it seems. Only inside-right Eisenhoffer scored before the interval, but Hirzer's double soon after half-time made the result secure, before Opata took the total to five.

Round Two

27 May	France 7-0 Latvia (3-0)	Stade de Paris, Saint-Ouen
	Crut 17, 28, 55	
	P. Nicholas 25, 50	
	Boyer 71, 87	

27 May	Netherlands 6-0 Romania (2-0)	Stade Colombes
	Hurgronje 8	
	Pijl 32, 52, 66; one other goal (time uncertain)	
	De Natris 69 (p)	

28 May	Ireland 1-0 Bulgaria (0-0)	Stade Colombes
	Duncan 75	

28 May	Switzerland 1-1 Czechoslovakia (0-1)	Stade Bergeyre
	(after extra time)	
	Dietrich 79 Stapl 21 (p)	

30 May   (Replay)

                   Switzerland 1-0 Czechoslovakia (0-0) Stade Bergeyre
                   Pache 87

29 May   Uruguay 3-0 USA (3-0)   Stade Bergeyre
                   Petrone 10, 15, 44

29 May   Italy 2-0 Luxembourg (2-0)   Stade Pershing
                   Baloncieri 20
                   Della Valle 38

29 May   Egypt 3-0 Hungary (2-0)   Stade de Paris
                   Yaghen 4
                   Hegazi 40
                   Ali Riad 58

29 May   Sweden 8-1 Belgium (4-0)   Stade Colombes
                   Kock 8, 24, 77   Larnoe 67
                   Rydell 20, 61, 83
                   Brommesson 30
                   Kaufeldt 46

Round Two

Against the Netherlands, Romania soon found it difficult to contain experienced forwards such as de Natris and Groosjohan, who had played in the 1920 Olympics. This time it was Pijl, the Dutch centre-forward, who hit the headlines with a goal on the half-hour and three more in the later stages of a 6-0 win.

15,000 flocked to watch France play Latvia, and the home fans were delighted as three French inside forwards shared seven goals, scored at regular intervals over the 90 minutes. Crut hit a hat-trick, Nicholas and Boyer two each.

Ireland v Bulgaria saw two more countries take their bow, and the Irish centre-forward Duncan scored the winner 15 minutes from time. It could have been more comfortable, but Ireland missed two penalties.

Two powerful teams, Switzerland and Czechoslovakia, produced a bruising encounter that was not resolved until two games were complete. A Stapl penalty gave the Czechs an early lead, but the Swiss equalised through a late goal from Dietrich. For the replay both teams made significant changes.

The Swiss forward Abegglen took over as captain from Schmiedlin, and three new colleagues started in attack. Czechoslovakia also introduced three new inside forwards, all named Novak. A single goal in 87 minutes won it for Switzerland – Pache, the new number 9, was their hero.

Against the USA, Uruguay were clear favourites, but the 3-0 result was a respectable one for the American team. Petrone scored two goals for Uruguay in the first 15 minutes and completed his hat-trick on the interval; but there were no more goals in the second half, and this was a better performance for the US side than many they put on in later Olympics.

Italy, having defeated Spain, found Luxembourg's defence difficult to open up and only Baloncieri and Della Valle hit the target, as the Italians struggled to find a fluency to match their skills.

Two of the biggest upsets in football history came in the last matches of this Round.

Belgium met Sweden as reigning champions and had no inkling of what was to ensue. Even when Kock, Sweden's outside-left, scored in eight minutes, there was plenty of time to recover. After all, gold medallists such as Coppee, Van Hege and Larnoe were in the Belgian line up.

But their defence could not cope with Swedish attacks as Sven Rydell and Rudolf Kock scored hat-tricks. 4-0 at the interval, 8-1 at the final whistle, with only Larnoe's goal to relieve the Belgian feelings of shock.

Almost as stunning was the demise of the well regarded Hungarian team, who lost 3-0 to Egypt. This was another fine performance by Egypt, who had finished eighth, ahead of most other teams, in 1920. Their inside-left Yaghen scored in four minutes and Hegazi, the centre-forward, added another just before the interval. With Riad's goal on the hour, the victory was sure – the first African win in the main Olympic tournament.

Quarter-Finals

1 June	Uruguay	5-1	France (2-1)	Stade Colombes
	Scarone 2, 24		P. Nicholas 12	
	Petrone 58, 68			
	Romano 83			

1 June	Sweden	5-0	Egypt (3-0)	Stade Pershing
	Kaufeldt 5, 71			
	Brommesson 31, 34			
	Rydell 49			

2 June	Netherlands	2-1	Ireland (1-1)	Stade de Paris
	(after extra time)			
	Formenoy 7, 104		Farrell 33	

2 June	Switzerland	2-1	Italy (0-0)	Stade Bergeyre
	Sturzenegger 47		Della Valle 52	
	Abegglen 60			

Quarter Finals

These matches were held on 1st and 2nd June in four stadia. By now Uruguay's fame had spread and, instead of 1,000 spectators at the Olympic Stadium six days before, 45,000 thronged to watch their French heroes play the South Americans.

Uruguay had put seven goals past Yugoslavia, while France had also scored seven against Latvia. France were in their own stadium, buoyed by a huge support. Who would prevail?

Late-comers missed a compelling start. Scarone, the Uruguayan inside-right, scored the opening goal within 120 seconds, but Nicholas, France's centre-forward, equalised soon after. The match continued evenly balanced in that first half, although Scarone scored his second in 24 minutes. From the hour mark, the game tilted Uruguay's way. It was then that Petrone scored twice, in 58 and 68 minutes, to put the result beyond doubt, and Romano, on the left wing, added a late fifth. For all their endeavours, with home advantage, France were the third team who could not stem Uruguay's forwards.

Against giant-killers Egypt, Sweden also scored five. Their number nine, Kaufeldt, scored in the fifth minute, and his right-wing colleague Brommesson trebled Sweden's lead just after half an hour. Three up at the interval, they never looked back. Rydell quickly made it four in the second half, and Kaufeldt added another in 71 minutes.

Next day, only 2,000 watched the Netherlands, who had scored six against Romania, struggle against Ireland. The match went into extra time and was only decided when Formenoy, the Dutch number 8, scored his second after 104 minutes. Now they had to play Uruguay and this tight quarter-final was not the prelude they hoped for.

Switzerland came through to face Italy after an easy First Round and two hard matches against Czechoslovakia. The Italians had beaten Spain and Luxembourg in two close contests.

The first half saw neither team gain the upper hand, but immediately after returning to the field, the Swiss inside-right, Sturzenegger, found the net and his earlier form, which had seen him score four against Yugoslavia.

Back came Italy to level, through Della Valle, within five minutes. It took another goal, by the reliable Abegglen at inside-left, to win the match, although there was still a third of the match to go.

Semi-Finals

5 June	Switzerland	2-1	Sweden (1-1)	Stade Colombes
	Abegglen 15, 77		Kock 41	
6 June	Uruguay	2-1	Netherlands (0-1)	Stade Colombes
	Cea 62		Pilj 32	
	Scarone 81 (p)			

Third Place match

8 June   Sweden 1-1 Netherlands (1-0)   Stade Colombes
              (after extra time)
              Kaufeldt 44   Le Fevre 77

9 June   (Replay)
              Sweden 3-1 Netherlands (2-1)   Stade Colombes
              Rydell 34, 77   Formenoy 43 (p)
              Lundquist 42

Semi-finals

The four teams left, Switzerland, Sweden, Uruguay and the Netherlands, now played their matches between 5 and 9 June in Stade de Colombes – a new continent contending with three European nations, all of whom had been neutral in the Great War.

Switzerland v Sweden was always likely to be closely fought. Abegglen once more rose to the occasion, opening his account in 15 minutes to put the Swiss into the lead, but late in the half Sweden's Kock equalised. Extra time beckoned, until Abegglen produced the winner with 13 minutes to go.

Over 7,000 had enjoyed the first semi-final, but 40,000 flocked to see the Uruguayan sensations play the Netherlands, bronze medallists in 1908, 1912 and 1920.

For the first time, a team took the lead against the South Americans. Pilj, the Dutch number 9, scored in 32 minutes, and the Dutch held that slender advantage until Cea, Uruguay's inside-left, equalised half an hour later. Then came a penalty for Uruguay, hotly disputed by the Netherlands, but converted by Scarone with only nine minutes left.

Uruguay had won by a single goal and shown they could overcome a deficit, in their most difficult match of the tournament.

Third place match

The bronze medals were decided between Sweden and the Netherlands in two keenly fought matches. First, 120 minutes could not bring a winner. Kaufeldt scored on the stroke of half-time for Sweden, while the Dutch right-half Le Fevre levelled the tie in 77 minutes.

While about 10,000 saw the 1-1 draw, 40,000 attended the replay, largely because they could watch both Sweden v the Netherlands and then the big event, Uruguay v Switzerland, in the Final. (Some reports put the attendance at 60,000 with 10,000 more unable to get in).

Sweden eventually took the bronze, thanks to the right-wing pair of Sven Rydell, with two goals, and Evert Lundquist. Their three goals were enough, although Dutch hopes flickered briefly with Formenoy's penalty goal, when it was 2-1. But even when Kaufeldt was sent off with 15 minutes left, the ten men added a third, from Rydell.

Final

9 June   Uruguay 3-0 Switzerland (1-0)   Stade Colombes
              Petrone 9
              Cea 65
              Romano 82

The Final

Immediately after the bronze medal match was replayed, the finalists took the field – Uruguay wearing blue and white, Switzerland red and white.

At first the Swiss dominated, but were knocked out of their stride by Petrone's goal in nine minutes. The early stages continued to be evenly contested, and Swiss chances were not turned into a precious equaliser. Both sides were able to counter-attack at speed, as the match enthralled a packed stadium.

The turning point was Cea's goal in 65 minutes, which put Uruguay 2-0 up and placed too heavy a burden on Switzerland's forward line, which became less well organised and effective. Eight minutes to go and Romano made the gold medals a certainty for his team. By then the Uruguayans were playing with flair and brio, in magnificent June sunshine which matched the South Americans' symbol of the sun.

After the three teams received their medals, with national flags flying, Uruguay introduced the 'lap of honour' followed by the Swiss team, as they ran round the Olympic Stadium, applauded by spectators lucky enough to see a sporting watershed.

The Medal Winners

Gold: Uruguay

Mazali	Scarone
Nasazzi	Petrone
Arispe	Cea
Andrade	Romano
Vidal	Tomasina
Ghierra	Naya
S. Urdinaran	Zibechi

Silver: Switzerland

Pulver	Pache	Kramer
Reymond	Dietrich	
Ramseyer	Abegglen	
Oberhauser	Fassler	
Schmiedlin	Bedouret	
Pollitz	Mengotti	
Ehrenbolger	Sturzenegger	

Bronze: Sweden

Lindberg	Rydell	Dahl
Alfredsson	Kaufeldt	Hirsch
Hillen	Keller	Lindquist
Holmberg	Kock	Mellgren
Friberg	Carlson	
Sundberg	Brommesson	
Lundquist	Svensson	

Top Goal Scorers

Petrone (Uruguay): 8
Abbeglen (Switzerland): 6
Sturzenegger (Switzerland): 5
Pijl (Netherlands): 5

Referees

P. Putz (Belgium)   USA v Estonia

A. Scamoni (Italy)	Switzerland v Lithuania
P. Andersen (Norway)	Czechoslovakia v Turkey
	Uruguay v France
M. Slawik (France)	Italy v Spain
	Switzerland v Czechoslovakia (replay)
	Uruguay v Switzerland (Final)
G. Vallat (France)	Uruguay v Yugoslavia
	Uruguay v Netherlands (Semi-Final)
J. Mutters (Netherlands)	Hungary v Poland
	Switzerland v Italy
	Switzerland v Sweden (Semi-Final)
H. Christophe (Belgium)	France v Latvia
	Sweden v Egypt
F. Herren (Switzerland)	Netherlands v Romania
A. Henriot (France)	Ireland v Bulgaria
C. Andersen (Norway)	Switzerland v Czechoslovakia
C. Barette (Belgium)	Uruguay v USA
J. Richard (France)	Italy v Luxembourg
L. Colina (Spain)	Egypt v Hungary
H. Retschury (Austria)	Sweden v Belgium
	Netherlands v Ireland
	Sweden v Netherlands (Bronze medal match)
Y. Mohamed (Egypt)	Sweden v Netherlands (replay)

8. Amsterdam, 1928

Return of the Comet

Amsterdam had been planning a bid for the Olympics since 1912, but the Dutch decided to support Antwerp as the host city in 1920 and Paris four years later, provided they were successful in 1928.

The IOC accepted that, although the USA countered with a bid for Los Angeles; reluctantly, the Americans accepted that it would be California's turn next, in 1932.

The Dutch built a new Olympic Stadium on land reclaimed from the North Sea. It housed most sports and all but one football matches in the main tournament. Jan Wils even won an architecture prize for its design, a personal medal in the Olympic arts competitions.

Wils's stadium introduced a huge results board, which spectators now take for granted, and the length of the athletics track was standardised at 400 metres. These Olympics also introduced a symbolic flame, continuously burning over the weeks of competition – the torch relay from Athens only began in 1936.

More fundamentally, women could now enter their own athletic events, in five track and field competitions, long after they were allowed to take part in tennis and yachting (1900) and swimming (1912). Football, however, remained a male event until the century was nearly over; the first women's tournament came about in 1996.

17 nations competed in the 1928 football tournament, five fewer than in Paris. Back came the champions Uruguay, and Germany; making their first entry were Portugal as well as Argentina, Chile and Mexico, enthused by the immediate success of Uruguay to travel across the Atlantic.

While those nations joined up, ten who had taken part in 1924 were not present. Estonia withdrew late in the day, while new nations such as Latvia, Lithuania, Ireland, Romania, Czechoslovakia and Bulgaria sat this one out. Hungary and Poland were absent, and Sweden, bronze medal winners last time, also missed the event, as did all the Scandinavian countries.

It was a sign of football's growing importance worldwide that 250,000 fans applied for tickets to see the final, and each of Uruguay's and the Netherlands' games attracted between 18,000 and 28,000. Taking the 1924 and 1928 tournaments together, 27 countries took part in one or both, with Europe, South America, Africa, Asia, Central and North America all represented.

That success ensured that a World Cup for all players, professional as well as amateurs, would soon be established. Once it was, in 1930, the Olympic tournament would never be the same again.

Preliminary Round

All matches in the main tournament were played in the Olympic Stadium, Amsterdam, except for Portugal v Yugoslavia (May 29).

May 27	Portugal	4-2	Chile (2-2)
	Vitor Silva 42		Subiabre 3
	Pepe 43, 52		Carbonell 16
	Fonseca 61		

With 17 nations competing, one preliminary match was essential before the First Round (the 'Round of 16'). Portugal won through, defeating the furthest travelled team, Chile.

This was doubly disappointing for the South Americans, since they had gone two up in the first few minutes. Portugal then rose to the occasion, equalising just before the interval and going on to win 4-2. Soares Lauro, known as Pepe, scored twice from the inside-right berth.

Chile's team, however, were able to stay on in Holland and were rewarded with a tangible consolation a few days later.

First Round

May 27	Belgium	5-3	Luxembourg (3-3)
	R. Braine 9, 72		Schutz 31
	Moeschal 20, 23, 67		Weisgerber 42
			Theissen 45
May 28	Germany	4-0	Switzerland (2-0)
	R. Hofmann 16, 75, 87		
	Hornauer 41		

May 28   Egypt 7-1 Turkey (2-0)
           Zubeir 20 (p)   Alaeddin 80
           Riad 27, 46, 63
       Ismail Mohamed 52, 65
              Mokhtar 86

May 29   Italy 4-3 France (3-2)
             Rosetti 19   Brouzes 15, 17
             Levratto 39   Pavillard 61
             Banchero 43
             Baloncieri 60

May 29   Portugal 2-1 Yugoslavia (1-1)   Old Stadium,
                                                Amsterdam

           V. Silva 20, 89   Bonacic 40

May 29   Argentina 11-2 USA (4-0)
        Cherro 9, 48, 50, 58   Deal 55
       Tarasconi 30, 63, 66, 85   Kuntner 75
              Orsi 41, 73
             Ferreira 35
          (approximate time)

May 30   Spain 7-1 Mexico (3-0)
           Regueiro 12, 44   Carreno 61
           Yermo 25, 46, 80
             Marculeta 50
             Mariscal 56

May 30   Uruguay 2-0 Netherlands (1-0)
            Urdinaran 21
             Scarone 83

First Round

Round One was played over three days, starting with Belgium winning against Luxembourg after a remarkable first 45 minutes. The Belgians were coasting, 3-0 up after 23 minutes, when their opponents suddenly sprang to life and equalised just on the interval. The 1920 champions needed two more goals from Braine and Moeschal, who scored a hat-trick, before they could breathe easily.

A much bigger crowd, 16,000, watched a straightforward victory for Germany, returning after 16 years. Switzerland could not revive their silver medal winning form of 1924. Hofmann collected the second hat-trick of the Round, and there were many more goals to come over the next 48 hours.

Egypt were once more the only African country to compete, and were drawn against Asia's representative, Turkey. There were only two goals in the first half for Egypt. Zubeir scored in 20 minutes from the penalty spot, and Riad doubled the lead soon afterwards. Soon after the break, Egypt took full control to win 7-1, with Riad the third hat-trick hero so far. His country were to experience a rollercoaster of a championship in 1928.

The closest match so far was a thrilling Italy v France contest. Like Chile two days earlier, France held the early advantage with goals in 15 and 17 minutes, but their grip slackened. Italy's forward line took back the initiative and powered into a 3-2 lead before half-time. The second half was evenly balanced, with each side adding a goal on the hour, and more always possible. Italy got through, to another difficult match in the Quarter-finals.

Portugal and Yugoslavia played their match in the Old Stadium, and neither could gain control. Silva opened the scoring, Bonacic equalised, and it took Silva's second to win it for Portugal, only seconds from the final whistle. By then both teams had one man sent off in the 80th minute, the result of a clash between Ivkovik and Mota.

The other three games all featured South and Central American teams – Argentina, Mexico, and the reigning champions Uruguay.

For 30 minutes Argentina v USA was still a contest, but once Argentina scored a third goal, it became a procession. They collected four goals before the interval, seven after; both Cherro and Tarasconi scored four. In the most one-sided game of the year, the USA kept trying for goals and they did manage two in the second half.

Mexico made their Olympic debut against Spain, who were untroubled in scoring six, before Carreno put Mexico on the scoresheet after an hour. Yermo recorded the hat-trick in this match.

Lastly came the host country's match against the champions, the one every fan wanted to see. 28,000 was an attendance greater than the combined total of six other First Round crowds.

Both teams were in good form, and there was no repeat of the controversies of their semi-final in Paris. Uruguay were just as skilful and fluent as in 1924, and Urdinaran gave them the lead in 21 minutes. The Dutch were never outplayed, however, and only Scarone's late strike ended their hopes.

There is always an element of luck in any draw. The Netherlands had high hopes of making progress at their own Olympic Stadium, if they had faced almost any team other than Uruguay.

Quarter-finals

June 1 Italy 1-1 Spain (0-1)
(after extra time)
Baloncieri 63   Zaldva 11

June 4 Italy 7-1 Spain (4-0)
(Replay)
Magnozzi 14   Yermo 47
Schiavio 15
Baloncieri 18
Bernardini 40
Rivolta 72
Levratto 76, 77

June 2 Argentina 6-3 Belgium (3-2)
Tarasconi 1, 10, 75, 89   R. Braine 24
Ferreira 4   Van Halme 28
Orsi 81   Moeschal 53

June 3 Uruguay 4-1 Germany (2-0)
Petrone 35, 39, 84   Hofmann 81
Castro 63

June 4 Egypt 2-1 Portugal (1-0)
Mokhtar 31, 48   V. Silva 79

Quarter-finals

Italy v Spain brought together teams with very different First Round experiences: Spain had sailed into the next stage, Italy had recovered from a torrid first half to win 4-3.

The Spaniards made an early breakthrough with Zaldva's goal, a great rarity from a full-back in the 1920s. Italy levelled through their captain Baloncieri, and there were no more goals in the next hour. A replay was arranged for three days later.

Amazingly, that second game was almost over in 18 minutes, when Italy were 3-0 in front. Their 7-1 victory remains one of football's greatest shocks, because of the margin. Every Italian forward scored, Levratto on the left wing hitting the net twice. When the Spanish captain Yermo scored a consolation goal, he could reflect on his hat-trick a few days before in a very different match.

Argentina defeated Belgium 6-3, but the scoreline is deceptive. The South Americans started faster than any other team, three up in 10 minutes, but even that was not enough. Belgians Braine and Van Halme soon reduced the deficit to 3-2 and Moeschal delighted their supporters by equalising in 53 minutes.

With 15 minutes to go, Argentina reclaimed the lead through Tarasconi, who ended with four after his goal against the USA. But for a long time this contest was a close-run thing.

Uruguay's prodigiously talented Pedro Petrone, still only 22, was their outstanding player against the German side. For over half an hour Germany, buoyed by a clear cut victory against the Swiss, held Uruguay, but then Petrone scored twice for a 2-0 lead at half-time.

Just before the second goal, Germany were depleted when their captain and centre-half Kalb was ordered off. The 10 men could not get back into the game, and Petrone completed his hat-trick. For the Germans, Hofmann scored in 81 minutes and was later sent off, following an incident with Uruguay's left-back and captain Nasazzi. In a tournament where there were few flare-ups, this match saw both sides lose their leader – Kalb and Nasazzi.

Egypt also reached the peak of their tournament, beating Portugal 2-1, thanks to Mokhtar's goals near the start of both halves. Silva scored in all three of Portugal's games, but his late strike did not change this result.

Semi-finals

June 6   Argentina 6-0 Egypt (3-0)

Cherro 11

Ferreira 38, 82

Tarasconi 40,
54, 61

June 7   Uruguay 3-2 Italy (3-1)

Cea 17   Baloncieri 9

Campolo 28   Levratto 60

Scarone 32

Bronze medal match

June 9   Italy 11-3 Egypt (6-2)

Schiavio 6, 14, 42   I. Mohamed 12, 16

Banchero 19, 35,   Hassan 60
44, 57

Baloncieri 50

Magnozzi 75, 80, 88

Semi-finals

It was satisfying to neutral supporters that the two South American teams were in different halves of the draw. Their record since 1924, and form in Amsterdam, made both favourites to reach the Final.

Egypt's achievement in reaching this stage was remarkable, but Argentina's Cherro scored in ten minutes to make their task very difficult. They kept the score to 1-0 until close to the break, when Ferreira and Tarasconi trebled their lead.

Argentina were comfortably in charge when the prolific Tarasconi, Amsterdam's top scorer by some distance, completed another hat-trick. The quietest period of the game was the last 30 minutes when only one goal, by Ferreira, was a feature. Egypt did win a penalty, but even that was saved, from Riad.

A much larger crowd attended the Uruguay v Italy semi-final and saw an enthralling contest. Italy scored first, through Baloncieri, in nine minutes. Uruguay bounced back and Cea, Campolo and their captain Scarone all scored within 15 minutes: 3-1 at half-time.

Italy's goal on the hour from Levratto made the second half outcome uncertain. Perhaps 3-2 flattered Italy, but they fielded stars of the 1930s such as Combi in goal and the centre-forward Schiavio, and this was easily their best tournament to date.

Bronze medal match

Egypt now had to face Italy, who had beaten France and Spain before challenging the mighty Uruguay.

6,000 spectators enjoyed 14 goals, the Italians sparkling in an 11-3 victory. The opening 20 minutes alone were worth the price of a ticket. Schiavio scored in the sixth minute, and Italy added more from Baloncieri and Banchero; for Egypt Riad matched them goal for goal in 12 and 16 minutes.

3-2 and a close match in prospect, yet the prelude was misleading. The main theme of the next 70 minutes was Egypt's defence struggling to contain Italy's inside-forwards, who added three goals before the interval, when it stood 6-2.

When the teams returned to the field, the score kept on rising until two minutes from the end, when Magnozzi netted an eleventh goal. He collected a hat-trick in the last 15 minutes alone. Schiavio equalled that tally in the first half, and Banchero hit four to become Italy's top scorer in the event, along with Baloncieri.

Final

June 10   Uruguay   1-1   Argentina (1-0)
                   (after extra time)
                   Petrone 20   Ferreira 51

June 13   Uruguay 2-1 Argentina (1-1)

   (Replay)

Figueroa 17   Monti 28
Scarone 73

The two strongest teams in the tournament met in the only all South-American final in Olympic history. They had rather different experiences in their earlier matches, Argentina scoring 23 goals to Uruguay's nine, but the 1924 champions had defeated the Netherlands, Germany and Italy, all powerful teams.

It required two matches to separate them, with the only drawn game in any final, as Petrone gave Uruguay the lead and Ferreira equalised early in the second half. The two defences dominated the next hour as extra time added no goals.

In three days before the replay, both sides took stock. Their regular contests in their own continent meant that they knew each other's play after two decades. Now Uruguay made a bold decision – to field a completely new forward line, with only inside-right Cea keeping his place. Out went Campolo, the prolific scorer Petrone, Castro, and Urdinaran – in came Figueroa, Tito, Scarone and Arremon. Argentina's only change was that Perducca, the inside-left, replaced Ganzarain.

Although the replay was still close, Uruguay won the match with their new forwards Figueroa and Scarone scoring the decisive goals. For Argentina, Monti equalised, after Figueroa's opener, and he went on to become a legendary defender for Argentina in the 1930 World Cup – and then for Italy when they won the 1934 Cup.

In that 1930 competition, held in Uruguay, the hosts proved once again that they were the best team in the world.

With several Olympians still in their team, they overcame Argentina 4-2 in Montevideo to complete a unique hat-trick of championships between 1924 and 1930. Remarkably, they did not enter the Olympic tournament again for many years, and when they did attempt to qualify, for example in 1992, they did not succeed.

But those earlier achievements were memorable for a small country, and their footballers won Uruguay's only gold medals at the Olympics.

Consolation tournament

Semi-finals

June 5   Netherlands 3-1 Belgium (2-0)   Sparta-Stadion, Het Kasteel, Rotterdam

Ghering 4   P. Braine 83
Smeets 6
Tap 63

June 5   Chile 3-1 Mexico (2-0)   Monnikenhuize, Arnhem

Subiabre 24, 48, 89   Sota 15

Final

June 8   Netherlands 2-2 Chile (0-0)   Sparta-Stadion, Rotterdam

Ghering 59   Bravo 55
Smeets 66   Alfaro 89

(Netherlands won the Consolation Trophy, after lots were drawn to decide the winner. However, they awarded the Trophy to Chile).

The Medal Winners

Gold: Uruguay

Mazali	S. Urdinaran	Borjas
Nasazzi	Castro	Scarone
Arispe	Petrone	Figueroa
Andrade	Cea	
Fernandez	Campolo	
Piriz	Canavesi	
Gestido	Arremon	

Silver: Argentina

Bossio	Orsi	Diaz
Paternoster	Ganzarain	Cherro
Bidoglio	Ferreira	Orlandini
Evaristo	Tarasconi	Calandra
Monti	Carricaberry	
Medice	Perducca	

Bronze: Italy

Combi	Baloncieri	Rosetta
Bellini	Banchero	Pietroboni
Caligaris	Schiavio	Janni
Pitto	Magnozzi	Rivolta
Bernardini	Levratto	Rossetti
Genovesi	De Pra	

Goal Scorers

(Main Tournament)

Tarasconi (Argentina): 11
Baloncieri (Italy): 5
Banchero (Italy): 5

Referees

Y. Mohamed (Egypt)	Portugal v Chile
	Uruguay v Germany
L. Martinez (Argentina)	Belgium v Luxembourg
W. Eymers (Netherlands)	Germany v Switzerland
	Uruguay v Italy (Semi-final)
M. Slawik (France)	Egypt v Turkey
H. Christophe (Belgium)	Italy v France
A. Birlem (Germany)	Portugal v Yugoslavia
P. Ruoff (Switzerland)	Argentina v USA
G. Boronkay (Hungary)	Spain v Mexico
J. Langenus (Belgium)	Netherlands v Uruguay
	Italy v Egypt
D. Lombardi (Uruguay)	Italy v Spain
H. Boekman (Netherlands)	Italy v Spain (replay)

G. Malcher (Italy)	Argentina v Belgium
	Netherlands v Belgium
G. Mauro (Italy)	Egypt v Portugal
P. Escartin (Spain)	Argentina v Egypt (Semi-final)
J. Mutters (Netherlands)	Uruguay v Argentina (Final)
	Uruguay v Argentina (replay)
	Chile v Mexico
G. Comorera (Spain)	Netherlands v Chile (Consolation Final)

9. Berlin, 1936

A tournament like no other

Berlin was awarded the Games in 1931, during the Weimar Republic, and received 43 votes from IOC members to Barcelona's 16. The result was a sign that Germany was once more part of the community of nations, and indeed several other German cities had bid for the 1936 Olympics.

By 1934 Hitler was Chancellor and dictator, hostile to the IOC and the Olympic ideals of reducing national conflicts through the Games. Once persuaded of the propaganda value to his regime, however, he ordered the most lavish building yet known for a sports festival. Football, which Hitler actively disliked, became part of the quest for medals, and German players spent a year in intensive preparation, far longer than genuine amateurs could afford. Although there were demands to boycott the Berlin Games (over Nazi treatment of Jewish people), the first such attempts since 1896 affected only Spain and some individual athletes. 49 countries sent teams and 16 of those entered football squads.

For a few weeks, in July and August 1936, the Third Reich was ordered to be on its 'best behaviour', removing offensive posters, but the swastika and Nazi symbols were ubiquitous.

In the event, Germany collected most medals, but their track and field competitors disappointed, easily outshone by the four golds of Jesse Owens, and the football team, of whom so much was expected, were soon eliminated. Extraordinary, then, that Hitler authorised a late bid to hold the World Cup in 1942, and claimed that from 1944 all Olympics would take place in a vastly expanded Berlin 'sports city'.

None of those bids was acceptable to FIFA or the IOC, for whom the peripatetic nature of tournaments and Olympics around the world every four years was central to their vision of international sport and sportsmanship, which could not be confined within one country or city.

There have been more books on 1936 than any other Olympiad, and their titles understandably focus on 'The Nazi Olympics' and 'Hitler's Olympics'. The football matches receive little attention in those studies, apart from the mayhem which followed the Peru v Austria game.

The XI Olympiad introduced the torch relay as well as full radio coverage, an official film, 'Olympia', and TV pictures to a tiny Berlin audience. Broadcasters were selective; US radio concentrated on athletics, while south American networks were especially interested in the football tournament, although Peru alone represented their continent in the sport.

The absence of a football competition in 1932 was probably the result of several factors. FIFA was now more concerned with its own World Cup, for professionals, which got underway in 1930, and disagreements between the IOC and FIFA rose to the surface in 1930-32.

The Los Angeles Olympic organisers also focussed on American football's presence as a demonstration sport, rather than worrying about soccer's absence.

For amateur footballers, the central issue was finance in the Depression years after 1929. As in 1904, Europeans were reluctant to take time off work for the long journey to, and across, the USA.

In 1936 four stadia in Berlin presented matches contested by 16 teams, 10 from Europe, three from Asia, and one each from North America, South America and Africa.

Round One

3 August	Italy 1-0 USA (0-0)	Post Stadium
	Frossi 58	

3 August	Norway 4-0 Turkey (1-0)	Mommsen Stadium
	Martinsen 30, 70	
	Brustad 53	
	Kvammen 80	

4 August	Japan 3-2 Sweden (0-2)	Hertha-BSC Field
	T. Kamo 49	Persson 24, 37
	Ukon 65	
	Matsunaga 85	

4 August	Germany 9-0 Luxembourg (2-0)	Post Stadium
	Urban 16, 54, 75	
	Simetsreiter 32, 48, 74	
	Gauchel 49, 89	
	Elbern 76	

5 August	Poland 3-0 Hungary (2-0)	Post Stadium
	Gad 12, 27	
	Wodarz 88	

5 August	Austria 3-1 Egypt (2-0)	Mommsen Stadium
	Steinmetz 4, 65 Kerim 85	
	Laudon 7	

6 August	Peru 7-3 Finland (3-1)	Hertha-BSC Field
	T. Fernandez 17, Kanerva (p) 42	
	33, 47, 49, 70	
	Villanueva 21, 67 Gronlund 76	
	Larvo 80	

6 August	Great Britain 2-0 China (0-0)	Mommsen Stadium
	Dodds 55	
	Finch 65	

The first matches got underway in Berlin's stadia on 3rd August. In the Official Report, there are descriptions of weather and temperature: this was a damp afternoon with an 'influencing wind'.

Italy had a difficult game against the USA, whose 1928 team had lost eleven goals to Argentina. Italy were fortunate to finish with eleven men after Piccini, their centre-half, was sent off, but refused to leave. The referee Mr Weingartner's arms were held by other Italians until he could do no more than accept the situation as it was.

Reprieved in such a manner, Italy scored the only goal in 58 minutes when their outside right Frossi claimed the first of his seven goals in the tournament. There was no mistaking Frossi, who played with a headband, and spectacles to correct short-sightedness.

Norway proved too strong for Turkey, their centre-forward Martinsen leading the 4-0 victory with two goals, and his colleagues on the left-wing Brustad and Kvammen netting one each.

Both Italy and Norway were to have successful tournaments.

4th August saw one of the great Olympic comebacks, leaving Sweden stunned and Japan in the quarter-finals.

Sweden's inside right Persson hit two goals to put them on easy street, but after half-time the game turned around. Kamo and Ukon scored for Japan, who even avoided extra time with a late goal from Matsunaga.

Germany v Luxembourg produced nine goals for the home team, the biggest score in the Olympiad. Surprisingly, the Germans were only two up at the interval, but shortly after the 45th minute they added three in nine minutes. Urban and Simetsreiter, their left-wing partnership, both collected hat-tricks and the teenager Gauchel two, although none of the team could guarantee his place in the next round.

Austria, guided by the pioneering English coach, Jimmy Hogan, were called the 'Wonderteam' and were one of the favourites to win gold. Against Egypt, Africa's single contestants, Steinmetz and Laudon scored in the first seven minutes and closed the game out when Steinmetz added a third after an hour. Egypt, who had a remarkable series of matches in 1928, mustered a consolation goal near the end.

Austria's great rivals, neighbours and 'brothers-in-law', Hungary, had a glittering future in football but on 5th August, as the weather cooled, they lost to Poland. Gad, the Polish inside-left, caught the eye with two early goals and Wodarz, his outside-left colleague, ensured the win with seconds left.

The last two games in Round One saw Peru face Finland, and Great Britain against China.

Peru had little difficulty in achieving a 7-3 win, although two late goals for the Finns made the score look respectable. Peru's Fernandez, at centre-forward hit five on his own, while Villanueva added two.

Great Britain lined up with four players from Queen's Park, Scotland's original club and still resolutely amateur. Gardiner was a strong tackling right half and three forwards, Crawford, Kyle and Dodds, were familiar with each other's approach in League and Cup matches.

Although they won 2-0, the British press and selectors were unimpressed. On the positive side, their wingers, Crawford and Finch, were superior to the Chinese full backs, but their accurate crosses were not turned into goals. Of greater concern were China's longer preparation – they had spent a year playing matches and raising essential funds in Asia – and fine ball control, although Britain's players were taller on average.

In a goalless 45 minutes, Kyle especially had good chances at inside-right and Sven, China's inside-left, saw a 'goal' disallowed for a foul. Eventually Dodds scored in 55 minutes from Crawford's pass, and ten minutes later Finch doubled their lead from Kyle's through ball.

Quarter Finals

7 August	Italy 8-0 Japan (2-0)		Mommsen Stadium

Frossi 14, 75, 80
Biagi 32, 57, 81, 82
Cappelli 89

7 August	Norway 2-0 Germany (1-0)		Mommsen Stadium

Isaksen 7, 83

8 August	Poland 5-4 Great Britain (2-1)		Post Stadium

Gad 33   Clements 26
Wodarz 43, 48, 53   Shearer 71
Piec 56   Joy 78, 80

8 August	Peru 4-2 Austria (0-2) (after extra time)		Hertha-BSC Field

Alcade 75   Werginz 23
Villanueva 81, 117   Steinmetz 37
T. Fernandez 119

In the quarter-finals, Japan played Italy, and their earlier, remarkable victory over Sweden may have proved too demanding for their players in the last 15 minutes of an 8-0 defeat.

Italy knew how fortunate they were to come through Round One and took little time to open their account. Frossi scored in 14 minutes against Japan and Biagi, his inside-left, doubled the lead. Although the Italians were in command, it was not until 75 minutes that the floodgates opened and they added five more. Biagi, with four in all, outpaced even Frossi's hat-trick.

While Italy powered into the semi-finals, another favoured team were losing. Germany had lost only once in three years at home, but Norway took full advantage of their hosts' off day.

Germany v Norway may be the only match ever attended by Hitler, and the German team must have been nervous. Selectors made five changes to the side who scored nine against Luxembourg, introducing a new keeper, one new defender and three new forwards. Gauchel, the young inside-right, was dropped after scoring twice.

Perhaps the five left out on 7th August were fortunate. The Nazi regime were not pleased, nor were 55,000 supporters, nearly five times the crowd who attended Germany v Luxembourg.

Norway's achievement was their finest at an Olympics, their 2-0 victory in Berlin more impressive even than their victory over Britain in 1920. Isaksen, their inside-left, scored early, in seven minutes, and late, seven minutes from the end, in a deserved win, which showed their friendly match victories over Austria and Hungary were not flukes.

Where Norway's result was sensational, the Peru-Austria match was both sensational and notorious.

Once again, Austria began strongly with goals from Werginz and Steinmetz setting up a 2-0 lead which lasted until 75 minutes. Only then did the Peruvian right winger, Alcade, score and six minutes later the prolific Villanueva took the match into extra time.

For almost the whole half hour of added time, neither team could score. Suddenly the stars of Round One, Villanueva and Fernandez, found the net and ensured Peru's progress. Or so it seemed.

What happened next remains disputed, but people encroached on the pitch, either to celebrate with Peru's scorers or to attack the crestfallen Austrians. Immediately after the final whistle, Austria protested about their team's treatment.

A five-man jury considered the appeal on behalf of the IOC and ordered the teams to replay on the 10th August, with no crowd allowed to watch. At this decision, Peru withdrew their team and went home, accompanied by Colombia's Olympians in sympathy. There were protests in Peru, initially against German 'intervention' in these events, which the Peruvian government later accepted had not occurred.

Austria did turn up on the 10th and 'won' the replay, once the referee had waited 15 minutes and awarded them the match. Soon afterwards, they went on to play Italy in their semi-final.

Great Britain v Poland offered nine goals and a result which surprised most of those who attended the match. Britain had won gold medals three times, Poland were playing in their first Olympic matches. But they had the advantage of army service, which enabled them to practise as a team and have State sponsorship. That did not match the scale of totalitarian regimes, such as Italy, Germany and post-1945 Soviet bloc countries, but it was a world apart from Britain's amateur team.

After that uncertain start against China, the selectors replaced all three inside forwards but retained the two wingers. It was their new number nine, Clements, who broke the deadlock against Poland in 26 minutes. Poland continue to press with swift attacks from the left-wing pair Gad and his captain Wodarz, who had ensured victory against Hungary. Now both scored before the interval to give the Poles a 2-1 lead.

The key minutes came just after the break, with Wodarz completing a hat-trick and Piec, on the right wing, making it 5-1. Britain now threw everything into attack, with their captain and centre-half Joy moving upfield (a rare move for a defender in the 1930s). He was involved in three goals, scoring twice himself between 70 and 80 minutes. The 5-4 score was disappointing to the British but, considering their lack of match practice both individually and as a team, it was not unexpected to observers such as Stanley Rous, one of the FA management.

Commenting on the Berlin matches twelve years later, he recalled that some countries put winning before other goals. 'Two or three were using football as part of a political campaign ... at the expense of the true spirit which should alone inspire those participating in the Olympiad'. (Rous, 1948, p.11).

Semi Finals

10 August   Italy 2-1 Norway (1-0)   Olympic Stadium
(after extra time)
Negro 15   Brustad 58
Frossi 96

10 August   Austria 3-1 Poland (1-0)   Olympic Stadium
K. Kainberger 14   Gad 73
Laudon 55
Mandl 88

Bronze medal match

13 August   Norway 3-2 Poland (1-0)   Olympic Stadium
Brustad 15, 21, 84   Wodarz 5
Peterek (p) 24

So the semi-finalists were Italy and Austria, clear favourites from day one to come back with medals, and the outsiders Poland and Norway.

Even though the hosts were out, attendances for Italy v Norway and Austria v Poland were huge, dwarfing the crowd numbers for any previous Olympic football game and showing what a money spinner the event was – even after two World Cups for professional players had apparently eclipsed the Olympic appeal for fans.

Italy's left-winger Negro got his team off to a flying start, but Norway showed their earlier performances were not forgotten. Brustad, their number eleven, equalised soon after the interval, and the match went to extra time. As before, Italy relied on Frossi to make the difference and win the match.

In a busy afternoon, Austria had 'won the replay' against Peru by turning up, and now faced Poland. This time they gained their usual early advantage, through the inside-forwards Kainberger and Laudon, but held on to it, until Gad contributed his customary goal a game for Poland. With almost the last move of the game, Austria's Mandl ensured a 3-1 victory.

The bronze medal match, between Norway and Poland, produced another thrilling first half in the Olympic Stadium. Two outstanding wingers, Wodarz and Brustad, scored in the first 15 minutes. 1-1. Brustad then put Norway ahead, only for Peterek to equalise with a penalty, itself a rarity in this event.

The medals were in doubt right to the end, even after Brustad's hat-trick gave Norway a 3-2 lead with six minutes left. The 1930s have been called Norway's 'Bronze years', which sounds ironic but is a compliment to their unexpected achievement in Berlin.

Final

15 August   Italy 2-1 Austria (0-0)   Olympic Stadium
                    (after extra time)
            Frossi 70, 92   K. Kainberger 79

Italy and Austria had reached the final and could breathe a sigh of relief that August was half-way through and they were still in the tournament.

Austria had played in two well fought contests against Egypt and Poland, with the infamous quarter-final to reflect upon. Italy had one eight goal canter and two difficult matches against the USA and Norway.

The Final was a very close-run thing for the whole 120 minutes. An even match produced no goals until Frossi scored with 20 minutes left, and Kainberger headed the equaliser.

Into extra time, and immediately Frossi moved from his right wing, eluded the Austrian defence and scored from close in, to give Italy that coveted gold, with Austria taking the silver.

Mussolini's regime subsidised football and other sports and Italy won three world tournaments in 1934-38, including both the World Cups. Frossi, however, only played once more for his country, although he was a successful forward in Italy's League, especially with Inter Milan, making goals and scoring many more.

There is a photograph in the Official Report, which shows Frossi about to score his seventh (and vital) goal in extra time. He is an unlikely forward, tall, thin and with spectacles, concentrated on the ball, just as he is launching it into the net. But so much of the 1936 Games was unexpected, then and now.

Top goal scorers

7: Frossi (Italy)
6: T. Fernandez (Peru)

The medal winners

Gold: Italy

Venturini	Frossi	Cappelli
Foni	Marchini	Negro
Rava	Bertoni	
Baldo	Biagi	
Piccini	Gabriotti	
Locatelli	Scarabello	

Silver: Austria

E. Kainberger	Werginz	Mandl
Kunz	Laudon	Kitzmuller
Kargl	Steinmetz	
Krehn	K. Kainberger	
Wahlmuller	Fuchsberger	
Hofmeister		

Bronze: Norway

Johansen	Monsen	Hansen
Eriksen	Kvammen	Isaksen

Holmsen   Martinsen
Ulleberg   Frantzen
Juve   Brustad
Holmberg   Horn

Referees

Round 1:	K. Weingarner (Germany)	Italy USA
	G. Scarpi (Italy)	Norway v Turkey
	W. Peters (Germany)	Japan v Sweden
	P. Hertzka (Hungary)	a. Germany v Luxembourg
		b. Italy v Norway (Semi-Final)
	R. Scorzoni (Italy)	Poland v Hungary
	A. Jewell (GB)	Austria v Egypt
	Barlassina (Italy)	Peru v Finland
	H. Fink (Germany)	Great Britain v China
Quarter-Finals:	O. Olsson (Sweden)	Italy v Japan
	A. Barton (GB)	a. Norway v Germany
		b. Austria v Poland (Semi-Final)
	R. Eklow (Sweden)	Poland v Great Britain
	T. Kristiansen (Norway)	Peru v Austria
Bronze Medal:	A. Bilem (Germany)	Norway v Poland
Final:	P. Bauwens (Germany)	Italy v Austria

10. London, 1948

Matt Busby's Britain

During the Second World War, Olympics were not a priority, and they were not held in 1940 or 1944. The IOC had awarded the 1940 Games to Tokyo, but that invitation was withdrawn because of Japanese aggression on the Asian mainland.

In 1939, the decision went to London for 1944, ahead of seven other contenders. When that could not take place, the 1948 Olympics went to London, once the IOC were sure that the city could stage the Games – and was willing to do so. If London had dropped out, several American cities would have taken the baton from her.

For the first time, people could watch at home on the new TV's, although very few owned the expensive sets with their small screens. The vast majority 'listened-in' to radio commentaries, heard across the world. The BBC paid £1,000 to cover the Games and were enthusiastic about them, unlike many people in Britain who felt that the country could not afford them in a post-war era of rationing, Government debt and 'Austerity'.

Lord Burleigh, Chairman of the British Olympic Committee and gold medallist in 1928, was a strong advocate of the London Olympics, which he described as a 'flame of hope for better understanding in the world'.

In the 'Radio Times' that July, Ian Orr-Ewing, the BBC's Outside Broadcasts Manager, called the Games a 'Shop Window for British Television'. There were engineering control vans at the Empire Stadium and Empire Pool, Wembley, next to a road called Olympic Way. The Radio Centre was based in the nearby Palace of Arts, with studios, control rooms, and a range of expert commentators.

The TV commentator for football was James Jewell, who was chosen after interviews and tests of his voice, reaction to events and sense of drama.

Ian Orr-Ewing encouraged TV viewers to watch some of the 50 hours of programmes over the Olympics – but not every programme, 'or viewers will be easily recognised ... by their pallid appearance'.

The British football team was still resolutely amateur, and their new manager was Matt Busby, appointed Manchester United's manager in 1945 and a man who shaped the club forever, winning every trophy available.

In 1957, writing 'My Story', he called his achievement with the Olympic team one of his best jobs of work. Winning the First Division, as his club did in 1956 and 1957, or the FA Cup (1948), was simple, compared to taking part-time players from England, Scotland, Wales and Northern Ireland into a team that finished fourth.

In particular he praised Bob Hardisty, the courageous Tommy Hopper, Harry McIlvenny, and Eric Lee. Such players who hardly knew one another before they were selected for Great Britain, worked with Busby and his trainer Tom Curry, to build team spirit and play warm-up matches.

Those results included narrow defeats to The Netherlands and a Basle XI, but just before the Olympics began GB went to Nantes and defeated France 3-2.

Journalists with memories of Britain's previous matches in 1920 and 1936, when they lost to Norway and Poland, did not have high hopes for the team. They did, however, have faith in the manager, whose Manchester United had just lifted the FA Cup against Stanley Matthews's Blackpool. 'Leave it to Busby' said the Press.

Preliminary Round

26 July   Luxembourg 6-0 Afghanistan (3-0) Goldstone Ground, Brighton

Gales 2
Paulus 2
Kettel
Schammel

(Times of goals are uncertain; other sources credit different players as scorers)

26 July   Netherlands 3-1 Ireland (2-0)   Fratton Park, Portsmouth

Wilkes 1, 74   O'Kelly 52

Roosenburg 11

Preliminary Round

With 18 teams taking part, there were two preliminary matches (before Round One could include the required 16) and both took place well outside London.

For once, Luxembourg were favourites to win, against a team making their only appearance, Afghanistan. The match remains one of Olympic football's most mysterious.

It ended 6-0 to Luxembourg (3-0 at the interval) with 5,000 watching at the home of Brighton and Hove Albion. But who scored the goals is disputed, and the times when they were scored are lost. Different sources agree only that four Luxembourg players were on the score-sheet, but some credit Konter and Kremer, with doubles, Wagner, and the captain V. Feller.

The Netherlands' 3-1 win over the Republic of Ireland was based on two swift goals from Wilkes and Roosenburg in the opening minutes. O'Kelly brought the Irish back into the match at 2-1, but another from Wilkes sealed the victory in 74 minutes. This match took place at Fratton Park, Portsmouth FC's stadium, and so the two earliest matches were played in Sussex and Hampshire.

First Round

31 July   Denmark 3-1 Egypt (0-0)   Selhurst Park, London
(after extra time)
K.A. Hansen 82, 95   El Guindy 83
Ploger (p) 119

31 July   Great Britain 4-3 Netherlands   Highbury, London
(1-1)
(after extra time)
McBain 22   Appel 20, 63
Hardisty 58   Wilkes 81
Kelleher 77
McIlvenny 111

31 July   France 2-1 India (1-0)   Ilford, London
Courbin 30   Raman 70
Persillon 89

31 July	Yugoslavia 6-1 Luxembourg (0-1)	Craven Cottage, Fulham, London
	Stankovic 57 Schammel 10	
	Mihajlovic 61	
	Zeljko, Cajkovski 65, 70	
	Mitic 74	
	Bobek 87	

2 August	Sweden 3-0 Austria (2-0)	White Hart Lane, London
	G. Nordahl 2, 10	
	Rosen 71	

2 August	Korea 5-3 Mexico (2-1)	Dulwich, London
	Choi 13 Cardenas 23	
	Bai 30 Figueroa 85	
	K. C. Chung 63, 66 Ruiz 89	
	N. S. Chung 87	

2 August	Italy 9-0 USA (2-0)	Griffin Park, Brentford, London
	Pernigo 2, 57, 88, 90	
	Stellin 25 (p)	
	Turconi 46	
	Cavigioli 72, 87	
	Caprile 90	

2 August	Turkey 4-0 China (1-0)	Walthamstow, London
	Gunduz 18, 61	
	Huseyin 72	
	Lefter 87	

First Round

Denmark v Egypt drew 12,000 to Crystal Palace's stadium, Selhurst Park, for the first match held in London. There were no goals until the last eight minutes, when Karl Aage Hansen, the Danish inside-right, seemed to have won it. Immediately, Egypt's number 8, El Guindy, a tall, skilful and strong ball player, equalised.

In extra time Hansen scored his second, but this contest was over only when Ploger made it 3-1 with a last minute penalty.

On the same, hot day in late July, Great Britain played the Netherlands before 21,000 at Arsenal's famous Highbury Stadium. This was a bruising encounter, and three British players received injuries but played on – Ronnie Simpson in goal, Gwyn Manning at left-back, and, most seriously, right-winger Tommy Hopper, who suffered a broken cheek-bone.

Against the more skilful Dutch, Britain showed spirit and strength of will. They had outstanding players in left-half Eric Fright and Denis Kelleher, a superb dribbler, and never gave up.

The Netherlands scored first through Appel, their centre-forward, in 20 minutes, but Dougie McBain equalised straight after; 1-1 at half-time. Then Bob Hardisty put GB ahead, only for Appel to level the match. Two inside-lefts now entered the fray, Kelleher for Britain and Wilkes for the Dutch, to make it 3-3 near the end.

Into extra time; when Harry McIlvenny won the tie in the 111st minute. Hardly surprising that Hopper collapsed at the final whistle.

France v India drew a big crowd of 17,000, only slightly less than the British match, and they almost witnessed a shock result. This was India's second tournament, and they played with skill and courage, almost all barefoot.

Courbin, France's left winger, gave them the lead in 30 minutes, but Raman equalised with 20 minutes left. Just before the referee could blow to begin extra time, Persillon scored the winning goal for France, but it was a very close-run thing.

At Fulham's ground, Craven Cottage, Luxembourg faced Yugoslavia with the confidence engendered by their recent 6-0 victory. Now they took an early lead through Schammel, and the Slav team could not turn their attacking play into goals for an hour.

Once they did score, however, they were not to be denied. Stankovic, the Yugoslav left back, showed his forwards the way, and four of them followed in a 6-1 victory: Zeljko Cajkovski, Mihajlovic, Mitic and Bobek. Once that awkward first match was behind them, the Slavs were to have a successful tournament. That success, by the first Communist regime to participate at the Olympics, caught the attention of Soviet bloc governments who started sending football teams in 1952 and immediately dominated the event.

Unlike the State-sponsored Yugoslavs, Sweden's footballers really were amateurs and they impressed fans at Tottenham Hotspur's stadium when they beat Austria 3-0. Even if the Austrians were not the 'wonderteam', built in the 1920s and 1930s by Hugo Meisl and Jimmy Hogan, they were still good enough to beat Hungary in 1949.

With their manager, George Raynor, Sweden embarked on a golden decade when they were one of the best teams in the world. This team benefited from the three Nordahl brothers, two in defence and Gunnar Nordahl at centre-forward. In this match, he put Sweden 2-0 ahead within 10 minutes. A superb forward line included Gren and Liedholm, as well as Carlsson and Rosen, their outside-right who scored the third goal in 71 minutes. Sweden were the top scorers in 1948, and every attacker contributed goals.

Korea met Mexico in a unique pairing at the Olympics, and the Asian side opened their account with Choi's goal, while Cardenas equalised for Mexico. Goals came in bursts, with eight in all, although none between 30 and 63 minutes.

Korea were coasting, 4-1 ahead, with only five minutes left, when Figueroa, Mexico's centre-half, left his defensive beat to score, and two more, very late goals meant it ended Korea 5, Mexico 3. That was the good news for the winners; the less good news meant they would now face Sweden in three days' time.

20,000 flocked to Brentford FC's Griffin Park to see Italy play the USA. In 1936 Italy were gold medallists, with their hardest match coming right at the start, against the Americans – they were lucky to win 1-0. In 1948, the result was the same, but the score very different.

Pernigo, the Italian centre-forward, scored in two minutes, and Stellin's penalty made it 2-0 at the interval. Just after the break, Turconi ensured Italy's progress with a third goal. What was unexpected was that Italy scored four times in the final three minutes, taking the score to 9-0. Pernigo collected four goals, Cavigioli two.

Lastly, Walthamstow welcomed Turkey, China, and the smallest attendance of the tournament – 3,000. China's players came from Singapore, Vietnam and the Philippines, and had raised funds for this exciting visit to the West by playing friendlies in countries such as Indonesia.

Turkey dominated the match after Gunduz's opener in 18 minutes, and he doubled their lead on the hour. Their right-half, Huseyin, and Lefter (appropriately, the inside-left) raised the score to 4-0 late in the match.

Six decades on, Chia Boon-Leong remembered that China were upset by their centre-forward Chu Wing-Keung's injury, but they knew that

Turkey were a strong team, with several army veterans. To compensate, the Chinese were delighted to visit Britain, especially London's Hyde Park, and defeat did not upset their strong team spirit.

Quarter-Finals

5 August   Sweden 12-0 Korea (4-0)   Selhurst Park, London

Liedholm 11, 62
G. Nordahl 25, 40, 78, 80
Gren 27
Carlsson 61, 64, 82
Rosen 72, 85

5 August   Denmark 5-3 Italy (1-0)   Highbury, London

J. Hansen 30, 53, 74, 82   Cavigioli 49
Ploger 84   Caprile 67
   Pernigo 81

5 August   Yugoslavia 3-1 Turkey (1-1)   Ilford, London

Zeljko Cajkovski 21   Sukru 33
Bobek 60
Wolfl 80

5 August   Great Britain 1-0 France (1-0)   Craven Cottage, Fulham, London

Hardisty 29

Quarter-Finals

When Korea came out to face Sweden at Selhurst Park, they knew they had outscored their opponents in Round One matches, but most observers could see only one outcome.

Both sides needed time to settle, but once Liedholm (nominally outside-left but usually in midfield) scored in eleven minutes, Sweden were off and running. Goals hit the net with regularity, and Korea could do little to stop the Scandinavian tide. Gunnar Nordahl, with two, and Gren made it 4-0 at the interval.

That might have satisfied some teams, but Carlsson hit a second half hat-trick and Nordahl added two late goals. The 12-0 score was like a throwback to pre-Great War days. No team now relished playing against Sweden.

Denmark, returning to the tournament for the first time in 28 years, knew that Italy had won by nine goals over the USA, while their own victory against Egypt was a struggle over 120 minutes.

Bestriding this match like a Colossus was John Hansen, who broke the deadlock in 30 minutes. The second half was full of goals, seven in all, as both teams strove for mastery. Cavigioli equalised for Italy, but Hansen put the Danes 2-1 up. Caprile's turn, to make it 2-2. Hansen moved on to his hat-trick and 3-2, only for Pernigo to level: 3-3.

Eight minutes left, and Hansen hit his fourth goal, Ploger making sure of Danish success on 5-3. It is not surprising that Italians were impressed by their opponents, and both Hansen brothers and Karl Aage Praest were signed by Juventus; John scored 124 goals in 187 matches for the Turin club. The Denmark v Italy match was the most entertaining of the whole tournament, but every game had crowds cheering.

When Yugoslavia and Turkey travelled to Ilford, the Slavs' outside-left Cajkovski was soon off the mark in 21 minutes, with Sukru equalising twelve minutes later. Only in the last half hour did Yugoslavia seal the win through Bobek and Wolfl; powerful as they were, they did not dominate the first half of any of their four matches.

Great Britain had won their first match only after two hours, when injuries reduced their effectiveness but not their outstanding spirit. Now they faced France, whom they last met in the 1900 Olympics. New players were required – McAlindon, McColl, and Donovan made their entrance, while all three half-backs and most of the forward line kept their places. France included only one new man, with some positional changes, after the unsatisfactory performance against India.

This match, at Craven Cottage, drew 25,000, who saw a nervous opening, punctuated by a free kick every minute or two. Both keepers made good saves, and McIlvenny, Britain's centre-forward, headed on to the bar. Then in 29 minutes Bob Hardisty, captain courageous, met Donovan's right-wing corner and powered a header into the net. It was the only goal, a rarity in this year of high scores, and Britain had reached the semi-finals, to the surprise and delight of home supporters.

Semi-Finals

10 August   Sweden 4-2 Denmark (4-1)   Wembley Stadium, London

       Carlsson 18, 42   Seebach 3
       Rosen 31, 37   J. Hansen 77

11 August   Yugoslavia 3-1 Great Britain (2-1) Wembley Stadium
       Bobek 19   Donovan 20
       Wolfl 24
       Mitic 48

Bronze medal match

13 August   Denmark 5-3 Great Britain (3-2) Wembley Stadium,
       Praest 12, 49   Aitken 5
       J. Hansen 16, 77   Hardisty 33
       Sorensen 41   Amor 63

Semi-finals

Wembley's Empire Stadium welcomed its first football match of the Games when Sweden met Denmark. The game sprang to life right from the kick-off, and Seebach put Denmark ahead in three minutes.

At first, Nordahl and Gren, the Swedish attacking hub, were allowed no room to set up chances, and so it was Carlsson on the left who found space to equalise. Then Rosen put Sweden 2-1 ahead, soon adding a third, while Carlsson made Denmark's task even harder in 42 minutes.

The Danes, who had started so well when Seebach ran half the length of Wembley to score, were now 4-1 down and not even John Hansen could save them; he scored only one consolation goal.

One of Carlsson's goals was a header past the onrushing Danish keeper, but its achievement owed much to Gunnar Nordahl. Clearly in an offside position, he walked into the Danish net to avoid play being stopped, and Carlsson's goal was the result.

Next day 40,000 came to Wembley to watch the hosts play Yugoslavia. In the Olympics Official Report, Bernard Joy (of Arsenal, and GB in 1936)

compared the Slav team to Moscow Dynamo, who had toured Britain in 1945. They strung passes across the field, moving the ball like chess pieces on a board. When a pass was needed to keep possession, there was a team mate to receive the ball.

Britain's amateurs, who hardly knew most of their colleagues two months before, offered heart and individual skills from the left sided players Fright and Kelleher. McIlvenny had two clear chances early on, but constant rain made the ball hard to control.

At the other end, GB's keeper McAlinden could not hold a Bobek shot, and Yugoslavia were 1-0 up. Immediately, Donovan hit a shot through the crowded Slav defence to make it 1-1. Intent on attack, Britain now left Wolfl unmarked and in 24 minutes he restored the 2-1 lead.

Britain fell 3-1 behind soon after the break with a Mitic strike, but there was still all to play for. Eventually, the hosts lost by that margin, but this was their finest performance of 1948. Matt Busby recognised that a State-funded team like Yugoslavia always had the advantage over genuine amateurs, but his team had given all they could.

The Bronze medal match

Busby wanted every man in his squad to experience the chance of playing at the Olympics, and for the third place match he selected everyone who had not yet taken the field. There were seven changes to the semi-final team, with six players coming in and Hardisty stepping back to a defensive role.

Their opponents, Denmark, fielded nine of the semi-finalists, while Sorensen and Lundberg came in for Liedholm and K.A. Hansen.

The small Wembley crowd soon had something to cheer, as Aitken scored for GB in five minutes, but Praest levelled the match. Play surged from one penalty area to the other, with Eric Fright again showing his class.

John Hansen put Denmark in front, Bob Hardisty equalised. 2-2 after half an hour, with more goals to come. On another rainy day, Sorensen put the Danes ahead and Praest made it 4-2. Back came Bill Amor with a penalty in 63 minutes, but Hansen scored the last goal. Denmark 5, Great Britain 3, and the Danes had won the bronze.

Both keepers, Nielsen and Simpson, found the conditions demanding, but they also made fine saves. Ronnie Simpson, Queen's Park's teenager, soon turned professional in an extraordinary career that brought him two FA Cup medals with Newcastle United, a host of trophies, including the European Cup, with Celtic, and five Scotland caps. When he helped them defeat England at Wembley, in 1967, it was nearly two decades since he had played for The Olympic side.

Final

13 August   Sweden 3-1 Yugoslavia (1-1)   Wembley Stadium,

Gren 24, 67 (p)   Bobek 42

G. Nordahl 48

The Final

Sweden v Yugoslavia represented the meeting of two definitions of amateur football. Scandinavian countries had no professional football leagues; the new Communist regime in the Balkans regarded all sportsmen as amateurs and, like the post-war Soviet bloc, paid them as members of the Army or civil servants.

En route to the Final, Yugoslavia had the easier draw; but their Achilles heel was that they slowed down the match with intricate passing, when powerful shots from distance could have brought more goals.

Sweden had their finest players in the 1940s and 1950s, with star forwards Gunnar Gren, Gunnar Nordahl and Nils Lieldholm, who later joined AC Milan, where they were known as the 'Gre-No-Li' trio. Nordahl's 210 goals make him Serie A's second top scorer of all time, and his strength and speed made him the ideal foil for Gren and Garvis Carlsson.

The other Nordahl brothers in defence showed that this was a team like a family, players who knew each other well and were managed with care by George Raynor, a Yorkshireman who never had a top post in England but coached Sweden to Olympic gold and a World Cup final ten years later.

In his chapter of the Official Report, Bernard Joy praised both finalists but remembered that Sweden won the title through their determination coupled with brilliant skills. Where they were weaker, on the two wings, they gambled by changing Rosen and Liedholm, superb at half-back and inside-forward, into the nation's outside-right and -left.

Against the Slav team, Gren opened the scoring in 24 minutes, but Bobek equalised just before the interval. The second half won it for Sweden, inspired by Nordahl's brilliant goal in 48 minutes. He won the ball, passed and received back several times before bringing the ball into the penalty area and hitting it into the net. Gren's penalty virtually ensured that the Swedish players would take the gold and Yugoslavia the silver. This was the last time that a fully amateur team won the title, and no Western country succeeded until Los Angeles in 1984.

Every team contributed its own style and strategy to this most diverse of tournaments. Crowds were rewarded with 102 goals. These were later called The Austerity Olympics, but there was no shortage of happy memories.

Top Scorers

7:   G. Nordahl (Sweden)
     J. Hansen (Denmark
5:   Rosen (Sweden)
     Carlsson (Sweden)
     Pernigo (Italy)

The Medallists

Gold: Sweden

Lindberg	Andersson	Liedholm
Lindberg	Andersson	Liedholm
K. Nordahl	Rosen	Leander
Nilsson	Gren	
Rosengren	G. Nordahl	
B. Nordahl	Carlsson	

Silver: Yugoslavia

Lovric	Cimermancic	Sostaric
Lovric	Cimermancic	Sostaric
Brozovic	Mitic	Mihajlovic
Stanovic	Bobek	Wolfl
Zlatko Cajkovski	Zeljko Cajkovski	Tomasevic
Jovanovic	Vukas	

Bronze: Denmark

Nielsen	I. Jensen	Sorensen
Nielsen	I. Jensen	Sorensen
V. Jensen	Ploger	Seebach
Overgaard	Lundberg	K.A. Hansen
Pilmark	Praest	
Ornvold	J. Hansen	

Referees

A.C. Williams (Great Britain)   Luxembourg v Afghanistan
G. Reader (Great Britain)   Netherlands v Ireland

S. Boardman (Great Britain)

V. Laursen (Denmark)
G. Dahlner (Sweden)
K. van der Meer (Netherlands)

W. Ling (Great Britain)

L. Lemesic (Yugoslavia)
C. de la Salle (France)
J. Beck (Austria)
G. Carpani (Italy)
V. Sdez (France)

Denmark v Egypt
Sweden v Denmark (Semi-Final)
GB v Netherlands
France v India
Yugoslavia v Luxembourg
GB v France
Yugoslavia v GB (Semi-Final)
Denmark v GB (Bronze medal)
Sweden v Austria
Denmark v Italy
Sweden v Yugoslavia (Final)
Korea v Mexico
Italy v USA
Turkey v China
Sweden v Korea
Yugoslavia v Turkey

11. Helsinki, 1952

The Magnificent Magyars

1952 was a turning point in Olympic history. For the first time, the USSR, and other East European states who were part of the Soviet bloc, sent teams to the Games.

At a stroke, the amateur ethos of Olympic tradition was undermined. Communist governments regarded all sportspeople as 'amateur' and employed them to play their elite sport, what other nations defined as 'professional'.

The effects were soon evident in football, where no team from a non-Communist country won gold between 1952 and 1980. Nominally members of the armed forces or civil service, players from the USSR, Hungary, Poland, Romania and Bulgaria, as well as non-aligned Yugoslavia, had a full-time job playing football for club and country.

Such a difference in definitions was far more basic than the debates of 1920's Olympic football, when the Football Associations in Britain and Scandinavia rejected 'broken time' payments for amateurs. These compensated amateurs for a few weeks' wages, lost when they trained and played for their countries. Britain and Denmark, in particular, sat out Olympic football in 1924 and 1928.

The 1952 matches benefit from a unique source, written by the victorious captain just over two years later. Ferenc Puskas's autobiography, 'Captain of Hungary', describes the Olympic final and other memorable games during the team's unbeaten run in 1950-54. He also explains the tactics that made the Magyars the best team in the world and changed international and club football.

Helsinki was a remarkable Olympics for Hungary, who won 16 golds, including four in women's swimming, and finished third behind the USA and USSR – all from a population of nine million.

For the first time there were two Olympic villages, the Soviet bloc insisting their teams live apart from the main village in Kapyla. Instead, the secluded town of Otaniemi was allotted to them, on the coast outside Helsinki.

The individual athlete whom the world took to its heart in 1952 was Emil Zatopek, the long-distance runner from Czechoslovakia. Having won a gold and silver in 1948, he won all three of his events – 5,000 metres, 10,000, and marathon.

Renowned for his ungainly style and crowds chanting his name at every opportunity, Zatopek improved his times over four years by 11.2 seconds and 42.6 seconds in the 5K and 10K races.

In the football tournament, only ten matches were played in Helsinki – five in the Olympic Stadium, five in the Pallokentta. Tampere, North of the city, hosted five; Turku, on the West coast, four; Kotka, East of Helsinki, four; and Lahti, two.

Preliminary Round

15 July	Hungary 2-1 Romania (1-0)	Kupittaa, Turku
	Czibor 21 Suru 86	
	Kocsis 73	

15 July	Denmark 2-1 Greece (2-0)	Ratina, Tampere
	P.E. Petersen 36 Emanuilidis 85	
	Seebach 37	

15 July	Poland 2-1 France (1-1)	Lahti
	Trampisz 31 Leblond 30	
	Krasowka 49	

15 July	Yugoslavia 10-1 India (5-0)	Pallokentta, Helsinki
	Vukas 2, 62 A. Khan 89	
	Mitic 14, 43	
	Zebec 17, 23, 60, 87	
	Ognjanov 52, 67	

16 July	Italy 8-0 USA (3-0)	Ratina, Tampere
	Gimona 3, 51, 75	
	Pandolfini 16, 62	
	Venturi 27	
	Fontanesi 52	
	Mariani 87	

16 July   Egypt 5-4 Chile (2-2)   Kotka
El Far 27   Jara Constanzo 7, 78
El Mekkawi 43   Vial Blanco 14, 88
El Dezwi 66, 75, 80

16 July   Luxembourg 5-3 Great Britain (0-1)   Lahti
(after extra time)
Roller 60, 95, 97   Robb 12
Letsch 91   Slater 101
Gales 102   Lewis 118

16 July   Brazil 5-1 Netherlands (3-1)   Kupittaa, Turku
Humberto 25   van Roessel 15
Larry 33 (p), 36
Jansen 81
Vava 86

16 July   USSR 2-1 Bulgaria (0-0)   Kotka
(after extra time)
Bobrov 100   Kolev 95
Trofimov 104

There were two walk-overs.
    Norway (w/o) v Mexico
    Austria (w/o) v Saarland

Both Mexico and Saarland withdrew after the draw was made. Saarland did compete in other Olympic events but only in 1952. In 1955 it became part of (West) Germany again.

Preliminary Round

Hungary's first match was probably their toughest of the year; a bruising encounter against Romania, making their own debut in Olympic football.

After 21 minutes, Czibor gave Hungary the lead but they could not be sure of victory, even when Kocsis scored a second with 17 minutes to go. That was his last contribution to the match, before being sent off, and against ten men Suru got a goal for Romania right at the end.

Although Hungary won the game, they suffered injuries and three players, Dalnoki, Kovacs and Budai, missed the next round. Kocsis, however, did play in all the matches; in 1952, a player sent off in one round did not miss the next stage.

Denmark were able to build on their experienced players and their bronze medals in London, to defeat Greece. It was their captain, Poul Petersen, who scored first in 36 minutes. Hardly had the match restarted when Seebach made it 2-0 to the Danes, and that was sufficient, although the Greek outside-right Emanuilidis made the last five minutes hectic with a late goal.

Poland, now behind the Iron Curtain, faced a French team who had lost to Britain four years earlier. On the half-hour Leblond gave France hope, but Trampisz equalised immediately. Soon after the interval Krasowka put Poland 2-1 ahead, and they went through to the First Round.

Yugoslavia v India required the team of skilful but barefooted young Indian players to meet the veteran silver medallists of 1948. The Slav team still included two defenders and three forwards from their London matches, including the captain Mitic.

Within 17 minutes they were 3-0 up and out of sight. Zebec and Mitic ended top scorers in the tournament, scoring four and two in this 10-1 result. (In 1956, India had a more enjoyable event with one unexpected victory in Melbourne).

One of the most entertaining matches proved to be Egypt's contest with Chile. As in 1928, Chile raced into a 2-0 lead; Constanzo and Blanco, their two wingers, scored within 14 minutes.

However, the next hour belonged to Egypt. El Far and El Mekkawi scored to level the match before half-time. Then, after the break, their inside-left El Dezwi was the key forward with a hat-trick. Although Constanzo and Blanco scored again to make it 5-4, the Egyptians held on.

The USA were unlucky to be drawn once more against Italy, who had won 9-0 four years earlier. In Tampere, there was only one team in it and this was an even more comfortable victory, despite the 8-0 score. In 1948 Italy had hit four very late goals, but here they scored at regular intervals. Gimona opened with a goal in three minutes and later attained his hat-trick, the captain Pandolfini scored twice, while four of the forward line contributed.

The Luxembourg-Great Britain result was a great surprise. The British team, captained by Bob Hardisty – the only veteran of London 1948 –

took an early lead through George Robb. Britain had other chances to produce a comfortable lead, but could not convert them.

Then, on the hour, they were shocked by Roller's equaliser, and the match went to extra time. Worse was to come, and within seven minutes Letsch, on Luxembourg's left wing, and Roller had made the score 4-1. The centre-forward now had a remarkable hat-trick.

Bill Slater, later to prove a great half-back for Wolverhampton and England, did reduce the deficit, but from the kick-off Gales added a fifth. Jim Lewis's last minute goal made no difference.

The result was not a fluke, as Luxembourg's next match (against Brazil) was to prove. Their right-back and captain Wagner was outstanding, and although Lahure, in goal, was blamed for the first British shot going in, he made amends by stopping a series of attempts.

Eight of the British amateurs decided to return home, but twelve stayed to play friendly matches against Greece, Norway and Finnish clubs. Just as important, they and Walter Winterbottom, manager of GB and of England, watched the rest of the Olympics and Hungary in particular. Bill Slater even wrote a report on Puskas's team which emphasised their new approach to football.

Brazil arrived at their first Olympic tournament with a highly talented team, including Vava and Carlos Alberto. They faced the Netherlands, who immediately caught the eye and took an early lead through van Roessel.

The South Americans, whose full professionals had been runners-up in the 1950 World Cup, employed a new 4-2-4 formation against the standard two full backs, three half-backs, five forwards of almost every team, except for Hungary.

Eventually all the Brazilian front four scored against the Dutch, led by Humberto and a double from Larry in the first half. 5-1 was a comprehensive result, but a flattering one because of Jansen's and Vava's goals in the last ten minutes.

Since 1917, the USSR (Soviet Union) had taken no part in the Olympics, while Tsarist Russia did compete in the 1912 matches. But now they sent a team, who faced another Soviet bloc nation, Bulgaria. 10,000 who turned up saw a goalless draw, only relieved by goals in extra time.

Kolev, Bulgaria's inside-right, gave them the lead, only for the Russian forwards Bobrov and Trofimov to win the day. The next USSR match could not have been more different.

First Round

19 July	Austria 4-3 Finland (2-3)		Olympiastadion, Helsinki
	Gollnhuber 8 (p), 30	Stolpe 11, 34	
	Sturnpf 59	Rytkonen 36	
	Grohs 79		

20 July	West Germany 3-1 Egypt (2-0)		Kupittaa, Turku
	Klug 33	El Dezwi 64	
	Schroder 38, 61		

20 July	Brazil 2-1 Luxembourg (1-0)		Kotka
	Larry 42	Gales 86	
	Humberto 49		

20 July	Yugoslavia 5-5 USSR (3-0)		Ratina, Tampere
	(after extra time)		
	Mitic 29	Bobrov 53, 77, 87	
	Ognjanov 33	Trofimov 75	
	Zebec 44, 59	Petrov 89	
	Bobek 46		

22 July	Yugoslavia 3-1 USSR (2-1)		Ratina, Tampere
	(Replay)		
	Mitic 19	Bobrov 6	
	Bobek (p) 29		
	Cajkovski 54		

21 July	Hungary 3-0 Italy (2-0)		Pallokentta, Helsinki
	Palotas 11, 20		
	Kocsis 83		

21 July   Turkey 2-1 Netherlands Antilles (1-0)   Lahti

             Muzaffer 9   Briezen 79
             Tekin 76 (p)

21 July   Sweden 4-1 Norway (2-0)   Ratina, Tampere
             Brodd 23, 35   Sorensen 83
             Rydell 81
             Bengtsson 89

21 July   Denmark 2-0 Poland (0-0)   Kupittaa, Turku
             Seebach 17
             S. Nielsen 69

First Round

Both Finland and Austria received byes and met in Helsinki's Olympic Stadium, cheered by the biggest crowds of the whole event, apart from the Final: 33,000.

The hosts had an outstanding first half, once they had got over Austria's penalty in eight minutes from Gollnhuber. His opposite number, Stolpe, another outside-left, equalised only three minutes later.

After half an hour, the pattern was repeated – Gollnhuber and then Stolpe scored. 2-2. Now Rytkonen struck to put Finland ahead, and this form was much better than their recent heavy defeat to Hungary in a friendly match.

Eventually, however, the Austrians regained their composure and Stumpf equalised before an hour had gone. Extra-time was likely until Grohs, Austria's centre-forward, hit the winner in 79 minutes. Although it is always disappointing for home crowds to see their team lose in an early round, the Finnish supporters were very fair and applauded skilful play. In 1952 they were happy to cheer teams like Hungary, Brazil and Sweden.

The Federal Republic of Germany (West Germany) took part, after German participation was barred in 1948. Now they were too strong for Egypt after an indecisive half hour. Klug, the German outside-left, and his centre-forward Schroder scored three goals to win the match. El Dezwi's fourth goal of the event did not alter the result for Egypt, but was an outstanding contribution.

Having played sparkling football for much of their victory over the Dutch, Brazil fielded the same eleven against tiny Luxembourg. The result should have been clear-cut, but Brazil's Olympic record over the decades was to prove inconsistent, and here it took 42 minutes to establish a lead. Larry claimed it, and Humberto netted a second just after the interval.

Even then Luxembourg scored a late consolation from Jules Gales, the centre-forward. He played four times in 1948 and 1952 and helped his country produce Olympic performances that belied their international record. (1952 even saw Luxembourg win a surprise athletics gold, when Josef Barthel won the 1,500 metres.)

A sizeable crowd of 17,000 came to watch Yugoslavia play the USSR. They witnessed a match so extraordinary that its British referee, Arthur Ellis, wrote about its quality in 'The Final Whistle' (1963). He called it 'the most honourable draw' in history and 'for once, sensational was justified' as a description.

The Yugoslavs had scored ten against India, while the Russians took 100 minutes to find a goal against Bulgaria.

Here, after a cautious opening, Yugoslavia took command with goals from Mitic and his two wingers, Ognjanov and Zebec, giving them a 3-0 lead at half-time.

Immediately the teams took the field again, Bobek made the score 4-0, and the USSR were apparently already out. Even when Bobrov, their centre-forward, reduced the lead to three, Zebec countered with a fifth goal.

After their narrow win over Bulgaria, the Russians had replaced most of their forwards, but now they had to rely on the dependable Trofimov and Bobrov, who kept their places. Arthur Ellis awarded the palm to Bobrov in his book, claiming that his hat-trick was an individual feat. The team scored four times between 75 and 89 minutes, against a most intransigent side, and the centre-half Petrov hit the equaliser with seconds left. Extra time added nothing to the ten goals.

In the replay, two days later, with the same referee in the same stadium, Bobrov started as he had ended the first match, with an opener in 6 minutes. But Yugoslavia, with an unchanged side, levelled through Mitic, and a Bobek penalty gave them the lead and the momentum. They went on to win 3-1 after Cajkovski's goal in 54 minutes. The USSR defeat was not officially publicised in their own country for over a year.

In their three matches, the Russians left their defence unchanged but fielded nine forwards. Yugoslavia chose the same eleven in each of their six fixtures.

An even bigger crowd flocked to see Hungary play Italy. Palotas, one of five quick-changing forwards, scored twice in the first 20 minutes, and

Kocsis again hit a late goal, for a 3-0 victory. Every team which faced the Hungarians in 1952 wondered what might have been if they had been drawn against any other side, and Italy, fresh from an eight goal result, had some justification to speculate.

It was ironic that, while the Netherlands lost in the Preliminary Round, their South American dependency the Netherlands Antilles played in the next stage.

After their long journey to Lahti, they lost to Turkey but it was a good performance from a team which played in this Olympic tournament and no other. Muzaffer's early goal separated the teams until Tekin's penalty made it 2-0 for Turkey. Even then, Briezen, the Antilles centre-forward, scored in 79 minutes, a unique goal for his side in the event.

Only 4,200 watched two Scandinavian sides – Sweden and Norway – play for a quarter-final place. Brodd scored two first-half goals for Sweden, and the match seemed to be ending in a straightforward 2-0 result, when there was a sudden flood of goals in the last nine minutes. Rydell and Bengtsson took Sweden's total to four, with Sorensen adding one for Norway.

The Norwegians stayed on in Finland, drawing 2-2 in a friendly with Britain. Their tournament was brief, as was their manager Frank Soo's tenure. At one time a wing-half with Stoke City and England, Soo was in charge only for that summer.

Both Denmark and Poland had come through narrow 2-1 victories to make the First Round. The Danes had a more comfortable match against Greece, whereas Poland had fallen behind to France, before equalising and forging a lead.

In this contest, Denmark were the stronger team, with a goal in each half from two left-sided players, Seebach and Svend Nielsen, their left-back. Although John Hansen, the number nine, could not recapture his scoring touch of 1948, Seebach scored a goal in each match he played. Poland went on to success in later tournaments.

Quarter Finals

23 July	Sweden 3-1 Austria (0-1)		Pallokentta, Helsinki
	Sandberg 80	Grohs 40	
	Brodd 85		
	Rydell 87		

24 July	Hungary 7-1 Turkey (2-0)		Kotka
	Palotas 18	Ercument 57	
	Kocsis 32, 90		
	Lantos 48		
	Puskas 54, 72		
	Boszik 70		

24 July	West Germany 4-2 Brazil (0-1)		Pallokentta, Helsinki
	(after extra time)		
	Schroder 75, 96	Larry 12	
	Klug 89	Zozimo 74	
	Zeitler 120		

25 July	Yugoslavia 5-3 Denmark (3-0)		Pallokentta, Helsinki
	Cajkovski 19	Lundberg 63	
	Ognjanov 35	Seebach 85	
	Vukas 41	Jens Hansen 87	
	Bobek 81		
	Zebec 81		

Quarter-Finals

Three quarter-finals took place in Helsinki's Pallokentta Stadium, the other in Kotka. Attendances ranged from 10,000 to 20,000, with goals to cheer the spectators at every game.

Having knocked Finland out, Austria faced another Scandinavian team, Sweden. At first goals were hard to find, but Grohs opened the scoring for Austria just before half-time.

The reigning champions were still 1-0 down with only ten minutes left, and Austria closing on a semi-final place or even their silver medal of 1936. At last Sandberg found the net to equalise in 80 minutes. His left-wing colleague Brodd quickly overturned the lead by putting Sweden 2-1 up, and Rydell scored a third to ensure they progressed.

Hungary, on the other hand, won a straightforward victory over Turkey. Even without their legendary forward Hidegkuti, they increased the score at regular intervals, until they reached seven.

In 18 minutes Palotas put them in front, Kocsis added the second in 32. There were two goals from the captain, Puskas, another from Kocsis, and two from half-backs Boszik and Lantos. From any other side, the defenders' goals would have raised eyebrows. But Hungarian teams were unique in 1952, switching positions and requiring each man to attack or defend, according to the match situation.

In losing, Turkey were one of many in the early 1950s who could not stem the Magyar tide, and they did score a goal, through Ercument, a feat many others did not emulate.

West Germany v Brazil promised a feast of goals, and there were six, almost all of them late in the day.

Larry put Brazil 1-0 in front after 12 minutes, and with 16 minutes left Zozimo came up from their back four to double that lead. Perhaps the key moment came now, when from the kick-off Schroder, the German inside-left, reduced the lead to 2-1. This offered his team new hope and Klug equalised on the final whistle.

Into extra time, and Germany proved stronger. Within six minutes, Schroder had made the score 3-2 and Brazil could not recover, losing another to Zeitler after two hours.

After their two matches against the USSR, 3½ hours in all, Yugoslavia had no intention of allowing Denmark to come back and upset their pattern of play.

Once again, the Slav team hit three without reply in the first half, through Cajkovski, Ognjanov and Vukas. Lundberg did respond in 63 minutes, but Yugoslavia's Bobek and Zebek took their total to five. Seebach and Jens Hansen improved the score to 5-3, but Yugoslavia had reached the semi-finals once more.

Semi-Finals

28 July   Hungary 6-0 Sweden (3-0)   Olympiastadion, Helsinki

Puskas 1
Palotas 16
Lindh (o.g.) 36
Kocsis 65, 69
Hidegkuti 67

29 July   Yugoslavia 3-1 West Germany (3-1)   Olympiastadion
Mitic 3, 24   Stollenwerk 12
Cajkovski 30

Bronze medal match

1 August   Sweden 2-0 West Germany (1-0)   Olympiastadion

Rydell 11
Lofgren 86

Semi-Finals

If anyone doubted that Hungary were a remarkable team, their display against Sweden swept those doubts aside. From the very first minute, the Hungarians took charge as Puskas gave them the perfect start. Soon it was 2-0 from Palotas.

They had a stroke of luck when Lindh, Sweden's left half, hit the single own goal of the tournament. On the hour mark, the Magyars were reaching their peak and Kocsis scored twice in four minutes, with Hidegkuti not to be denied.

Puskas later wrote that the 1948 Swedish team was a better side than that of 1953, after gold medallists such as Gren, Gunnar Nordahl and Liedholm had migrated to Italy. Even so, two friendlies between Hungary and Sweden the year after Helsinki were close, ending 2-2 and 4-2 to Puskas' team.

For Yugoslavia v West Germany, also in the Olympic Stadium, there was a 20,000 attendance, slightly less than for Hungary v Sweden. Most unusually in this event, all four goals were scored in the first half, Mitic opening Yugoslavia's account in three minutes. Stollenwerk, the German inside-right, quickly equalised, but the decisive strikes went to the Slavs. Again their captain Mitic was behind the second goal, followed by Cajkovsky, and 3-1 it ended as the Slavs reached their second Final in a row.

The Bronze medal match

After three days of strong criticism in their national Press over the 6-0 defeat, Sweden now met West Germany to decide third place.

Something about Helsinki's Olympic Stadium encouraged early goals: five matches produced seven goals in their first quarter of an hour. Here Rydell broke through to score for Sweden in eleven minutes, but it took Lofgren's second right at the end to bring Sweden (and their manager, George Raynor) the triumph and more medals after London's gold.

Final

2 August   Hungary 2-0 Yugoslavia (0-0)   Olympiastadion

Puskas 70
Czibor 88

The Final

Ferenc Puskas's disappointment at losing the World Cup Final of 1954 to West Germany was clear in his book, but he did not regard the Olympic gold as a secondary achievement.

Winning the championship was immensely important in August 1952, and for once even the Hungarians were nervous. In 36 minutes, Kocsis was tripped, and Puskas stepped up to take the penalty. For the only time in his career, he hit a weak shot, saved by the Yugoslav keeper Beara. Visibly upset and with a painful hip, Puskas saw out the next few minutes till the interval.

Revived by new tactics and greater confidence, Hungary began to control the match, as Yugoslavia were frustrated by defenders' breaking up their attacks. Still, there were no goals and just 20 minutes left. Finally, Puskas took a pass from Czibor and shot; Beara let the ball drop; Puskas scored at the second attempt.

Looking more like their usual selves, Hungary went 2-0 up through Czibor in 88 minutes. But this victory was founded on solid defensive work against the Slav players who were averaging five goals a game.

Hungary took the train home, with their gold medals, and a huge crowd welcomed them in Budapest – 400,000 was the captain's estimate.

Hungary remained undefeated from 1950 to 1954. Puskas played for his country and his club Honved until the Hungarian uprising in 1956 – later he played for Real Madrid till the age of 40.

'The galloping major', 'Ocsi' (kid brother) Puskas was a goal provider as well as scorer throughout his career. This makes his tally even more astonishing, a goal a game on average for Hungary, Honved and Real – 83, 358 and 324 respectively.

Top Scorers

7: Mitic (Yugoslavia), Zebec (Yugoslavia)
6: Kocsis (Hungary)
5: Bobrov (USSR)

The Medal Winners

Gold: Hungary

Grosics	Boszik	Palotas
Geller	Kovacs	Puskas (Captain)
Lantos	Zakarias	Czibor
Buzansky	Budai	Csordas
Dalnoki	Kocsis	
Lorant	Hidegkuti	

Silver: Yugoslavia

Beara	Cajkovski	Ognjanov
Cvetkovik	Horvat	Mitic (Captain)
Stankovik	Boskov	Vukas
Crnkovik	Lustica	Bobek
Colic	Diskic	Zebec
Firm	Conc	Rajkov

Bronze: Sweden

K. Svensson	Hansson	Rydell
T. Svensson	Gustavsson	Brodd
Carlsson	Lindh	Sandberg
Samuelsson	Ahlund	A. Jonsson

Nilsson (Captain)	Bengtsson	Eriksson
Andersson	Lofgren	Sandell
Hjertsson	E. Jonsson	

Referees

N. Latichev (USSR)	Hungary v Romania
W. Karni (Finland)	Denmark v Greece
	Yugoslavia v Denmark
	Yugoslavia v West Germany (Semi-Final)
	Hungary v Turkey
K. van der Meer (Netherlands)	Poland v France
	Hungary v Italy
J. Best (USA)	Yugoslavia v India
A. Ellis (Great Britain)	Italy v USA
	Yugoslavia v USSR (both matches)
	West Germany v Brazil
	Hungary v Yugoslavia (Final)
J. Nilsson (Sweden)	Egypt v Chile
V. Orlandini (Italy)	Luxembourg v Great Britain
	Sweden v Austria
	Sweden v West Germany (Bronze medal)
G. Bernardi (Italy)	Brazil v Netherlands
	West Germany v Egypt
I. Zsolt (Hungary)	USSR v Bulgaria
W. Ling (Great Britain)	Austria v Finland
	Hungary v Sweden (Semi-Final)
M. Macancic (Yugoslavia)	Brazil v Luxembourg
C. Jorgensen (Denmark)	Turkey v Netherlands Antilles
J. Alho (Finland)	Sweden v Norway
F. Balstad (Norway)	Denmark v Poland

12. Melbourne, 1956

Beneath the Southern Cross

Melbourne was awarded these games in 1949, by one vote ahead of Buenos Aires. It was the first Southern hemisphere city to host the Olympics, and the only one which had to share events with another country. (Equestrian competitions had to take place abroad, because of Australia's quarantine laws, and Stockholm was chosen to host them, in June 1956.)

These Summer Games were held in November and December, and the football final was the latest event in any Olympiad, on 8th December. Soon after, the closing ceremony saw every athlete enter the Olympic Stadium as a mixed group, rather than marching in national teams. That inspired innovation was in keeping with the 'Friendly Games', as they were called.

The world outside was less friendly, and political events in late 1956 caused some nations to withdraw from the Olympics or specifically from football matches.

Initially, 28 nations entered the football tournament, and qualifying matches were played for the first time, so that only 16 teams would travel to Melbourne. However, the Soviet invasion of Hungary, an international crisis over Suez Canal intervention, and disputes between China and Taiwan reduced the number who finally took part. The cost of travelling from other continents also lowered participation, until it came to only eleven countries, the least since 1912.

The champions, Hungary, did not send a football team, but there were debuts for Australia, Indonesia and Thailand. There was also representation from four continents, and the final drew the biggest attendance ever for a football match in Australia. It was also the largest crowd to see an Olympic tie up to that point.

The Qualifying Tournament (1955-56)

Byes to the final stages in Melbourne:

Australia (host nation), Poland, Turkey, West Germany (as members of a United German team for the whole Olympics).

(Poland and Turkey later withdrew)

Qualifying matches : aggregate scores over two legs.

Bulgaria 5-3 Great Britain (2-0 and 3-3)
Yugoslavia walkover – Romania withdrew
Hungary v East Germany (Both withdrew)
USSR 7-1 Israel (5-0 and 2-1)
Egypt 9-3 Ethiopia (4-1 and 5-2) (Egypt later withdrew)
Iran v Afghanistan (Both withdrew)
China v Philippines (Both withdrew)
India v Thailand (Both qualified, when other teams withdrew)
Indonesia walkover – Taiwan withdrew
Japan 2-2 South Korea (2-0 and 0-2) (Japan won by drawing lots)
USA walkover – Mexico withdrew
Great Britain agreed to take part after Poland withdrew, but South Korea turned down the invitation to replace Hungary.

The September 1956 draw in Zurich produced:

USSR v West Germany
Great Britain v Thailand
Australia v Japan
Yugoslavia v USA
Bulgaria v Egypt
Hungary v India
Indonesia v Vietnam
China v Turkey

But by November even this depleted draw had become a nightmare for FIFA officials, as Egypt, Hungary, Vietnam, China and Turkey withdrew. The three men supervising the tournament, Kurt Gassman, Sir Stanley Rous and James McGuire, produced this revised version at the last minute.

First Round

USSR v West Germany
Great Britain v Thailand
Australia v Japan

Quarter Finals

Yugoslavia v USA
USSR or West Germany v Indonesia
Bulgaria v Great Britain or Thailand
India v Australia or Japan

First Round

24 November   USSR 2-1 West Germany   Olympic Park,
                                    (0-1)   Melbourne

                              Isaev 23   Habig 89
                            Strelzov 86

26 November   Great Britain 9-0 Thailand (4-0)   Olympic Park
                          Twissell 12, 20
                              Lewis 21 (p)
                       Laybourne 30, 82, 85
                          Bromilow 75, 78
                                 Topp 90

27 November   Australia 2-0 Japan (1-0)   Olympic Park
                         McMillan 26 (p)
                             Loughran 61

First Round

USSR v West Germany brought together two of the strongest teams in Melbourne. The German amateurs, representing a unified German Olympic squad in their sport, had seen their professionals lift the World Cup in 1954.

However, according to the Official Report for these Olympics, the Germans played only two forwards with everyone else in defence. Such a counter-attacking plan, now standard when clubs play away matches in European competitions, did not succeed. The Russians employed three defenders to mark their two opponents, who needed greater speed and skill to break away.

That pattern of play discouraged high scores and only Isaev, the USSR inside-right, found the net until four minutes from time. Then his centre-forward Strelzov made it 2-0, and for once Habig evaded his markers to score a consolation for Germany.

Australia's first ever Olympic match was against Japan, who had played two games in 1936. The host country scored once in each half, with McMillan's penalty after 26 minutes and another on the hour from Loughran.

The third match of this truncated Round set Great Britain against a skilful but small Thailand eleven, who made a promising start. Soon, the stronger British team, well marshalled by their captain (and veteran of 1948 and 1952) Bob Hardisty, took control of the match. In particular, Charlie Twissell had a powerful shot and he scored with two piledrivers before 20 minutes had passed. Jim Lewis was a tireless runner on the right wing and in 21 minutes he added a third from the penalty spot.

After centre-forward Jack Laybourne made it 4-0 in 30 minutes, there were no more goals until the last quarter of an hour. Then Britain added five late goals from George Bromilow, Laybourne, and even right-half Topp, coming out of defence with seconds left.

The hat-trick for Laybourne and the 9-0 score remain the highest achievements for Britain in any post-1912 match.

However, there was a cost, when their captain Hardisty sustained a groin injury and could not play against Bulgaria.

Quarter-Finals

28 November   Yugoslavia 9-1 USA (5-1)   Olympic Park, Melbourne

  Veselinovic 10, 84, 90   Zerhusen 42
  Antic 12, 73
  Mujic 16, 35, 56
  Papec 20

29 November   USSR 0-0 Indonesia (0-0) Olympic Park
                     (after extra time)

1 December (Replay)	USSR 4-0 Salnikov 17, 59 Ivanov 19 Netto 43	Indonesia (3-0)	Olympic Park

30 November	Bulgaria 6-1 Dimitrov 6 Kolev 40, 85 Milanov 45, 75, 80	Great Britain (3-1) Lewis 30	Olympic Park

1 December	India 4-2 D'Souza 9, 33, 50 Kittu 80	Australia (2-2) Morrow 17, 41	Olympic Park

Quarter-finals

Having lost twice to Italy (by nine and eight goals) in 1948 and 1952, the USA had an unenviable task against Yugoslavia, silver medallists in London and Helsinki.

Within 20 minutes, the Slav team were 4-0 ahead, goals coming from four players, Veselinovic, Antic, Mujic and Papec. Even without some of their best players, left in Europe for World Cup qualifying matches, Yugoslavia scored at every stage of the match. Their captain Mujic collected a hat-trick, as did Veselinovic with two very late goals, in the 9-1 victory. To their credit, the USA scored through Zerhusen.

The match drew 20,000, double the crowd who attended the USSR's match against Indonesia. The Asian team followed West Germany in relying on counter-attacks, with three forwards on the half-way line and everyone else massed in defence.

Although Indonesia were rarely in a position to score, the Russians found no way to goal, and two hours ended goalless. In the replay three days later, the USSR used more finesse instead of going forward in numbers. As a result, they scored twice in the first 20 minutes and won 4-0. They also rested their goalkeeper, Razinski replacing the legendary Lev Yashin.

Against Britain, during the qualifying tournament, Bulgaria had won 2-0 in Sofia and drawn 3-3 at Wembley. In Melbourne, the East Europeans took the early initiative with Dimitrov's goal in six minutes, and threatened to run off with the match. However, as so often, the British amateurs showed great spirit and hard work against a faster, tactically superior team who knew each other's play far better.

Jim Lewis managed to equalise in 30 minutes, and, even without Hardisty, the defenders Stoker, Topp, and Prince held their opponents until near the interval. Then Kolev and Milanov hit two quick goals to give Bulgaria a 3-1 lead at half-time.

The disappointment of losing those goals led 80 sailors from HMS 'Newcastle' to come on to the field, carrying three Union Flags, but they saw none of the second half after police removed them from the Olympic Park.

Once again, Bulgaria controlled the match after the interval, but could not increase their tally until late on, when Milanov completed his hat-trick and Kolev a double; they were flattered by the 6-1 scoreline.

After leaving Melbourne, Britain won three friendly matches at hot and humid stadia in Singapore, Kuala Lumpur and Rangoon. On 20th December, they landed back in a cold, foggy home country.

After the shock of Indonesia's draw with USSR came another surprise as Australia lost to India. The Asian country regards this as its best football performance, and the hat-trick by Neville D'Souza as a fine achievement.

The Indian centre-forward gave them the lead in nine minutes and his opposite number, Morrow, equalised twice for Australia, as the hosts never gained control of play as they had hoped. After the interval, D'Souza scored his third and the inside-left Kittu ended the goals with an 80th minute counter.

This was a controversial match, because the Indonesian referee disallowed two Australian 'goals' and, like many other officials at the time, did not speak English.

Even so, Australian journalists were disappointed that their team was not better prepared and had not taken their chances on a world stage.

Semi-Finals

4 December	Yugoslavia 4-1 India (0-0)	Olympic Stadium, Melbourne Cricket Ground
	Papec 54, 65	D'Souza 52
	Veselinovic 57	
	Salaam (og) 78	

5 December   USSR 2-1 Bulgaria (0-0) Olympic Stadium,
(after extra time)
Strelzov 112   Kolev 95
Tatushin 116

Bronze Medal Match

7 December   Bulgaria 3-0 India (2-0)   Olympic Stadium,
Diev 37, 60
Milanov 42

Semi-Finals

It is a measure of how well the Indian team played in 1956 that, after their victory over Australia in front of a Melbourne crowd, they yielded nothing to Yugoslavia for nearly an hour. In fact, D'Souza gave them the lead in 52 minutes.

This was reminiscent of 1948, when the Slavs could not score against Luxembourg and went a goal down. As happened in London, however, they did eventually find the net. Papec and Veselinovic scored within five minutes of India's goal to put them 2-1 ahead. The prospect of losing had spurred them on, and two more goals followed, from Papec and the unfortunate midfielder Salaam, with an own goal.

As the Official Report pointed out, the Indian players were used to shorter matches and only reluctantly wore boots. Their 'showing was far better than anticipated'.

The USSR v Bulgaria match was, for some observers, the 'real' Final between the two best teams. In a result which virtually copied these sides' encounter in Helsinki, there were no goals in the 90 minutes.

Into extra time, and Bulgaria's inside-left Kolev gave them the lead after five minutes. With eight minutes to go and facing elimination, the Russians equalised and right at the end won the match 2-1.

Not only was the result the same as in 1952, but Kolev also scored then in the same minute of the match, the 95th. Once more, the Russian centre-forward and outside-right gave them victory – in Melbourne Strelzov and Tatushin were the scorers.

One important difference in 1956 was that the USSR's right-back

Tischenko suffered a collar-bone injury, and played much of the game as a passenger.

One curious point, noted by the Official Report, is that all three goals were scored at the same end of the Olympic Stadium, when both keepers had the sun in their eyes.

Bronze Medal Match

Bulgaria appeared to be certain winners against India after coming so close to defeating the Russians. But India, with seven changes, fielded a fresh team and their third goalkeeper in three games. As a result, they stopped the Bulgarians from scoring until Diev, the new outside-left, broke through in 37 minutes.

The veteran Milanov doubled their lead just before half-time and Diev's second won the medals.

Final

8 December　　　　　USSR 1-0 Yugoslavia (0-0) Olympic Stadium,

Ilyin 48

The Final

The largest crowd for a football match in Australia flocked to the Olympic Stadium in the Melbourne Cricket Ground, to see Yugoslavia face the USSR. It was probably over 100,000, although FIFA gives a figure of 87,000.

Like the other Russian matches, this was unlikely to produce many goals. Both sides were cautious and aware of each other's strengths, and the pace of this game was noticeably slower than those in earlier rounds.

One goal was likely to prove the decider, and the honour went to Ilyin, on Russia's left wing, in 48 minutes. The USSR team did play five times, twice more than any other side, and they proved to be adaptable against defensive and attacking sides.

Yugoslavia won their third silver medal in a row, and the clean sweep of medals for Communist-run countries set the pattern until 1984. Even so, the achievements of Indonesia and India showed that underdogs could sometimes challenge the best funded and most experienced teams from Eastern Europe.

The Medal Winners

Gold: USSR

Yashin	Isaev	Betza
Kuznetsov	Simonian	Strelzov
Bashashkin	Salnikov	Ivanov
Ogonikov	Ilyin	Rishkin
Netto (captain)	Razinski	
Maslenkin	Tischenko	
Tatushin	Paramonov	

Silver: Yugoslavia

Radenkovic	Papac
Koscak	Antic
Radovic	Veselinovic
Santek	Vidinic
Spajic	Biogradlic
Krstic	Liposinovic
Sekularac	Mujic (captain)

Bronze: Bulgaria

Yosifov	Dimitrov	Kolev
Rakarov	Panayotov	Diev
Manolov	Naidenov	
Kovatschev	Kirchev	
Bojkov (captain)	Goranov	
Stoyanov	Kovacev	
Milanov	Yanev	

Top Scorers

4: D'Souza (India)
Milanov (Bulgaria)
Veselinovic (Yugoslavia)

Referees

R.H. Mann (Great Britain)   USSR v West Germany
                                 USSR v Bulgaria (semi-final)

N. Latishev (USSR)   GB v Thailand
Yugoslavia v India (semi-final)
Bulgaria v India
(Bronze medal match)

R. Lund (New Zealand)   Australia v Japan
USSR v Indonesia (replay)

M. Swain (New Zealand)   Yugoslavia v USA

S. Takenokoshi (Japan)   USSR v Indonesia (first match)

R. Wright (Australia)   Bulgaria v GB
USSR v Yugoslavia (Final)

H. Wensveen (Indonesia)   Australia v India

13. Rome, 1960

All roads lead to Rome

In a recent book David Maraniss called these 'The Olympics that changed the world'. Certainly they were the Games that changed the Olympics to a recognisably modern phenomenon.

They were the first to be televised in a significant number of countries, including the UK and the USA, where CBS paid nearly 400,000 dollars for broadcasting rights.

Rome also shared events with other cities, some far from the capital, such as Naples. Melbourne provided all the venues in 1956, and although earlier Games employed a few stadia outside London and Helsinki, for example, 1960 introduced a new scale and dispersal. In 2012, football will be staged in six grounds all over the UK.

The IOC chose Rome in 1955, ahead of Lausanne and Detroit. Vesuvius' eruption had cost her the 1908 Olympics, when funding had to go to essential reconstruction for Southern Italy.

In Italy, it was not surprising that late August and early September were very hot, especially for footballers playing matches that began at 4pm.

Another drawback for some athletes was that they missed the opening or closing ceremonies. British and Brazilian footballers, preparing for their game in Livorno, had to settle for TV coverage, and not join their national teams as they entered the Olympic Stadium in Rome.

Despite international tensions, these were generally less than in 1956, and 83 nations took part. So many entered the football tournament – 52 initially – that there were qualifying matches in every continent in 1959-60, to produce 16 for the final stages.

In retrospect, the most famous gold medallist in Rome was a young light-heavyweight boxer, later known as Muhammad Ali, who was cheered by American supporters in the arena. One celebrity who added a distinctive voice to the US national anthem, when Edward Crook received his middleweight gold, was Bing Crosby.

On the track, Australia and New Zealand won all three men's middle-distance races, thanks to Herb Elliott, Peter Snell and Murray Halberg. Not only did Elliott win the 1500 metres by 2.8 seconds, but he made running look as easy as Emil Zatopek (and the 400 metres legend Eric Liddell) had made it look hard in earlier decades.

In the summer heat Britain's Olympians benefited from energy drinks, supplied by the manufacturers of Horlicks and Lucozade. Smaller firms also provided biscuits and boiled sweets, all welcome when footballers lost an average of nine calories every minute.

After 1956, when eleven teams travelled to Melbourne with no certainty of more than one match, FIFA and the IOC accepted a plan from the FA. This proposed arranging the final stages in Italy with 16 teams in four groups. Each side played at least three games, the winner of a group progressing straight to the semi-finals.

The qualifying tournament was divided into continents – Europe, the Americas (North, Central and South), Africa and Asia, plus 'The Near East', for 1960 only.

52 teams entered and there were three withdrawals – Afghanistan and Australia (placed within Asia), and Lebanon, in the Near East. South Korea were disqualified after arguments led to their match in Taiwan being abandoned.

The 16 qualifiers were:

Italy (host nation)
Europe (7): Denmark, Poland, Bulgaria, Yugoslavia, Great Britain, France, Hungary
The Americas (3): Argentina, Peru, Brazil
Africa (2): UAR (United Arab Republic), Tunisia
Asia (2): Taiwan (Formosa), India
The Near East: Turkey

The Football Tournament

First Round

Group One

26 August	Bulgaria 3-0 Turkey (1-0)	Stadio Olimpico Comunale, Grosseto

Diev 13, 58
Iliev 67

26 August	Yugoslavia	6-1	UAR (3-0)	Stadio Adriatico, Pescara
	Rifal o.g. 3		Attia 72	
	Galic 30 (p)			
	Kostic 32, 61, 63			
	Knez 49			
29 August	Bulgaria	2-0	UAR (1-0)	Stadio Comunale, L'Aquila
	Yordanov 42			
	Diev 88			
29 August	Yugoslavia	4-0	Turkey (1-0)	Stadio Comunale, Florence
	Kostic 10, 89			
	Galic 46			
	Knez 61			
1 September	UAR	3-3	Turkey (1-2)	Stadio di Ardenza, Livorno
	Attia 10		Bilge 15	
	Qotb 58, 65		Ugur 30	
			Ibrahim 69	
1 September	Yugoslavia	3-3	Bulgaria (0-0)	Stadio Flaminio, Rome
	Galic 50, 57, 69		Kovachev 59	
			Debarski 81, 89	

Qualified	Yugoslavia	5 points	(13 goals for – 4 against)
	Bulgaria	5 points	(8-3)
	UAR	1 point	(4-11)
	Turkey	1 point	(3-10)

The United Arab Republic (UAR) was the name of the country formed by a temporary merger of Egypt and Syria. All the players in the football team were Egyptian. The UAR competed under that title in 1960-68.

Group One

With only one team progressing from each group, the match between Bulgaria and Yugoslavia was always likely to be decisive in Group One.

First, however, they encountered the other teams. In Grosseto, **Bulgaria** took an early lead over **Turkey** through Diev, but could not capitalise on it until his second goal, after almost an hour. Iliev ensured the two points in a straightforward 3-0 result.

At the same time in Pescara, **Yugoslavia** benefited from an own goal in just three minutes, from **UAR's** right-back Rifai, and then a penalty from their captain Milan Galic. The match was effectively over in 32 minutes, when Kostic added a third.

In the second half, there was time for him to complete a hat-trick, with Knez and Turkey's Attia also on the 6-1 scoresheet.

Three days later **Bulgaria** found **UAR** had a new keeper and full-backs; although the Europeans won 2-0, their achievement was hard fought. The goals came at the end of each half from a new centre-forward, Yordanov, and the prolific outside-right Diev.

Against **Turkey**, **Yugoslavia** had another big victory. Kostic took ten minutes to score the opener, and in a second half controlled by the Slavs, Galic, Knez and Kostic raised the total to four without reply.

After their two matches, only Bulgaria and Yugoslavia could reach the semi-finals. Both had four points, with the better goal average that of Yugoslavia – goal difference was not used until several Olympiads later. The two other teams still had no points.

On 1st September, 15,000 came to Rome's Stadio Flaminio to find out which of the East Europeans would prevail. At first, neither **Yugoslavia** nor **Bulgaria** dominated, and there were no goals for 50 minutes. Then Galic scored twice within seven minutes.

Bulgaria had to win this encounter. Now they pushed more men forward, and left-half Kovachev reduced the lead to 2-1. Back came Galic for his hat-trick with 20 minutes to go. The Bulgarians should have been even further behind on chances created by the sides, but in a hectic last few minutes Debarski, on the left wing, threw his team a lifeline with two goals. 3-3 was the final score, and Yugoslavia were through.

That was also the result in Livorno between **UAR** and **Turkey**. In an exciting match, two sides eliminated three days earlier showed the value of taking part in an Olympics was more than just about medal winning. The game ebbed and flowed, UAR leading twice and Turkey once. Only 600 spectators enjoyed the spectacle and six goals.

Group Two

26 August	Brazil 4-3	Great Britain (1-1)	Stadio di Ardenza, Livorno
	Gerson 2	B. Brown 32, 87	
	China 61, 72	Lewis 47	
	Wanderley 64		
26 August	Italy 4-1	Taiwan (Formosa) (2-1)	Stadio di Fuorigrotta, Naples
	Rivera 10, 33	C.W. Mok 29	
	Fanello 49		
	Tomeazzi 67		
29 August	Yugoslavia 4-0	Turkey (1-0)	Stadio Comunale, Florence
	Kostic 10, 89		
	Galic 46		
	Knez 61		
1 September	UAR 3-3	Turkey (1-2)	Stadio di Ardenza, Livorno
	Attia 10	Bilge 15	
	Qotb 58, 65	Ugur 30	

29 August	Brazil 5-0 Taiwan (2-0)		Stadio Flaminio, Rome
	Gerson 13, 16, 47		
	Dias 73, 87		

29 August	Great Britain 2-2 Italy (1-1)		Stadio Flaminio, Rome
	B. Brown 23	Rossano 11, 55	
	Hasty 75		

1 September	Italy 3-1 Brazil (0-1)		Stadio Comunale, Florence
	Rivera 69	Valdir 4	
	Rossano 70, 86		

1 September	Great Britain 3-2 Taiwan (1-0)		Stadio Olimpico Comunale, Grosseto
	Lewis 35	Y.C. Yin 70, 88	
	B. Brown 58		
	Hasty 85		

Qualified	Italy	5 points	(9-4)
	Brazil	4 points	(10-6)
	Great Britain	3 points	(8-8)
	Taiwan	0 points	(3-12)

Group Two

Italy had not won a medal since their 1936 gold, but they were assured of vocal support in their own stadia. They had defeated Britain's amateurs in a friendly match a few weeks before, 5-1.

Brazil qualified, despite losing to Colombia, Peru and Argentina, and their full professional team were the toast of sport after the World Cup triumph of 1958. Vicente Feola coached the winners and this young

Olympic team, mostly aged 21 or less.

Britain and Taiwan (then called Formosa) had the unenviable task of trying to win points from such formidable opposition.

Italy's match in Naples drew 36,000 to see them play **Taiwan**, and the hosts soon took a lead through Giani Rivera. Mok, Taiwan's outstanding forward, equalised, and Rivera needed a second goal to give Italy a 2-1 advantage at half-time.

As so often in these Olympics, vital goals were scored just after the interval, and Fanello hit the decisive shot in 49 minutes. Taiwan could not recover, and Tomeazzi's fourth added a grace note as Italy finished in style.

Brazil included players who later became legendary, such as Gerson, a scorer in the 1970 World Cup Final, and Roberto Dias, a defender whom Pele esteemed. Against **Great Britain** they scored almost immediately, from a free kick taken by Gerson.

The South Americans ran and passed faster than Britain, and David Holt (later a full Scottish international) twice cleared off the line. In danger of being swamped, the British found a lifeline when Bobby Brown, their young inside-right, outran his two markers and scored from 18 yards. The 1-1 score, and the interval, brought his team the chance to regroup.

Two minutes after restarting, Brazil were shocked when Jim Lewis, veteran of 1952 and 1956, made the score 2-1 and another British shot hit the bar. Now came the turning-point of this match, and perhaps of Britain's campaign, in 52 minutes.

Their right-back Tommy Thompson was tackled and suffered a broken leg. No action was taken by the referee, and the ten men lost two goals in the next 12 minutes from China and Wanderley. 3-2 ahead, Brazil soon added another from their centre-forward China, although Bobby Brown completed the scoring near the end. The Brazilians had won 4-3, but their weaknesses had been exposed by a team playing at their peak, especially in defence, where centre-half Laurie Brown and keeper Mike Pinner were heroic.

Brazil's match against **Taiwan** was notable for Gerson's hat-trick, two in the first 16 minutes and another in 47 minutes. The Brazilian right-half Roberto Dias was not taxed in defence, and was able to score two late goals by moving forward, to complete the 5-0 victory.

In Rome, **Italy** faced **Britain** with the best of the country's under 21s from Serie A, such as Giovanni Trapattoni, Rivera and Burgnich. Within eleven minutes, the 18 year old inside-left Rossano, of Juventus, put Italy 1-0 ahead – from a possibly offside position. However, this was not the prelude to a home victory.

Instead, Bobby Brown benefited from an interpassing move, between Willie Neil and Jim Lewis, and took his chance to equalise.

BBC TV showed the second half via Eurovision to millions of British viewers, their first chance to see an Olympic match. (The 1948 TV coverage was received by the tiny number of households with sets).

Kenneth Wolstenholme praised 'a great British side' in his commentary. Rossano scored his second controversial goal in 55 minutes – after the outstanding Hugh Lindsay was fouled, British players stopped for a free kick that was not given, letting the inside-left run in and shoot past Mike Pinner.

Even then there was a second equaliser, Paddy Hasty taking Hunter Devine's left-side corner and driving home from six yards.

Brazil now stood on four points, Italy on three and Britain one. To progress to the semi-finals, a draw would suffice for **Brazil**, **Italy** required to win when they met in Florence.

For much of that evening, nearly 25,000 supporters were forlorn as Brazil's Valdir found the net in just four minutes. It seemed for over an hour that bringing in Rancati and Ferrini to refresh the Italian attack was not working. Then at last, with 20 minutes left, Rivera and Rossano scored twice in 60 seconds, to put Italy 2-1 ahead.

Now Brazil had to go all out for an equaliser, leaving room for Rossano to make the score 3-1 near the end. Italy went through to play Yugoslavia, and experience a unique form of disappointment, in their semi-final.

In Grosseto, before a small crowd, **Britain** won 3-2 against **Taiwan**, but this was their least inspired performance of the event. It took them 35 minutes to score through Lewis, and the second half was evenly contested, goals from Brown and Hasty cancelled out by Yiu's double.

In 2010, British players held a reunion in Much Wenlock, Shropshire, home of Dr Brookes's Olympics, and reminisced over what happened, and what might have been, fifty years earlier.

One teenager who turned out for Great Britain in a warm-up match against Northampton, but was not selected for competitive fixtures, later became an England international and manager. That was Chelsea's Terry Venables.

Bobby Brown, whose goals and general skills had impressed in all the matches, almost moved from Barnet to A.C. Milan. Then Giuseppe Viani, the Milan, and Italian Olympic, manager fell ill – and the offer lapsed. Instead, his career continued at Fulham, Watford and Cardiff.

In July 2011, Mike Greenwood told the 'Sunday Sun' newspaper, 'it was very exciting ... We're proud of what we did'.

Group Three

26 August	Denmark 3-2 Argentina (1-1)		Stadio Flaminio, Rome
	Sorensen 31	Oleniak 20	
	H. Nielsen 46, 85	Bilardo 88	

26 August	Poland 6-1 Tunisia (3-1)		Stadio Flaminio, Rome
	Pol 7, 40, 42, 84, 89	Kerrit 3	
	Hachorek 67		

29 August	Denmark 2-1 Poland (1-0)		Stadio di Ardenza, Livorno
	H. Nielsen 15	Gadecki 62	
	Pedersen 86		

29 August	Argentina 2-1 Tunisia (1-1)		Stadio Adriatico, Pescara
	Oleniak 15, 82	Kerrit 25	

1 September	Argentina 2-0 Poland (1-0)		Stadio di Fuorigrotta, Naples
	Oleniak 38		
	Perez 55		

1 September	Denmark 3-1 Tunisia (2-0)		Stadio Comunale, L'Aquila
	F. Nielsen 24	Cherif 48	
	H. Nielsen 27, 88		

Qualified   Denmark   6 points   (8-4)
            Argentina 4 points   (6-4)
            Poland   2 points   (7-5)
            Tunisia   0 points   (3-11)

Group Three

This group brought together two past silver medal winners, Denmark and Argentina, with Poland, and Tunisia making their debut.

This skilful **Argentina** side had won every qualifying match and for 45 minutes were a class ahead of **Denmark**. But they could not make it count in goals. Oleniak gave the South Americans the lead after 20 minutes, but Sorensen levelled eleven minutes later. Argentina just missed the target, they hit the post, Henry From made save after save for the Danes. 1-1 at half-time.

Immediately the game restarted after the interval, Denmark's teenaged centre-forward, Harald Nielsen, scored – and their defence held out for almost the whole second half. Nielsen even broke away to make victory secure in 85 minutes, although Bilardo then added Argentina's second. The outstanding goal in the 3-2 win for Denmark went to Nielsen when he counter-attacked, dribbling upfield past three defenders and shooting home from 25 yards.

Tunisia could not have asked for a better start to their first tournament. Against **Poland**, Kerrit scored in three minutes, but that was a false dawn, for Poland soon equalised, and Pol went on to score five times in a 6-1 victory. The essential goals were his double just before the interval, making it 3-1.

Poland knew the significance of goal average in these groups, and Pol scored two more in the last six minutes, with Hachorek collecting the other.

Denmark v Poland was the most difficult of games to forecast. Harald Nielsen again showed his power with a goal in 15 minutes, but Poland conceded no more in the 45. Then, on the hour, Polish outside-right Gadecki levelled the score, and any result was possible.

Neither would accept a draw, but Poland still had to play Argentina, and their need to risk all-out attack was greater than the Danes'. In 86 minutes Pedersen had the chance to win the match, which ended 2-1 to Denmark.

In Pescara, **Argentina** found their match with **Tunisia** far more demanding than Poland had. Although Oleniak put Argentina ahead in only 15 minutes, Kerrit's goal brought the African team back into contention. A 1-1 draw would have seen both sides go out, but Oleniak scored the winner with just eight minutes left.

With one game left for each team, Denmark were obvious favourites to go through. They had four points, Argentina and Poland two. Only a Tunisian win over the leaders gave the others any opportunity.

However, Flemming Nielsen moved up front to give **Denmark** the lead over **Tunisia** in 24 minutes; they were not under threat of losing out in Group Three. Harald Nielsen scored another three minutes later and Denmark's third right at the end of the match. Cherif replied for Tunisia early in the second half.

Argentina played **Poland** in Naples, and the South Americans scored through Oleniak, his fourth in three games, and Perez, to take the runners-up position in their group.

Group Four

26 August	France 2-1 Peru (0-1)	Stadio Comunale, Florence
	Giamarchi 67 Uribe 1	
	Quedec 80	

26 August	Hungary 2-1 India (1-0)	Stadio Comunale, L'Aquila
	Gorocs 23 Balaram 79	
	Albert 56	

29 August	France 1-1 India (0-0)	Stadio Olimpico Comunale, Grosseto
	Coincon 82 Banerjee 71	

29 August	Hungary 6-2 Peru (3-1)	Stadio di Fuorigrotta, Naples
	Albert 17, 87 Ramirez 25, 79	
	Rakosi 27	
	Gorocs 33	
	Dunai 46, 63	

1 September   Peru 3-1 India (1-0)   Stadio Adriatico, Pescara
              Nieri 27, 53   Balaram 88
              Iwasaki 85

1 September   Hungary 7-0 France (3-0) Stadio Flaminio, Rome
              Albert 12, 85
            Gorocs 34, 59, 77
              Dunai 41, 79

Qualified   Hungary   6 points   (15-3)
                France   3 points   (3-9)
                 Peru   2 points   (6-9)
                 India   1 point   (3-6)

Group Four

This group included Hungary, France, India and Peru.

Hungary, champions in 1952, had suffered upheavals since then and famous players, notably Puskas, had left the country. They won four qualifying ties, over Austria and Czechoslovakia, and included four full internationals in the team. Clearly they were favourites to win the group and perhaps the gold.

Peru had defeated Uruguay and Brazil en route to reaching the group stages, India hoped to improve on their fourth place in 1956, and France returned, despite losing one match to Luxembourg.

Sometimes an outstanding team finds their first match the most difficult, and that was true when **Hungary** met **India** in L'Aquila. Gorocs put Hungary 1-0 ahead in 23 minutes, but India's defenders did not concede a second time until Florian Albert, the new star at centre-forward, hit home in the 56th minute.

India were not outclassed in any of their contests, and Balaram's late goal produced a tense few minutes before the end.

Peru's Olympic endeavour began against **France** and they received a flying start in 60 seconds from Uribe's goal. France only improved when they were reduced to ten men in 58 minutes, after the inside-left Arab was dismissed. Soon Giamarchi equalised and in the very last moments Quedec won France the game.

Against **India**, **France** once more had to respond to being 1-0 down. India's captain, Banerjee, put them in front 19 minutes from the end, only for Coincon to equalise. France were so unhappy with their earlier performance that they fielded new full-backs, half-backs, two new forwards and a new keeper.

When they met **Peru**, **Hungary's** captain Varhidi moved from full-back to centre-half, and the Magyars did improve with three goals in just over half an hour. Albert, Rakosi and Gorocs all found the net, although Ramirez did equalise at 1-1.

Once the veteran Dunai got a fourth after the interval, the points were secure, and Dunai, Albert and Ramirez all collected doubles in a 6-2 win for Hungary.

With two matches played by every team, Hungary had four points, France three, and India one. Only **France** could stop the **Hungarians'** progress by winning against them in Rome.

But the French dream lasted barely 41 minutes. By then the Magyars were 3-0 up from Albert, Gorocs and Dunai. The second half became a procession, as the same players scored again – Gorocs's hat-trick was the individual highlight.

Peru 3-1 **India** completed the group, when Nieri scored twice and Iwasaki added a late third goal – Balaram added a consolation for the Indian team.

Semi-Finals

5 September   Italy 1-1 Yugoslavia (0-0)) Stadio di Fuorigrotta, Naples

(after extra time:
Yugoslavia won on the toss of a coin)
Tumburus 109   Galic 107

6 September   Denmark 2-0 Hungary (1-0)   Stadio Flaminio, Rome

H. Nielsen 19
Enoksen 81

Bronze medal match

9 September   Hungary 2-1 Italy (1-0)   Stadio Flaminio, Rome
               Orosz 32   Tomeazzi 84
               Dunai 69

Semi-Finals

Italy's fans knew that their team had reached the Naples semi-final only in the last 20 minutes of their group and that **Yugoslavia** had won three silver medals in three Olympics.

But the Slavs had come close to defeat against Bulgaria, and no one in the Stadio di Fuorigrotta could imagine what the next two hours would produce.

Yugoslavia had amassed 13 goals to Italy's nine, but now they introduced two new right-side attackers, as well as a new right-half and keeper. Italy retained the side who beat Brazil, except that Tomeazzi replaced Fanello at centre-forward.

There were no goals for 107 minutes, and then Galic, the Slav captain, scored his sixth goal of the event. Italy threw more men into attack, and Tumburus came out of midfield to equalise two minutes later. At 11 pm the match ended 1-1. With no replay or penalty deciders in 1960, a coin was tossed and Yugoslavia called right, to reach the Final.

Denmark v **Hungary** was probably the finest match in these Olympics. The Danes, authentically amateurs, came through group Three with three wins, eliminating Argentina and Poland. Hungary had outscored every team so far, albeit against weaker sides.

The Magyars were favourites, with new stars upfront in Florian Albert and Janos Gorocs, but Denmark had a settled squad, well organised by the coach Arne Sorensen. In 18 year-old Harald Nielsen they had a goal-scorer, and he gave them the lead in 19 minutes.

Both sides missed a penalty, and when the Danish keeper, From, saved Varhidi's shot, the Hungarian captain might have recalled Puskas's miscue in the 1952 Final. A second goal for Denmark near the end ensured they would play for the gold.

Willy Meisl, veteran journalist and brother of Hugo, wrote that no team could have matched the Danes that night. With technique, speed and spirit they were a revelation, worthy of medals just as much as their predecessors of 1906, 1908 and 1912.

Bronze Medal Match

Almost 19,000 came to see if Italy could at least win the bronze after losing out by the toss of a coin. Hungary were just as eager to overcome their shock at Denmark's victory. Both introduced two new men to their forward line – Satori and Orosz for the Magyars, Cella and Bulgarelli for Italy.

Orosz put Hungary ahead in 32 minutes and Dunai made it 2-0 with 20 minutes left. Italy did respond but too late, when Tomeazzi scored in 84 minutes. The Italians were unfortunate not to go into extra time, as Gabor Torek saved Hungary time and again. The keeper was inspired, and deserved his medal more than anyone.

Final

10 September   Yugoslavia 3-1 Denmark (2-0) Stadio Flaminio, Rome

                            Galic 1   F. Nielsen 90
                            Matus 11
                            Kostic 69

In Rome, Yugoslavia took seconds to produce a goal, something that took them an hour and three quarters against Italy in the semi-final. Milan Galic led the way, and his inside-right Matus, fresher after sitting out the group matches, doubled the lead in eleven minutes.

Well into the second half, Kostic confirmed the victory with a third goal. The one blot on the Slav's gold was that their captain, 21 year old Galic, was sent off in 40 minutes. He refused to accept an offside decision that disallowed a Kostic 'goal'.

Even with ten men, Yugoslavia remained the stronger side and won the title after three successive runners-up positions. Denmark were noticeably tired after four demanding contests, although Flemming Nielsen scored on the final whistle.

Medal Winners

Gold: Yugoslavia

Vidinic	Matus	Sombolac
Roganovic	Galic (captain)	Kozlina
Jusufi	Knez	Bego

Perusic	Kostic	
Durkovic	Soskic	
Janetic	Maravic	
Ankovic	Takac	

Silver: Denmark

From	Troelsen	Hellbrandt
Andersen	H. Nielsen	Krog
Jensen (captain)	Enoksen	Kurtzweil
B. Hansen	Sorensen	Larsen
H.C. Nielsen	Danielsen	Mejer
F. Nielsen	Gaardhoje	Sterobo
Pedersen	J. Hansen	

Bronze: Hungary

Torok	Gorocs	Farago
Dudas	Albert	T. Pal
Dalnoki	Orosz	
Solymosi	Dunai	
Varhidi (captain)	Novak	
Kovacs	Vilezsal	
Satori	Rakosi	

Top Goal-scorers

7: Galic (Yugoslavia)
6: Kostic (Yugoslavia)
6: Harald Nielsen (Denmark)

Referees

C. Jonni (Italy)	Bulgaria v Turkey
	Yugoslavia v Bulgaria
R. Leafe (Great Britain)	Yugoslavia v UAR
	Denmark v Hungary
	(Semi-Final)
	Hungary v Italy
	(Bronze medal)
L. Helge (Denmark)	Bulgaria v UAR
	Italy v Taiwan

V. Orlandini (Italy)	Yugoslavia v Turkey
	Hungary v France
L. van Nuffel (Belgium)	UAR v Turkey
	GB v Italy
J. Kandlbinder (West Germany)	Brazil v GB
	GB v Taiwan
	Italy v Yugoslavia
	(Semi-Final)
E. Erlih (Yugoslavia)	Brazil v Taiwan
	France v Peru
P. Schwinte (France)	Italy v Brazil
F. Liverani (Italy)	Denmark v Argentina
C. lo Bello (Italy)	Poland v Tunisia
	Denmark v Poland
	Yugoslavia v Denmark
	(Final)
I. Zsolt (Hungary)	Argentina v Tunisia
S. Garan (Turkey)	Argentina v Poland
G. Campanati (Italy)	Denmark v Tunisia
B. Ben Said (Tunisia)	Hungary v India
R. Morgan (Canada)	France v India
P. Bonetto (Italy)	Hungary v Peru
H. Imam (United Arab Republic)	Peru v India

The qualifying tournament

In qualifying, the only teams with 100% records were Poland, Hungary and Argentina. The greatest surprise was that the gold medallists in 1956, the USSR, did not qualify, losing out to Bulgaria. From 1964, the reigning champions did not have to qualify for the next Olympics, and Yugoslavia were offered a place in Tokyo.

Individual matches produced shocks, with Finland defeating West Germany, Luxembourg winning 5-3 over France, and Israel winning in Yugoslavia.

(In the final stages in Italy, Groups Two, Three and Four included two European teams, one from South America, and one from Africa or Asia. Group One included Turkey, but none from South America.)

Europe (every team played four matches).

Group 1

Denmark: 7 points (11 goals for − 6 against): Qualified
Iceland: 3 points (5-7)
Norway: 2 points (5-8)
Iceland 2-4 Denmark, Denmark 1-1 Iceland
Denmark 2-1 Norway, Norway 2-4 Denmark
Iceland 1-0 Norway, Norway 2-1 Iceland

Group 2

Poland: 8 points (15-4): Qualified
West Germany: 2 points (5-10)
Finland: 2 points (7-13)
Finland 1-3 Poland, Poland 6-2 Finland
West Germany 2-1 Finland, Finland 3-2 West Germany
West Germany 0-3 Poland, Poland 3-1 West Germany

Group 3
Bulgaria: 5 points (4-3): Qualified
USSR: 4 points (3-2)
Romania: 3 points (2-4)
USSR 1-1 Bulgaria, Bulgaria 1-0 USSR
USSR 2-0 Romania, Romania 0-0 USSR
Romania 1-0 Bulgaria, Bulgaria 2-1 Romania

Group 4
Yugoslavia: 5 points (12-4): Qualified
Israel: 5 points (7-6)
Greece: 2 points (3-12)
Israel 2-2 Yugoslavia, Yugoslavia 1-2 Israel
Yugoslavia 4-0 Greece, Greece 0-5 Yugoslavia
Israel 2-1 Greece, Greece 2-1 Israel

Group 5

Great Britain: 7 points (13-6): Qualified
Republic of Ireland: 3 points (9-9)
Netherlands: 2 points (6-13)
Netherlands 0-0 Ireland, Ireland 6-3 Netherlands

Great Britain 3-2 Ireland, Ireland 1-3 Great Britain
Netherlands 1-5 Great Britain, Great Britain 2-2 Netherlands

Group 6

France: 6 points (7-6): Qualified
Luxembourg: 4 points (7-6)
Switzerland: 2 points (3-5)
France 1-0 Luxembourg, Luxembourg 5-3 France
Switzerland 1-2 France, France 1-0 Switzerland
Luxembourg 0-0 Switzerland, Switzerland 2-2 Luxembourg

Group 7

Hungary: 8 points (10-3): Qualified
Czechoslovakia: 3 points (4-5)
Austria: 1 point (2-8)
Czechoslovakia 0-0 Austria, Austria 1-2 Czechoslovakia
Hungary 2-1 Austria, Austria 0-4 Hungary
Czechoslovakia 1-2 Hungary, Hungary 2-1 Czechoslovakia

The Americas

Round One

Mexico, Surinam, Brazil, Argentina and Peru went into Round Two, on two-leg aggregates.
Mexico 3-1 USA (2-0 and 1-1)
Surinam 6-3 Netherlands Antilles (4-1 and 2-2)
Colombia 3-7 Brazil (2-0 and 1-7)
Chile 1-11 Argentina (1-5 and 0-6)
Peru 9-2 Uruguay (6-0 and 3-2)

Round Two

(4 matches each)
Argentina: 8 points (14-5): Qualified
Peru: 6 points (7-3): Qualified
Brazil: 4 points (7-7): Qualified
Mexico: 2 points (6-6)
and Surinam: 0 points (4-17)
Peru 1-0 Mexico

Argentina 6-2 Surinam
Peru 3-1 Surinam
Brazil 2-1 Mexico
Mexico 4-0 Surinam
Argentina 3-1 Brazil
Surinam 1-4 Brazil
Peru 1-2 Argentina
Peru 2-0 Brazil
Mexico 1-3 Argentina
(All matches played in Peru in Round Two)

Africa

(Every team played four games in each Round)

Round One: Group One

Tunisia: 5 points (5-3) (Tunisia into Round Two on goal average)
Morocco: 5 points (7-6)
Malta: 2 points (3-6)
Malta 0-0 Tunisia, Tunisia 2-0 Malta
Malta 2-2 Morocco, Morocco 2-1 Malta
Tunisia 2-0 Morocco, Morocco 3-1 Tunisia

Round One: Group Two

UAR: 6 points (11-5) (UAR into Round Two)
Ghana: 4 points (8-6)
Nigeria: 2 points (6-14)
Nigeria 3-1 Ghana, Ghana 4-1 Nigeria
UAR 2-1 Ghana, Ghana 2-0 UAR
Nigeria 2-6 UAR, UAR 3-0 Nigeria

Round One: Group Three

Sudan: 7 points (6-2) (Sudan into Round Two)
Ethiopia: 4 points (5-6)
Uganda: 1 point (2-5)
Uganda 1-2 Ethiopia, Ethiopia 1-1 Uganda
Sudan 3-1 Ethiopia, Ethiopia 1-1 Sudan
Sudan 1-0 Uganda, Uganda 0-1 Sudan

Round Two

(UAR and Tunisia qualified)
UAR: 7 points (7-1)
Tunisia: 3 points (3-4)
Sudan: 2 points (1-6)
Sudan 1-0 Tunisia, Tunisia 2-0 Sudan
UAR 3-1 Tunisia, Tunisia 0-0 UAR
Sudan 0-1 UAR, UAR 3-0 Sudan

Asia

Round One

(Aggregate scores over two legs)
India walk-over: Afghanistan withdrew after the fist leg (India 5-2 Afghanistan)
Indonesia walk-over: Australia withdrew
Taiwan 6-2 Thailand (3-1 and 3-1)
South Korea 2-1 Japan (2-0 and 0-1)

Round Two

(Taiwan and India qualified)
Taiwan 1-2 South Korea (First leg)
In the second leg, played in Taipei, the match was abanadoned after 35 minutes, with Taiwan leading 1-0. Taiwan were awarded the tie.
India 6-2 Indonesia (4-2 and 2-0)

The Near East

(Turkey qualified)
Turkey 2 games: 4 points (10-3)
Iraq 4 games: 4 points (14-10)
Lebanon 2 games: 0 points (0-11)
Lebanon 0-3 Iraq, Iraq 8-0 Lebanon
Turkey 7-1 Iraq, Iraq 2-3 Turkey
Lebanon then withdrew.

14. Tokyo, 1964

Tokyo Melody

In 1964 the British hit parade was dominated by home-grown groups such as the Beatles, Searchers, and Animals, but that October the German bandleader Helmut Zacharias had great success with 'Tokyo melody'. When viewers awoke to the BBC's morning broadcasts of Olympic events (long before Breakfast TV began in 1983), they heard this theme. A vocal version was appropriately named 'Good Morning, Tokyo'.

No other Olympiad has produced such a successful tune, with claims that the record sold 13 million over the years. Tokyo's Games were the first shown via a geostationary satellite, Syncom 3, around the globe – and Japan may have spent $3 billion on stadia and transport links.

Tokyo was awarded the Olympics in 1959, ahead of Detroit, which consoled itself with the global success of Motown records. Japan's capital had the 1940 Games withdrawn when the country invaded China. A moving reminder of the Second World War was that the Olympic Flame was lit in the National Stadium by 19 year old Yoshinori Sakai.

He was born the day that Hiroshima was devastated in 1945. The flame itself, and Tokyo's successful bid, expressed reconciliation within the Olympian aim of friendship between peoples.

A record 93 nations took part, 14 for the first time, and the Olympic flagpole measured 15.21 metres, the precise distance cleared by triple jumper Mikio Oda in 1928, when he won Japan's first gold medal.

Now the hosts achieved 16 golds, surpassed only by the USA and USSR, but the new discipline of judo was not a clean sweep for Japan. The Netherlands' Anton Geesink shocked everyone by winning the Open category (unlimited weight).

Another heavyweight champion, Joe Frazier, was soon challenging his fellow Olympian, Muhammad Ali, in the professional ring. The American basketball team won their sixth title in a row, captained by Bill Bradley, who later represented New Jersey in the Senate.

In athletics, these were the last Olympics to feature a cinder track, on which New Zealand's Peter Snell again won the 800 metres – and this time the 1500 as well. No one has won both since, although Sebastian Coe came close in 1980 and 1984.

British women achieved their first athletics golds, thanks to Mary Rand's long jump and Ann Packer in the 800. Lynn 'the leap' Davies made it a British double by winning the men's long jump.

The football tournament

16 teams qualified – of whom 14 took part in Tokyo.
(1) Host nation: Japan
(2) Holders: Yugoslavia (1964 introduced this automatic qualification for the title holders).
(3) Europe (five): Romania, Hungary, (East) Germany, Italy, Czechoslovakia. (Italy were later withdrawn for fielding professional players).
(4) South America (two): Argentina, Brazil
(5) North and Central America (one): Mexico
(6) Africa (three): UAR, Ghana, Morocco
(7) Asia (three): South Korea, North Korea, Iran. (North Korea later withdrew when their athletes in other sports were not allowed to take part).

Football matches took place in five cities – Tokyo, Yokohama, and Saitama for the main tournament, and Kyoto and Osaka for three Consolation games.

Tokyo stadia:	Olympic Stadium, Shinjuku
	Chichibunomiya rugby stadium, Minato
	Komazawa stadium, Setagaya
	Nishigaoka National Stadium, Kita
Yokohama:	Mitsuzawa Stadium, Kanagawa-ku
Saitama:	Omiya Park soccer stadium
Kyoto:	Nishikyogoku Athletic Stadium
Osaka:	Nagai Stadium

In 1960 winners of the four groups progressed to a semi-final place, but in 1964 two teams moved from each group to the quarter-finals. This reduced the pressure to win any single match, and the five European sides were expected to get through.

On paper, the strongest of the other nine teams were Argentina, Brazil and possibly the hosts, Japan.

The draw for the quarter-finals read:
Group A winners v Group B runners-up
Group B winners v Group A runners-up

Group C winners v Group D runners-up
Group D winners v Group C runners-up

Round One

Group A

11 October	Romania 3-1 Mexico (2-0)		Tokyo
	Creiniceanu 20	Fragoso 73	
	Pircalab 33		
	Ionescu 47		

11 October	East Germany 4-0 Iran (3-0)		Yokohama
	Bauchspiess 7		
	Vogel 20, 63		
	Frenzel 44		

13 October	Iran 1-1 Mexico (0-0)		Tokyo
	Nirlou 59	Gonzalez 54	

13 October	East Germany 1-1 Romania (1-1)		Tokyo
	Frenzel 22	Pavlovici 27	

15 October	East Germany 2-0 Mexico (1-0)		Yokohama
	Barthels 37		
	Noldner 66		

15 October	Romania 1-0 Iran (1-0)		Saitama
	Pavlovici 26		

Qualified:	East Germany:	5 points	(7 goals for – 1 against)
Qualified:	Romania:	5 points	(5-2)
	Mexico:	1 point	(2-6)
	Iran:	1 point	(1-6)

Group A

Within the unified German Olympic team, footballers were the East German squad, who had defeated West Germany in the qualifying tournament. Their State-funded 'amateurs' and those of Romania were regarded as the strongest teams in Group A, which included Mexico and Iran.

East Germany effectively won their match against **Iran** in the first half, when they went 3-0 ahead. Bauchspiess scored in seven minutes, Vogel doubled the lead after 20, and Frenzel added a third on the half-time whistle. The left-winger Vogel made the final score 4-0 in a comfortable opening match for the Germans.

Romania took 20 minutes to dominate their match with **Mexico** but they were not seriously troubled after their wingers, Creiniceanu and Pircalab, both scored. Straight after half-time, the centre-forward Ionescu put the game beyond Mexico, even when Fragoso scored in 73 minutes. The 3-1 victory could have been greater, had Romania converted a second half penalty.

Iran and **Mexico** gained their only point in a 1-1 draw between the teams, left-half Gonzalez scoring for Mexico in 34 minutes and the Iranian inside-right Nirlou equalising just before the hour. Iran also missed a penalty in the second half.

A far bigger attendance, 25,000 watched **East Germany** and **Romania** draw 1-1, after goals midway through the first half by Frenzel, the German number nine, and then Pavlovici, Romanian right-half.

In the British Olympic Association's Report, Doug Gardner described this 'bruising battle' as 'a mockery of Olympic football', a poor introduction to world football for the 'polite' spectators.

With one match to go for each team, none was sure of progressing, but the European teams had three points, the others one point. East Germany's victory over Mexico, 2-0, with Barthels and Noldner the scorers, won them the Group ahead of Romania, whose 1-0 win over Iran was hard-fought, with only Pavlovici's 26th minute goal separating the teams.

Group B

(North Korea withdrew when their athletes in some other sports were not allowed to compete)

11 October   Hungary 6-0 Morocco (2-0) Tokyo
Bene 13, 38 (p), 70, 74, 78, 87

13 October   Yugoslavia 3-1 Morocco (2-1) Yokohama
Samardzic 8   Bouachra 2
Belin 12, 59

15 October   Hungary 6-5 Yugoslavia (5-4) Tokyo
Csernai 5, 11, 44, 63 (p)   Osim 1, 82
Farkas 18   Belin 12, 35
Bene 25 (p)   Zambata 31

Qualified: Hungary   4 points   (12-5)
Qualified: Yugoslavia   2 points   (8-7)
                  Morocco   0 points   (1-9)

Group B

When North Korea withdrew, because some of their athletes could not compete in Japan, the task of other teams was made easier. Hungary, Yugoslavia and Morocco played only two matches. The champions from 1952 and 1960 were drawn alongside the African team, who had defeated Nigeria after a remarkable comeback in the qualifiers.

The first game marked one of football's most astonishing individual achievements. When **Hungary** defeated **Morocco** 6-0, Ferenc Bene scored every goal. Starting in the 13th minute, he added a penalty close to the interval. As Morocco could not contain the Magyar forwards, Bene completed a hat-trick in 70 minutes. That was his first hat-trick, because he then collected a second in the next 20 minutes. Not surprisingly, he finished the event as its top scorer and played a key role in later games.

Morocco also lost to **Yugoslavia** but they opened the proceedings with a second minute goal from Bouachra, their outside-right. His Slav opposite number, Samardzic, equalised soon after, and their right-half Belin gave Yugoslavia a 2-1 lead, all in the first 12 minutes. A second goal by Belin, on the hour, decided the match, but Morocco's form had improved in their second game.

Before **Hungary** met **Yugoslavia**, both had qualified, but there was no question of either saving energy for the next round. In some respects – notably the goal torrent – this game resembled Yugoslavia's 5-5 draw with the USSR in 1952.

Osim scored for Yugoslavia within the first minute, but Csernai, man of the moment, equalised almost immediately and then put Hungary 2-1 ahead.

Now the Slav defender Belin equalised at 2-2, continuing his goal-scoring skills. Farkas, Hungary's right-winger, restored their lead and Bene scored from a penalty. 4-2, and just 25 minutes gone.

Zambata and Belin levelled the match at 4-4 in the next ten minutes, and at half-time it stood Hungary 5, Yugoslavia 4 as Csernai completed his hat-trick.

If nine goals in 45 minutes were not enough to tax the (newly-invented) pocket calculators in the 15,000 crowd, the referee Mr Fukushima had to prevent players squaring up to each other.

The second half could hardly match the first – and only two goals were added. Csernai's fourth was another penalty in 63 minutes, and Osim made the last eight minutes even more hectic before Hungary 6 Yugoslavia 5 was the final score. An astonishing game, with Csernai's four goals and only one from Bene this time.

In the next few days, both teams were to score six goals against other sides, but this was a football equivalent of the Paris Exhibition 'Flip-Flop', the Ferris Wheel of 1900.

Group C

12 October   Brazil 1-1 UAR (1-0)   Tokyo

       Roberto Miranda 10   Shahin 90

12 October   Czechoslovakia 6-1 South Korea (4-0)   Saitama

       Lichtnegl 25   Lee Yi-Woo 59

       Vojta 26

       Mraz 32, 68

       Masny 43, 71

14 October   Czechoslovakia 5-1 UAR (3-0)   Tokyo

       Vojta 5, 27   Riad 53

       Urban 36

       Mraz 83

       Cvetler 84

14 October   Brazil 4-0 South Korea (2-0)   Yokohama

       Ze Roberto 30

       Elizeu 44, 54

       Roberto Miranda 73

16 October   UAR 10-0 South Korea (3-0)   Tokyo

       Riad 14, 17, 40, 48, 72, 77

       Shehta 50

       Elfanagili 61

       Etman 66

       Hassan 78

16 October   Czechoslovakia 1-0 Brazil (0-0)   Saitama

       Valosek 77

Qualified:	Czechoslovakia	6 points	(12-2)
Qualified:	UAR	3 points	(12-6)
	Brazil	3 points	(5-2)
	South Korea	0 points	(1-20)

UAR finished ahead of Brazil on a superior goal difference.

Group C

The strongest teams in this group seemed to be Czechoslovakia, who qualified by defeating France 8-2 over two legs, and Brazil, whose professionals were the best in the world after winning another World Cup in 1962. The UAR (United Arab Republic) and South Korea represented Africa and Asia.

The first match, between **Brazil** and the **UAR**, proved to be the key to this group, specifically the very last minute. Roberto put Brazil in front after ten minutes, but then the African team stood firm. Instead of Brazil increasing their lead, they lost an equaliser to Shahin in the final seconds.

Czechoslovakia took longer to score against **South Korea**, but once their centre-forward Lichtnegl hit the net in 25 minutes, three more goals followed before the interval. Right-half Vojta and inside-forwards, Mraz and Masny, won the plaudits.

Lee Yi-Woo scored the Koreans' only goal of the event, but Mraz and Masny doubled their own tally in the 6-1 win.

Brazil had a similar victory over **South Korea** 48 hours later. The 4-0 result came from goals by Ze Roberto and Elizeu, late in the first half, and by Elizeu and Roberto in the second phase.

The matches on 16 October required UAR to play South Korea first; Czechoslovakia faced Brazil an hour later.

The Czechs, with four points, were already in the quarter-finals. Brazil (three) and UAR (one) both hoped to join them. Brazil needed a draw to finish second in the group, a victory to finish at the top.

However, if Brazil lost to the Czechs, there was just a possibility that UAR could finish runners-up in the group. It was, admittedly, a remote possibility. Brazil had a goal difference of plus four, the UAR's was minus four, so that the African side had to produce a result nine goals better than the South Americans'. As yet they had only scored twice.

In fact, **UAR** won by the largest margin of the whole tournament, 10-0, against **South Korea**. Five days earlier, Bene had scored six times for Hungary. Now the UAR's inside-right Riad equalled that feat. Opening the goal spree in 14 minutes, he added another double in the first half, when the score was only 3-0.

That would not suffice, and seven goals came after the interval from the Egyptian forwards Shehta, Etman and Hassan, and wing-half Elfanagili. Between 61 and 78 minutes alone, they scored five. Riad scored another hat-trick, in a performance as fine as Bene's and under the unique pressure of this situation.

Czechoslovakia defeated **Brazil** 1-0 in the other match, the only goal coming from Valosek, their outside-left, in 77 minutes. By then the UAR v South Korea match was over, and Brazil did not have time to find the equaliser they needed.

The reversal of fortunes in this group can stand as one of the greatest shocks in any Olympic event. The UAR finished second in Group C, with a goal difference three better than Brazil.

The Czech victory over Brazil reversed the result in 1962, when Brazil defeated Czechoslovakia 3-1 in the World Cup Final. None of the players took part in both matches, but national prestige and Olympic prowess mattered to all these countries.

Group D

(Italy were disqualified)

12 October	Argentina 1-1 Ghana (0-0)	Yokohama
	Bulla 26 E. Acquah 80	
14 October	Japan 3-2 Argentina (0-1)	Tokyo
	Sugiyama 54 Dominguez 24, 62	
	Kawabuchi 81	
	Ogi 82	
16 October	Ghana 3-2 Japan (1-1)	Tokyo
	Agyemang 27 Sugiyama 12	
	S. Acquah 69 Yaegashi 52	
	Aggrey-Fynn 80	

Qualified:	Ghana:	3 points	(4-3)
Qualified:	Japan:	2 points	(5-5)
Qualified:	Argentina:	1 point	(3-4)

Group D

The second South American team, Argentina, had won all five qualifying games and would expect to top Group D.

The hosts, Japan, and Ghana were their opponents, after Italy were disqualified for including professionals in their matches against Turkey and Poland.

Argentina v **Ghana** drew one of the largest attendances to Yokohama – 25,000 – and Bulla put the South Americans ahead after 26 minutes. With ten minutes left, Edward Acquah equalised with the first goal for a team from sub-Saharan Africa in the Olympics. The point gave them an excellent chance of reaching the quarter-finals.

Japan's opening match against **Argentina** saw the home side, cheered on by their Tokyo fans, face an uphill task throughout the first half, after Dominguez scored in 24 minutes. But in the second period Sugiyama levelled the match, only for Dominguez to put Argentina 2-1 ahead.

Time was running out, ten minutes were left, when Kawabuchi on the right wing broke through to equalise. Japan then regained possession straight from the kick-off and their centre-half Ogi came forward to net the decider – 3-2.

Argentina, with only one point, could qualify, but only if **Japan** beat **Ghana**. That seemed likely, thanks to Sugiyama, who delighted the home crowd with an early goal, and Yaegashi, when he restored Japan's lead in 52 minutes after Agyemang's leveller.

Well aware that they faced an early elimination, Ghana attacked in strength and their right-back Sam Acquah equalised with 21 minutes left. Had the match ended at 2-2, both sides would make the quarter-finals, but Ghana made sure they did with a late winner from Aggrey-Fynn. Neither of the South American giants would feature in a quarter-final.

Quarter-finals

18 October   Germany 1-0 Yugoslavia (1-0)   Tokyo
Frenzel 1

18 October   Hungary 2-0 Romania (1-0)   Yokohama
Csernai 2, 84 (p)

18 October   UAR 5-1 Ghana (1-1)   Saitama
Badawi 42, 61   Mfum 37
Riad 65
Elfanagili 69, 85

18 October   Czechoslovakia 4-0 Japan (1-0)   Tokyo
Brumovsky 43, 59
Vojta 69 (p)
Mraz 86

Quarter-finals

All four matches kicked off at noon on 18 October. **Germany's** Frenzel put them ahead in 60 seconds and their packed defence stopped **Yugoslavia** from converting any chances for the other 89 minutes. Although the Slavs then announced they would not enter the 1968 tournament, they did participate in consolation matches a few days later.

Hungary v **Romania** was never likely to be a classic. Puskas's winners in 1952 found Romania their toughest opponent, and the Magyar Csernai was the difference between the teams. He scored in the second minute, and six minutes from the end, from a penalty. This match was far easier for Mr Ashkenazi to referee than the Final five days later.

Instead of **Ghana's** quarter-final against **UAR**, most spectators would have expected an Argentina v Brazil or Japan v Brazil contest. During the first half Ghana looked the stronger team, Mfum putting them ahead and it could have been 2-0, for they missed a penalty. UAR took advantage of that reprieve and Badawi equalised before half-time. 1-1.

However, the defining few minutes were between 60 and 70 minutes.

Badawi, Riad and defender Elfanagili took UAR to a 4-1 lead, before the right-half added his second. UAR now prepared to meet Hungary in the semi-finals.

Japan's huge support were delighted with their team against **Czechoslovakia** for almost the entire first half, but two minutes before the interval, Brumovsky gave the Czechs the lead. His second goal on the hour, and Vojta's penalty in 69 minutes, put the game beyond the home team, and Mraz scored a fourth.

All four teams who lost on 18 October took part in the Consolation event two days later.

Semi-finals

20 October   Hungary 6-0 UAR (3-0)   Tokyo

Bene 7, 20, 66, 77
Komora 29, 58

20 October   Czechoslovakia 2-1 East Germany (0-1)   Tokyo

Lichtnegl 47   Noldner 25

Mraz 89

Bronze Medal Match

23 October   East Germany 3-1 UAR (1-0)   Olympic Stadium, Tokyo

Frenzel 17   Attia 75 (p)
Vogel 48
Stocker 56

Semi-finals

Hungary's three wins began with Ferenc Bene's six goals, but since then Tibor Csernai had outshone him. Now, against the **UAR**, Bene showed the way with two goals in the first 20 minutes. Once their inside-left Komora made it 3-0, Hungary were too skilful to let their opponents come back.

There was time for Komora to hit a second goal, and for Bene to complete four, taking his total to eleven so far.

For a long spell **East Germany's** semi-final against **Czechoslovakia** resembled their match against Yugoslavia. Noldner gave the Germans a lead in 25 minutes, and they stopped the prolific Czech forwards until Lichtnegl's goal soon after the interval.

The most significant incident was an injury to Urbanczyk, the outstanding German right-back, who had to go off. Against a re-organised defence and ten men, Mraz scored the Czechs' winner with seconds left. For the second major tournament in two years, Czechoslovakia were into the final.

Bronze Medal Match

In the match for third place Germany did not consider defence in depth, as they had against Yugoslavia. Instead they played five forwards, and Frenzel scored their first goal in 17 minutes. Against them UAR maintained a 4-2-4 line up, and German miscues in front of goal kept the score down to 1-0 at the interval.

Early in the second half, Vogel and Stocker raised the total to 3-0, as the UAR keeper lacked authority in coping with high crosses, and chances came to the German strikers. Attia's penalty in 75 minutes reduced the leeway, with the final result 3-1. 60,000 people watched the contest in Yokohama's Mitsuzawa Stadium.

Final

23 October   Hungary 2-1 Czechoslovakia (0-0) Olympic Stadium,
                                                                    Tokyo
          Farkas 47   Brumovsky 80
          Bene 59

Final

Hungary (20 goals) and Czechoslovakia (18 goals) deservedly reached the final, after scoring more than any other team, and this should have been a match to enthral 75,000 people.

Yet the Olympic Stadium pitch was softened by heavy rain, and neither side compromised in tackling and bodychecking. Mr Ashkenazi awarded an astonishing 60 free kicks – one every 90 seconds on average.

The Czechs had the better defence, especially on the left side, with Picman and Geleta, but Hungary were unpredictable, with an exceptional centre-forward in Bene. Gardner called him 'quick-thinking, quick-moving ... with a deadly shot'.

Farkas, the outside-right, put Hungary ahead in 47 minutes, and in the 59th minute Bene lit up the early Tokyo afternoon with a run from 40 yards out to the Czechs' penalty area; there he drove the ball from an acute angle past Schmucker in goal.

Unlike some other teams, Hungary continued to attack until Brumovsky's late goal, ten minutes from time, reduced their lead to 2-1. The Magyars had won gold again, and if Bene was the scoring legend, his captain Dezso Novak at right-back was superb.

Once again, the tournament was dominated by East European teams, who won the medals, and the Consolation Fifth Place final was their contest also. Only UAR, in fourth place, had interrupted that story in Tokyo.

Consolation Matches

Round One

20 October   Yugoslavia 6-1 Japan (4-0)   Osaka

Zambata 3, 5, 43, 63   Kamamoto 61

Osim 28, 60

20 October   Romania 4-2 Ghana (3-2)   Kyoto

Pavlovici 12, 19, 74   Aggrey-Fynn 25, 44

Creiniceanu 41

Final (Fifth place match)

22 October   Romania 3-0 Yugoslavia (0-0)   Osaka

Pavlovici 50

Pircalab 52

Constantin 78

1964 saw the return of a Consolation event, involving the four losing quarter-finalists, in matches played in Osaka and Kyoto.

Yugoslavia assuaged some of the disappointment at relinquishing their title with a 6-1 victory against **Japan**. Zambata and Osim shared the goals, with four and two respectively.

Romania struggled to hold **Ghana** in the first half, when they led 3-2, and it took Pavlovici's hat-trick to see them into the final.

The 'Fifth place' match – or Consolation Final – was held in Osaka between the East European sides. After a goalless 45 minutes, the **Romanians** won the day over **Yugoslavia** with two swift counters from Pavlovici and Pircalab in 50 and 52 minutes, and a late addition from Constantin.

Medal Winners

Gold: **Hungary**

Szentmihalyi	Palotai	Dunai
Gelei	Csernai	Farkas
Novak (captain)	I. Nagy	Katona
Kaposzta	Komora	Orosz
Orban	Varga	Bene
Ihasz	Nogradi	
Szepesi	G. Nagy	

Silver: **Czechoslovakia**

Schmucker	Geleta	Masny
Svajlen	Mraz	Valosek
Urban (captain)	Lichtnegl	Brumovsky
Weiss	Knesl	
Picman	Nepomucky	
Vojta	Knebort	
Matlak	Cvetler	

Bronze: **East Germany**

Heinsch	Pankau	Lisiewicz	Stocker
Weigang	Rock	Barthels	
Urbanczyk	Unger	Backhaus	
Walter	Korner	Bauchspiess	
Geisler	Engelhardt	Frenzel	
Seehaus	Noldner	Frassdorf	
Vogel			

Top goal scorers (Main tournament)

12: Bene (Hungary)
8: Riad (UAR)
6: Csernai (Hungary)

Referees

Y. Yokoyama (Japan)	Romania v Mexico
	East Germany v UAR (Bronze medal match)
De Queiroz (Brazil)	East Germany v Iran
	Czechoslovakia v Japan
J. Wontumi (Ghana)	Iran v Mexico
V. Korelus (Czechoslovakia)	East Germany v Romania
G. De Silva (Malaysia)	East Germany v Mexico
	East Germany v Yugoslavia
	Romania v Ghana
M. Comesana (Argentina)	Romania v Iran
	Hungary v UAR (Semi-final)
K. D. Chun (Korea)	Hungary v Morocco
H. Imam (United Arab Republic)	Yugoslavia v Morocco
	Yugoslavia v Japan
G. Fukushima (Japan)	Hungary v Yugoslavia
R. Glockner (East Germany)	Brazil v UAR
	UAR v South Korea
R. Valenzuela (Mexico)	Czechoslovakia v South Korea
I. Zsolt (Hungary)	Czechoslovakia v UAR
	Romania v Yugoslavia
S. Boukkili (Morocco)	Brazil v South Korea
A. Tehrani (Iran)	Czechoslovakia v Brazil
M. Ashkenazi (Israel)	Argentina v Ghana
	Hungary v Romania
	Czechoslovakia v East Germany (Semi-final)
	Hungary v Czechoslovakia (Final)
A. Skoric (Yugoslavia)	Japan v Argentina
C. Nitescu (Romania)	Japan v Ghana

The Qualifying Tournament (1963-4)

Most matches were played over two legs, and the aggregate score decided which team progressed. Bulgaria 2-0 Albania, for example, is the aggregate, and Bulgaria went into the next round after winning both home and away (1-0 and 1-0).

In South America, matches were played in a single group of seven teams, in Lima, Peru.

Europe

Group One: Romania qualified
Preliminary: Bulgaria 2-0 Albania (1-0 and 1-0)
Round 1: Bulgaria walk-over – Luxembourg withdrew.
Romania 5-5 Denmark (3-2, 2-3)
Romania 2-1 Denmark (play-off in Turin)
Round 2: Romania 3-1 Bulgaria (1-0, 2-1)

Group Two: Hungary qualified
Round 1: Hungary 6-2 Sweden (4-0, 2-2)
Spain 7-0 Switzerland (6-0, 1-0)
Round 2: Hungary 5-1 Spain (2-1, 3-0)

Group Three: East Germany qualified
Preliminary: East Germany 4-2 West Germany (3-0, 1-2)
Round 1: USSR 11-0 Finland (7-0, 4-0)
East Germany 4-1 Netherlands (1-0, 3-1)
Round 2: East Germany 2-2 USSR (1-1, 1-1)
East Germany 4-1 USSR (play-off in Warsaw)

Group Four: Italy qualified. When they were disqualified, Poland declined the offer to replace them.
Round 1: Italy 9-3 Turkey (2-2, 7-1)
Poland: Bye
Round 2: Italy 4-0 Poland (3-0, 1-0)

Group Five: Czechoslovakia qualified
Preliminary: Great Britain 10-0 Iceland (6-0, 4-0)
Round 1: Czechoslovakia 8-2 France (4-0, 4-2)
Greece 5-3 Great Britain (1-2, 4-1)

Round 2: Czechoslovakia walk-over – Greece were disqualified by their own country's Federation for including professional players against Great Britain.

South America: Argentina and Brazil qualified.

Seven teams competed for two qualification places in a single group, all the fixtures played in Lima, Peru. After the Peru v Argentina match was abandoned, no more fixtures were played in the group.

Argentina qualified with 10 points from 5 games, Brazil and Peru both had five points and played off in Rio de Janeiro, Brazil winning 4-0.

Other results were:

Peru 1-1 Ecuador
Uruguay 0-0 Chile
Argentina 1-0 Ecuador
Uruguay 1-1 Ecuador
Argentina 4-0 Chile
Chile 2-0 Colombia
Colombia 4-1 Ecuador
Uruguay 1-1 Colombia

Argentina 2-0 Colombia
Peru 3-0 Colombia
Brazil 2-0 Chile
Brazil 1-1 Colombia
Peru 2-0 Uruguay
Brazil 3-1 Ecuador
Argentina 3-1 Uruguay
Argentina 1-0 Peru (abandoned after 85 minutes)

North and Central America: Mexico qualified

Preliminary: Surinam 4-2 Netherlands Antilles (1-2, 3-0)
Group matches, played in Mexico City.
Mexico 5-1 Panama
Surinam 1-0 USA
Mexico 6-1 Surinam
USA 4-2 Panama
Mexico 2-1 USA
Surinam 6-1 Panama

Mexico:	6 points	(13 goals for – 2 against)
Surinam:	4 points	(7-7)
USA:	2 points	(5-5)
Panama:	0 points	(4-15)

Africa: UAR, Ghana and Morocco qualified

Group One: UAR qualified
Round 1: UAR 7-2 Uganda (4-1 and 3-1)
Sudan walkover v Rhodesia
Round 2: UAR 7-4 Sudan (4-1, 3-3)

Group Two: Ghana qualified
Round 1: Ghana 6-4 Liberia (5-4, 1-0)
Tunisia 3-3 Dahomey (2-2, 1-1)
Play-off: Tunisia 1-1 Dahomey (in Casablanca – Tunisia won on toss of a coin)
Round 2: Ghana 3-2 Tunisia (2-0, 1-2)

Group Three: Morocco qualified
Round 1: Ethiopia 10-5 Kenya (3-4, 7-1)
Morocco 4-4 Nigeria (0-3, 4-1)
Play-off: Morocco 2-1 Nigeria (in Dakar)
Round 2: Morocco 2-0 Ethiopia (1-0, 1-0)

Asia: South Korea, North Korea and Iran qualified. North Korea later withdrew.

Group One: South Korea qualified
Preliminary: South Korea 2-2 Taiwan (2-1, 0-1)
Play-off: South Korea walkover v Taiwan
Round 1: South Korea walkover v Philippines
South Vietnam 2-1 Israel (0-1, 2-0)
Round 2: South Korea 5-2 South Vietnam (3-0, 2-2)

Group Two: North Korea qualified
Preliminary: Thailand 4-3 Malaysia (1-1, 3-2)
Round 1: North Korea 1-0 Burma (0-0, 1-0)
Thailand walk-over v Indonesia
Round 2: North Korea 7-0 Thailand (2-0, 5-0)
(Both legs played in Rangoon, Burma)

Group Three: Iran qualified
Preliminary: Iran 4-2 Pakistan (4-1, 0-1)
India 12-3 Sri Lanka (Ceylon) (5-3, 7-0)
Round 1: Iran 4-0 Iraq (4-0, 0-0)
India walk-over v Lebanon
Round 2: Iran 6-1 India (3-0, 3-1)

15. Mexico City, 1968

South of the Border

When Mexico City's bid succeeded – Detroit the runner-up once more – its altitude was a prime concern. A city 7,300 feet (2,240 metres) above sea level was sure to increase the already considerable strain on competitors' bodies, and that included footballers', whose 90 minutes of exertion lasted longer than almost all athletes experienced.

In fact, October 1968 produced a clear divide between shorter track, and field, events, where performances often broke records, and long distance competitions, where times were slower than four years earlier.

Bob Beamon's long jump remains the Olympic record and could not be measured by standard equipment, at 8.90 metres. High jumpers reached their own altitudes unreached before, none higher than Dick Fosbury with his backward 'Flop', now standard but then unknown.

On the other hand, the gold medal times for steeplechase, 5,000 metres and 10,000 metres were all markedly slower than in Tokyo, by 20, 16 and 63 seconds respectively. Mamo Wolde won the marathon in a time eight minutes slower; a true Olympian spirit was shown by Tanzanian John Akhwan, who managed to complete over 26 miles with a dislocated knee.

These were also momentous Olympics for Janice Romary, who was the first woman to carry the U.S. flag into the stadium, in her sixth Olympics as a fencer.

Felipe Munoz won Mexico's first gold in swimming. The 200 metres breast-stroke champion was nicknamed 'warm water', because his parents came from two towns whose names meant 'hot water' and 'cold river'.

Whenever athletes from West and East Germany appeared in Mexico City's stadium – no longer part of a unified German team – Beethoven's 'Ode to joy' from his Ninth Symphony was played. The music was not heard during football matches, and JS Bach's keyboard work, 'The well-tempered klavier', would also have been inappropriate. Good temper was in short supply in the 1968 tournament.

FIFA allowed substitutes for the first time, two per side, and the first to come on was Ghana's Abukari against Israel. He was later involved in an incident which rendered this match memorable for the wrong reasons.

The football tournament

A record 78 countries entered the event, and 17 later withdrew. The 16 teams who reached the final stages were:
Hosts: Mexico
Holders: Hungary
Europe: Czechoslovakia, Bulgaria, France, Spain
North and Central America: Brazil, Colombia
South America: Guatemala, El Salvador
Africa: Guinea, Nigeria, Ghana
Asia: Japan, Thailand, Israel
Six teams made their debut – Columbia, Guatemala, El Salvador, Guinea, Nigeria, and Israel.

Four stadia hosted the matches, all newly built except for Leon's, constructed in 1952.

The Azteca Stadium, Mexico City (10 matches)
Cuauhtemoc Stadium, Puebla (7 matches)
Nou Camp, Leon (7 matches)
Jalisco Stadium, Guadalajara (8 matches)

Group A

13 October	Mexico 1-0 Colombia (1-0)		Mexico City
	Estrada 6		
13 October	France 3-1 Guinea (0-0)		Puebla
	Hallet 61	Maxime Camara 79	
	Horlaville 64		
	Perigaud 70		
15 October	Guinea 3-2 Colombia (1-0)		Puebla
	Mama douba	Santa 49	
	Camara 26		
	Bouya 58, 84	Mosquera 66	

15 October	France 4-1 Mexico (3-1)		Mexico City
	Kanyan 20, 69	Victorino 26	
	Tamboueon 30		
	Medina (o.g.) 36		

17 October	Mexico 4-0 Guinea (0-0)		Mexico City
	Pereda 70, 85		
	Pulido 86, 88		

17 October	Colombia 2-1 France (2-0)		Puebla
	Tamayo 14	Tamboueon 59	
	Jaramillo 35		

Qualified:	France	4 points	(8 goals for – 4 against)
Qualified	Mexico	4 points	(6-4)
	Colombia	2 points	(4-5)
	Guinea	2 points	(4-9)

Group A

Mexico got the event underway in the Azteca Stadium, with a narrow win over **Colombia** who had qualified ahead of Uruguay (Argentina did not enter). The hosts took both points with Jose Estrada's sixth minute goal. No team found Colombia easy to compete against, and there was no addition to the score.

In Puebla, **France** and **Guinea** could not find the net for an hour, but when Gerard Hallet put the French in the lead, they soon went 3-0 up, through two midfielders and club colleagues, Horlaville and Perigaud. Maxime Camara reduced the leeway, and it finished 3-1 to France.

With **Mexico** and **France** on two points, the next match between them would ensure progress to the quarter-final for its victor. France took control of this game when Marc Case, known as Kanyan, scored in 20 minutes. Victorino swiftly equalised, but Tamboueon restored the French advantage, and full back Medina's own goal put Mexico 3-1 down at half-time. Kanyan's second in 69 minutes gave France their perfect result, a 4-1 win.

Guinea v Colombia was both teams' best opportunity to secure two points. The African team went ahead in 26 minutes through M.N. Camara – one of four Camaras in the squad, and after the interval Santa levelled the score. Bouya became the third Camara to score in the event, but Mosquera equalised. Guinea were not to be denied, however, and Bouya's late goal gave them a 3-2 victory.

France had ensured a place in the next stage with four points, Colombia had none and could not make it. **Mexico** and **Guinea** both had two points, the African team with a better goal difference, and they needed only a draw against the home team to be in the quarter-finals.

For 70 minutes, Mexico could not find a goal, and faced the unthinkable, elimination in their own Azteca Stadium. But Vicente Pereda gave them the lead. 1-0 was too close for comfort until a remarkable burst of three goals in five minutes from Pereda and Hector Pulido, with a double.

Colombia v France could not influence the Group A table, but the South Americans, having suffered two narrow defeats, won the day through Tamayo and Jaramillo.

France still won the group on goal difference from Mexico, and now faced Group B's runners-up.

Group B

14 October	Spain 1-0 Brazil (0-0)	Mexico City
	Juan 77	
14 October	Japan 3-1 Nigeria (1-1)	Puebla
	Kamamoto 24, 72, 89	Okoye 33
16 October	Spain 3-0 Nigeria (1-0)	Mexico City
	Ortuno 27	
	Grande 52, 69	
16 October	Brazil 1-1 Japan (1-0)	Puebla
	Ferretti 9	Watanabe 83

18 October   Brazil 3-3 Nigeria (0-3)   Puebla
                 Ferretti 50   Olayombo 10, 41
                 Tiao 59, 65   Anieke 19

18 October   Spain 0-0 Japan   Mexico City

Qualified: Spain   5 points   (4-0)
Qualified: Japan   4 points   (4-2)
              Brazil   2 points   (4-5)
              Nigeria   1 point   (4-9)

Group B

This Group brought together Japan, who achieved fourth place in 1964, with Spain, Brazil and Nigeria, in their debut.

What might have been a goal-feast produced the fewest goals of any group – 16 from the six matches. **Spain** conceded none of the goals, and their defence was the foundation for their success. They had qualified by scoring once against Great Britain in two matches.

Now they defeated **Brazil** with a single goal from Juan in 77 minutes, a narrow victory eased by the South Americans' losing their midfielder Manoel Maria, who was sent off just before half-time.

As in the Tokyo tournament, **Japan** could not be taken lightly. Eleven of their squad took part in both 1964 and 1968 events, and in Kunishige Kamamoto they had an outstanding centre-forward. Now representing Yanmar Diesel FC after leaving Waseda University, he scored Japan's first goal against **Nigeria** in 24 minutes. Okoye came up from his full back post to score a leveller nine minutes later.

Kamamoto won the match in the last 18 minutes, when he collected a hat-trick, and he was to finish the event as the top scorer, the only Asian player to achieve that feat.

Nigeria's next game was against **Spain**, who won 3-0 and made certain of their place in the quarter-finals. Ortuno, Sabadell's winger, opened the scoring midway through the first half, and a double by Grande, one of five Real Madrid players in the squad, completed the Spanish success.

Brazil met **Japan** in Puebla and took a ninth minute lead through Ferretti, but neither team scored again until Japan's coach, Ken Naganuma, brought on Watanabe to the forward line in 81 minutes. Within two minutes, he scored the equaliser.

After their two matches, **Spain** (4 points) were already through, **Japan**, on 3 points, needed a draw to progress. When the sides met in the Azteca Stadium, there were no goals, one of very few Olympic matches to finish on that disappointing score.

Japan fielded virtually the same players against both Brazil and Spain. The Spanish, by contrast, chose a new midfield, goalkeeper and two new forwards.

Brazil (on one point) had to beat **Nigeria** to stand any chance of finishing second in Group B.

Even that slim chance seemed to evaporate when Nigeria went 3-0 up before the interval. None of the goals went to their forwards – instead, midfielders Olayombo, with two, and Anieke led the charge.

The second half was very different, and within 20 minutes of restarting, Brazil were level on 3-3. Ferretti and a double from Tiao went on to the scoresheet. Ferretti's dismissal soon after his goal left Brazil to play with ten men for 35 minutes, and the match ended even.

France and Japan finished first and second, leaving Brazil to rue missed chances against Japan.

Group C

Morocco withdrew, and were replaced by Ghana.

13 October   Israel 5-3 Ghana (3-2)   Leon

Spiegel 11, 75 (p)   Malik 18, 79
Feigenbaum 16, 30, 70   Amusa 35

13 October   Hungary 4-0 El Salvador (1-0)   Guadalajara

Menczel 19

A. Dunai 47

Fazekas 51

Sarkozi 68

15 October	Hungary 2-2 Ghana (2-2)		Guadalajara
	A. Dunai 15	Sunday 12	
	Menczel 17	Stevens 33	

15 October	Israel 3-1 El Salvador (2-1)		Leon
	Talbi 20	Martinez 35 (p)	
	Spiegler 44		
	Bar 85		

17 October	Ghana 1-1 El Salvador (0-1)		Leon
	Kofi 55	Rodriguez 42	

17 October	Hungary 2-0 Israel (1-0)		Guadalajara
	A. Dunai 40, 75		

Qualified:	Hungary	5 points	(8-2)
Qualified:	Israel	4 points	(8-6)
	Ghana	2 points	(6-8)
	El Salvador	1 point	(2-8)

Group C

Several matches in this Group brought little credit to the event. **Israel** v **Ghana** produced eight goals but also some of the worst incidents in the tournament's history.

In the first 16 minutes, Israel went two up through Spiegel and Feigenbaum, although Malik reduced the lead within two minutes. After half an hour, Feigenbaum made it 3-1, while Amusa came through from midfield to score. 3-2 at the interval.

On the hour, Attuquayefio, another Ghanaian midfielder, was dismissed, and, soon after, Feigenbaum completed a hat-trick. Spiegel's penalty took the score to 5-2, before Malik hit the net for a final score of 5-3 to Israel.

With seconds of the match left, Alhassan was the second of Ghana's team to be sent off. Two of his colleagues then attacked the referee, and they were later suspended for six months by their own Football Association.

None of the four players involved in those incidents appeared in Ghana's other matches in Mexico.

When **Hungary** played **El Salvador** in Guadalajara, they scored only once in the first half, through Menczel, but three goals after half-time eventually saw them through to a comfortable 4-0 result. Characteristically, the Magyars' goals could come from anywhere – Menczel, a defender; two midfielders, Antal Dunai and Fazekas; and one forward, Sarkozi.

This game might have ended differently had Mendez netted for El Salvador with a 42nd minute penalty to produce a 1-1 score at the interval, but the shot was saved.

Ghana's next match was against **Hungary**, who found this a difficult contest. Sunday, the Africans' defender, moved into attack to score the opener in 12 minutes.

Immediately Dunai and Menczel hit back to give Hungary a 2-1 lead, but they could not capitalise on it, and Stevens, on the left wing, equalised for Ghana. Hungary's Novak, their full back and captain, did not play against Ghana, and his experience was missed.

Israel's 3-1 win over **El Salvador** ensured that, with four points, they reached a quarter-final place. Talbi scored for them in 20 minutes, but Martinez levelled for El Salvador with a penalty. Their captain, Spiegler, put the Asian team ahead just before the interval, and Bar completed the scoring in 85 minutes after coming on as Israel's first substitute. The Central Americans' task was made more difficult when Villalta, midfielder and captain, was sent off after 67 minutes.

Hungary (3 points) were not certain to progress ahead of Ghana (one point) unless they took a point from their last match, against **Israel**. It was Antal Dunai's goals – in 40 and 75 minutes – which secured a 2-0 victory and top place in the group. Talbi, Israel's midfielder, became yet another player not to finish a match when he was sent off on 58 minutes.

El Salvador v **Ghana** ended in a 1-1 draw, Rodriguez scoring three minutes before half-time as the captain showed El Salvador the route to goal, and Kofi equalising in 55 minutes.

Group D

14 October   Guatemala 1-0 Czechoslovakia (1-0)   Guadalajara
                         Valdez 28

14 October   Bulgaria 7-0 Thailand (1-0)   Leon
                         Gjonin 25
                         Zhekov 55
                Mikhajlov 56, 61
                         Zafirov 73
                     Nikodimov 85
                         Ivkov 88

16 October   Bulgaria 2-2 Czechoslovakia (1-2)   Guadalajara
                       Georgiev 44   Jarabinsky 25
                         Zhekov 77   Petras 42

16 October   Guatemala 4-1 Thailand (1-1)   Leon
                 N. Melgar 23, 85   Sornbutnark 44
                         Roldan 55
                   Lopez Oliva 67

18 October   Bulgaria 2-1 Guatemala (0-0)   Leon
                     Nikodimov 50   Lopez Oliva 88
                         Zhekov 84

18 October   Czechoslovakia 8-0 Thailand (6-0)   Guadalajara
                         Herbst 12
                   Petras 17, 18, 67
                     Stratil 28, 34
                     Vecerek 38
                     Krnac 83

Qualified:	Bulgaria	5 points	(11-3)
Qualified:	Guatemala	4 points	(6-3)
	Czechoslovakia	3 points	(10-3)
	Thailand	0 points	(1-19)

Group D

Czechoslovakia, runners-up in 1964, faced a powerful challenge in Bulgaria, but the other Group members seemed to pose fewer difficulties. Guatemala had qualified by defeating Bermuda in a play-off and Costa Rica, on the toss of a coin. Thailand's experience of the 1956 event was a 9-0 loss to Great Britain.

Guatemala's victory over **Czechoslovakia** was shocking, not only for the 1-0 result, but because only 19 players remained on the pitch at the final whistle. No matter how often the Czechs attacked, the only goal came in 28 minutes from Valdez, the left-side midfielder. But Guatemala ended with only nine men, for Pena and Torres were sent off in the last few minutes, and the Czech substitute Pajerchin was also dismissed.

At the same time, **Bulgaria** made **Thailand's** opening match one to forget. Only one goal, from Gjonin, in the first half, but six more in the second period, all for Bulgaria. Six players hit the net, with Zhekov, their captain, Mikhajlov with two, Zafirov, Nikodimov, and Ivkov completing the victory. Goals came from all sections of the team, from defence to left wing.

Eventually **Thailand** did score, through Sornbutnark, against **Guatemala**, to equalise Melgar's opening goal. It was 1-1 after 45 minutes, an improvement for Thailand, but when Paholpat was sent off, Guatemala quickly took the lead through Roldan, their captain, and won the match 4-1.

Even though they were also reduced to ten men when Hasse was dismissed, Lopez Oliva and Melgar made their victory certain – with the four points to see them into the next round.

Bulgaria (3 points) were likely to make the quarter-finals too. Only if they lost to Guatemala, and the Czechs beat Thailand, could Czechoslovakia progress. Even then, the goal difference was in Bulgaria's favour (plus seven, compared to minus one).

The **Czech** team did all they could to improve their goal tally. They went three up against **Thailand** in 18 minutes, six ahead at half-time. The final score, 8-0, included goals from five players – Petras, with a hat-trick, Herbst, Stratil's double, Vecerek, and Krnac. What would any of them have given for one goal against Guatemala?

Bulgaria did win Group D by a 2-1 victory over **Guatemala**, but not without a struggle. There were no goals till Nikodimov's in 50 minutes. Zhekov added a second, six minutes from the end, and Lopez Oliva scored the last goal in the Group, his second of the event and a rare achievement for a full-back.

Quarter-finals

20 October   Mexico 2-0 Spain (1-0)   Puebla

Morales 34
Pereda 48

20 October   Hungary 1-0 Guatemala (0-0)   Guadalajara

Szucs 69

20 October   Japan 3-1 France (1-1)   Mexico City

Kamamoto 27, 59   Tamboueon 32
Watanabe 70

20 October   Bulgaria 1-1 Israel (1-0)   Leon

(after extra time)
Khristakiev 5   Feigenbaum 89

(Bulgaria went through on the toss of a coin)

The quarter-finals

All four matches took place on 20 October in the noonday heat, and **Mexico** played **Spain** in Puebla, the hosts' first game in that stadium. Spain still had not conceded a goal, while Mexico had lost four in one match, against France.

But past form was unimportant and the home team had their best result of the year, winning 2-0 as Morales and Pereda, club colleagues at CD Toluca, scored after 34 and 48 minutes.

Hungary were now familiar with Guadalajara, where they played the three Group matches, and with **Guatemala's** form. Neither side dominated the match, and one goal by Szucs, Ferencuaros's midfielder, gave the

Magyars their victory in a game which was their most demanding of all.

Japan v **France**, in Mexico City, was a rare encounter of the teams, and this produced a contest between two centre-forwards – Kamamoto and Tamboueon. The Japanese scored his first in 27 minutes, Tamboueon equalising within five minutes. 1-1 at half-time, but from the hour mark this became Japan's match. Kamamoto and then Watanabe made it 3-1, and their team had reached a semi-final for the second time.

By 2pm, Mexico, Hungary and Japan had completed their wins, but in Leon's Nou Camp **Bulgaria** and **Israel** could not score a decider. For 89 minutes it seemed that Khristakiev's early goal was sufficient, but then Feigenbaum scored the equaliser. Since extra time was goalless, it went to the toss of a coin, and Bulgaria's captain Gajdarski called correctly.

Semi-finals

22 October		Bulgaria 3-2 Mexico (2-1)		Guadalajara

Zhekov 8			Morales 39
Mikhajlov 9		Pulido 48
T. Dimitrov 58

22 October		Hungary 5-0 Japan (1-0)		Mexico City

Szucs 30, 60, 75
Novak 53, 65

Bronze Medal match

24 October		Japan 2-0 Mexico (2-0)		Mexico City

Kamamoto 20, 40

The semi-finals

To defeat **Mexico**, **Bulgaria** had to outplay their opponents and face a huge support. The Europeans had the ideal start, going two up in nine minutes, thanks to their captain, Zhekov, and Mikhajlov. But that did not guarantee a victory, because Morales scored in 39 minutes and Pulido levelled the match soon after the interval break.

The winner came from Tsvetan Dimitrov, who had not previously started any match in the tournament, just before an hour had elapsed.

Bulgaria then packed their defence for 30 minutes and, despite Mexico's attacking formation, won 3-2.

Hungary had a difficult first half against **Japan**, with only Lajos Szucs's goal in 30 minutes. The significant period was in the 12 minutes between the 53rd and 65th, when Szucs scored another and his captain Dezso Novak adding two more. Szucs's hat-trick was a remarkable achievement, especially when he lined up in the back four, but his colleague Pancsics was just as important, for he marked Kamamoto out of the game.

The Bronze medal match

Two days later, Japan's spirits were raised when they defeated Mexico in the Azteca Stadium. In 1968, Japan won matches only when Kamamoto scored, and he netted both goals in 20 and 40 minutes. He finished top scorer in the event with seven goals in six matches. Only Hungary were able to control him.

Kamamoto's height, speed, skills and self-belief were notable, and he was the dynamo behind victories against France and Mexico.

Japan are the only Asian team to win a football medal at the Olympics. They were also the only medallists from outwith Europe between Uruguay (1928) and Nigeria (1996).

The Final

26 October   Hungary 4-1 Bulgaria (2-1)   Mexico City

Menczel 41   T. Dimitrov 20
A. Dunai 42, 62
Juhasz 49

Hungary confirmed their position as the best team in Olympic football, retaining their championship, as Great Britain and Uruguay had done in previous generations.

Bulgaria were always likely to be awkward opponents, and that was true in the first half-hour, when Tsvetan Dimitrov, their central midfielder, scored the opening goal. Although on the back foot, Hungary kept pressing. Menczel, the left-sided defender, equalised just before half-time, and top scoring Antal Dunai put them 2-1 ahead, almost from the kick-off.

Hungary then dominated the second half, with an early goal from their left-winger Juhasz and Dunai's second. But this match was remembered less for the scorers than for those who left the field early. Bulgaria did finish the match, unlike the Czech team in 1920, but with only eight players; Hungary with ten.

In the British Olympic Authority's report, John Ballantine saw a potentially great match spoiled by refereeing decisions and players' reaction to them.

Hungary had shown their class, even against Guatemala. Defeating a fine Japanese side 5-0 four days earlier showed why they were favourites for the gold.

Bulgaria were more enigmatic, packing their defence to preserve a 1-0 lead against Israel, and going through by deciding whether a coin showed heads. In Guadalajara, they won 3-2 over Mexico, but lost an early two goal advantage in the second half.

For the Final, conditions were ideal – dry, sunny, about 70 degrees Fahrenheit, with the magnificent Azteca Stadium full of neutral enthusiasts eager for skilful football.

At first, Bulgaria were the better side and deserved to lead with Dimitrov's powerful header. Tackles, according to Ballantine, were hard but fair, and Leo de Diego, the Italian referee, was hardly noticed.

All that changed when Bulgaria fell behind, to goals from Menczel in a goal area scramble, and Dunai. Immediately after the goals, Dimitrov tackled Hungary's right-winger Nosko, and was dismissed. His team-mates surrounded Mr de Diego, without result.

After some time, when Dimitrov had left the pitch, the game restarted, only to be stopped again within seconds. The Bulgarian defender, Ivkov, fouled Dunai, and he had to go as well. His colleagues and their coach, who ran on to the field, could not change the decision, but the centre-forward Mikhajlov kicked the ball towards the referee, and he joined Ivkov off the pitch.

The first half ended with eight lining up against eleven. By the time Hungary led 4-1, they slowed the game down and spent 30 minutes passing the ball around as if in a training match. With five minutes to go, Juhasz was also sent off for what Ballantine called 'a simple barge' familiar in League football in his own country. Only 18 were left on the park – ten Hungarians, eight Bulgarians.

On a happier note, the Hungarian manager, Dr Lakat, praised his defence and looked to them as the foundation for their 1970 World Cup team when the event was held in Mexico. (In fact, they did not qualify, losing in a playoff to Czechoslovakia).

The Medal Winners

Gold: Hungary

Fater	Keglovich	Varga
Bicskei	Szucs	Nagy
Szarka	Fazekas	Nosko
Novak	Kocsis	Sarkozi
L. Dunai	A. Dunai	Basti
Pancsics	Juhasz	
Menczel	Szalai	

Silver: Bulgaria

Yordanov	Georgiev	Nikodimov
Krastev	Yanchovski	Gjonin
Gerov	Mikhajlov	Tsvetkov
Khristakiev	Stankov	Zafirov
Gajdarski	Y. Dimitrov	
Ivkov	Zhekov	
T. Dimitrov	Vasilev	

Bronze: Japan

Yokoyama	Suzuki	Kuwahara
Hamazaki	Tomizawa	Kamamoto
Katayama	Ogi	Matsumoto
M. Miyamoto	Yuguchi	Sugiyama
Yamaguchi	Yaegashi	
Kamata	T. Miyamoto	
Mori	Watanabe	

Top goal scorers:

7: Kamamoto (Japan)
6: A. Dunai (Hungary)
4: Szucs (Hungary), Feigenbaum (Israel)

Referees

I. Zsolt (Hungary)	Mexico v Colombia
M. Gugulovic (Yugoslavia)	France v Guinea
	Mexico v Spain
D. Rumenchev (Bulgaria)	Guinea v Colombia
E. Hieger (Peru)	France v Mexico
	Spain v Japan
S. Wanchai (Thailand)	Mexico v Guinea
K. Galba (Czechoslovakia)	Colombia v France
A. Klein (Israel)	Spain v Brazil
	Japan v Mexico (Bronze medal match)
R. Marmol (El Salvador)	Japan v Nigeria
A. Robles (Guinea)	Spain v Nigeria
G. Lamptey (Ghana)	Brazil v Japan
S. Tarekegn (Ethiopia)	Brazil v Nigeria
	Japan v France
	Bulgaria v Mexico (Semi-final)
M. Kitabdjian (France)	Israel v Ghana
	Bulgaria v Israel
D. de Leo (Mexico)	Hungary v El Salvador
	Hungary v Bulgaria (Final)
Y. Maruyama (Japan)	Hungary v Ghana
T. Badru (Nigeria)	Israel v El Salvador
M. Iglesias (Spain)	El Salvador v Ghana
A. Yamasaki (Peru)	Hungary v Israel
	Hungary v Guatemala
R. Filho (Brazil)	Guatemala v Czechoslovakia
	Hungary v Japan (Semi-final)
G. Velasquez (Colombia)	Bulgaria v Thailand
A. Elizalde (Mexico)	Bulgaria v Czechoslovakia
J-L. Faber (Guinea)	Guatemala v Thailand
R. Osiris (Mexico)	Bulgaria v Guatemala
F. Elcuaz (Mexico)	Czechoslovakia v Thailand

Europe

Group One: Czechoslovakia qualified
Round 1: USSR walkover – Albania withdrew
Round 2: USSR 3-1 Poland (2-1, 1-0)
Czechoslovakia walk-over – Yugoslavia withdrew
Final: Czechoslovakia 5-3 USSR (3-0, 2-3)

Group Two: Bulgaria qualified
Round 1: East Germany 10-0 Greece (5-0, 5-0)
Round 2: Bulgaria 6-2 Turkey (3-0, 3-2)
East Germany 2-0 Romania (1-0, 1-0)
Final: Bulgaria 6-4 East Germany (4-1, 2-3)

Group Three: France qualified
Round 1: Finland 1-0 Netherlands (0-0, 1-0)
Round 2: Austria 4-2 Switzerland (4-1, 0-1)
France 4-2 Finland (3-1, 1-1)
Final: France 4-2 Austria (3-1, 1-1)

Group Four: Spain qualified
Round 1: Spain 6-4 Iceland (1-1, 5-3)
Round 2: Great Britain 2-1 West Germany (2-0, 0-1)
Spain walk-over – Italy withdrew
Final: Spain 1-0 Great Britain (1-0, 0-0)

North and Central America

Group One: Guatemala qualified
Round 1: Bermuda 2-1 USA (1-0, 1-1)
Haiti 14-0 Domican Republic (8-0, 6-0)
Round 2: Guatemala 1-1 Bermuda (1-1, 0-0)
(play-off) Guatemala 2-0 Bermuda
Costa Rica 5-4 Haiti (3-1, 2-3)
Final: Guatemala 3-3 Costa Rica (1-0, 2-3)
Guatemala won on the toss of a coin.

Group Two: El Salvador qualified
Round 1: Cuba 3-2 Canada (2-1, 1-1)
El Salvador walk-over – Honduras withdrew
Trinidad and Tobago 3-5 Surinam, but Surinam withdrew (1-0, 2-5)
Round 2: El Salvador 5-1 Cuba (3-0, 2-1)
Trinidad and Tobago 4-3 Netherlands Antilles (4-0, 0-3)
Final: El Salvador 4-1 Trinidad and Tobago (2-0, 2-1)

South America

Group One:

Brazil 3-0 Venezuela
Paraguay 1-0 Chile
Paraguay 3-0 Venezuela
Brazil 0-0 Chile
Brazil 0-0 Paraguay
Chile 1-0 Venezuela

Paraguay (5 points) and Brazil (4 points) went through to a Final group, ahead of Chile (3 points) and Venezuela (0 points).

Group 2:

Colombia 1-0 Ecuador
Uruguay 0-0 Peru
Colombia 2-1 Peru
Uruguay 2-0 Ecuador
Peru 1-1 Ecuador
Colombia 1-1 Uruguay

Colombia (5 points) and Uruguay (4 points) went through to the Final group, ahead of Peru (2 points) and Equador (1 point).

Final Group:

Uruguay 2-1 Brazil
Colombia 4-2 Paraguay
Brazil v Paraguay (match awarded to Brazil)
Uruguay 3-3 Paraguay
Colombia 2-0 Uruguay
Brazil 3-0 Colombia

Brazil (4 points) and Colombia (4 points) qualified for Mexico, ahead of Uruguay (3 points) and Paraguay (1 point).

Africa

Group One: Guinea qualified
Round 1: Libya 4-2 Niger (2-0, 2-2)
Guinea 6-1 Gabon (0-0, 6-1)
Round 2: Guinea walk-over – UAR withdrew
Algeria 3-2 Libya (2-1, 1-1)
Final: Guinea 5-4 Algeria (3-2, 2-2)

Group Two: Nigeria qualified
Round 1: Nigeria walk-over – Uganda withdrew
Madagascar 6-2 Tanzania (4-2, 2-0)
Round 2: Nigeria 2-2 Sudan (Nigeria won on the toss of a coin) (1-0, 1-2)
Ethiopia 8-4 Madagascar (0-1, 8-3)
Final: Nigeria 4-1 Ethiopia (3-1, 1-0)

Group Three: Morocco qualified, but later withdrew. They were replaced by Ghana.
Round 1: Cameroon walk-over – Mali withdrew
Round 2: Morocco 1-1 Tunisia (Morocco won on the toss of a coin) (1-1, 0-0)
Ghana 3-3 Cameroon – Cameroon withdrew before the play-off, and Ghana went through (0-1, 3-2)
Final: Morocco 3-2 Ghana (1-1, 2-1)

Asia

Group One: Japan qualified

South Korea 4-2 Taiwan
South Korea 5-0 Philippines
Lebanon 11-1 Philippines
Japan 4-0 Taiwan
South Korea 2-0 Lebanon
South Vietnam 3-0 Taiwan
Taiwan 7-2 Philippines
Japan 15-0 Philippines
Japan 3-1 Lebanon
Japan 3-3 South Korea
Japan 1-0 South Vietnam
South Korea 3-0 South Vietnam

Lebanon 5-2 Taiwan
South Vietnam 10-0 Philippines
Lebanon 1-1 South Vietnam

Japan (9 points) qualified ahead of South Korea (9 points) on a higher goal difference (+22, compared to +12). Lebanon finished Group One with 5 points, South Vietnam 5, Taiwan 2, and The Philippines 0 points.

Group Two: Thailand qualified

Iraq 4-0 Thailand
Indonesia 2-1 Iraq
Thailand 2-1 Iraq
Thailand 1-0 Indonesia
Thailand 2-1 Indonesia
Iraq 1-1 Indonesia
Hong Kong, Malaysia and Pakistan withdrew from Group Two.

Thailand qualified with 6 points, ahead of Iraq (3 points) and Indonesia (3 points).

Group Three: Israel qualified

Israel 11-0 Ceylon (Sri Lanka) (7-0, 4-0)

Burma, India, Iran and North Korea withdrew from Group Three.

16. Munich, 1972

Football in perspective

Although these Olympics were completed, they could not be the same after the tragic events in early September, when eleven Israeli team members, and most of their attackers, were killed. Several teams went home, but the great majority continued to compete, after a solemn memorial service in the Olympic Stadium.

In 1966 Munich's bid had succeeded over those of Madrid, Montreal, and Detroit. Their opening ceremony saw the German athlete, Heidi Schuller, become the first woman to take the Olympic oath on behalf of everyone concerned. There were soon to be starring roles for Mary Peters, the first Briton to win a pentathlon; Shane Gould, Australia's swimming triple gold medallist who took part in a record 12 races; and the first world legend of gymnastics, Olga Korbut of the USSR.

Others not content with one victory were Valery Borzov, the Soviet winner of 100 and 200 metres, and a new flying Finn, Lasse Viren, outlasting the field in both 5,000 and 10,000 metres. Though he fell in the longer race, he picked himself up and started all over again.

Powering through the pool for the USA was Mark Spitz, who received a record seven golds – in three relays and four individual events, sending spray and world records in all directions. This one swimmer contributed to 20% of the US total of 33 gold medals.

The 1972 football tournament

Six stadia housed matches – the brand-new Olympic Stadium in Munich (11 matches) and another new construction in Passau, the Drei Flusse Stadium (6).

Four older grounds hosted football – Nuremberg's Municipal Stadium (6), Jahnstadium, Regensburg (6), the Rosenau Stadium, Augsburg (5), and Ingolstadt's ESV Stadium (4 matches).

A new structure was tried for the second stage of the event. Instead of quarter-finals, teams entered another Group, in Round Two.

The following received entry to Group One in Round Two:
  Group A winners,
  B runners-up,
  C winners,
  D runners-up.

These entered Group Two in Round Two:
  Group A runners-up,
  B winners,
  C runners-up,
  D winners.

Then Group One and Group Two winners progressed to the Final, the runners-up to the Bronze medal game.

Round One

Group A

27 August	USA 0-0 Morocco	Augsburg
27 August	West Germany 3-0 Malaysia (0-0) Worm 56 Kalb 71 Seliger 82	Munich
29 August	Malaysia 3-0 USA (1-0) Shaharuddin 8 Salleh 67 Zawawi 77	Ingolstadt
29 August	West Germany 3-0 Morocco (2-0) Nickel 30, 33 (both penalties) Hitzfeld 53	Passau

31 August   Morocco 6-0 Malaysia (4-0)   Ingolstadt
               Benkhrif 16
              Faras 19, 21, 25
               El Filali 56
               Zouita 85

31 August   West Germany 7-0 USA (2-0)   Munich
             Nickel 17, 43, 70, 86
               Hitzfeld 47
               Seliger 62
                Bitz 79

Qualified: West Germany   6 points   (13 goals for – 0 against)
Qualified: Morocco   3 points   (6-3)
                Malaysia   2 points   (3-9)
                  USA   1 point   (0-10)

West Germany went into Round Two, Group One – Morocco into Round Two, Group Two.

Group A

For the first time West Germany and East Germany both took part in the tournament and the Federal Republic were strong favourites to win Group A in the first round of matches.

They had automatic entry as hosts, and this was a stronger team than the one who lost to Great Britain in 1967 qualifying matches.

The USA qualified by defeating Barbados and El Salvador, but also drew twice with the Central American side en route. Morocco had narrowly beaten Nigeria and then finished ahead of Tunisia and Mali. In Asian qualifiers, Malaysia caused a shock by winning 3-0 against Japan, bronze medallists in 1968, and taking one of the two places from their continent.

For the American team, the good news was that they gained a point, their first since St Louis in 1904. The draw against **Morocco** in Augsburg, however, was goalless, and the **US** side did not score in this event.

In Munich's Olympic Stadium, a crowd 15 times as large – 60,000 – saw an uncertain start for the home team, who could not turn attacks into goals for almost an hour. At last, supporters cheered when the left-winger Worm put **West Germany** one up on **Malaysia**.

Immediately Jupp Derwall, the coach, brought on a substitute, the midfielder Kalb, and he repaid that confidence with the second goal in 71 minutes. Seliger, his central midfield colleague, came up with the third, eight minutes from time.

In their second match, **West Germany** ensured progress to the next stage when they won by the same 3-0 score, against **Morocco**. This victory was easier, with Morocco conceding two penalties which the striker Nickel converted, in 30 and 33 minutes. Hitzfeld added a third soon after half-time, and the African team had their forward Mouhoub sent off with 19 minutes left.

At the same time, **Malaysia** collected two points against the **USA** in Ingolstadt. Shaharuddin opened the scoring in only 14 minutes, and two more late in the match came from Salleh and Zawawi, in the third 3-0 result in Group A.

With one fixture left for the sides, West Germany had four points, Malaysia two, and only those teams could win the group. The greatest interest was in who would claim the runners-up spot.

Morocco finished second, by a 6-0 win against **Malaysia**. There was little doubt of that, once they went four ahead in the first 25 minutes, notable for Faras's hat-trick within six minutes, after their captain Benkhrif opened the scoring. Not only was his goal unusual for a right-back, but once his team went 3-0 up, Benkhrif was substituted to save him for the next round.

Replacing the captain after 22 minutes showed their coach's confidence in his team.

West Germany played **USA** before a Munich crowd of 65,000, and an upset was not likely, once Nickel scored in 17 minutes. He ended with four goals in the fixture, and three more arrived from Hitzfeld, Seliger (who only appeared after half-time), and Bitz.

Group B

28 August	USSR 1-0 Burma (0-0) Kolotov 51		Regensburg
28 August	Mexico 1-0 Sudan (1-0) Manzo 16		Nuremberg
30 August	Mexico 1-0 Burma (0-0) Cuellar 86		Nuremberg
30 August	USSR 2-1 Sudan (2-0) Evryuzhikin 42 (p) Jaksa 59 Zanazanian 44		Munich
1 September	Burma 2-0 Sudan (1-0) T. Soe 7 T. Moe 61		Passau
1 September	USSR 4-1 Mexico (3-0) Blokhin 7, 13, 14 Razo 60 Semjonov 58		Regensburg

Qualified:	USSR	6 points	(7-2)
Qualified:	Mexico	4 points	(3-4)
	Burma	2 points	(2-2)
	Sudan	0 points	(1-5)

USSR progressed to Round Two, Group Two, and Mexico to Round Two, Group One.

Group B

The USSR, who did not qualify in 1968, were back, and looked to be the strongest team in this Group by some distance. Mexico qualified after narrowly heading off strong challenges from Canada and Jamaica, who both won matches against them.

Sudan's route to Munich came through victories over Uganda and then Ethiopa and the Malagasy Republic, also known as Madagascar. Burma's first appearance in the tournament was the result of matches in Rangoon, where they won every game against Taiwan, Sri Lanka, India, Indonesia and Thailand.

Group B provided a predictable winner, via an unpredictable route, in front of crowds varying from 500 to 25,000.

The **USSR** defeated **Burma** by the slimmest margin; the Soviet midfielder Kolotov hit the only goal in 51 minutes. His defence was the team's foundation for success when forward play was not inspiring.

Mexico won by the same score in Nuremberg over **Sudan**. In a stadium devoid of atmosphere, the match lived down to its surroundings with Manzo, the right-winger, winning the game in 16 minutes.

The niggardly goal count continued when **Mexico** beat **Burma** with one goal, and that came right at the end from Cuellar, left-winger and captain. Once more, hardly 1,000 turned up at Nuremberg, but Mexico at least were sure to qualify if USSR won against Sudan.

In Munich, before the largest attendance in Group B, **Sudan** put up a good performance before losing 2-1 to the **USSR**. Although the Russians guaranteed they would make the next stage, their result depended on 120 seconds just before the interval. First, Evrjuzhikhin scored from a penalty and then Zanazanian made it 2-0. However, Jaksa's counter in the second half made the last half-hour uncomfortable for the USSR.

Now, since both had four points, the winner of the group would be decided by **USSR** v **Mexico**. The Russians' 4-1 success was largely thanks to a midfielder who had played only 22 minutes so far – Oleg Blokhin. Starting this match, he produced a hat-trick in the opening quarter of an hour, and the match was over. A team which had struggled upfront was transformed, and Semjonov scored a fourth just before the hour. Razo's consolation came too late, but Mexico went ahead as runners-up.

Burma finally scored and won 2-0 over **Sudan**. Than Soe's goal came at exactly the same moment as Blokhin's first Russian goal (seven minutes in) and his left-winger T.A. Moe doubled the lead, to give Burma third place. Both teams were new to the event, their defences generally held firm, and there were no one-sided encounters for them.

Group C

27 August   Hungary 5-0 Iran (1-0)   Nuremberg
A. Dunai 31, 48, 90
Varadi 52
Kozma 81

27 August   Denmark 3-2 Brazil (1-0)   Passau
Simonsen 28, 83   Dirceu 68
Rontved 50   Ze Carlos 69

29 August   Hungary 2-2 Brazil (1-0)   Augsburg
A. Dunai 4   Pedrinho 67
Juhasz 84   Dirceu 73

29 August   Denmark 4-0 Iran (3-0)   Munich
Heino Hansen 16, 58
Simonsen 39
Nygaard 44

31 August   Hungary 2-0 Denmark (1-0)   Augsburg
E. Dunai 17, 84

31 August   Iran 1-0 Brazil (0-0)   Regensburg
Halvaei 63

Qualified: Hungary   5 points   (9-2)
Qualified: Denmark   4 points   (7-4)
             Iran   2 points   (1-9)
             Brazil   1 point   (4-6)

Hungary went through to Round Two, Group One, and Denmark to Round Two, Group Two.

Group C

Group C offered spectators probably the best chance of good football, from Hungary, Brazil, Denmark and Iran.

Hungary had not played a qualifying match since 1960 and once more they entered the tournament as reigning champions. They were able to prepare in their usual ultra-methodical manner, playing only friendlies to assist their build-up to August 1972.

Denmark, one of the few medallists from outside Eastern Europe since 1952, had qualified by defeating Switzerland and Romania, after a play-off.

Brazil came through a series of matches in Colombia, which produced very few goals. They won games against Bolivia, Chile, Argentina, and Peru, all by a single goal.

In Asia, Iran overcame Kuwait and then North Korea, in a Rawalpindi decider.

Hungary v **Iran** produced five goals, all for the Magyars. Antal Dunai, very much the elder statesman of the team, scored his first in 31 minutes, and added two more, at the start and finish of the second period, for the tournament's first hat-trick. His colleagues in attack, Varadi and Kozma, also scored, in front of a surprisingly low attendance in Nuremberg, just 2,000.

Denmark's match against **Brazil** was as evenly contested as the other game was one-sided. Simonsen, the Danish left-winger, put them in front after 28 minutes, with his captain and full-back Rontved doubling their lead soon after the interval.

But Brazil's coach Antoninho brought on midfielder Ze Carlos in 62 minutes, and the South Americans swiftly came back into the match with goals from Dirceu and Carlos. In a tense finale, Simonsen scored the winner for Denmark with just seven minutes to go.

The **Danes'** next match against **Iran** was easier, and they held a 3-0 advantage at half-time. Heino Hansen, one of three Hansens in the team, gave them the lead in 16 minutes and scored the fourth and last, in 58. In between, Simonsen and centre-forward Nygaard added two more, to ensure Denmark had four points out of four.

Hungary v **Brazil** drew 50,000 to the Olympic Stadium and rightly so, such was the reputation of these nations. One was outstanding in the Games, the other in the World Cup – Hungary had won three football golds, Brazil three trophies with their senior professionals.

Dunai showed Hungarian attacking intentions from the kick off and scored inside four minutes, but 1-0 was never sufficient. Again, Ze Carlos did not start the match but was a substitute in 46 minutes. When Pedrinho levelled after 67 minutes, both sides brought on substitutes – Bolivar for Brazil, and Balint for Hungary.

Dirceu quickly put Brazil 2-1 ahead, only for Juhasz, the Magyar's left back, to equalise six minutes from the whistle.

With four points, Denmark would go into the next round, and Hungary's three points meant they were sure to progress with a draw in their third game. Brazil (one point) now had to win decisively, and hope the Danes overcame Hungary. Neither happened.

Only 2,200 in Regensburg saw one of the great upsets of Olympic football, as **Iran** defeated **Brazil** 1-0. The result in itself and its effect, placing the Asian team above the South American in Group C, were remarkable. Iran's midfielder Halvaei scored in 63 minutes. That was his side's only goal, while Brazil had previously hit four, only to prop up the table.

Hungary finished at its head, with a goal in each half as they won 2-0 against **Denmark**. Ede Dunai took the goal honours in his first match of the event, in 17 and 84 minutes. Hungary fielded Dunai and Balint as wing halves, in a new combination for this match, and retained it throughout the rest of the event.

One unusual feature of the second half was that Denmark fielded their substitute goalkeeper Hildebrandt after the interval. This was his only appearance in the event, for three days later Thorkildsen was fit to return between the posts.

Group D

28 August   East Germany 4-0 Ghana (2-0)   Munich
                 Kreische 19, 89
                 Streich 45
                 Sparwasser 66

28 August   Poland 5-1 Colombia (3-0)   Ingolstadt
                 Deyna 16, 32   Moron 63
                 Gadocha 42, 49, 72

30 August	East Germany 6-1 Colombia (4-1)		Passau
	Streich 1, 10	Espinosa 38	
	Sparwasser 9		
	Ducke 31		
	Vogel 85		
	Kreische 88 (p)		

30 August	Poland 4-0 Ghana (1-0)		Regensburg
	Lubanski 40		
	Gadocha 59, 89		
	Deyna 86		

1 September	Colombia 3-1 Ghana (0-0)		Munich
	Moron 56	Sunday 79	
	Torres 60		
	Montano 82		

1 September	Poland 2-1 East Germany (1-1)		Nuremberg
	Gorgon 6, 63	Streich 45	

Qualified:	Poland	6 points	(11-2)
Qualified:	East Germany	4 points	(11-3)
	Colombia	2 points	(5-12)
	Ghana	0 points	(1-11)

Poland went through to Round Two, Group Two, and East Germany to Round Two, Group One.

Group D

Poland and East Germany were drawn with Colombia and Ghana and, like all the East European teams sponsored by their governments, were strong favourites to reach the next round.

Poland qualified by beating Greece, Spain and Bulgaria in their European section, while East Germany overcame Italy and Yugoslavia.

Playing their qualifiers at home, Colombia came through to the tournament with Brazil, from a group where they drew every match.

Group D produced 28 goals, the highest-scoring of the groups, and 22 went to the Europeans, who coasted into the next stage.

East Germany v **Ghana** attracted 40,000 to Munich, and Kreische, the German left-half, scored first in 19 minutes. His left winger Streich collected the second as the whistle blew for the interval. They were not taxed by Ghana's forwards in the second half, and Sparwasser settled the issue in 66 minutes with a third goal. Kreische made it 4-0 right at the end.

Poland's 5-1 victory over **Colombia** in Ingolstadt was even more straightforward. Deyna, the Polish central midfielder, was to be a highly influential player, and he scored twice early on, with Gadocha, on the left wing, making it 3-0 at half-time. Then Gadocha caught the eye with a hat-trick, while Moron, Colombia's winger, made the score more respectable.

The next two matches followed a similar path, as East Germany and Poland both won – and booked their Round Two places.

East Germany could not draw more than 4,500 to Passau (compared to Munich's 25,000 to watch Colombia v Ghana) for their game against **Colombia**. Those who stayed away missed a phenomenal opening ten minutes when Streich, with two, and Sparwasser put the Germans 3-0 up. Ducke, their centre-forward, scored his only goal of the event, and Vogel – his substitute in the second half – made it 5-1. Espinosa collected one for Colombia in 38 minutes, and Kreische's last minute penalty completed a 6-1 result.

Poland's 4-0 win over **Ghana** took longer to achieve, since the Poles' captain Lubanski hit their opener only after 40 minutes. Gadocha and Deyna were the second half scorers, but two came in the last four minutes to produce a result which flattered the Europeans.

Colombia v **Ghana** in the Olympic Stadium was a contest for third place, and neither team could gain supremacy for nearly an hour. Then Moron scored for Colombia in 56 minutes, and Torres doubled their lead. Ghana's captain Sunday moved up to make it 2-1 but Montano, a very late substitute, secured the win in 82 minutes.

Only 10,000 watched **Poland** v **East Germany** decide who would top the group: a draw would put the Germans just ahead on goal difference. The Polish full-back Gorgon was their match winner, with two goals, opening his account in just six minutes. Streich equalised just as the Canadian referee was about to sound the interval. But Gorgon had the final say, scoring the winner in 63 minutes, and Poland won Group D.

Round Two

Group One

3 September   Hungary 2-0 East Germany (0-0)   Passau
                   A. Dunai 60
                   Toth 66

3 September   Mexico 1-1 West Germany (0-1)   Nuremberg
                   Cuellar 69   Hitzfeld 5

5 September   East Germany 7-0 Mexico (2-0)   Ingolstadt
                   Ganzera 34
                   Sparwasser 39, 51, 89
                   Streich 48
                   Kreische 72
                   Hafner 79

6 September   Hungary 4-1 West Germany (2-1)   Munich
                   E. Dunai 14   Hitzfeld 33
                   A. Dunai 43
                   Ku 75, 87

8 September   East Germany 3-2 West Germany (1-1)   Munich
                   Pommerenke 10   Hoeness 31
                   Streich 53   Hitzfeld 68
                   Vogel 82

8 September   Hungary 2-0 Mexico (1-0)   Regensburg
                   A. Dunai 35
                   Kocsis 53

Hungary:	6 points	(8-1)
East Germany	4 points	(10-4)
West Germany	1 point	(4-8)
Mexico	1 point	(1-10)

Hungary progressed to the Final, while East Germany moved to the bronze medal match.

Round Two

Group One

This group brought together the hosts, West Germany, who had won their matches without conceding a goal, and Hungary, whose one hiccough was a draw against Brazil.

Joining them were two teams who had finished second in their Round One sections – Mexico and East Germany. This meant that for the first time in the final stages of a tournament, the two halves of disunited Germany would contest a match.

But first **West Germany** had a flying start against **Mexico** in Nuremberg's Frankenstadion, before 40,000 spectators. Hitzfeld scored in five minutes, and the crowd's expectations rose, only to be dashed when the Mexican left-winger and captain, Cueller, equalised over an hour later. This, their only goal in Round Two, gained them a draw.

Hungary found **East Germany** a difficult side to break down, and the match was goalless for 60 minutes. Then Dunai gave the Magyars a lead which his right-winger Toth doubled soon after. After one match, Hungary were already entrenched at the top of Group One.

East Germany, like the hosts, did not at first find **Mexico** easy to overcome. But once their full-back Ganzera showed his forwards the way in 34 minutes, they soon followed suit. Sparwasser hit the first of his three goals before half-time, and after the interval Streich made victory sure within three minutes. Midfielders Kreische and Hafner, a substitute, added more goals in the 7-0 result. Hafner had been on the field a few seconds when he scored in 79 minutes.

Hungary v **West Germany** drew 70,000 to the Olympic Stadium for a match which, especially in the first half, lived up to its Champions v Hosts billing. Ede Dunai put Hungary ahead in 14 minutes, but Hitzfeld equalised after half-an-hour. Just before the interval, Antal Dunai gave Hungary the advantage. Later the Magyar's centre-half Ku showed he could be a match winner with two goals in a 4-1 victory. West Germany brought on both substitutes, Hungary employed none.

With one match to go, Hungary (four points) would top the group and reach the Final unless East Germany (two points) defeated West (one), and Mexico (one point) won against the Hungarians.

Hungary completed three wins out of three, 2-0, over **Mexico**, before a sparse crowd in Regensburg. Antal Dunai again scored a decisive goal, after 35 minutes, and a second half substitute Kocsis netted their second.

The contest between the two Germanies, of course, was held in Munich before the biggest crowd so far – 80,000. There was much more at stake than finishing second, or even first, in the group.

First came Pommerenke's goal in 12 minutes, then the leveller from Hoeness, a legendary figure in Germany's World Cup win in 1974. 1-1 at half-time and, in many senses, all to play for. Streich put East Germany in front soon after the break, but Hitzfeld again proved his mettle in 68 minutes to make it 2-2. At last the match was decided by Vogel, brought on to replace Streich, eight minutes from time. The Eastern team now went into a 3rd place match, while the hosts rued the chances they had missed, especially against Mexico.

Round Two

Group Two

3 September   USSR 3-0 Morocco (2-0)   Munich
            Semjonov 1
            Kolotov 15
            Eliseev 69

3 September   Denmark 1-1 Poland (1-1)   Regensburg
            Heino Hansen 27   Deyna 36

5 September   Poland 2-1 USSR (0-1)   Augsburg
            Deyna 79 (p)   Blokhin 28
            Szoltysik 87

5 September	Denmark 3-1 Morocco (0-0)		Passau
	Bak 55, 83 Merzaq 89		
	Printzlau 90		

8 September	USSR 4-0 Denmark (2-0)		Augsburg
	Kolotov 20		
	Semjonov 28		
	Blokhin 55		
	Szabo 88		

8 September	Poland 5-0 Morocco (3-0)		Nuremberg
	Kmiecik 3		
	Lubanski 10		
	Deyna 45 (p), 63		
	Gadocha 53		

Poland:	5 points	(8-2)
USSR:	4 points	(8-2)
Morocco:	0 points	(1-11)

Poland went on to the Final, and USSR to the bronze medal match.

Round Two

Group Two

Three European teams took their places in Group Two – The USSR and Poland, as winners of their Round One groups, and Denmark, who finished second. Morocco were the outsiders.

USSR v **Morocco** was watched by 55,000 in Munich, far more than had attended the African team's previous fixtures. The Soviet right-winger Semjonov received the ball almost from the kick-off and scored in 60 seconds. His right-midfield colleague, Kolotov, made it 2-0 in 15 minutes, and Morocco could not find a goal. Compared with their outstanding win over Malaysia, their coach Sabino Barinaga placed Faras – a hat-trick hero

– and Hadri back into midfield. He then restored forwards who had not scored in their earlier matches. 3-0 was the final score, as the USSR's substitute Eliseev scored with almost his first move.

Poland's match with **Denmark** saw two teams in fine form but who rarely faced each other. The Danes had a settled formation, and did not use substitutes in this match, while Poland used both, and made several changes throughout the tournament.

Heino Hansen had scored twice against Iran, and here he gave Denmark the lead in 27 minutes. Deyna equalised nine minutes later and the match finished 1-1, with neither side out of the running to win this group.

Poland v **USSR** brought the two favourites in Group Two to Augsburg, and Blokhin opened the Russians' account in 28 minutes. For almost the whole match, 1-0 seemed to be enough and two points were heading the Soviets' way. Yet in a remarkable turn-round, Deyna scored from a penalty in 79 minutes to equalise. With three minutes left, the substitute Szoltysik won the match for Poland.

Denmark won their match against **Morocco** 3-1, but goals were slow in arriving, and their central mid-fielder Bak scored the first in 55 minutes. As in the Polish victory, 1-0 seemed to be the final score until the last few minutes. Then Bak hit a second in 83 minutes, and although Merzaq collected Morocco's one goal of the group, Printzlau made the result more comfortable for the Scandinavians.

Denmark and Poland now had three points, the USSR two, Morocco none. Any of the European sides could reach the Final, and the Danes had a better goal difference than Poland. However, **Poland** v **Morocco** was expected to give the Polish team another victory, and five points. Denmark had to defeat the Russians and keep their advantage in goal difference – a lot to ask of the amateurs.

Within ten minutes Poland were 2-0 ahead of Morocco, through Kmiecik and his captain Lubanski. Deyna added a penalty on the half-time whistle, and his team could relax, since the USSR were in charge of their match against Denmark. Early in the second half, Gadocha and the reliable Deyna completed a 5-0 win. Poland would contest the Final, against Hungary.

Denmark's tournament ended with disappointment, losing 4-0 to the **USSR** in Augsburg. Kolotov took 20 minutes to put the Russian team ahead, with Semjonov following up eight minutes later. Oleg Blokhin's third, in 55 minutes, ensured the USSR would go into the Bronze medal match, and Szabo was able to come out of central midfield to score the fourth.

The Bronze Medal Match

10 September   USSR 2-2 East Germany (2-1)   Munich

Blokhin 10   Kreische 33 (p)
Khurtsilava 30 Vogel 78

(After extra time. Since no replay had been scheduled, both teams received medals).

In this third place match, the USSR took an early lead through Blokhin and his defender Khurtsilava put them 2-0 ahead in half an hour. East Germany were on the back foot, and their left-back Ganzera had to go off after just 20 minutes, to be replaced by Kurbjuweit, who had not played a Round Two match.

But the Germans gained a chance to regroup with a penalty, scored by Kreische in 33 minutes. This was a bruising 90 minutes with 40 fouls causing constant interruptions, and with 12 minutes left Vogel, a late substitute, levelled it at 2-2.

The crowd were informed, by public address, that there would be no replay and a draw after extra time would see both sides receive bronze medals.

After the storms, came a strange calm in the extra 30 minutes as players accepted a draw and passed the ball around, to the counterpoint of whistles and complaints. The match dwindled into a training session and anti-climax.

The Final

10 September   Poland 2-1 Hungary (0-1)   Munich

Deyna 47, 68   Varadi 42

20,000 of the crowd at the Bronze medal match did not stay for the final, and missed a fine match.

Two skilful teams had to master their opponents and the elements – powerful wind and pouring rain. Hungary, going for three championships in a row, won the toss and chose to play with a gale at their backs. Significantly, they could not take advantage of the conditions until Varadi, the left winger, scored from an acute angle after 42 minutes.

1-0 for Hungary at the interval was an insecure lead. Immediately the game restarted, Poland gained the upper hand. Deyna beat the defence and from 18 yards his wind-assisted shot sped past Geczi for the equaliser in 47 minutes.

Deyna scored a second 21 minutes later, as the Hungarian keeper found clutching the ball awkward and his punch did not clear the danger. Poland's Gadocha then hit a shot over an open goal. Poland won their first championship in a game worthy of the term Olympian.

Top goal scorers

9: Deyna (Poland)
7: Antal Dunai (Hungary)
   Streich (East Germany)

The medal winners

Gold: Poland

Kostka	Gut	Lubanski
Szeja	Cmikiewicz	Gadocha
Szymanowski	Maszczyk	Kmiecik
Gorgon	Szymczak	Lato
Anczok	Szoltysik	Marx
Kraska	Deyna	
Ostafinski	Jarosik	

Silver: Hungary

Geczi	Balint	Toth
Rapp	Szucs	A. Dunai
Rothermel	Kozma	Varadi
Vepi	Ku	Branikovits
Pancsics	Kovacs	Basti
Juhasz	E. Dunai	
Vidats	Kocsis	

In a unique result, two teams received bronze medals in 1972.

USSR:

Rudakov	Olshanskij	Onishchenko
Pilguj	Kolotov	Yakubik
Istomin	Semjonov	Evrjuzhikhin
Khurtsilava	Kuksov	Eliseev
Lovchev	Zanazanian	Blokhin

Kaplichnyj
Dzodzuashvili

Andreasian
Szabo

East Germany:

Croy	Ganzera	Schulenberg
Schneider	Irmscher	Sparwasser
Kurbjuweit	Pommerenke	Streich
Zapf	Kreische	Ducke
Weise	Hafner	Vogel
Bransch	Seguin	
Watzlich	Tyll	

Referees

R. Gluckner (East Germany) USA v Morocco
A. Marques (Brazil) West Germany v Malaysia
Hungary v East Germany
East Germany v USSR
(Bronze medal match)
H. Oberg (Norway) Malaysia v USA
Poland v USSR
D. Babacan (Turkey) West Germany v Morocco
USSR v Denmark
M. Dorantes (Mexico) West Germany v USA
K. Palotai (Hungary) Morocco v Malaysia
J. Namdar (Iran) USSR v Burma
East Germany v Mexico
F. Francescon (Italy) Mexico v Sudan
Poland v Morocco
R. Quarshie (Ghana) Mexico v Burma
F. Biwersi (West Germany) USSR v Sudan
M. Srodecki (Poland) Burma v Sudan
L. Pestarino (Argentina) USSR v Mexico
Hungary v West Germany
G. Velasquez (Colombia) Hungary v Iran
USSR v Morocco
P. Kazakov (USSR) Denmark v Brazil
A. Ziani (Morocco) Denmark v Iran
W. Mullan (Great Britain) Hungary v Brazil
East Germany v
West Germany

G. Schulemburg (West Germany) Iran v Brazil
O.P. Hwa (Malaysia) Hungary v Denmark
　　Mexico v West Germany
M. Wuertz (USA) East Germany v Ghana
A. Gindil (Sweden) Poland v Colombia
A. Aouissi (Algeria) East Germany v Colombia
　　Denmark v Poland
K-C. Lee (Hong Kong) Poland v Ghana
　　Hungary v Mexico
K. Tschenscher (West Germany) Colombia v Ghana
　　Poland v Hungary (Final)
W. Winsemann (Canada) Poland v East Germany
　　Denmark v Mexico

The Qualifying Tournament

Teams who qualified for Munich were:

Hosts: West Germany
Champions: Hungary
Europe: USSR, Poland, East Germany, Denmark
South America: Brazil, Colombia
North and Central America: Mexico, USA
Africa: Morocco, Ghana, Sudan
Asia: Malaysia, Burma, Iran

Europe

Round One

(Aggregate scores over two matches)

Great Britain	1-5	Bulgaria	(1-0, 0-5)	
Luxembourg	3-3	Austria	(1-0, 2-3)	
Austria	2-0	Luxembourg	(play-off in Marburg)	
Switzerland	2-5	Denmark	(2-1, 0-4)	
East Germany	5-0	Italy	(4-0, 1-0)	
Spain	2-0	Turkey	(1-0, 1-0)	
Iceland	0-1	France	(0-0, 0-1)	

Poland	8-0	Greece	(7-0, 1-0)
USSR	4-0	Netherlands	(4-0, 0-0)
Ireland	0-3	Yugoslavia	(0-1, 0-2)
Romania	4-2	Albania	(2-1, 2-1)

Round Two

Group One

USSR	4-0	Austria
Austria	0-1	USSR
USSR	5-1	France
France	1-3	USSR
France	5-1	Austria
Austria	0-3	France

USSR (8 points) qualified, ahead of France (4 points) and Austria (0 points).

Group Two

Spain	0-2	Poland
Poland	3-0	Spain
Bulgaria	3-1	Poland
Poland	3-0	Bulgaria
Bulgaria	8-3	Spain
Spain	3-3	Bulgaria

Poland (6 points) qualified ahead of Bulgaria (5 points) and Spain (1 point).

Group Three

East Germany	2-0	Yugoslavia
Yugoslavia	0-0	East Germany

East Germany qualified.

Group Four

Denmark	2-1	Romania
Romania	2-3	Denmark

Denmark qualified.

South America

All qualifying matches were played in Colombia.

Group One

Brazil	1-1	Ecuador
Bolivia	1-1	Chile
Brazil	2-1	Bolivia
Argentina	2-2	Ecuador
Brazil	0-0	Argentina
Ecuador	0-0	Chile
Argentina	2-0	Chile
Bolivia	2-1	Ecuador
Argentina	1-1	Bolivia
Brazil	1-0	Chile

Brazil (6 points) and Argentina (5 points) progressed to the next stage ahead of Bolivia (4 points), Ecuador (3 points) and Chile (2 points).

Group Two

Colombia	2-1	Uruguay
Paraguay	4-1	Venezuela
Colombia	2-0	Venezuela

Peru	2-1	Paraguay
Peru	3-0	Venezuela
Paraguay	1-1	Uruguay
Colombia	1-1	Peru
Uruguay	2-0	Venezuela
Colombia	0-0	Paraguay
Peru	1-0	Uruguay

Peru (7 points) and Colombia (6 points) progressed, ahead of Paraguay (4 points), Uruguay (4 points) and Venezuela (0 points).

Final Stage

Colombia	1-1	Brazil
Argentina	1-1	Peru
Brazil	1-0	Argentina
Colombia	0-0	Peru
Colombia	1-1	Argentina
Brazil	1-0	Peru

Brazil (5 points) and Colombia (3 points) qualified for the Munich tournament, ahead of Argentina (2 points) and Peru (2 points).

North and Central America

Round One

Group One

Bermuda	0-2	Mexico
Bermuda	0-3	Canada
Mexico	1-0	Canada
Canada	1-1	Bermuda

Mexico	3-0	Bermuda
Canada	1-0	Mexico

Mexico progressed to Round Two, with 6 points, ahead of Canada (5 points) and Bermuda (1 point).

Group Two

Guatemala	2-2	Dutch Guyana (Surinam)
Guatemala	4-1	Panama
Panama	4-1	Dutch Guyana
Dutch Guyana	3-0	Panama
Dutch Guyana	0-1	Guatemala

Panama v Guatemala was not played.

Guatemala progressed (5 points), ahead of Dutch Guyana (3 points) and Panama (2 points).

Group Three

USA	1-1	El Salvador
USA	3-0	Barbados
Barbados	0-3	El Salvador
El Salvador	4-2	Barbados
El Salvador	1-1	USA
Barbados	1-3	USA

USA (6 points) and El Salvador (6 points) finished equal, with the same goal difference, ahead of Barbados (0 points).

USA	1-0	El Salvador (play-off in Kingston)

USA went through to Round Two.

Group Four

Jamaica	2-1	Netherlands Antilles
Netherlands Antilles	1-1	Jamaica

Jamaica went into Round Two.

Round Two

Guatemala	1-2	Mexico
Jamaica	1-1	USA
Mexico	1-1	USA
Guatemala	1-0	Jamaica
Mexico	4-0	Jamaica
Guatemala	3-2	USA
USA	2-1	Guatemala
Jamaica	1-0	Mexico
Jamaica	0-0	Guatemala
USA	2-2	Mexico
Mexico	3-1	Guatemala
USA	2-1	Jamaica

Mexico (8 points) and USA (7 points) qualified for the Munich tournament ahead of Guatemala (5 points) and Jamaica (4 points).

Africa

Round One

Tunisia	3-2	United Arab Republic	(3-0, 0-2)
Mali	3-2	Algeria	(1-0, 2-2)
Morocco	8-3	Niger	(5-2, 3-1)
Togo	6-5	Guinea	(1-1, 5-4)
Ghana	3-1	Liberia	(2-1, 1-0)

Senegal	3-2	Nigeria	(2-1, 1-1)
Cameroon	3-2	Gabon	(3-2, second match not played)
Malagasy Republic	6-3	Malawi	(2-1, 4-2)
Ethiopia	6-4	Zambia	(6-3, 0-1)
Sudan	5-1	Uganda	(4-0, 1-1)

Round Two

Group One

Tunisia	3-3	Morocco
Morocco	0-0	Tunisia
Mali	2-0	Tunisia
Tunisia	4-0	Mali
Morocco	2-1	Mali
Mali	1-4	Morocco

Morocco (6 points) qualified for Munich, ahead of Tunisia (4 points) and Mali (2 points)

Group Two

Senegal	1-1	Cameroon
Cameroon	3-2	Senegal
Ghana	1-1	Togo
Togo	0-2	Ghana
Ghana	1-0	Senegal
Senegal	2-0	Ghana
Cameroon	0-3	Ghana
Ghana	0-0	Cameroon
Togo	1-3	Senegal
Senegal	0-0	Togo

Togo	1-2	Cameroon
Cameroon	1-0	Togo

Ghana (8 points) qualified for Munich, ahead of Cameroon (8 points), on goal difference, Senegal (6 points) and Togo (2 points).

Group Three

Malagasy Republic	1-2	Ethiopia
Ethiopia	2-2	Sudan
Sudan	3-0	Malagasy Republic
Ethiopia	3-2	Malagasy Republic
Sudan	1-0	Ethiopia

Sudan (7 points) qualified ahead of Ethiopia (5 points) and the Malagasy Republic (0 points). The Malagasy Republic v Sudan was not played – Sudan were awarded a 2-0 win.

Asia

Group One

(matches played in Seoul, South Korea).

Malaysia	3-0	Japan
South Korea	0-1	Malaysia
Philippines	3-0	Taiwan
Malaysia	3-0	Taiwan
Japan	8-1	Philippines
South Korea	6-0	Philippines
Japan	5-1	Taiwan
Malaysia	5-0	Philippines
South Korea	2-1	Japan
South Korea	8-0	Taiwan

Malaysia qualified for Munich with 8 points, ahead of South Korea (6 points), Japan (4 points), The Philippines (2 points) and Taiwan (0 points).

Group Two

(matches played in Rangoon, Burma)

Burma	7-0	Thailand
Israel	3-0	Sri Lanka
Indonesia	4-2	India
Indonesia	4-0	Thailand
Israel	1-0	India
Burma	5-1	Sri Lanka
Burma	4-3	India
Israel	1-0	Indonesia
Thailand	5-0	Sri Lanka

The top four teams out of these six – Burma, Israel, Indonesia and Thailand – progressed to semi-finals:

Semi-finals:	Burma	3-0	Indonesia
	Thailand	0-0	Israel

(after extra-time – Thailand qualified after a penalty decider, the first in Olympic football).

Final stage:	Burma	1-0	Thailand

Burma qualified for Munich.

Group Three

Round One

	Iraq	1-1	Lebanon	(0-1, 1-0)
Play-off:	Iraq	2-1	Lebanon	(in Kuwait)
	North Korea	1-0	Syria	(0-0, 1-0)

Round Two

North Korea	3-1	Iraq	(0-1, 3-0)
Iran	4-0	Kuwait	(2-0, 2-0)

Final

	Iran	0-0	North Korea
Play-off	Iran	2-0	North Korea (in Rawalpindi)

Iran qualified for Munich.

17. Montreal, 1976

Maple Leaf Matches

Montreal's bid succeeded in 1970 against those of Moscow and Los Angeles, whose turns came immediately afterwards in 1980 and 1984. The city's Mayor, Jean Drapeau, was the bid's principal enthusiast but the cost rose skywards from $310 million to $1,400 million. The new Olympic Stadium alone cost $485 million, and its doughnut shape was nicknamed 'The Big O' and later, as debts mounted, 'The Big Owe'.

Only 92 countries took part, after 20 nations, mostly African, boycotted the Games over New Zealand's presence. This dispute concerned a non-Olympic sport, rugby, for the All-Blacks had toured South Africa, itself ousted from the Olympics in 1964. In football, no African sides came to Montreal, and they could not be replaced at very short notice. Even then, over 6,000 competitors was the second highest total, after 1972.

Two young runners carried the torch into the Stadium for the opening ceremony, a girl of British, a boy of French, ancestry to symbolise their Canadian heritage. (Some years later, they were married).

Stars of Montreal included the Romanian gymnast Nadia Comaneci, whose perfect scores baffled the scoreboard, which presented her 10.00 as 1.00. David Wilkie won Britain's first swimming gold for men since 1908, in the 200 metres breaststroke. The 100 metres, where he came second, went to the USA, as did every other men's swimming event. Hungary's Miklos Nemeth won the javelin contest 28 years after his father Imre's gold in the hammer, when Nemeth junior was three months old. In another family occasion, the Italian brothers Raimondo and Piero D'Inzea competed in their eighth Olympics. From 1948-76 they never missed their equestrian event and received 12 medals between them over 28 years.

Host nations usually perform well, but Canada's eleven medals did not include a gold. In Los Angeles, however, just eight years on, their team won 44 medals – ten of them gold.

The football tournament

With all three African teams withdrawn, only 13 competed in the event, reminiscent of the 1956 tournament with eleven in Melbourne.

The 13 were:

Hosts: Canada
Reigning Champions: Poland
Europe: France, Spain, East Germany, USSR
South America: Brazil
North and Central America: Mexico, Guatemala, Cuba
Asia: Israel, Iran, North Korea

As had become standard, there were four Groups in Round One, of three or four teams. The quarter-finals comprised:

Winners of Group A v Runners-up in Group B
Winners of Group B v Runners-up in Group A
Winners of Group C v Runners-up in Group D
Winners of Group D v Runners-up in Group C

The new, the very new, Olympic Stadium in Montreal had easily the largest capacity of the four stadia used. It housed ten matches, Ottawa's Lansdowne Park five, Toronto's Varsity Stadium five, and the smaller Sherbrooke Municipal Stadium, East of Montreal, three.

Over 71,000 watched the Final and no Montreal attendance fell below 29,000. Ottawa's largest crowd was 20,000, and Toronto's 21,000. Sherbrooke drew between 3,000 and 6,000 to its matches.

First Round

Group A

18 July	Brazil 0-0 East Germany	Toronto

20 July   Brazil 2-1 Spain (1-1)   Montreal
           Rosemiro 7   Idigoras 14
      Chico Fraga 47 (p)

22 July   East Germany 1-0 Spain (0-0)   Montreal
           Dorner 46

Qualified: Brazil :   3 points   (2 goals for – 1 against)
Qualified: East Germany :   3 points   (1-0)
                Spain :   0 points   (1-3)

Nigeria withdrew.

Group A

Even with only three teams, Group A was the strongest of the four sections. East Germany, bronze medallists in 1972, qualified just in front of Czechoslovakia after the teams drew twice. Spain had impressive wins over West Germany and Bulgaria, while Brazil played every qualifying game at home and headed the South American teams.

Remarkably, three Groups got underway with an identical score. Unfortunately, the score was a 0-0 draw, as teams played it safe to avoid a first defeat.

In **Brazil's** goalless match, against **East Germany**, they were hampered by losing their captain and central defender Tecao after 28 minutes, and he missed their next match.

Over 38,000 came to see **Spain** play **Brazil**. Once again the South Americans lost a defender early on, when Rosemiro was replaced, but only after an eventful 19 minutes. He scored the opener in seven minutes.

This was an even contest, and the Spanish captain, centre-forward Idigoras, quickly levelled the scores. Only a penalty from Brazil's Chico Fraga, just after half-time, separated the teams and ensured Brazil would progress to the quarter-finals with three points.

Either **East Germany** or **Spain** would join them, and it was the Germans who finished runners-up with a goal from their captain Dorner in 46 minutes. Group A was more notable for early substitutes than for goals; Spain's Camus had to be replaced in 22 minutes.

Group B

19 July   Israel 0-0 Guatemala   Toronto

19 July   France 4-1 Mexico (2-0)   Ottawa
                  Schaer 14   Hugo Sanchez 81
                  Baronchelli 33
                  Rubio 78
                  Amisse 90

21 July	France 4-1 Guatemala (2-0)	Sherbrooke
	Platini 7, 86 Fion 58	
	Amisse 41	
	Schaer 82	

21 July	Mexico 2-2 Israel (2-0)	Montreal
	Rangel 19, 44 Oz 51	
	Shum 55 (p)	

23 July	Mexico 1-1 Guatemala (1-1)	Sherbrooke
	Rangel 36 Rergis (o.g.) 8	

23 July	Israel 1-1 France (0-0)	Montreal
	Peretz 75 Platini 80 (p)	

Qualified:	France	5 points	(9-3)
Qualified:	Israel	3 points	(3-3)
	Mexico	2 points	(4-7)
	Guatemala	2 points	(2-5)

Group B

In this, the only four-team Group, France and Mexico were favoured to reach the next stage, despite the best efforts of Israel and Guatemala.

France, with the 21 year old Michel Platini at the heart of their midfield, had come through in front of Romania and The Netherlands.

Mexico had faced Guatemala twice en route to Montreal, with each winning their home fixture, while Israel faced only two other countries in qualifying.

In Toronto, 9,000 saw **Israel** and **Guatemala** produce a goalless draw. Perhaps those who had attended the previous day's 0-0 encounter between Brazil and East Germany expected the same result, and they were right.

However, 14,000 headed to Ottawa's match, **France** v **Mexico**, and were rewarded with five goals. The French went 2-0 up in the first half, thanks to their forwards Schaer and Baronchelli.

Mexico introduced two new players when the second half started, but it made little difference. France added two late goals, and Hugo Sanchez's consolation for Mexico resulted in a fine 4-1 victory for the European team.

Against **Israel**, **Mexico** effectively lost their chance to progress to the next stage in a genuine 'two-halves' game in Montreal. The first 45 saw Mexico in charge and Rangel, their striker, score early and late. But the second period was very different – Israeli midfielders Oz and Shum, with a penalty, levelled the score at 2-2 within 20 minutes.

Then an incident involving Lev, the Israeli full-back, and Lopez Malo, his Mexican counterpart, saw both dismissed. No more goals followed, but Oz also received a red card with seconds to go.

In Sherbrooke's small stadium, just over 3,000 came to see **France** play **Guatemala**. They were fortunate to witness Platini's first goals on the world stage. He put the French ahead in seven minutes and ended the game with their fourth.

France's second 4-1 victory was the result they needed to ensure progress, and Amisse and Schaer added the other goals. In 58 minutes Fion's counter brought Guatemala into the game, but it was not sufficient.

France (4 points) would win Group B unless they lost heavily to Israel (2 points). In theory, any of the teams could finish second; Mexico and Guatemala had a point each.

In the end, France's two wins were the only ones in the group, which saw four draws. **Mexico** v **Guatemala** finished 1-1, with an own goal from Mexican defender Rergis cancelled out by Rangel, who scored his third in the event.

France also drew 1-1 with **Israel**, both goals arriving in the last 15 minutes, from Peretz, Israel's forward, and Platini's penalty. This was a rare contest without any substitutions. Israel took second place, just ahead of the two Central American teams.

Group C

18 July	Poland 0-0 Cuba	Ottawa
20 July	Iran 1-0 Cuba (1-0) Mazloumi 28	Ottawa

22 July	Poland 3-2 Iran (0-1)	Montreal
	Szarmach 48, 75 Parvin 6	
	Deyna 51 Rowshan 79	

Qualified:	Poland	3 points	(3-2)
Qualified:	Iran	2 points	(3-3)
	Cuba	1 point	(0-1)

Ghana withdrew.

Group C

When Poland were drawn alongside Iran and Cuba, the champions of 1972 seemed to have an easy task of winning Group C. Cuba were present after Uruguay's withdrawal, and had won none of their four matches at the final qualifying stage. Iran, playing at home, had won three out of four games.

Surprisingly, **Poland** made hard work of reaching the next round. **Cuba** denied them goals, and then **Iran** went to the top of the Group by a single goal victory over **Cuba**.

Since two teams would progress, Iran (2 points) were already through. Either Cuba (1 point) or Poland (1 point) would join them, but Poland had to avoid losing by two clear goals to Iran.

That may seem unlikely, but for 45 minutes **Iran** led **Poland** 1-0 courtesy of their captain Parvin's goal. After the interval, however, the prolific Szarmach and his captain Deyna gave Poland a 3-1 advantage. Even then, Rowshan scored a second for Iran and Poland won 3-2, if unconvincingly, to head the section, with Iran runners-up.

Group D

19 July	USSR 2-1 Canada (2-0)	Montreal
	Onishchenko 8, 11 Douglas 88	

21 July	North Korea 3-1 Canada (1-0)	Toronto
	An Se-ook 18 Douglas 51	
	Hong Sung-nam 66, 80	

23 July   USSR 3-0 North Korea (0-0) Ottawa
Kolotov 76 (p)
Veremeev 81
Blokhin 89

Qualified:	USSR	4 points	(5-1)
Qualified:	North Korea	2 points	(3-4)
	Canada	0 points	(2-5)

Zambia withdrew.

Group D

In qualifying, USSR won five times and North Korea four, although they defeated Indonesia only after penalty deciders. Canada were in the event as hosts, without needing to qualify, but they had rarely featured in the tournament since Galt FC won the gold in 1904.

Canada's opening match against the **USSR** ended in a creditable 2-1 defeat. The crowd of 34,000 – the largest so far – were doubly disappointed because Onishchenko took only eleven minutes to establish an invincible 2-0 lead for the Russians.

Possibilities of a draw flickered in the second half, when the hosts' defence held firm, and Jimmy Douglas, their captain, even scored in 88 minutes.

North Korea also took an early lead over **Canada**, in 18 minutes, from An Se-ook. Douglas again inspired his team with an equaliser soon after half-time, but the key midfielder was Hong Sung-nam, whose two late goals gave the Koreans a 3-1 victory and entry to the next stage.

Who would head Group D? Since Canada were already out, the winners of **USSR** v **North Korea** would decide the Group standings. As Poland knew, there were no easy matches, and this one lacked a goal until the last 15 minutes.

Then An Kil-hwan, North Korea's right-back, was sent off, and Kolotov put the Russians in front from the penalty spot. Next, Veremeev celebrated his goal to make the score 2-0, although he soon received a red card, and Blokhin's third made the result secure and the USSR claimed top place.

Quarter-finals

25 July	East Germany 4-0 France (1-0)	Ottawa
	Lowe 27	
	Dorner 60, 68	
	(both penalties)	
	Riediger 77	

25 July	USSR 2-1 Iran (1-0)	Sherbrooke
	Minaev 40 Ghelichkhani 82 (p)	
	Zvyagintsev 67	

25 July	Brazil 4-1 Israel (0-0)	Toronto
	Jarbas 56, 74 Peretz 80	
	Erivelto 72	
	Junior 88	

25 July	Poland 5-0 North Korea (1-0)	Montreal
	Szarmach 13, 49	
	Lato 59, 79	
	Szymanowski 64	

The Quarter-Finals

The last eight teams included four from Europe – France, Poland, and USSR, winners of their Groups, and East Germany. Brazil, the only Americas team left, had also won their Group, but Israel, Iran and North Korea had come through as runners-up and would do exceptionally well to go into the semi-finals.

A feature of these four matches was the imbalance of goals scored before and after the interval – only three goals in the first 45, 14 in the second period. In particular, eleven goals hit the net in the last 30 minutes of the games, as differences between teams' abilities were emphasised.

In Toronto **Brazil** v **Israel** saw the South Americans unable to score till the 56th minute, when their striker Jarbas hit the opener. His right-winger Erivelto doubled the lead, and when Jarbas put Brazil 3-0 ahead, his coach took him off to save him for the next round. Peretz's goal reduced the lead, but Junior's fourth on the whistle produced a convincing victory, 4-1, for the Brazilians.

East Germany and **France** drew 20,000 to Ottawa, and for nearly an hour this was evenly balanced, only Lowe's first-half goal for the Germans on the board.

In 58 minutes, France's midfield line was reduced from three to one, Platini, as both Fernandez and Rubio were sent off. Seconds later, Dorner scored a penalty to give East Germany a two-goal (and a two man) advantage.

The French coach Gaby Robert soon replaced two forwards with fresh players, Pecout and Couge. This was a rare example of what is now common, bringing on two substitutes together, but the unusual circumstances made it an essential change. It did not help – Dorner added another penalty, and Riediger scored the Germans' fourth a minute after leaving the bench.

In Sherbrooke, the **USSR** took 40 minutes to score against **Iran**, and won 2-1 without a forward hitting the net. Minaev, the Russians' left-half, and a defender, Zvyagintsev, were the scorers and then two forwards were substituted. Iran's penalty goal from Ghelichkhani late in the day made this too close for the Soviet team's comfort.

Easily the biggest crowd, over 46,000, gathered in Montreal, where **Poland** were not seriously troubled by **North Korea**. Their 5-0 win was founded on Szarmach's two goals in 13 and 49 minutes. The Korean centre-half An Se-ook was dismissed soon afterwards, and Lato's double and Szymanowski took Poland's tally to five.

Semi-finals

27 July   East Germany 2-1 USSR (0-0)   Montreal
Dorner 59 (p)   Kolotov 84 (p)
Kurbjuweit 66

27 July   Poland 2-0 Brazil (0-0)   Toronto
Szarmach 51, 82

Poland v **Brazil** appeared to be the pick of the tournament to watch, judging by the teams' performances 48 hours earlier. There was to be no goal fest, in fact, and not until Szarmach (the top scorer of all) hit form did any result but a draw seem likely. He netted twice in 51 and 82 minutes, and it is a measure of the low scoring in 1976 that no one equalled his overall total of six goals.

In the 1974 World Cup Poland had defeated the full Brazilian team 1-0 and taken third place. They fielded virtually the same side two years later, and there may have been doubts as to whether they were improving.

East Germany's match with the **USSR** promised to be a struggle between two powerful defences, and no goals appeared till 59 minutes had passed. Once more, the Germans' captain Hans-Jurgen Dorner broke the deadlock with his third penalty, and his left-back Kurbjuweit soon doubled the lead.

Despite making two substitutions, the USSR could score only once – a penalty, taken by their captain, Kolotov, brought the goal six minutes from the close.

Bronze medal match

29 July   USSR 2-0 Brazil (1-0)   Montreal
                          Onishchenko 5
                          Nazarenko 49

Both teams chose one new player for this third-place match. **Brazil** gave Julinho, the Flamengo forward, his opportunity after his eight minutes of play against Spain. Junior, his club colleague, showed versatility by moving away from the forward line to left-back.

The **USSR** replaced Veremeev with Fomenko in defence.

After just five minutes, the Russians took the lead as Onishchenko, their striker, caught Brazil's defence cold. Before half-time, however, he was replaced by Nazarenko, who scored after four minutes of the second period. The only tarnish on their bronze medals, was that Troshkin saw two yellow cards and missed the last five minutes.

The Final

31 July   East Germany 3-1 Poland (2-0)   Montreal
                            Schade 7   Lato 59
                            Hoffman 14
                            Hafner 84

The final was between the reigning champions, **Poland,** and **East Germany,** bronze medallists in 1972.

The Polish coach, Kazimierz Gorski, brought in Wieczorek and Kmiecik, and German coach Georg Buschner started Riediger up front, dropping Heidler.

As in the USSR v Brazil match, this leapt into life immediately as Schade and Hoffmann scored for East Germany in seven and 14 minutes. To make matters worse for Poland, their experienced keeper, Jan Tomaszewski had to go off, but his understudy Mowlik coped well with the German forwards' pressure.

Poland's reliable Szarmach was closely marked but on the hour the astute Lato did take his chance to give the team hope. At 2-1, the German coach replaced two forwards with Grobner and Bransch, both defenders, as they determined to hold the lead. Hafner eased any concerns with a late third goal.

East Germany had played well in the two Munich events of 1972 and 1974, and now they had won gold to place beside West Germany's two World Cups in 1954 and 1974.

The medal winners

Gold: East Germany

Croy	Grobner	Hoffmann
Grapenthin	Weber	Lowe
Dorner (captain)	Lauck	Riedel
Weise	Heidler	
Kurbjuweit	Hafner	
Bransch	Schade	
Kische	Riediger	

Silver: Poland

Tomaszewski	Maszczyk	Szarmach
Mowlik	Kasperczak	Kmiecik
Szymanowski	Deyna (captain)	Ogaza
Gorgon	Wieczorek	
Rudy	Cmikiewicz	
Zmuda	Benigier	
Wawrowski	Lato	

Bronze: USSR

Astapovsky	Zvyagintsev	Blokhin
Prokhorov	Kipiani	Fyodorov
Konkov	Kolotov	Nazarenko
Matvienko	Veremeev	
Fomenko	Buryak	
Reshko	Minaev	
Troshkin	Onishchenko	

Goal scorers

6: Szarmach (Poland)
4: Dorner (East Germany)
3: Platini (France)
   Lato (Poland)
   Onishchenko (USSR)
   Rangel (Mexico)

Referees

J. Paterson (GB)   Brazil v East Germany
                                Poland v Brazil (semi-final)

P. Schiller (Austria)   Brazil v Spain
                                Poland v North Korea

W. Winsemann (Canada)   East Germany v Spain
V. Rudnev (USSR)   Israel v Guatemala
A. Coerezza (Argentina)   France v Mexico
J. Namdar (Iran)   France v Guatemala
A. Michelotti (Italy)   Mexico v Israel
                                East Germany v France

M. Kuston (Poland)   Mexico v Guatemala
R. Barreto (Uruguay)   France v Israel
                                East Germany v Poland (Final)

A. Klein (Israel)   Poland v Cuba
                                USSR v Brazil
                                (Bronze medal match)

A. Prokop (East Germany)   Iran v Cuba
A. Coelho (Brazil)   Poland v Iran
R. Helies (France)   USSR v Canada
M. Dorantes (Mexico)   North Korea v Canada
                                East Germany v USSR (semi-final)

E. Guruceta-Muro (Spain)   USSR v North Korea
G. Velasquez (Colombia)   USSR v Iran
K. Palotai (Hungary)   Brazil v Israel

The qualifying tournament (1975-76)

16 places were allotted for the Montreal event, including the hosts (Canada) and the 1972 champions (Poland).

Four places went to Europe, two to South America, two to North and Central America, three to Africa, three to Asia.

77 nations entered, but 12 withdrew during the qualifying stage or after it.

Uruguay qualified for Montreal but then withdrew. No South American team would replace them, and Cuba took their place.

The three African qualifiers – Ghana, Zambia and Nigeria – all withdrew.

Europe

Round One

East Germany	5-0	Greece	(1-0, 4-0)
Netherlands	3-1	Luxembourg	(1-0, 2-1)
Spain	3-2	West Germany	(0-0, 3-2)
USSR	4-1	Yugoslavia	(1-1, 3-0)
Bulgaria	4-2	Hungary	(0-2, 4-0)
Czechoslovakia	3-1	Ireland	(2-1, 1-0)
Norway	6-4	Finland	(5-3, 1-1)
Romania	6-1	Denmark	(4-0, 2-1)

Byes – Austria, France, Iceland, Turkey

Round Two

Group One

Iceland	1-1	Norway
Norway	2-3	Iceland
Iceland	0-2	USSR
USSR	1-0	Iceland
Norway	3-1	USSR
USSR	4-0	Norway

USSR qualified for Montreal (8 points) ahead of Iceland (3) and Norway (1).

Group Two

East Germany	1-0	Austria
Austria	0-2	East Germany
East Germany	0-0	Czechoslovakia
Czechoslovakia	1-1	East Germany
Czechoslovakia	5-0	Austria
Austria	0-0	Czechoslovakia

East Germany (6 points) qualified for Montreal ahead of Czechoslovakia (5) and Austria (1).

Group Three

Spain	2-1	Bulgaria
Bulgaria	1-1	Spain
Spain	2-0	Turkey
Turkey	0-0	Spain
Turkey	0-3	Bulgaria
Bulgaria	2-0	Turkey

Spain (6 points) qualified for Montreal ahead of Bulgaria (5) and Turkey (1).

Group Four

France	4-0	Romania
Romania	1-0	France
Netherlands	2-3	France
France	4-2	Netherlands
Romania	5-1	Netherlands
Netherlands	0-3	Romania

France (6 points) qualified on goal difference, ahead of Romania (6) and Netherlands had no points.

South America

(all matches played in Brazil)

Brazil	1-1	Uruguay
Brazil	3-0	Peru
Brazil	4-0	Colombia
Brazil	2-0	Argentina
Brazil	2-1	Chile
Uruguay	3-0	Peru
Uruguay	2-2	Colombia
Uruguay	2-0	Argentina
Uruguay	1-1	Chile
Argentina	3-1	Peru
Argentina	2-2	Colombia
Argentina	2-1	Chile
Colombia	0-1	Peru
Colombia	1-0	Chile
Chile	2-1	Peru

Brazil (9 points) and Uruguay (7) qualified for Montreal ahead of Argentina (5), Colombia (4), Chile (3) and Peru (2). Uruguay withdrew in June 1976, Argentina declined their place, and it was accepted by Cuba.

North and Central America

Preliminary Round

Jamaica 2-0 Haiti (1-0, 1-0)

Round One

Barbados	1-1	Trinidad and Tobago	(1-0, 0-1)
Play-off: Trinidad and Tobago	3-1	Barbados	
El Salvador	5-2	Nicaragua	(4-0, 1-2)
Jamaica	3-1	Dominican Republic	(1-0, 2-1)

Round Two

USA	4-3	Bermuda	(2-3, 2-0)
Guatemala	2-0	Honduras	(0-0, 2-0)
Cuba	1-1	Jamaica	(1-0, 0-1)
Play-off: Cuba	4-1	Jamaica (in Panama)	(1-0, 2-1)
Costa Rica	3-1	El Salvador	(0-2, 4-0)
Surinam	3-1	Trinidad and Tobago	(2-0, 1-1)

Bye: Mexico

Round Three

Mexico	12-2	USA	(8-0, 4-2)
Guatemala	3-2	Costa Rica	(1-1, 2-0)
Cuba	7-1	Surinam	(1-0, 6-1)

Final stage

Mexico	4-2	Cuba
Cuba	1-1	Guatemala
Mexico	4-1	Guatemala
Guatemala	1-1	Cuba
Cuba	1-1	Mexico
Guatemala	3-2	Mexico

Mexico (5 points) and **Guatemala** (4) qualified for Montreal, ahead of Cuba (3). (Cuba also went to Montreal, replacing Uruguay when they withdrew.)

Africa

Round One

Ghana	10-1	Liberia	(6-0, 4-1)
Zambia	9-0	Mauretania	(5-0, 4-0)
Nigeria walkover –		Cameroon withdrew	
Morocco	3-1	Libya	(2-1, 1-0)
Zaire	6-2	Upper Volta	(4-1, 2-1)
Guinea	7-0	Gambia	(1-0, 6-0)
Mali	7-0	Mauritius	(6-0, 1-0)
Senegal	2-1	Togo	(1-0, 1-1)
Sudan	2-1	Egypt	(1-1, 1-0)
Tunisia	3-2	Algeria	(1-1, 2-1)
Tanzania	3-0	Ethiopia	(0-0, 3-0)

Malawi walkover – Malagasy Repulbic withdrew

Round Two

Ghana	6-3	Guinea	(0-1, 6-2)
Zambia	5-2	Malawi	(1-1, 4-1)
Nigeria walkover –		Mali withdrew	
Sudan	2-1	Tanzania	(0-1, 2-0)
Senegal	3-3	Zaire	Senegal won on penalties
Morocco	2-0	Tunisia	(1-0, 1-0)

Round Three

Ghana	2-1	Senegal	(0-0, 2-1)
Zambia	2-2	Sudan	(2-2, 0-0) Zambia won on penalties
Nigeria	3-2	Morocco	(3-1, 0-1)

Ghana, Zambia, and **Nigeria** qualified for Montreal. All withdrew before the Olympics began.

Asia

Group One

(all matches played in Iran)

Iran	3-0	Bahrain
Iran	3-0	Saudi Arabia
Iran	1-1	Kuwait
Iran	1-0	Iraq
Kuwait	2-1	Bahrain
Kuwait	4-2	Saudi Arabia
Kuwait	1-2	Iraq
Saudi Arabia	1-0	Bahrain
Saudi Arabia	2-0	Iraq
Iraq	4-0	Bahrain

Iran qualified for Montreal with 7 points, ahead of Kuwait (5), Saudi Arabia (4), Iraq (4), and Bahrain (0 points).

Group Two

Round One

(all matches played in Indonesia)

Indonesia	8-2	Papua New Guinea
Indonesia	2-1	Malaysia
Indonesia	0-0	Singapore
Indonesia	1-2	North Korea
North Korea	4-0	Papua New Guinea
North Korea	2-0	Malaysia
North Korea	2-0	Singapore
Malaysia	10-1	Papua New Guinea
Malaysia	6-0	Singapore
Singapore	7-0	Papua New Guinea

North Korea (8 points) and Indonesia (5) progressed to the final stage of Group Two. Malaysia had 4, Singapore 3, Papua New Guinea 0 points.

Final stage: North Korea 0-0 Indonesia

North Korea qualified for Montreal, on penalty kicks.

Group Three

Israel	0-0	South Korea
South Korea	0-3	Israel
Israel	4-1	Japan
Japan	0-3	Israel
South Korea	2-2	Japan
Japan	0-2	South Korea

Israel qualified (7 points), with South Korea on 4, Japan 1 point.

18. Moscow, 1980

Boycotting the Bear

In 1974 Moscow were awarded these Olympics, the only other bidders being Los Angeles. But in 1979 the USSR's decision to invade Afghanistan led to the largest boycott of any Games, by the USA, West Germany, Japan and about 40 other nations.

It is uncertain how many countries joined the boycott, because nations have always entered the Olympics and then withdrawn for various reasons, especially lack of funds. Certainly 80 nations were represented, compared with 121 in 1972 and 169 in 1992.

The Moscow organisers used Russian associations with a bear to produce their ursine mascot Misha but he did not win the hearts of those who stayed away.

Despite their Government's advice, British athletes did travel to Moscow, and TV audiences were fascinated by some outstanding competitors. Allan Wells won the 100 metres, Britain's first gold in the sprint since Harold Abrahams's in 1924. The greatest of middle-distance duels saw Steve Ovett win the 800 and Sebastian Coe the 1500.

If Coe and Ovett were the 'twins' on the track, four sets of real twins featured in 1980. The Landvoigts (East Germany) beat Russia's Pimenov brothers in coxless pairs rowing; the German Diessner twins won the coxed fours; and the Beloglasov brothers both won freestyle wrestling golds.

The Football Tournament

Although seven nations withdrew from the tournament when they boycotted the Olympics, 16 did take part in Moscow.

Hosts: USSR
Champions: East Germany
Europe: Czechoslovakia, Spain, Yugoslavia, Finland
North and Central America: Cuba, Costa Rica
South America: Venezuela, Colombia
Africa: Zambia, Nigeria, Algeria

Asia: Kuwait, Syria, Iraq

As in 1976, Cuba stepped in as a late replacement. The full list of replacements was:

Finland (for Norway)
Cuba (for USA)
Venezuela (for Argentina)
Nigeria (for Ghana)
Zambia (for Egypt)
Iraq (for Malaysia)
Syria (for Iran)
Five stadia hosted football matches –
The Lenin (or Luzhniki) Stadium in Moscow, (4 matches)
The Dynamo Stadium, Moscow, (7)
Kirov Stadium, Leningrad, (now St Petersburg), (7)
Republican Stadium, Kiev (now in Ukraine), (7)
Dynamo Stadium, Minsk (now Belarus), (7)

The great distances between these four cities were matched in 1984, when the Los Angeles tournament included games on both coasts of the USA.

One feature of the football was the rarity of unruly incidents on the field. Some teams, such as Finland, received no cards, yellow or red. Another memorable fact was the size of attendances, over 1.8 million officially, with an average of almost 58,000.

Group A

20 July   USSR 4-0 Venezuela (3-0)   Lenin Stadium, Moscow
          Andreev 3
          Cherenkov 25
          Oganesian 51

20 July   Cuba 1-0 Zambia (0-0)   Kirov Stadium, Leningrad
          Roldan 58

22 July   USSR 3-1 Zambia (1-1)   Lenin Stadium
        Khidiatullin 9, 51   Chitalu 13
        Cherenkov 87

22 July   Cuba 2-1 Venezuela (0-0) Leningrad
        Hernandez 49   Zubizarreta 68
        Nunez 71

24 July   USSR 8-0 Cuba (5-0)   Dynamo Stadium,
                                            Moscow
        Andreev 8, 27, 44
        Romantsev 40
        Shavlo 43
        Cherenkov 55
        Gavrilov 75
        Bessonov 77

24 July   Venezuela 2-1 Zambia (0-0) Leningrad
        Zubizarreta 86   Chitalu 73
        Elie 90 (p)

Qualified:	USSR	6 points	(15 goals for – 1 against)
Qualified:	Cuba	4 points	(3-9)
	Venezuela	2 points	(3-7)
	Zambia	0 points	(2-6)

Group A

In Group A all three of the USSR's original opponents withdrew from the 1980 Olympics – USA, Argentina and Egypt. Two of those teams could have offered a sterner test for the Russians than the sides who took part.

Against **Venezuela**, **USSR** were out of sight by half-time. 3-0 ahead, their midfielder Andreev led the way with the opener in three minutes, followed by strikers Cherenkov and Gavrilov. Both were substituted, and Oganesian came on, scoring soon after to cap an easy victory.

The contest with **Zambia**, however, was more taxing. Although the **Russians** took the lead in nine minutes, Chitalu quickly levelled the match, and the USSR forwards could not find the net. It was the defender Khidiatullin who scored twice, while a substitute forward Cherenkov clinched a 3-1 victory right at the end.

Cuba begin their tournament with a win over **Zambia**, the only goal coming from their defender Roldan, and overcame **Venezuela** 2-1. Again, the winner for Cuba came from a defender, Dreke, after earlier strikes by Hernandez and – the equaliser for Venezuela – Zubizarreta.

Both **Russia** and **Cuba** had already qualified for the quarter-finals with two victories and four points each. Any ideas that the Caribbean team could top the group were dissipated after 20 minutes, when they were 2-0 behind. In the 8-0 win, more Russian players (six) scored than did not.

Andreev scored a first-half hat-trick and his fellow midfielders Shavlo and Bessonov also added a goal, while Cherenkov and Gavrilov reminded the Moscow spectators that there were forwards present. Romantsev came up from defence to collect the fourth.

Both Venezuela and Zambia, who did not reach the next stage, had better goal differences than Cuba, and gave good accounts of themselves. The **Zambian** striker Chitalu scored both his team's goals, and they lost to **Venezuela** only through a last minute penalty.

Group B

21 July	Czechoslovakia 3-0 Colombia (2-0)	Leningrad
	Pokluda 14	
	Berger 18	
	Vizek 85	

21 July	Kuwait 3-1 Nigeria (2-1)	Dynamo Stadium
	Al-Dakhil Mubarak (o.g.) 25	
	16, 40, 85 (p)	

23 July	Czechoslovakia 1-1 Nigeria (1-0)	Leningrad
	Vizek 25 Nwosu 84	

23 July   Colombia 1-1 Kuwait (0-0)   Dynamo Stadium
            Molinares 73   Yaqoub Sultan 64

25 July   Czechoslovakia 0-0 Kuwait   Leningrad

25 July   Colombia 1-0 Nigeria (0-0)   Dynamo Stadium
            Cardona 55

Qualified:	Czechoslovakia	4 points	(4-1)
Qualified:	Kuwait	4 points	(4-2)
	Colombia	3 points	(2-4)
	Nigeria	1 point	(2-5)

Group B

Few teams who eventually won gold have struggled as hard to reach the quarter-finals as Czechoslovakia. On paper they should have had little difficulty in overcoming Colombia, Kuwait and Nigeria, far less familiar with Olympic tournaments.

The **Czechs** began with two quick goals against **Colombia** from Pokluda and Berger, and Vizek's late addition completed a straightforward win.

However their results against both **Nigeria** and **Kuwait** proved to be disappointing draws. Vizek put them in front against the African team, who were a late replacement and had not played any qualifying matches, but they paid for missed chances when Nwosu equalised in 84 minutes.

Against **Kuwait**, **Czechoslovakia** could not break down a defence which conceded only two goals in the group, and there was a goalless stalemate.

Kuwait reached the semi-finals along with the Czechs, thanks to a 3-1 victory over **Nigeria**, in which their left-winger Al-Dakhil scored a hat-trick, and a 1-1 draw with **Colombia**.

The South Americans defeated **Nigeria**, with Cardona scoring the only goal.

Group C

20 July	East Germany	1-1	Spain (0-0)	Republican Stadium, Kiev
	Kuhn 49		Marcos 50	
20 July	Algeria	3-0	Syria (1-0)	Dynamo Stadium, Minsk
	Belloumi 36			
	Madjer 48			
	Merzekane 73 (p)			
22 July	East Germany	1-0	Algeria (0-0)	Kiev
	Terletzki 61			
22 July	Spain	0-0	Syria	Minsk
24 July	East Germany	5-0	Syria (3-0)	Kiev
	Hause 6		Chitalu 73	
	Netz 25, 45			
	Peter 75			
	Terletzki 82			
24 July	Spain	1-1	Algeria (1-0)	Minsk
	Rincon 38		Belloumi 63	

Qualified:	East Germany	5 points	(7-1)
Qualified:	Algeria	3 points	(4-2)
	Spain	3 points	(2-2)
	Syria	1 point	(0-8)

Group C

As 1976 champions, **East Germany** had played no competitive matches to reach Moscow, and their early group matches suggested a slight rustiness in their play. Against **Spain**, it took 49 minutes for Kuhn to open the scoring – but they were then caught off-guard by Marcos Alonso, Athletico Madrid's midfielder, losing a goal and a point.

Next, the **Germans** took 61 minutes to gain the advantage over **Algeria**. Terletzki, their centre-half and captain, scored the only goal.

Syria did not score in their matches, and began with a 3-0 defeat to **Algeria**, for whom Belloumi, Madjer and Merzekane scored.

After two encounters each, East Germany led Group C (3 points), Spain and Algeria both had two, and Syria one. The Germans needed one point to reach the quarter-finals, while Spain and Algeria had to contest the other place.

At last the **German** side got off to a flying start, when Hause, their full-back, scored against **Syria** in six minutes. His left-winger Netz added two more before the interval, with late goals from Peter and Terletzki building a 5-0 win.

Spain's Rincon, from Real Madrid, put them ahead of **Algeria**, but they responded with Belloumi's leveller. The 1-1 draw gave Algeria second place in Group C, on goal difference ahead of the Spanish.

Spain's young team, drawn from clubs such as Barcelona, Real Madrid, and Real Zaragoza, drew all three matches and scored only twice.

East Germany were through, but their uncertainty in attack showed when they fielded different forward lines in each of the group games.

Group D

21 July	Yugoslavia 2-0 Finland (0-0)	Minsk
	Secerbegovic 56	
	Sestic 58	

21 July	Iraq 3-0 Costa Rica (1-0)	Kiev
	Ahmed 45	
	Saeed 49	
	Hassan 75	

23 July	Yugoslavia 3-2 Costa Rica (2-1)	Minsk
	Z. Vujovic 6, 54 White 35	
	Primorac 24 Aarroyo 90	

23 July	Finland 0-0 Iraq	Kiev

25 July	Finland 3-0 Costa Rica (1-0)	Kiev
	Tissari 18	
	Alila 58	
	Soini 88	

25 July	Yugoslavia 1-1 Iraq (0-0)	Minsk
	Z. Vujovic 63 Hassan 61	

Group D

Once again, the East European team were the most experienced, by some distance, in a group including Yugoslavia, Finland, Iraq and Costa Rica.

Yugoslavia took almost an hour to overcome **Finland**, playing at this stage for the first time since 1952. Two quick goals, from the Slavs' substitute Secerbegovic and Sestic, put two points on the board.

Against **Costa Rica**, **Yugoslavia** fielded a different trio upfront. Vujovic scored in six minutes, Primorac – moved from a defender to a striker now – hit the second in 24. The Central American side were not out of it, and White cut the lead before half-time. Vujovic's second made it 3-1 and the Slav team controlled the game, although Arroyo's goal for Costa Rica in the final minute put a better complexion on the score.

After two victories, **Yugoslavia** were sure to reach the quarter finals, and reverted to a more familiar line-up. The result was an unsatisfactory draw against **Iraq**, who took the lead on the hour through Hassan, with Vujovic equalising almost from the resumption of play.

Iraq's first match produced a 3-0 win over **Costa Rica** with goals either side of the interval and a third in 75 minutes.

The **Iraq-Finland** goalless match meant that Iraq (3 points) would qualify with a point against Yugoslavia, as they in fact achieved.

The **Finns** had one match to savour, 3-0 against **Costa Rica**, with goals from Tissari, Alila and Soini. They did not progress, largely because they could not find the net when it mattered most.

Costa Rica lost three goals in each match and, like several teams in 1980, kept changing their forwards to compensate.

Qualified:	Yugoslavia	5 points	(6-3)
Qualified:	Iraq	4 points	(4-1)
	Finland	3 points	(3-2)
	Costa Rica	1 point	(2-9)

Quarter-finals

27 July   USSR 2-1 Kuwait (1-0)   Dynamo Stadium, Moscow

    Cherenkov 30   Yaqoub Sultan 59

    Gavrilov 51

27 July   Czechoslovakia 3-0 Cuba (1-0)   Leningrad

    Vizek 29, 59

    Pokluda 90

27 July   East Germany 4-0 Iraq (4-0)   Kiev

         Schnuphase 4 (p)
         Netz 11
         Steinbach 17
         Terletzki 22

27 July   Yugoslavia 3-0 Algeria (2-0)   Minsk

         Mirocevic 5
         Sestic 19
         Z. Vujovic 70

Quarter-finals

Having strolled through Group A, the **USSR** faced **Kuwait**, unbeaten in Group B. The Asian side had held Czechoslovakia, and now the Russians struggled for a goal against a defence breached only twice in three games.

Eventually, Cherenkov put USSR ahead after half an hour, and his fellow striker Gavrilov doubled the lead in 51 minutes. Yaqoub reduced the deficit soon after, and their 2-1 victory was too close for the Soviet team's comfort.

The other quarter-finals all produced more comfortable wins for East European teams.

Czechoslovakia needed 29 minutes to score against **Cuba**, through their versatile defender Vizek, and he added another in 59 minutes. Pokluda, his centre-half, clinched a 3-0 win in the last seconds. Once again, however, the Czech forward line did not produce goals, as they fielded yet another new combination up front.

East Germany accomplished their 4-0 victory over **Iraq** in just 22 minutes. Four players scored – Schnuphase with a penalty in four minutes, Netz after eleven, Steinbach and Terletzki soon after. Three German midfielders were on the scoresheet. With Iraq four goals down, Alaa Ahmed was booked and in 80 minutes he was sent off. Reaching this stage was an achievement for his team, although the result was one to forget.

Yugoslavia's win over **Algeria** was almost as straightforward. Mirocevic put the Slav team ahead in five minutes, Sestic doubled the advantage after 19, and the left winger Zoran Vujovic sealed the victory with 20 minutes to go.

Semi-finals

29 July   East Germany 1-0 USSR (1-0)   Lenin Stadium, Moscow
           Netz 16

29 July   Czechoslovakia 2-0 Yugoslavia (2-0)   Dynamo Stadium, Moscow
           Licka 4
           Sreiner 18

Semi-finals

Matches between the four European teams, who had conceded so few goals, did not promise a feast for neutral observers.

East Germany were fortunate to have their striker Netz, while the team formation was changed around him. In 16 minutes he disappointed the huge **USSR** support by scoring the only goal. Although they were losing, the Russians fielded no substitutes, while the Germans brought on two.

Czechoslovakia won their match against **Yugoslavia** in the first 18 minutes, when Licka and Sreiner hit the net, and showed clear improvement over their Group performances.

Bronze Medal Match

1 August   USSR 2-0 Yugoslavia (0-0)   Dynamo Stadium, Moscow
           Oganesian 67
           Andreev 82

Bronze medal match

In their first home tournament, the **USSR** had to be content with third place. They defeated **Yugoslavia** with two late goals. Oganesian, a substitute, opened the scoring in 67 minutes, while Andreev doubled the lead with eight minutes left.

The Russians scored most goals in 1980 – 19, compared to the Czechs' ten – but that was scant consolation when they were expected to win gold in their own stadia.

The Final

2 August   Czechoslovakia 1-0 East Germany (0-0)   Lenin Stadium, Moscow

Svoboda 77

The Final

Czechoslovakia v **East Germany** brought two low scoring attacks and powerful defences together – the 1-0 score was not surprising. The Czechs' Svoboda claimed the decisive goal in 77 minutes, a notable achievement for a player who had been a substitute three times and started just one previous match. He was only on the field four minutes when he scored.

(Uncharacteristically for 1980, both teams lost a player to red cards, when Steinbach (East Germany) and the Czech Berger were dismissed just before the hour mark, after the midfielders clashed).

The gold medal must have been particularly welcome for Czechoslovakia, a team which recalled the disqualification in 1920. This was the eighth win in a row for Eastern European countries. There was to be only one more, and it came in 1988 for the USSR.

The Medal-winners

Gold: Czechoslovakia

Seman	Kunzo	Sreiner
Netolicka	Nemec	Vizek
Macela	Berger	Svoboda
Mazura	Pokluda	Licka
Radimec	Vaclavicek	Stambachr
Rygel	Rott	

Silver: East Germany

Rudwaleit	Trieloff	Trautmann
Jacobowski	Muller	Bahringer
Ullrich	Schnuphase	Peter
Hause	Terletzki	Kuhn

Uhlig	Steinbach	Netz
Baum	Liebers	

Bronze: USSR

Dasaev	Baltacha	Prokopenko
Pilguj	Nikulin	Andreev
Sulakvelidze	Shavlo	Cherenkov
Chivadze	Bessonov	Gazzaev
Khidiatullin	Gavrilov	Chelebadze
Romantsev	Oganesian	

Top goal scorers

5: Andreev (USSR)
4: Vizek (Czechoslovakia)
   Netz (East Germany)
   Cherenkov (USSR)

Referees

F. Wohrer (Austria)	USSR v Venezuela
	Czechoslovakia v Yugoslavia (semi-final)
M. Raus (Yugoslavia)	Cuba v Zambia
E. Guruceta-Muro (Spain)	Cuba v Venezuela
M. Arafat (Syria)	USSR v Zambia
R. Valentine (Great Britain)	USSR v Cuba
	USSR v Yugoslavia (Bronze medal match)
L. Calderon (Costa Rica)	Venezuela v Zambia
B. Lacarne (Algeria)	Czechoslovakia v Colombia
K. Schevrell (East Germany)	Kuwait v Nigeria
	Yugoslavia v Algeria
E. Revoredo (Peru)	Czechoslovakia v Nigeria
	Czechoslovakia v Cuba
A. Mattsson (Finland)	Colombia v Kuwait
R. Lattanzi (Italy)	Czechoslovakia v Kuwait
S. Al-Hachami (Iraq)	Colombia v Nigeria
U. Eriksson (Sweden)	East Germany v Spain
	East Germany v USSR (Semi-final)
V. Christov (Czechoslovakia)	Algeria v Syria

R. Filho (Brazil)	East Germany v Algeria
	East Germany v Iraq
J. Lozada (Venezuela)	Spain v Syria
G. Ramirez (Colombia)	East Germany v Syria
E. Azim-Zade (USSR)	Spain v Algeria
	Czechoslovakia v East Germany (Final)
M. Rubio (Mexico)	Yugoslavia v Finland
	USSR v Kuwait
N. Chayu (Zambia)	Iraq v Costa Rica
B. Eyo-Honesty (Nigeria)	Yugoslavia v Costa Rica
R. Castro (Cuba)	Finland v Iraq
A. Abdulwahab (Kuwait)	Finland v Costa Rica
A. Daina (Switzerland)	Yugoslavia v Iraq

The Qualifying Tournament (1979-80)

16 teams to take part in the Football Tournament in Moscow comprised:

Hosts: USSR
Champions of 1976: East Germany
Europe: Four teams
North and Central America: Two
South America: Three
Africa: Three
Asia: Three

Europe

Round One

(Byes – Poland, Yugoslavia, France, West Germany)

Group One

| Czechoslovakia | 4-1 Bulgaria | (0-1, 4-0) |
| Hungary | 3-2 Romania | (0-2, 3-0) |

Group Two

Italy	4-1	Greece	(0-1, 4-0)
Turkey	3-3	Austria	(0-1, 2-1)

Turkey won on penalties)

Group Three

(Four teams each played six games)

Belgium	3-1	Spain
Spain	1-1	Belgium
Belgium	0-0	Israel
Israel	0-2	Belgium
Belgium	1-0	Netherlands
Netherlands	1-2	Belgium
Spain	1-1	Israel
Israel	0-3	Spain
Spain	3-0	Netherlands
Netherlands	1-1	Spain
Israel	1-1	Netherlands
Netherlands	3-4	Israel

Belgium (10 points) and Spain (7) progressed to Round Two, ahead of Israel (5 points) and Netherlands (2).

Group Four

Norway	2-1	Ireland	(0-0, 2-1)
Finland	5-2	Denmark	(1-1, 4-1)

Round Two

(All teams played four games)

Group One

Czechoslovakia	3-2	Hungary
Hungary	3-0	Czechoslovakia
Czechoslovakia	1-0	Poland
Poland	0-1	Czechoslovakia
Hungary	2-0	Poland
Poland	1-0	Hungary

Czechoslovakia qualified for Moscow (6 points), ahead of Hungary (4) and Poland (2).

Group Two

Yugoslavia	5-2	Italy
Italy	1-0	Yugoslavia
Yugoslavia	3-0	Turkey
Turkey	0-1	Yugoslavia
Italy	5-0	Turkey
Turkey	0-2	Italy

Yugoslavia (6 points) qualified, ahead of Italy (6) on goal difference, and Turkey (0 points).

Group Three

Spain	3-0	Belgium
Belgium	2-0	Spain
Spain	3-1	France
France	1-1	Spain
Belgium	4-2	France
France	3-1	Belgium

Spain (5 points) qualified, ahead of Belgium (4) and France (3).

Group Four

Norway	2-0	West Germany
West Germany	0-1	Norway
Norway	1-1	Finland
Finland	0-1	Norway
West Germany	2-0	Finland
Finland	0-0	West Germany

Norway (7 points) qualified, ahead of West Germany (3) and Finland (2). Norway later withdrew, as did West Germany, but Finland did take part in Moscow.

North and Central America

Round One

Surinam	7-2	Barbados	(2-1, 5-1)
Bermuda	8-2	Canada	(3-0, 5-2)
Costa Rica	6-0	Panama	(4-0, 2-0)
Trinidad	9-3	Netherlands Antilles	(3-2, 6-1)

Guatemala	2-1	El Salvador	(2-0, 0-1)
Haiti	7-1	Dominican Republic	(4-1, 3-0)
Cuba	5-0	Jamaica	(3-0, 2-0)
Mexico	6-0	USA	(4-0, 2-0)

(Mexico then withdrew, and USA progressed to Round Two).

Round Two

USA	8-0	Bermuda	(3-0, 5-0)
Costa Rica	2-2	Guatemala	(1-2, 1-0)
Haiti	1-0	Cuba	(1-0, 0-0)
Surinam	3-3	Trinidad	(0-2, 3-1)

Play-offs:

Costa Rica	1-0	Guatemala
Surinam	2-0	Trinidad

Round Three

Surinam	2-2	Haiti	(0-2, 2-0)

Play-off:

Surinam	2-0	Haiti

Round Four

Costa Rica	0-1	USA
USA	1-1	Costa Rica
Costa Rica	3-2	Surinam
Surinam	2-3	Costa Rica
USA	2-1	Surinam
Surinam	4-2	USA

Costa Rica and **USA** qualified for Moscow, both with 5 points, ahead of

Surinam (2). When USA withdrew, Cuba took their place.

South America

(All matches played in Colombia in 1980).

Colombia	2-1	Peru
Colombia	0-1	Venezuela
Colombia	3-1	Chile
Colombia	0-1	Bolivia
Colombia	5-1	Brazil
Colombia	0-0	Argentina
Argentina	1-0	Chile
Argentina	1-0	Venezuela
Argentina	4-1	Peru
Argentina	3-1	Brazil
Argentina	4-0	Bolivia
Peru	3-0	Brazil
Peru	1-0	Chile
Peru	2-0	Venezuela
Peru	1-1	Bolivia
Venezuela	1-2	Brazil
Venezuela	5-1	Bolivia
Venezuela	0-0	Chile
Brazil	4-0	Bolivia
Brazil	0-0	Chile
Chile	2-0	Bolivia

Argentina (11 points) and **Colombia** (7 points) qualified for Moscow ahead of Peru (7), whose goal difference was inferior to Colombia's, Venezuela (5), Brazil (5), Chile (4), and Bolivia (3). When Argentina withdrew, Venezuela took their place.

Africa

Round One

(Byes – Ghana, Zambia)

Algeria	1-1	Mali (Algeria won on penalties) after (1-0, 0-1)
Egypt	walk-over	Tanzania withdrew
Kenya	walk-over	Sudan withdrew
Lesotho	7-3	Mauritius (4-1, 3-2)
Liberia	walk-over	Ivory Coast withdrew
Madagascar	3-2	Ethiopa (2-1, 1-1)
Morocco	1-1	Senegal (Morocco won on penalties) after (1-0, 0-1)
Siera Leone	walk-over	Guinea withdrew
Libya	3-1	Tunisia (0-1, 3-0)

Round Two

(Bye – Libya)

Algeria	8-1	Morocco (5-1, 3-0)
Ghana	5-1	Kenya (4-1, 1-0)
Zambia	5-0	Lesotho (0-0, 5-0)
Liberia	walk-over	Sierra Leone withdrew
Egypt	2-2	Madagascar (1-1, 1-1) Egypt won on penalties

Round Three

Algeria	walk-over	Libya withdrew
Egypt	5-2	Zambia (4-1, 1-1)
Ghana	4-2	Liberia (2-0, 2-2)

Algeria, **Egypt** and **Ghana** qualified for Moscow.

After Egypt and Ghana withdrew, Zambia and Nigeria agreed to take their places.

Asia

Group One

(all matches played in Iraq)

Iraq	0-0	Kuwait
Iraq	1-0	Syria
Iraq	3-0	Yemen
Iraq	4-0	Jordan
Kuwait	1-0	Syria
Kuwait	5-1	Yemen
Kuwait	1-0	Jordan
Syria	2-1	Yemen
Syria	2-0	Jordan
Yemen	2-1	Jordan

Iraq and Kuwait ended with 7 points, ahead of Syria (4), Yemen (2), and Jordan (0).

Kuwait qualified for Moscow by beating Iraq 3-2 in a play-off.

Group Two

(All matches played in Malaysia)

Malaysia	3-0	South Korea
Malaysia	1-1	Japan
Malaysia	3-1	Brunei
Malaysia	6-1	Indonesia

Malaysia	8-0	Philippines
South Korea	3-1	Japan
South Korea	3-0	Brunei
South Korea	1-0	Indonesia
South Korea	8-0	Philippines
Japan	2-1	Brunei
Japan	2-0	Indonesia
Japan	10-0	Philippines
Brunei	3-2	Indonesia
Brunei	2-0	Philippines
Indonesia	4-0	Philippines

Malaysia (9 points) qualified for Moscow in a play-off against South Korea, 2-1. (South Korea had 8 points).

Japan had 7 points, Brunei 4, Indonesia, Philippines 0.

Group Three

(all matches played inSingapore)

Iran	3-0	Singapore
Iran	2-2	China
Iran	0-0	North Korea
Iran	2-0	India
Singapore	1-0	China
Singapore	3-1	North Korea
Singapore	1-0	India
Singapore	3-0	Sri Lanka

China	1-1	North Korea
China	1-0	India
China	7-0	Sri Lanka
North Korea	2-1	India
North Korea	7-0	Sri Lanka
India	4-0	Sri Lanka

Iran (8 points) qualified for Moscow by winning 4-0 in a play-off against Singapore (8 points).

China had 6 points, North Korea 6, India 2, Sri Lanka 0 points.

In Asian groups the top two teams played off to decide who would qualify. Both Malaysia and Iran withdrew, however, and their places were taken by Iraq and Syria.

After the qualifying tournament, the 14 qualifying teams were:
Europe: Czechoslovakia, Yugoslavia, Spain, Norway
North and Central America: Costa Rica, USA
South America: Argentina, Colombia
Africa: Algeria, Egypt, Ghana
Asia: Kuwait, Malaysia, Iran
However, seven teams later boycotted the Moscow event – Norway, USA, Argentina, Egypt, Ghana, Malaysia and Iran. Eventually, these teams took part.
Europe: Czechoslovakia, Yugoslavia, Spain, Finland
North and Central America: Costa Rica, Cuba
South America: Colombia, Venezuela
Africa: Algeria, Zambia, Nigeria
Asia: Kuwait, Iraq, Syria.
82 nations entered for the 1980 football tournament, of which seven withdrew before the boycott, and the seven teams above joined that boycott.

19. Los Angeles, 1984

California, here I come

Los Angeles won these Games in 1978, but only after the IOC had worked diligently to avoid another debt-ridden 'big owe' like 1976. Companies decided to sponsor aspects of the 1984 Olympics, and ABC TV paid most of all to screen events for its US audiences.

There were 221 events, the largest number so far, and almost half the planet is believed to have tuned in to watch one or more contests.

It might be thought that, after the Moscow Olympiad closed in 1980, the USSR would have taken no part in the Los Angeles Games and made that position clear immediately. Not so, as the football qualifiers indicate. All the Soviet bloc took part in matches up to April 1984.

However, less than three months before the Games began, on 8 May 1984, when the Olympic flame arrived in the USA, the Russians declared they would not go after all. Days later, their allies also withdrew.

140 countries did accept their invitations, compared to 80 in Moscow and 121 in Munich, 1972. Comparison with 1976, when there was no boycott, shows that the USSR won 49 golds and East Germany 40 in Montreal. In 1984 other countries benefited from the Soviets' absence: Romania moved up from four golds (1976) to 20, China won their first golds (15), but the US won more than any other nation. Their total of 83 golds outnumbered their five closest rivals' added together – Romania, West Germany, China, Italy and Canada.

Both opening and closing ceremonies were Hollywood-style spectaculars, produced by David Wolper, with 85 pianos, and a 'space man' with jet pack arriving out of the blue.

Britain's Sebastian Coe became the first man to retain his 1500 metres title, in an Olympic record 5.8 seconds faster than his Moscow time. The hosts' star was Carl Lewis, repeating Jesse Owen's four golds (1936) in 100 metres, 200, 4 x 100 relay, and long jump.

Largest of all the Olympic attendances was for France v Brazil, when over 101,000 saw the final in Pasadena's Rose Bowl. This 1922 stadium was one of four housing football matches. Harvard Stadium, Boston and the Navy-Marine Corps Memorial Stadium, Annapolis, Maryland date from 1903 and 1959, a continent's breadth away from the Rose Bowl and

Stanford Stadium (1921) in San Francisco.

The football tournament

After last-minute changes caused by the Soviet countries' withdrawal, these teams took part:

Hosts: USA
Europe: France, Norway, Yugoslavia, West Germany, Italy
North and Central America: Canada, Costa Rica
South America: Chile, Brazil
Africa: Cameroon, Morocco, Egypt
Asia: Qatar, Iraq, Saudi Arabia

First (Preliminary) Round

Group A

29 July	Norway 0-0 Chile		Boston
29 July	France 2-2 Qatar (1-0)		Annapolis
	Garande 43	K. Al-Mohammadi 55, 60	
	Xuereb 61		
31 July	France 2-1 Norway (1-1)		Boston
	Brisson 5, 56	Ahlsen 33 (p)	
31 July	Chile 1-0 Qatar (0-0)		Annapolis
	Baeza 52		
2 August	Norway 2-0 Qatar (1-0)		Boston
	Vaadal 21, 52		
2 August	Chile 1-1 France (1-0)		Annapolis
	Santis 5	Lemoult 50	

242

Qualified: France   4 points   (5 goals for – 4 goals against)
Qualified: Chile   4 points   (2-1)
              Norway   3 points   (3-2)
              Qatar   1 point   (2-5)

Group A

This group included France, who had qualified by defeating Spain and West Germany. Weeks before the Olympics, their full professional squad had become champions of Europe. Norway arrived at the games by a circuitous route, third in a section behind East Germany, who withdrew, and Poland, who declined to replace them.

Chile qualified only on goal difference, ahead of Ecuador and Paraguay, while Qatar came through with wins over Malaysia, Thailand, Iraq and Japan.

France v **Qatar** produced no goals until Garande scored near the interval to put the French one up. A single goal hardly reflected his team's control of a match constantly interrupted by free-kicks. But soon after half-time Khalid al-Mohammadi turned the contest around with two goals, to give Qatar a 2-1 lead. Within seconds France equalised through their centre-forward Xuereb, and the game ended 2-2.

Norway's match with **Chile** also finished level, a goalless draw giving no clue to 90 minutes so one-sided that Norway had 27 shots on goal, hit the post twice, had one 'goal' disallowed, and drew eleven saves from the South American keeper, Fournier.

Much more evenly contested was **Norway** v **France**, but the French had the benefit of a goal-scorer in Brisson, who replaced Garande on the left wing. He hit the opener in five minutes and the winner in 56. Norway's centre-half Ahlsen converted a penalty after 33 minutes, but inability to score from open play cost the Norwegians dear.

Chile were the better side against **Qatar**, who conceded over 100 free kicks in three matches, but only Baeza found the target for them in 52 minutes. At least Chile had created more opportunities than in their first match, partly because they completely recast their forward line.

After two games each, France (3 points) and Chile (3) were favourites to reach the quarter-finals. Norway and Qatar both had one point; they now had to win and rely on there being a victor between Chile and France.

Norway did play their part, defeating **Qatar** 2-0. Both goals came from Vaadal, who had only played eleven minutes as a late substitute in the first match. He scored in 21 and 52 minutes, but time and again the eager Norwegian forwards were caught offside. Qatar rarely troubled Norway's keeper Thorstvedt, even missing a penalty, and had two midfielders sent off. Al-Khater left in 40 minutes and Issa al-Mohammadi in 55.

Chile's 1-1 draw with **France** meant both teams progressed, the South Americans taking the lead in five minutes through Santis. France's Lemoult levelled the match soon after half-time, and there were no more goals. Chile produced their best performance in this game and created the lion's share of scoring opportunities.

Group B

30 July	Canada 1-1 Iraq (0-0)	Boston
	Gray 70 Saeed 83	

30 July	Yugoslavia 2-1 Cameroon (1-1)	Annapolis
	Nikolic 39 Milla 32	
	Cvetkovic 70	

1 August	Cameroon 1-0 Iraq (1-0)	Boston
	Bahoken 7	

1 August	Yugoslavia 1-0 Canada (0-0)	Annapolis
	Nikolic 76	

3 August	Canada 3-1 Cameroon (1-0)	Boston
	Mitchell 43, 82 (p) M'Fede 76	
	Vrablic 72	

3 August	Yugoslavia 4-2 Iraq (0-2)	Annapolis
	Deveric 55, 76, 87 Saeed 17	
	Nikolic 86 A. Hussein 44	

Qualified:	Yugoslavia	6 points	(7-3)
Qualified:	Canada	3 points	(4-3)
	Cameroon	2 points	(3-5)
	Iraq	1 point	(3-6)

Group B

Yugoslavia, former gold medallists, were expected to reach the quarter-finals with ease, in a group which included Canada, Cameroon and Iraq. But, as so often, Olympic contests did not follow a script.

The Slav team qualified by defeating Romania, Italy and the Netherlands, Canada overcame Bermuda, Mexico and Cuba en route to Los Angeles, while Cameroon played only against Angola and Ethiopa.

Iraq travelled the longest distance to qualify in Singapore, where they came through ahead of Thailand, Japan, Malaysia and South Korea.

Yugoslavia were the better team against **Cameroon**, winning 2-1, but the African side opened the scoring in 32 minutes through one of the world's great strikers, Roger Milla. Nikolic took advantage of a fine move by Yugoslav forwards to equalise seven minutes later, and his left-winger Cvetkovic won the game in 70. Instead of adding another goal, they soon had to cope with losing a defender, when Eisner was sent off.

Canada v **Iraq** saw no goals until the 70th minute, when Gray, the Canadian centre-half, put them in front. Saeed, however, levelled the match at 1-1 in 83 minutes.

So **Yugoslavia** led Group B and they built on that advantage with a second victory, over **Canada**. Like teams in Group A, they created chances but only scored once; Nikolic hit the net in 76 minutes.

Iraq had most of the possession and opportunities against **Cameroon**, but it was Bahoken who gave Cameroon the lead in seven minutes and they never relinquished it, though the Asian team should have won at least a point.

Yugoslavia (4 points) were already sure to progress, but any one of Cameroon (2), Canada (1) and Iraq (1) could still join them.

Cameroon v **Canada** was one of the best and most evenly matched contests of 1984, but Canada's Mitchell made the breakthrough just on half-time. Cameroon quickly brought on two new forwards to play alongside Milla.

The 72nd minute was the key moment of this match. Vrablic gave Canada a 2-0 lead and immediately Abega was shown a red card, depleting Cameroon's midfield. Although M'Fede did reduce the deficit, Canada won 3-1 with Mitchell adding a late penalty.

Iraq could still qualify ahead of Canada on goal difference, but only if they won convincingly over **Yugoslavia**. The first half belonged to Iraq, who scored twice, through Saeed and Ali Hussein. Yugoslavia fielded a new look forward trio, including Katanec, usually a midfielder.

However, the Slavs started the second half with two fresh players, including their striker Nikolic, and gradually the game turned in their favour. Deveric scored in 55 minutes and 76, to level the match at 2-2. Two very late goals from Nikolic and Deveric (for his hat-trick), flattered Yugoslavia with a 4-2 win and three wins out of three.

Canada were runners-up on 3 points, their best performance since winning the title in St Louis, eighty years before.

Group C

30 July		West Germany	2-0	Morocco (1-0)	San Francisco
		Rahn 43			
		Brehme 52 (p)			
30 July		Brazil	3-1	Saudi Arabia (1-0)	Pasadena
	Gilmar Popoca 12			Abdullah 69 (p)	
		Silvinho 50			
		Dunga 59			
1 August		Brazil	1-0	West Germany (0-0)	San Francisco
	Gilmar Popoca 86				
1 August		Morocco	1-0	Saudi Arabia (0-0)	Pasadena
		Merry 72			
3 August		West Germany	6-0	Saudi Arabia (4-0)	San Francisco
		Schreier 8, 66			
		Bommer 22, 72			
		Rahn 24			
		Mill 32			

3 August   Brazil 2-0 Morocco (0-0)   Pasadena
                  Dunga 64
                  Kita 70

Qualified:	Brazil	6 points	(6-1)
Qualified:	West Germany	4 points	(8-1)
	Morocco	2 points	(1-4)
	Saudi Arabia	0 points	(1-10)

Group C

Brazil and West Germany have never repeated their World Cup triumphs on the Olympic stage but were confident of reaching the quarter-finals now. Brazil's qualification depended on victories over Colombia, Paraguay, Ecuador and Chile.

West Germany received their invitation, despite losing to France, after the USSR pulled out. In Africa's qualifying event, Morocco defeated Guinea, Senegal, and (in a penalty decider) Nigeria. Saudi Arabia came through with wins against India, Singapore, Indonesia and Malaysia.

Against **Morocco**, **West Germany** created most of the attacks but took time to convert them. Their 2-0 victory came from the midfielder Rahn, just before half-time, and their striker Brehme's penalty in 52 minutes; they also hit a post. Morocco's good defensive performance was spoiled right on the final whistle when El-Biyaz was sent off.

Brazil were off the mark against **Saudi Arabia** in just 12 minutes through their prolific striker Gilmar Popoca. They extended the lead to 3-0 from Silvinho and Dunga in 50 and 59 minutes. Saudi Arabia reduced the leeway with a penalty scored by their centre-half, Abdullah.

The most significant encounter in Group C brought 75,000 to see **Brazil** play **West Germany**. Gilmar Popoca won it for Brazil after 86 minutes, during which neither side could turn their skilful play into goals.

Morocco also took the points, 1-0, against **Saudi Arabia** when Merry scored the African team's only goal in the event, although another was disallowed.

Brazil (4 points) were almost sure to reach the quarter-finals, while West Germany (2) and Morocco (2) could still progress. Only Saudi Arabia (no points) were out of contention. Morocco's task was to produce a better result than the Germans' in their third match.

Brazil scored a 2-0 win over **Morocco**, even if their goals took over an hour to arrive from Dunga and Kita. If there was a flaw in the South Americans' play, it was their difficulty in establishing a convincing lead in the first 45 minutes of matches.

West Germany took only eight minutes to open their account against **Saudi Arabia**, with Schreier's goal. The Asian side's forwards made chances but could not take any, and the Germans took full advantage. Within 32 minutes, Bommer, Rahn and Mill put them four up and on the way to a 6-0 victory, easily the biggest of 1984.

Schreier and Bommer both scored doubles, and their coach Erich Ribbeck was able to rest two midfielders after half-time. With eight minutes left, the Saudi defence lost Abdul-Shakoor to a red card.

Brazil and West Germany showed their class in finishing first and second, although Morocco had conceded only four goals in total.

Group D

29 July		USA 3-0 Costa Rica (2-0)	San Francisco
	Davis 23, 86		
	Willrich 35		

29 July		Italy 1-0 Egypt (0-0)	Pasadena
	Serena 63		

31 July		Egypt 4-1 Costa Rica (2-0)	San Francisco
	El-Khatib 32	Coronado 87	
	Abdel-Ghani 35		
	Soliman 62		
	Gadallah 71		

31 July		Italy 1-0 USA (0-0)	Pasadena
	Baresi 58		

2 August	USA 1-1 Egypt (1-1)	San Francisco
	Thompson 8 Soliman 27	

2 August	Costa Rica 1-0 Italy (1-0)	Pasadena
	Rivers 33	

Qualified:	Italy	4 points	(2-1)
Qualified:	Egypt	3 points	(5-3)
	USA	3 points	(4-2)
	Costa Rica	2 points	(2-7)

Group D

While the USA appeared without needing to qualify, Italy only joined the event when Soviet teams withdrew. Yugoslavia had won their section, Romania were second but did not take up the offer of replacing one of the boycotting teams. Italy came third without winning a qualifier, as they drew four out of six matches.

Egypt qualified with victories over Sudan, Zambia and Algeria, while Costa Rica defeated Honduras, Guatemala and Cuba.

Rarely has a host nation started so promisingly without going on to the next stage. The **USA** took the lead against **Costa Rica** in 23 minutes through their midfielder, Davis, before 78,000 spectators. His centre-forward Willrich doubled the Americans' lead in 35 minutes, and, although Costa Rica had chances to score, Davis got the third right at the end. A 3-0 victory cheered the great majority of the San Francisco crowd.

At the same time, **Italy** made hard work of a slender victory over **Egypt**. The Italians had two 'goals' ruled out, and their forwards often fell into the offside trap. Serena, their centre-forward, scored the only goal in 63 minutes soon after two substitutes came on.

There was then an altercation which saw Nela, of Italy, and Sedqi, of Egypt, shown red cards. Egypt were eventually reduced to eight, as Nabil and Abdov – on the field two minutes – were dismissed.

Egypt's refashioned team next faced **Costa Rica** and could have won by more than 4-1. In 32 minutes they took the lead and swiftly made it 2-0, as their midfielders El-Khatib and Abdel-Ghani hit the target. In 62 minutes Soliman ensured the points, and his defender Gadallah was able to add a fourth, before Costa Rica scored a late goal through Coronado.

Gadallah's goal was soon to prove important for his team.

Italy v **USA** attracted 63,000 to a contest where the Europeans created nearly four times as many chances as their hosts, whose keeper made a series of fine saves before Baresi left his cenetre-half position to score the only goal.

So Italy led Group D on 4 points, with Egypt and USA on 2 points. Costa Rica could not progress (with no points), but **Egypt** v **USA** proved to be a cliffhanger.

The 1-1 draw was a fair reflection of an evenly fought match between two attacking sides – both hit the post. The US right-back, Thompson, delighted the crowd by scoring after eight minutes, while Soliman equalised in 27. There were no more goals and Egypt finished second in this group : their goal difference and 3 points exactly matched the Americans', but they had scored five times, the USA just four.

Meanwhile, one of the great Olympic shocks occurred when Rivers's goal in 33 minutes gave **Costa Rica** a 1-0 victory over **Italy**, who made 25 chances but missed 16, while Rojas in the Costa Rican goal saved the rest.

Italy reached the quarter-finals with the absolute minimum of two goals in two wins, but they did progress with Egypt. The USA were stunned after their best performances since 1904.

Quarter-Finals

5 August   France 2-0 Egypt (1-0)   Pasadena
           Xuereb 29, 52

5 August   Italy 1-0 Chile (0-0)   San Francisco
                     (after extra time)
           Vignola 95 (p)

6 August   Yugoslavia 5-2 West Germany (2-2)   Pasadena
        Cvetkovic 21, 58, 70   Bommer 1
              Radanovic 27   Bockenfeld 28
              Gracan 46 (p)

6 August   Brazil 1-1 Canada (0-0)   San Francisco
Gilmar Popoca 72   Mitchell 58
(after extra time Brazil won on penalty kicks, 4-2)

Quarter-finals

France were the better side against Egypt and they had Xuereb to thank for both goals in 29 and 52 minutes. With 15 minutes left, France were confident enough to substitute their striker and rest him for the semi-final.

Italy found **Chile's** defence difficult to break through – the South Americans lost only one goal in Group matches. Chile also showed attacking flair and tested the Italian back four, in a match which saw the referee produce eight yellow cards, the most of any game.

Italy selected the three forwards who started the match against USA, and again, none found the net. There were scoring opportunities galore before Vignola's penalty in 95 minutes won Italy the match in extra time.

Yugoslavia v **West Germany**, by contrast, provided seven goals, the zenith of 1984's scoring rate. And they came without delay, Bommer putting the Germans ahead in 60 seconds. Yugoslavia weathered other early pressure and Cvetkovic equalised in 21 minutes. His colleague, Radanovic, put the Slav team in front, but soon Bockenfeld took the match back to square one: 2-2 at the interval.

The second half began like the first, with a goal in seconds, as Gracan converted a Yugoslav penalty. Cvetkovic collected a hat-trick with two more goals by the 70th minute, in a 5-2 victory which flattered the winners but did no justice to a fine German performance.

Brazil had won every group match and now faced **Canada**. This match lasted 120 minutes and was the only one in the tournament decided by penalty kicks. Mitchell put Canada ahead in 58 minutes with his third goal of the event, but Gilmar Popoca levelled the match in 72.

On to the penalty shoot-out, where Brazil netted every time and their keeper Gilmar Rinaldi saved two spot kicks to see them through.

Semi-finals

8 August   France 4-2 Yugoslavia (2-0)   Pasadena
(after extra time)
Bijotat 7   Cvetkovic 63
Jeannol 15   Deveric 74
Lacombe 106
Xuereb 119

8 August   Brazil 2-1 Italy (0-0)   San Francisco
(after extra time)
Gilmar Popoca 53   Fanna 62
Ronaldo 95

Semi-Finals

The first semi-final was an extraordinary match between **France** and **Yugoslavia**. The French captain and centre-half Bijotat gave his side an early lead in seven minutes and another defender, Jeannol, put them 2-0 up after 15.

Soon after half-time, Yugoslavia lost Nikolic to a red card, but remarkably they came back to equalise through their two remaining forwards, Cvetkovic and Deveric. However, with 13 minutes to go, the Slavs were reduced to nine men and one striker, as Cvetkovic was sent off. Seconds earlier, his coach had taken the unusual step of substituting a substitute, Mrkela.

Even with a two man advantage, France needed 106 minutes to regain the lead, through Lacombe, and ensured the victory with a Xuereb goal in the final minute. Yugoslavia collected four yellow and two red cards.

Later that evening, **Brazil** v **Italy** also required extra time. No goals in the first 45, but Gilmar Popoca put Brazil one up in 53 minutes, with Fanna equalising in 62. At last, in the 95th minute, Ronaldo came out of the right-back position to win the match for Brazil.

Bronze medal match

10 August   Yugoslavia 2-1 Italy (0-1)   Pasadena

Baljic 59   Vignola 27 (p)
Deveric 81

Over 100,000 packed the Rose Bowl, the largest ever crowd for a third-place contest, to see **Yugoslavia** play **Italy**. Vignola put Italy in front after 27 minutes, with another penalty, but Yugoslavia – missing the two forwards sent off two days before – rallied with Baljic's equaliser in 59 minutes. There were only nine minutes left when Deveric won the game for the Slav team.

The Final

11 August   France 2-0 Brazil (0-0)   Pasadena

Brisson 55
Xuereb 60

In a final without an East European team for the first time since 1936, **France** and **Brazil** were cheered by over 101,000 as they produced an evenly contested match. Brisson scored first for France in 55 minutes, and Brazil quickly replaced two left-sided players. But it was Xuereb who broke through the reshaped defence in 60 minutes, and France took the gold to add to their European nations championship.

Top Scorers

5 – Xuereb (France), Cvetkovic (Yugoslavia), Deveric (Yugoslavia)
4 – Gilmar Popoca (Brazil)

Medal Winners

Gold: France

Rust	Bijotat (captain)	Cubaynes
Jeannol	Rohr	Thouvenel
Bibard	Lemoult	Senac

Zanon
Ayache
Lacombe

Brisson
Xuereb
Garande

Toure

Silver: Brazil

G. Rinaldi
Ronaldo
Pinga
M. Galvao
A. Luis
Dunga

Ademir (captain)
T. Gil
Silvinho
G. Popoca
Kita
Chicao

M. Cruz
Winck
Davi
P. Santos

Bronze: Yugoslavia

Ivkovic
Pudar
Capljic
Elsner
Radanovic
Baljic
Miljus

Mrkela
Katanec
Gracan
Deveric
Bazdarevic
Stojkovic
Nikolic

Smajic
Durovski
Cvetkovic

Referees

D. Socha (USA)

Norway v Chile
Cameroon v Iraq
Brazil v Italy (semi-final)

R. Filho (Brazil)
V. Roth (West Germany)
L. Calderon (Costa Rica)

France v Qatar
France v Norway
Chile v Qatar
Brazil v Canada

B. Kalombo (Malawi)
J. Keizer (Netherlands)

Norway v Qatar
Chile v France
Yugoslavia v Cameroon
France v Brazil (Final)

J. Palacios (Colombia)
M. el-Din (Egypt)
E. Barbaresco (Italy)
T. Sano (Japan)
T. Evangelista (Canada)

Canada v Iraq
Yugoslavia v Canada
Canada v Cameroon
Yugoslavia v Iraq
West Germany v Morocco

B. McGinlay (Great Britain)   Brazil v Saudi Arabia
                                           Italy v Chile
                                           Yugoslavia v Italy (Bronze
                                           medal match)

C. Kyung-bok (South Korea)   Brazil v West Germany
                                           France v Egypt

E. Sostaric (Yugoslavia)   Morocco v Saudi Arabia
I. Igna (Romania)   West Germany v Saudi Arabia
V. Arminio (Spain)   Brazil v Morocco
J. Quiniou (France)   USA v Costa Rica
G. Castro (Chile)   Italy v Egypt
A. Ramirez (Mexico)   Egypt v Costa Rica
                                           France v Yugoslavia
                                           (semi-final)

A. al Salmi (Kuwait)   Italy v USA
J. Romero (Argentina)   USA v Egypt
                                           Yugoslavia v West Germany

T. Gebreyesus (Ethiopia)   Costa Rica v Italy

The qualifying tournament (1983–84)

The teams entitled to join the 1984 Los Angeles event were:

Hosts: USA
Reigning champions: Czechoslovakia
Europe: four teams
North and Central America: two teams
South America: two teams
Africa: three teams
Asia: three teams

Europe

Group One

Bulgaria	1-1	Hungary
Hungary	3-1	Greece
Bulgaria	2-2	USSR
USSR	3-0	Greece
Hungary	0-1	USSR
Greece	1-2	Hungary
Greece	1-3	USSR
USSR	0-0	Bulgaria
Bulgaria	0-0	Greece
Hungary	1-1	Bulgaria
Greece	1-3	Bulgaria
USSR	0-1	Hungary

Turkey withdrew before playing any fixtures.

USSR (8 points) qualified on goal difference ahead of Hungary (8), Bulgaria (7) and Greece (one point).

Group Two

Denmark	1-2	East Germany
Finland	0-4	Poland
Finland	0-1	East Germany
Denmark	2-2	Norway
Poland	3-2	Finland
Finland	1-1	Norway
Denmark	3-0	Finland
Norway	0-1	Poland
Norway	1-1	Denmark

Finland	0-0	Denmark
East Germany	3-1	Poland
East Germany	1-0	Finland
Denmark	0-1	Poland
Norway	4-2	Finland
Norway	1-1	East Germany
Poland	1-0	Norway
East Germany	1-0	Norway
Poland	2-1	East Germany
East Germany	4-0	Denmark
Poland	0-0	Denmark

East Germany (13 points) qualified on goal difference ahead of Poland (13), Norway (6), Denmark (6) and Finland (2).

Group Three

Preliminary Matches

Netherlands 6-1 Liechtenstein (over two legs: 3-0, 3-1)

Byes: Italy, Yugoslavia, Romania

Yugoslavia	4-1	Romania
Romania	3-0	Netherlands
Italy	2-2	Yugoslavia
Netherlands	0-0	Romania
Romania	0-0	Italy
Yugoslavia	5-1	Italy
Yugoslavia	2-1	Netherlands
Italy	2-2	Netherlands
Italy	1-2	Romania
Netherlands	0-1	Yugoslavia
Romania	1-0	Yugoslavia
Netherlands	1-1	Italy

Yugoslavia (9 points) qualified ahead of Romania (8), Italy (4) and Netherlands (3).

Group Four

Subgroup A (won by West Germany, 6 points)

Portugal	3-1	West Germany
West Germany	2-0	Israel
West Germany	3-0	Portugal
Israel	1-0	Portugal
Israel	0-1	West Germany
Portugal	2-1	Israel

Subgroup B (won by France, with 7 points)

Belgium	0-0	Spain
Spain	0-1	France
France	2-0	Belgium
Spain	0-0	Belgium
Belgium	1-1	France
France	3-1	Spain

Final

France 2-1 West Germany (played over two legs: 1-1, 1-0)
   France qualified.
   The four qualifiers were therefore USSR, East Germany, Yugoslavia and France. When the first two teams withdrew, they were replaced by West Germany and Norway. (Poland would have replaced East Germany but they also withdrew). Czechoslovakia also withdrew, and Italy accepted an invitation to Los Angeles.

North and Central America

First preliminary round

Barbados	3-1	Antigua and Barbuda	(1-0, 2-1)
Cuba	5-1	Jamaica	(1-0, 4-1)

Second preliminary round

Cuba	2-0	Barbados	(2-0, 0-0)

First round

Canada	7-1	Bermuda	(6-0, 1-1)
Mexico	6-0	Bahamas	(6-0, 0-0)
Guatemala	6-1	El Salvador	(2-0, 4-1)
Cuba	3-1	Surinam	(0-1, 3-0)
Costa Rica	4-2	Honduras	(1-0, 3-2)
Trinidad and Tobago	1-0	Netherlands Antilles	(1-0, 0-0)

Second round

Costa Rica	2-1	Guatemala	(1-0, 1-1)
Canada	2-2	Mexico	(1-0, 1-2)
Canada	1-0	Mexico	(play-off)
Cuba	2-2	Trinidad and Tobago	(2-0, 0-2)
Cuba	1-0	Trinidad and Tobago	(play-off)

Final stage

Costa Rica	1-0	Cuba
Cuba	0-0	Costa Rica
Costa Rica	0-0	Canada
Canada	3-0	Cuba
Canada	0-0	Costa Rica

Cuba v Canada was not played.
 Costa Rica (5 points) and Canada (4 points) qualified, ahead of Cuba (one point).

South America (games held in Ecuador)

Peru and Argentina withdrew without playing matches.

Group One (Ecuador and Brazil progressed)

Ecuador	3-0	Colombia
Brazil	2-1	Colombia
Ecuador	0-0	Brazil

Group Two (Paraguay and Chile progressed)

Chile	1-0	Venezuela
Paraguay	4-0	Venezuela
Paraguay	0-0	Chile

Final Round

Brazil	2-0	Paraguay
Brazil	2-0	Ecuador
Brazil	3-2	Chile
Ecuador	3-2	Paraguay
Paraguay	3-2	Chile
Chile	2-0	Ecuador

Brazil (6 points) and Chile (2 points) qualified. Chile had a better goal difference than Ecuador and Paraguay, both on 2 points.

Africa

Preliminary Round

Gambia	6-2	Mauritania	(3-1, 3-1)
Mozambique	3-0	Lesotho	(3-0, 0-0)
Angola	walk-over	Niger withdrew	
Benin	w.o.	Sierra Leone withdrew	
Mauritius	w.o.	Madagascar withdrew	
Uganda	w.o.	Congo withdrew	

Round One

Tunisia	4-1	Gabon	(3-0, 1-1)
Libya	2-1	Kenya	(0-1, 2-0)
Morocco	3-0	Guinea	(0-0, 3-0)
Algeria	4-4	Uganda	(1-4, 3-0) (Algeria won on away goals scored)
Zimbabwe	3-0	Mozambique	(1-0, 2-0)
Senegal	4-0	Benin	(2-0, 2-0)

Egypt	2-1	Sudan	(0-0, 2-1)
Ghana	3-0	Gambia	(2-0, 1-0)
Nigeria	3-2	Togo	(2-1, 1-1)
Cameroon	4-3	Angola	(1-1, 3-2)
Ethiopa	w.o.	Tanzania withdrew	
Zambia	w.o.	Mauritius withdrew	

Round Two

Morocco	2-1	Senegal	(1-0, 1-1)
Ethiopia	3-3	Zimbabwe	(2-3, 1-0) (Ethiopia won on away goals scored)
Egypt	2-1	Zambia	(0-1, 2-0)
Algeria	3-2	Libya	(1-2, 2-0)
Nigeria	2-1	Ghana	(0-0, 2-1)
Cameroon	w.o.	Tunisia withdrew	

Round Three

Egypt	2-1	Algeria	(1-1, 1-0)
Cameroon	5-1	Ethiopa	(4-0, 1-1)
Morocco	0-0	Nigeria	(Morocco qualified on penalty kicks)

Egypt, Cameroon and Morocco qualified.

Asia

Round One

Group One

Qatar	1-0	Syria
Kuwait	3-0	Jordan
Syria	3-2	Jordan

Kuwait	2-2	Qatar
Syria	1-3	Kuwait
Jordan	0-0	Qatar
Jordan	0-2	Kuwait
Syria	1-1	Qatar
Jordan	0-1	Syria
Qatar	0-0	Kuwait
Qatar	2-1	Jordan
Kuwait	1-3	Syria

Kuwait (8 points) and Qatar (8) progressed ahead of Syria (7) and Jordan (1).

Group Two

Lebanon withdrew.

Iraq	0-0	UAE
Iraq	0-0	Bahrain
Bahrain	0-0	UAE
Bahrain	1-2	Iraq
UAE	2-2	Iraq
UAE	1-2	Bahrain

Iraq (5 points) and Bahrain (4) progressed ahead of UAE (3).

Group Three

India	1-2	Saudi Arabia
Indonesia	1-1	Saudi Arabia
Malaysia	3-1	Saudi Arabia

Singapore	0-3	Saudi Arabia
Malaysia	1-1	Indonesia
Singapore	2-1	India
India	4-0	Indonesia
Malaysia	2-0	Singapore
Malaysia	3-3	India
Singapore	1-0	Indonesia
Malaysia	2-0	India
Indonesia	1-1	Singapore
Indonesia	0-2	Malaysia
Singapore	0-1	India
Indonesia	0-1	India
Singapore	0-1	Malaysia
Saudi Arabia	1-0	India
Saudi Arabia	2-0	Malaysia
Saudi Arabia	5-0	Singapore
Saudi Arabia	3-0	Indonesia

Saudi Arabia (13 points) and Malaysia (12) progressed ahead of India (7 points), Singapore (5) and Indonesia (3).

Group Four (Matches played in Bangkok, Thailand)

Thailand	2-1	South Korea
China	4-0	Hong Kong
Thailand	3-0	Hong Kong
South Korea	3-3	China
Thailand	0-0	China
South Korea	4-0	Hong Kong
China	0-0	South Korea
Thailand	1-0	Hong Kong
Hong Kong	0-2	South Korea

Thailand	1-0	China
Thailand	0-2	South Korea
Hong Kong	1-3	China

Thailand (9 points) and South Korea (8) progressed ahead of China (7) and Hong Kong (no points).

Group Five

Preliminary Round (First Stage)

Taiwan	3-3	Papua New Guinea	(3-3, 0-0)

Taiwan progressed on penalty kicks.

Japan	17-1	Philippines	(7-0, 10-1)

Bye - New Zealand

Preliminary Round (Final Stage)

Japan	2-0	Taiwan
Taiwan	1-1	Japan
New Zealand	3-1	Japan
New Zealand	2-0	Taiwan
Japan	0-1	New Zealand
Taiwan	1-1	New Zealand

New Zealand (7 points) and Japan (3) progressed ahead of Taiwan (2).

Final Round (matches played in Singapore)

From those five groups, 10 teams reached the Singapore round:
    Kuwait, Qatar, Iraq, Bahrain, Saudi Arabia, Malaysia, Thailand, South Korea, New Zealand, Japan.
    They were now divided into two new groups, A and B, with the group winners qualifying for Los Angeles, and a third qualifier the winner of a play-off between the two runners-up in A and B.

Group A

Kuwait	2-0	Bahrain
Saudi Arabia	3-1	New Zealand
South Korea	0-0	Kuwait
Saudi Arabia	1-1	Bahrain
Kuwait	2-0	New Zealand
South Korea	1-0	Bahrain
Saudi Arabia	4-1	Kuwait
South Korea	2-0	New Zealand
Saudi Arabia	5-4	South Korea
Bahrain	1-0	New Zealand

Saudi Arabia (7 points) qualified for Los Angeles.

South Korea (5) finished second, ahead of Kuwait (5) on goal difference. Bahrain had 3 points, New Zealand none.

Group B

Qatar	2-0	Malaysia
Thailand	5-2	Japan
Qatar	1-0	Thailand
Malaysia	2-1	Japan
Iraq	2-1	Thailand
Iraq	2-1	Japan
Thailand	0-0	Malaysia
Qatar	2-0	Iraq
Qatar	2-1	Japan
Iraq	2-0	Malaysia

Qatar (8 points) qualified for Los Angeles.

Iraq (6) finished second, ahead of Malaysia (3), Thailand (3) and Japan (no points).

Play-off for the runners-up of Groups A and B

Iraq   1-0   South Korea

Iraq took the third qualifying place for Los Angeles.

This Asian qualifying competition, involving 23 teams to produce three qualifiers, was one of the most complex of any Olympic Games. There were five groups, and then two more groups in Singapore. In all, no fewer than 79 matches were played between September 1983 and the end of April 1984, and Saudi Arabia alone played 12 matches to reach Los Angeles.

20. Seoul, 1988

The Last Eastern Victory

South Korea's capital Seoul, was awarded the Olympics in 1981, with 52 votes, to 27 for the Japanese city Nagoya. This could have sparked the next major boycott of the decade, since Communist governments rarely had diplomatic links with South Korea. Eventually, only North Korea – who demanded the status of co-hosts – did not take part, along with Ethiopa and Cuba.

The opening ceremony in 1988 featured taekwondo athletes in unison, as their sport entered the Games as a demonstration event. Table tennis made its debut, and tennis returned after 64 years. The world organisations overseeing each sport now decided whether to allow open entry to professionals as well as amateurs, so that Steffi Graf added a singles gold to her tennis majors.

Other women to make the Seoul headlines were Olga Bondarenko, first ever winner of the 10,000 metres, Kerstin Palm, Sweden's veteran fencer and the first female contestant in seven Olympiads, and the riders who won every dressage gold from their male counterparts.

Unfortunately, Ben Johnson ran off with the negative headlines soon after finishing first in the 100 metres. Two failed drug tests led to his disqualification. The Official Report of the 1988 Games described shock and disillusion felt by billions of TV viewers that September day.

As had become common by the 1980's, Seoul shared Olympic football with other cities. The sport was now uniquely valuable in enabling spectators across a nation to feel part of the Olympic experience, and this will again be important in London 2012, with matches played in six British cities. (The Olympics have always been awarded to one city, but everyone throughout a host nation is encouraged to support such a massive enterprise.)

Pusan offered its 1954 stadium, Kwangju used one opened in 1966, while Taegu and Taejon arenas dated from 1975 and 1979. Seoul staged football at the 1984 Olympic Stadium and the country's oldest, Tongdaemun, from 1926.

In all, 111 countries entered the football qualifiers, with 13 later withdrawing. Attendances in South Korea were lower than those in Moscow and Los Angeles, but football remained a huge draw for the Olympics, in spectator numbers and on TV.

The football tournament

16 teams took part in Seoul.

Hosts: South Korea
Europe: West Germany, Italy, Sweden, USSR, Yugoslavia
North and Central America: USA, Guatemala
South America: Brazil, Argentina
Africa: Zambia, Tunisia, Nigeria
Asia: Iraq, China
Oceania: Australia
(France, the 1984 gold medallists, did not qualify).

Group A

17 September	West Germany	3-0	China (1-0)	Pusan
	Wuttke 31			
	Mill 60, 89			

17 September	Sweden	2-2	Tunisia (2-2)	Taegu
	Thern 44		Dhiab 15	
	Hellstrom 45		Maaloul 43 (p)	

19 September	West Germany	4-1	Tunisia (1-1)	Pusan
	Grahammer 5		Maaloul 28 (p)	
	Fach 50			
	Mill 55			
	Wuttke 76 (p)			

19 September	Sweden	2-0	China (2-0)	Taegu
	Lonn 19			
	Hellstrom 42			

21 September   Tunisia 0-0 China   Pusan

21 September   Sweden 2-1 West Germany (0-0)   Taegu
                    Engquist 73   Walter 70
                    Lonn 86

Qualified: Sweden   5 points   (6 goals for – 3 against)
Qualified: West Germany   4 points   (8-3)
            Tunisia   2 points   (3-6)
            China   1 point   (0-5)

Group A

West Germany qualified for Seoul with victories over Denmark, Poland, Romania and Greece, but the Danes would have taken their place except for one thing. Denmark fielded an ineligible player in their win over Poland, who were then awarded the victory instead.

Sweden came through ahead of Hungary, Spain, Ireland and France, losing only once, to the Magyars.

The group's African team, Tunisia, had narrow victories over Sierra Leone, Egypt and Morocco in matches that could have gone the other way. China's big wins, over Philippines and Nepal, ended against Japan, whom they just edged out.

In Group A **West Germany**'s victory over **China**, by three goals, was flattering. They were the better team, but China also made opportunities and the two keepers were equally busy during the match. The German midfielder Wuttke gave them the lead in 31 minutes, but, despite chances at both ends, there were no more goals until an hour had passed. Then Mill, playing upfront with Jurgen Klinsmann, made it 2-0 and scored another in the last minute.

At the same time, **Sweden** were playing **Tunisia**. The North African team took an early lead in 15 minutes, through Tarak Dhiab, and they went two up when his colleague Maaloul converted a penalty. Then, within barely 60 seconds, Sweden transformed the match and perhaps their chances of heading Group A. First, Thern and then Hellstrom scored to level the game: 2-2 at half-time.

In the second half, Sweden had most shots and corners, though the result ended in a draw. Both sides saw a player dismissed, after an altercation in 73 minutes between Thern and Tunisia's forward Liman.

West Germany found their match against **Tunisia** more comfortable, at least after the interval. The German defender, Grahammer, hit the opener in just five minutes, but Maaloul equalised with another of his penalties. West Germany did regain control, and after 50 minutes they benefited from Fach's shot to go 2-1 up. Soon after, Mill opened a two goal lead, and Wuttke clinched the win in 76 minutes with a penalty. The Germans even missed another spot kick.

Sweden also discovered that **China** produced good moves without troubling the scoresheet. If they had converted several misses in front of goal, the Chinese would have created an upset, but it was Sweden who took both points. Lonn, their defender, opened the scoring in 19 minutes and Hellstrom doubled the lead after 42, in a 2-0 win.

At that point, West Germany had 4 points, Sweden 3, Tunisia one, China none. The German team were sure to reach the quarter-finals, but Tunisia could still finish second ahead of Sweden in the group.

In fact, **Tunisia's** goalless draw with **China** was a game of few chances, and meant both sides were eliminated, China without a goal in three matches.

Sweden required at least a point from **West Germany** to progress, but they went one better and won the match. There were no goals until the last 20 minutes. Then Walter, a German substitute, put his team in front, but Engquist quickly equalised. A draw seemed likely until Lonn, Sweden's defender with an instinct for goals, won them the match in the 86th minute.

On the chances they created, West Germany deserved to win, but they missed almost all of them, while others were saved by S. Andersson.

Sweden shook off their disappointing first match to win the group, with Germany runners-up, and Tunisia a creditable third with one loss and two draws.

Group B

17 September	Zambia	2-2	Iraq (1-1)	Taejon
	Nyirenda 44		Radhi 39 (p)	
	K. Bwalya 65		Alawi 71	

17 September   Italy 5-2 Guatemala (4-1) Kwangju
               Carnevale 3   Castaneda 7
               Evani 12   Paniagua 80
               Virdis 34
               Ferrara 38
               Desideri 75

19 September   Zambia 4-0 Italy (1-0)   Kwangju
          K. Bwalya 41, 56, 90
          J. Bwalya 64

19 September   Iraq 3-0 Guatemala (0-0) Taejon
               Radhi 58
               Mudhafer 72
          Mazariegos (og) 77

21 September   Italy 2-0 Iraq (2-0)   Tongdaemun
                                             Stadium,
                                             Seoul
               Rizzitelli 59
               Mauro 64

21 September   Zambia 4-0 Guatemala (0-0) Kwangju
               Makinka 53, 85
          K. Bwalya 79 (p), 82

Qualified:	Zambia	5 points	(10-2)
Qualified:	Italy	4 points	(7-6)
	Iraq	3 points	(5-4)
	Guatemala	0 points	(2-12)

Group B

Group B's European team, Italy, qualified thanks to victories over Portugal, the Netherlands and Iceland, as well as their nearest rivals, East Germany, losing in Reykjavic.

Guatemala had the most extraordinary path to this stage. They seemed to have lost out to Mexico, but then FIFA banned the Mexicans for two years from their competitions. They were found to have played four overage players in the CONCACAF Under 20 championships in 1988, and Guatemala took their place in Seoul.

Zambia's victories over Botswana, Uganda and Ghana saw them through; Iraq defeated Qatar and Kuwait.

Zambia and **Iraq** were both unused to tournament football at this level, but they were enterprising and tried to attack whenever possible. Radhi opened the scoring for Iraq with a penalty in 39 minutes. Zambia's forward Nyirenda soon equalised, leaving the interval score 1-1. Just after an hour had gone, Kalusha Bwalya gave the African side the lead, only for Alawi to restore equality, and the match ended 2-2.

Italy's rare encounter with **Guatemala** produced five goals in the first half, four coming to the Italians. Carnevale scored for them in three minutes, although Castenada quickly equalised. Goals continued to flow, as Evani put Italy back in front in 12 minutes. The key time came just after half an hour, when Virdis and Ferrara added another two to put Italy 4-1 ahead and in full control.

There it remained until Desideri, an Italian substitute, scored a fifth goal soon after joining his team. By then 15 minutes were left, and only Paniagua could find a late consolation for Guatemala.

Guatemala's event did not improve against **Iraq**. Iraq created over three times as many goal chances as their opponents, but could not score for almost an hour. At last Radhi put them ahead, and they went on to win 3-0, adding goals from Mudhafer and the unfortunate Mazariegos's own goal.

One of the greatest Olympic surprises came when **Zambia** defeated **Italy** 4-0. That seemed unlikely in a first half without goals until K. Bwalya put Zambia ahead in 41 minutes. Bwalya hit a second in the 55th minute, and Italy brought on two substitutes.

A feature of the game was that the Italians created almost as many chances as Zambia, but kept missing the target. Instead, J. Bwalya made the victory sure, and his namesake completed his hat-trick just before the end. An extraordinary result from the youngest team in the event, aged on average only 18.

Zambia (3 points), Iraq (3), and Italy (2) still had hopes of reaching the next round, but Guatemala (no points) could not progress.

To **Italy's** credit, they put aside that unexpected defeat 48 hours earlier, and produced a solid performance to beat **Iraq** 2-0. It took them an hour to find the net, but then Rizzitelli and Mauro scored within four minutes, to ensure their quarter-final place at Iraq's expense.

Zambia scored another four goal victory, this time against **Guatemala**, whose defence kept the African forwards at bay throughout the first 80 minutes, except for Makinka's goal soon after the interval. In the last few minutes of the match, Makinka scored another, and Kalusha Bwalya took his personal total to six goals in Group B, as he added a late double.

Zambia won the group, with Italy runners-up. The first African team to make such an impression at the Olympics outscored all other 15 teams at this stage.

Group C

18 September	South Korea 0-0 USSR	Pusan

18 September	USA 1-1 Argentina (0-0)	Taegu
	Windischmann 79 A. Moreno 84 (p)	

20 September	USSR 2-1 Argentina (2-0)	Taegu
	Dobrovolski 7 A. Moreno 78 (p)	
	Mikhailichenko 22	

20 September	South Korea 0-0 USA	Pusan

22 September	Argentina 2-1 South Korea (1-1)	Pusan
	A. Moreno 4 Soo-Jin 15	
	Fabbri 73	

22 September	USSR 4-2 USA (3-0)	Taegu
	Mikhailichenko 6, 47 Goulet 65	
	Narbekovas 18 Doyle 84	
	Dobrovolski 44 (p)	

Qualified:	USSR	5 points	(6-3)
Qualified:	Argentina	3 points	(4-4)
	South Korea	2 points	(1-2)
	USA	2 points	(3-5)

Group C

In qualifying for their last Olympics as a team, the USSR dropped only two points in topping a section which included Bulgaria, Switzerland, Norway and Turkey. In eight matches they conceded only two goals.

Argentina qualified, as expected, along with Brazil, although they lost to Colombia en route.

The USA, after hosting the 1984 Games, survived a defeat in Canada to win the tie 3-2 on aggregate, and then came through ahead of Trinidad and Tobago, and El Salvador.

South Korea were the unknown quantity in the world stage, but were assured of their home crowds' support.

The hosts drew 30,000 to their opening fixture, but neither **South Korea** nor the **USSR** were on scintillating form in the goalless draw. The Russians hit a post, but there were few chances for either team. With hindsight, the Korean defence did better than any other team against the eventual winners of the tournament. As in 1956, the USSR began their successful event by struggling to find the net.

On paper the other favourites to win Group C were **Argentina**, but they could not score in the first half against the **USA**. The Americans were more than a match for Argentina, creating as many chances and seeing one shot rebound from the post. Only 11 minutes were left when Windischmann, a late substitute, put USA in front. There was relief for the South Americans when an even later penalty was hit home by Alfaro Moreno to level the game.

USSR then played **Argentina** in a contest likely to decide the group winners. After their disappointing opening match, the Russians introduced new strikers and played a 4-4-2 formation. This time Dobrovolski scored in the seventh minute, while Mikhailichenko doubled the lead in 22. Argentina struggled to make an impression, while USSR broke upfield time and again, hitting the post twice.

Alfaro Moreno's late penalty gave the Argentines a respectable 2-1 score, but the gap could have been wider.

South Korea's best chance of victory came against the **USA** but this was another match without goals. The home team was in charge, with far more of the play and nine corners to the Americans' two, but the result was another draw.

The USSR (3 points) led Group C with one match to go, USA and South Korea (2 points) still had a chance of reaching the next stage, while Argentina (one point) were not out of contention. Any two teams could find themselves in the quarter-finals.

When **Argentina** met **South Korea**, there were two firsts before 15 minutes had passed. Moreno scored his first goal from open play in the seventh minute, and Soo-Jin quickly replied with the Koreans' first goal. 1-1 was the score until 73 minutes, when Fabbri came up from his right-back position to win the game for Argentina.

The South Americans were never in control of their three group matches, and their hosts were unlucky not to win this game.

Even before the **USSR** played **USA**, they knew that a draw would suffice. However, they were 2-0 up in the first 18 minutes, thanks to Mikhailichenko and Norbekovas. In the last moments of the first half, Dobrovolski's penalty put the result out of the Americans' reach.

Soon after Mikhailichenko made it 4-0, early in the second half, the Russians rested him and his fellow striker Dobrovolski. Only then were the Americans able to turn their attacks into goals from a substitute, Goulet, in 65 minutes, and Doyle in 84. Spirited as their revival was, and though they had many chances to score, the USA lost their chance to progress.

In Group C the two qualifiers were the USSR and Argentina, as expected, but there had been some unexpected vagaries on the way.

Group D

18 September	Australia 1-0 Yugoslavia (0-0)	Kwangju
	Farina 50	

18 September	Brazil 4-0 Nigeria (0-0)	Taejon
	Edmar 56	
	Romario 74, 84	
	Bebeto 88	

20 September	Yugoslavia	3-1	Nigeria (0-0)	Taejon
	Stojkovic 46, 67		Yekini 88	
	Sabanadzovic 49 (p)			

20 September	Brazil	3-0	Australia (1-0)	Tongdaemun Stadium, Seoul
	Romario 19, 56, 59			

22 September	Brazil	2-1	Yugoslavia (1-0)	Taejon
	A. Cruz 25		Sabanadzovic 69	
	Bebeto 56			

22 September	Australia	1-0	Nigeria (0-0)	Tongdaemun Stadium, Seoul
	Kosmina 75			

Qualified:	Brazil	6 points	(9-1)
Qualified:	Australia	4 points	(2-3)
	Yugoslavia	2 points	(4-4)
	Nigeria	0 points	(1-8)

Group D

In Yugoslavia's final tournament, they reached Seoul just ahead of Czechoslovakia, the only team to defeat them, as well as Belgium, Austria, and Finland.

Brazil had an uncomfortable qualifying event, losing to Colombia and Argentina en route, but winning enough points against the other South American sides.

Nigeria's wins over Liberia, Zimbabwe and Algeria (a narrow 2-1 result) saw them through. The Oceania section was headed by Australia, in front of Israel, New Zealand and Taiwan.

As with the USSR, **Yugoslavia** were playing in their last tournament before huge changes to their country. Their opening match, against **Australia**, was evenly contested with defences on top. The Australians had a few more goal scoring opportunities and hit the post – they claimed the only goal soon after the interval, with their striker Farina scoring. The Slav keeper Levkovic played only half an hour before he had to be replaced by Stojanovic, who was then in goal throughout the group matches.

Brazil v **Nigeria** was the most one-sided match in Group D, yet Brazil struggled to turn their outfield dominance into goals. It took their midfielder Edmar 56 minutes to give them the lead, and two of Nigeria's few opportunities hit woodwork. Only in the last quarter of an hour were the South Americans secure. Bebeto, who went on to captain the side in 1996, came on as a substitute striker in the 73rd minute. Immediately, Romario scored to make it 2-0, and converted another chance in 84 minutes, with Bebeto hitting a fourth.

In a group where supporters had to be patient – only two goals out of 16 came before the interval – **Yugoslavia** defeated **Nigeria** with pivotal strikes in 46 and 49 minutes. Both were scored by midfielders – Stojkovic and Sabanadzovic, with a penalty. Stojkovic ensured the victory with their third in the 67th minute. Yugoslavia were the better team by some distance, but Yekini's goal with two minutes left was a consolation.

A 3-0 win for **Brazil** against **Australia** came from Romario's hat-trick, scored before the hour mark. The match could have been very different if Australia had scored from a penalty or taken advantage of several good chances and a plethora of corners.

Brazil were then on 4 points, both Australia and Yugoslavia on 2. Even Nigeria were not eliminated, since they could surpass their rivals on goal difference to finish second in the group. However, that was improbable – they had no points and their goal difference was minus 6, compared to minus 2 and plus 1.

Brazil achieved a 100% record by winning against **Yugoslavia** with goals from Andre Cruz, the defender, and Bebeto. Although the Brazilians were 1-0 ahead at half-time, the Slavs pressed hard for an equaliser, and two substitutes took the field at the restart for both teams. Yugoslavia reduced the deficit, through Sabanadzovic, with 20 minutes left, but the match finished 2-1 to Brazil, who won the group.

Australia took the second qualifying place with their 1-0 victory over an improving **Nigeria**. Both teams had their chances to take the lead before Kosmina's late winner in 75 minutes. The Africans' glory year was to be 1996.

Quarter-finals

25 September   Italy 2-1 Sweden (0-0)   Taegu
(after extra time)
Virdis 50   Hellstrom 85
Crippa 98

25 September   West Germany 4-0 Zambia (3-0)   Kwangju
Funkel 18 (p)
Klinsmann 34, 43, 89

25 September   USSR 3-0 Australia (0-0)   Pusan
Dobrovolski 50 (p), 54 (p)
Mikhailichenko 62

25 September   Brazil 1-0 Argentina (0-0)   Tongdaemun Stadium, Seoul
Geovani 76

Quarter-finals

Sweden met **Italy** with the more impressive group performance of the two. The first half saw no goals, but Virdis put the Italians in front just after the restart, and they had the better scoring opportunities, as well as hitting the post.

A feature of the match was that Italy's forwards were constantly running into offside positions. A single goal lead was tenuous, and five minutes from the end, Sweden's Hellstrom took the game into extra time. In the 98th minute, Crippa restored Italy's lead and they held on for a narrow victory. (One source gives the final goal to Sweden's Arnberg putting through his own net).

After mixed fortune in Group B, **West Germany** faced the high-scoring **Zambia**. Although the young African team had as many opportunities as Germany, the European side were generally in charge once Funkel scored with a penalty in the 18th minute. One later star of the 1990 World Cup success, Jurgen Klinsmann, now scored the second hat-trick of 1988, to rival Romario's. His goals after 34 and 43 minutes were too much for Zambia, who introduced two substitutes early in the second half. In the last minute, Klinsmann collected his third goal, and his side were through to the semi-finals.

Against the **USSR**, **Australia** continued their fine group form until the interval. Admittedly, the Russians – playing three forwards, with midfield support – had most of the possession, but they could not penetrate the 4-4-2 formation of their opponents.

The result turned on two penalties awarded to USSR early in the second half, and the reliable Dobrovolski scored in the 50th and 54th minutes. Mikhailichenko added a decisive third goal after an hour, and Australia's forward Mitchell was sent off with 22 minutes left to play.

Easily the biggest crowd of the quarter-finals, over 21,000, came to watch the top South Americans play. **Brazil** had won Group D, the only side to win every match, while **Argentina** had struggled in Group C before finishing second, with only one win. Now the single goal came from Brazil's Geovani in 76 minutes, but they should have won by a bigger margin.

While Taffarel, the Brazilian keeper, had to make four saves, Islas, in Argentina's goal, was called on for a dozen. Brazil's strikers and midfielders missed half-a-dozen more chances and hit the post. Still, that record was intact, and Brazil had won four times out of four.

Semi-finals

27 September   USSR 3-2 Italy (0-0)   Pusan
                 (after extra time)
                  Dobrovolski 78   Virdis 50
                  Narbekovas 93   Carnevale 120
              Mikhailichenko 107

27 September   Brazil 1-1 West Germany   Olympic
                                    (0-0)   Stadium, Seoul
                 (after extra time)
                     Romaria 80   Fach 51

Brazil won 4-3 on penalty kicks

Semi-finals

Both the **USSR** and **Italy** had been initially slow to find their form, but were improving. Once again, the crowd of 10,000 were not rewarded with a goal until the second half. Then Virdis gave Italy the lead in 50 minutes; in an end-to-end contest Dobrovolski levelled the game in the 78th minute. 1-1 and on to extra time.

The Russians played three strikers to Italy's two, and Narbekovas put them ahead in 93 minutes. Ferrara was then sent off within three minutes, and Mikhailichenko took advantage of the depleted Italian defence to make it 3-1. Carnevale's last seconds reply could not change the result.

Brazil v **West Germany** attracted 55,000 to Seoul's Olympic Stadium. In a match notable for 27 corners, most gained by Brazil, it was Germany's Fach who gave them the lead in 51 minutes. Brazil's free flowing attacks had a late reward in Romario's equaliser with 10 minutes to go. Extra time was approaching when West Germany were awarded a penalty; Funkel stepped up, but Taffarel saved his shot.

There were no goals in extra time, and again Taffarel was Brazil's hero, saving three of the German penalty deciders. The South Americans were in the Olympic final for the first time.

Bronze medal match

30 September   West Germany 3-0 Italy (2-0) Olympic Stadium, Seoul

Klinsmann 6

Kleppinger 17

Schreier 70

Bronze Medal Match

West Germany v **Italy** played for the bronze before a crowd of only 8,000 in the Olympic Stadium, but this was an evenly contested game, despite two early goals for the Germans. Klinsmann scored after just 6 minutes and Kleppinger doubled their lead in 17. Italy forced several corners, hit the woodwork, but could not find the net. With 20 minutes left, the substitute Schreier made the final result 3-0; he never started a match in 1988.

It was not the gold, but West Germany would progress to World Cup triumph under two years later.

The Final

USSR 2-1 Brazil (0-1) Olympic Stadium, Seoul
(after extra time)
Dobrovolski 62 (p) Romario 30
Savichev 104

The Final

73,000 applauded as the **USSR** and **Brazil** took the field on 1st October. No team had created more goal scoring oportunities than the Brazilians in their previous matches, but the USSR had scored 12 goals to Brazil's 11.

Within three minutes, Brazil were pushing forward and won the first of ten corners. Gradually the Russians replied, Dobrovolski's free kick drew a good save from Taffarel, and Liuty forced another stop from Brazil's keeper.

Then the breakthrough for Brazil, as Romario took a pass and hit the opener. His team finished the half on the upbeat as Aloisio hit a powerful free kick, saved by Kharine in the Russian goal.

Immediately after the interval, Savichev's shot was saved, and there were two USSR corners, as they strove to level the match. In 62 minutes, Dobrovolski was given the chance to score his fourth penalty goal, and in so doing he equalised. For almost half an hour, Brazil's strikers and midfield hit shots and free-kicks at Kharine, who dealt with them all.

In extra time, both sides continued to attack, and there were fine attempts by Luiz Carlos, Edmar, Andre Cruz for Brazil and Mikhailachenko for USSR. Only one counted – Savichev's goal after 104 minutes. In the last ten minutes, Tatarchuk and Edmar were sent off: it was the ten USSR players who won the match over ten Brazilians.

This was to be the last victory for a team from the Soviet bloc, as world and regional politics changed, and the term 'amateur' almost disappeared from Olympic sport. The Brazilians' silver medals were stepping stones for the World Cup stars of 1994, such as Taffarel, Bebeto and Romario.

Top goal scorers

7: Romario (Brazil)
6: Dobrovolski (USSR)
   K. Bwalya (Zambia)

The medal winners

Gold: USSR

Kharine	Fokin	Mikhailichenko
Prodnikov	Lossev	Narbekovas
Ketachvili	Gorlukovich	Borodiuk
Skjarov	Tishchenko	Lioutyi
Cherednik	Kuznetsov	Tatarchuk
Ianonis	Ponomarev	Savichev
Yarovenko	Dobrovolski	

Silver: Brazil

Taffarel	Aloisio	Romario	
Ze Carlos	Ademir	Joao Paulo	
Jorginho	Mazinho	Milton	
Batista	Valdo	Neto	
Ricardo	Gomes	Geovani	Andrade
Andre Cruz	Edmar	Bebeto	
Luiz Carlos	Careca		

Bronze: West Germany

Kamps	Kleppinger	Schreier
Reck	Sauer	Sievers
Schulz	Janssen	Klinsmann
Gortz	Bommer	Mill
Funkel	Fach	Walter
Horster	Wuttke	Riedle
Grahammer	Hassler	

Referees

J. Cardellino (Uruguay)   West Germany v China
                                   USSR v Australia
E. Codesal (Mexico)   Sweden v Tunisia
K. Hope (Great Britain)   West Germany v Tunisia
B. Sene (Senegal)   Sweden v China
L. Sirjvesingh (Trinidad and Tobago) Tunisia v China

K. Rothlisberger (Switzerland)	Sweden v West Germany
	Brazil v Argentina
J. Diaz (Colombia)	Zambia v Iraq
	West Germany v Zambia
S. Takada (Japan)	Italy v Guatemala
K. Hackett (Great Britain)	Zambia v Italy
	Brazil v West Germany (Semi-final)
J-F. Diramba (Gabon)	Iraq v Guatemala
M. Jassim (Bahrain)	Zambia v Guatemala
H. Arce (Chile)	Italy v Iraq
T. Lanese (Italy)	South Korea v USSR
J. Al-Sharif (Syria)	USA v Argentina
	USSR v Italy (Semi-final)
B. Laovissi (Morocco)	South Korea v USA
G. Biguet (France)	USSR v Argentina
	Italy v Sweden
	USSR v Brazil (Final)
C. Bambridge (Australia)	Argentina v South Korea
A. Coelo (Brazil)	USSR v USA
J. Loustau (Argentina)	Australia v Yugoslavia
	West Germany v Italy (Bronze medal match)
V. Mauro (USA)	Brazil v Nigeria
C. Gil-Soo (South Korea)	Yugoslavia v Nigeria
K-H. Tritschler (West Germany)	Brazil v Australia
A. Spirin (USSR)	Brazil v Yugoslavia
M. Listkiewicz (Poland)	Australia v Nigeria

The qualifying tournament

Europe

5 teams qualified, one from each group.

Group A

Preliminary tie: Greece 4-1 Cyprus (aggregate score over two legs)

Romania	1-0	West Germany
West Germany	3-0	Greece
West Germany	5-1	Poland

Denmark	0-1	West Germany
Greece	0-2	West Germany
West Germany	1-1	Denmark
Poland	1-1	West Germany
West Germany	3-0	Romania
Greece	0-5	Denmark
Denmark	8-0	Romania
Romania	1-2	Denmark
Poland	0-2	Denmark

This match was later awarded to Poland 2-0 by FIFA, who decided Denmark had fielded an ineligible player)

Denmark	4-0	Greece
Denmark	3-0	Poland
Romania	0-0	Poland
Greece	0-1	Poland
Poland	5-1	Greece
Poland	1-0	Romania
Romania	0-1	Greece
Greece	2-3	Romania

West Germany (12 points) qualified for Seoul, ahead of Denmark (11), Poland (10), Romania (5) and Greece (2).

Group B

Italy	1-0	Portugal
East Germany	0-0	Italy
Italy	2-0	Iceland
Italy	1-1	East Germany
Portugal	0-0	Italy
Netherlands	0-1	Italy

Italy	3-0	Netherlands
Iceland	0-3	Italy
Netherlands	0-1	East Germany
Portugal	0-0	East Germany
Iceland	2-0	East Germany
East Germany	4-2	Netherlands
East Germany	3-0	Portugal
East Germany	3-0	Iceand
Portugal	1-1	Netherlands
Portugal	2-1	Iceland
Netherlands	0-0	Portugal
Iceland	0-1	Portugal
Iceland	2-2	Netherlands
Netherlands	1-0	Iceland

Italy qualified for Seoul, with 13 points. East Germany had 11, Portugal 8, the Netherlands 5, and Iceland 3.

Group C

Spain	1-1	Sweden
Sweden	1-0	Ireland
Sweden	4-2	France
Ireland	0-1	Sweden
Hungary	2-1	Sweden
Sweden	1-0	Hungary
Sweden	2-0	Spain
France	1-2	Sweden

Ireland	1-2	Hungary
France	0-2	Hungary
Hungary	2-1	Spain
Spain	1-0	Hungary
Hungary	2-2	France
Hungary	3-1	Ireland
Ireland	2-2	Spain
Spain	1-2	France
France	1-1	Spain
Spain	2-2	Ireland
France	1-1	Ireland
Ireland	3-0	France

Sweden (13 points) qualified, ahead of Hungary (11), Spain (6), Ireland (5), and France (5).

Group D

Norway	0-0	USSR
Turkey	0-2	USSR
Bulgaria	0-1	USSR
USSR	1-0	Norway
Switzerland	2-4	USSR
USSR	2-0	Turkey
USSR	2-0	Bulgaria
USSR	0-0	Switzerland
Switzerland	1-1	Bulgaria
Norway	0-0	Bulgaria
Bulgaria	4-0	Norway

Turkey	0-3	Bulgaria
Bulgaria	2-0	Switzerland
Bulgaria	3-1	Turkey
Switzerland	1-0	Norway
Switzerland	2-0	Turkey
Norway	0-0	Switzerland
Turkey	3-2	Switzerland
Norway	1-1	Turkey
Turkey	0-0	Norway

USSR (14 points) qualified, with Bulgaria second (10), Switzerland (7), Norway (5), and Turkey (4).

Group E

Austria	0-1	Yugoslavia
Yugoslavia	2-1	Austria
Yugoslavia	5-0	Finland
Belgium	2-2	Yugoslavia
Czechoslovakia	1-0	Yugoslavia
Yugoslavia	4-0	Belgium
Yugoslavia	1-0	Czechoslovakia
Finland	1-2	Yugoslavia
Czechoslovakia	2-0	Belgium
Austria	2-0	Czechoslovakia
Finland	0-2	Czechoslovakia
Czechoslovakia	2-0	Finland
Belgium	0-2	Czechoslovakia
Czechoslovakia	1-0	Austria

Finland	0-2	Belgium
Belgium	2-3	Austria
Belgium	1-0	Finland
Austria	0-1	Belgium
Finland	2-1	Austria
Austria	0-2	Finland

Yugoslavia (13 points) qualified, ahead of Czechoslovakia (12), Belgium (7), Austria (4), and Finland (4).

North and Central America

2 teams qualified.

Round 1

(aggregate scores over two legs)

(Preliminary ties:

Guyana	6-1	Bahamas
Dominican Republic	1-1	Antigua/Barbuda

(Dominican Republic won on away goals rule)

Barbados	1-0	Jamaica

(Trinidad and Tobago walk-over: Surinam withdrew)

Guyana	6-1	Dominican Republic
Trinidad and Tobago	3-1	Barbados

Group B

USA	3-2	Canada
Mexico	7-2	Bermuda

Group C

El Salvador	4-3	Panama
Guatemala	4-3	Honduras

Round 2

Group 1

USA	4-1	Trinidad and Tobago
Trinidad and Tobago	0-1	USA
El Salvador	2-4	USA
USA	4-1	El Salvador
El Salvador	0-1	Trinidad and Tobago

USA (8 points) qualified for Seoul ahead of Trinidad and Tobago (2) and El Salvador (0). The Trinidad and Tobago v El Salvador match was not played.

Group 2

Guatemala	6-0	Guyana
Guyana	0-3	Guatemala
Guyana	0-9	Mexico
Mexico v Guyana	(match awarded to Mexico: Guyana withdrew)	
Mexico	2-1	Guatemala
Guatemala	0-3	Mexico

Mexico (8 points) finished top of Group 2 ahead of Guatemala (4) and Guyana (no points).

However, in June 1988 FIFA banned Mexico from its competitions for two years, after they fielded four over-age players in the Under-20 Championships for the CONCACAF region. In July **Guatemala** took Mexico's place in the tournament in Seoul.

South America

Group A

(played in Bolivia)

Colombia	1-0	Peru
Colombia	2-0	Brazil
Colombia	0-0	Uruguay
Colombia	1-0	Paraguay
Brazil	3-1	Paraguay
Brazil	1-1	Uruguay
Brazil	1-1	Peru
Paraguay	2-0	Peru
Paraguay	1-0	Uruguay
Uruguay	1-0	Peru

Colombia (7 points) and Brazil (4) progressed, Brazil having a better goal difference than Uruguay (4). Paraguay (4 points) had the same goal difference as Brazil, but scored one goal fewer. Peru finished with one point.

Group B

Argentina	1-1	Chile
Argentina	0-0	Ecuador
Argentina	2-0	Venezuela
Argentina	3-0	Bolivia
Bolivia	3-0	Venezuela
Bolivia	1-0	Chile
Bolivia	1-0	Ecuador

Chile	2-1	Ecuador
Chile	3-1	Venezuela
Ecuador	1-0	Venezuela

Argentina (6 points) and Bolivia (6) went through to the next stage. Chile were on 5 points, Ecuador 3, and Venezuela none.

Final Group

Brazil	0-2	Argentina
Brazil	2-1	Colombia
Brazil	2-1	Bolivia
Argentina	0-0	Bolivia
Argentina	0-1	Colombia
Bolivia	2-1	Colombia

Brazil (4 points) and **Argentina** (3) qualified for Seoul. Bolivia (3) were next on goal difference, Colombia had 2 points.

Africa

(3 teams qualified)

Preliminary Round

(Scores in all rounds were aggregates, over two legs.)

Malawi	8-2	Rwanda
Botswana	walk-over	– Madagascar withdrew
Swaziland	walk-over	– Mauritius withdrew

Round 1

Zambia	7-0	Botswana
Tunisia	2-1	Sierra Leone
Nigeria	5-3	Liberia
Zimbabwe	8-1	Swaziland
Egypt	7-1	Kenya
Cameroon	4-1	Malawi
Uganda	6-2	Mozambique
Algeria	4-2	Sudan
Ghana	3-0	Senegal
Ivory Coast	walk-over	– Guinea withdrew
Libya	walk-over	– Ethiopia withdrew
Morocco	walk-over	– Gambia withdrew

Round 2

Zambia	6-2	Uganda
Tunisia	1-0	Egypt (after extra time in the second leg)
Nigeria	2-0	Zimbabwe
Ghana	2-2	Cameroon (Ghana won on the away goals rule)
Morocco	2-1	Ivory Coast
Algeria	walk-over	– Libya withdrew

Round 3

Zambia	2-1	Ghana
Tunisia	3-2	Morocco
Nigeria	2-1	Algeria (after extra time in the second leg)

Zambia, **Tunisia**, and **Nigeria** qualified for Seoul.

Asia

2 teams qualified, one from each zone.

West Asia Zone

Round 1

Group 1

(played in Saudi Arabia)

Bahrain	2-0	Oman
Saudi Arabia	1-0	Oman
Saudi Arabia	2-0	Bahrain
Oman	2-1	Bahrain
Saudi Arabia	3-0	Oman
Saudi Arabia	2-1	Bahrain

Saudi Arabia (8 points) progressed, ahead of Oman (2) and Bahrain (2).

Group 2

Iraq	1-1	UAE (United Arab Emerites)
Jordan	1-1	UAE
UAE	3-0	Jordan
Jordan	1-2	Iraq
Iraq	2-0	Jordan
UAE	0-3	Iraq

Iraq (7 points) progressed, while UAE had 4, and Jordan one.

Group 3

Qatar	2-0	Syria
Syria	1-0	Qatar

South Yemen withdrew.
   Qatar progressed.

Group 4

Iran	2-1	Kuwait
Kuwait	1-0	Iran

North Yemen withdrew.
   Kuwait progressed, on away goals scored.

Round 2 (Final round)

Saudi Arabia	0-0	Iraq
Qatar	1-3	Iraq
Kuwait	2-1	Iraq
Iraq	1-1	Saudi Arabia
Iraq	4-1	Qatar
Iraq	1-0	Kuwait
Qatar	0-0	Kuwait
Kuwait	1-0	Saudi Arabia
Kuwait	0-0	Qatar
Saudi Arabia	0-0	Kuwait
Saudi Arabia	1-1	Qatar
Qatar	1-0	Saudi Arabia

Iraq (8 points) qualified for Seoul, ahead of Kuwait, on 7, Qatar (5) and Saudi Arabia (4).

East Asia Zone

Round 1

Group 1

(matches played in Nepal)

Pakistan	2-2	Nepal
Nepal	1-0	Pakistan

India withdrew.
    Nepal progressed.

Group 2

(matches played in Malaysia)

Malaysia	0-1	Thailand
Thailand	2-2	Malaysia

North Korea withdrew.
    Thailand progressed.

Group 3

Japan	3-0	Indonesia
Japan	1-0	Singapore
Singapore	0-1	Japan
Indonesia	1-2	Japan
Singapore	2-0	Indonesia
Indonesia	2-1	Singapore

Brunei withdrew.
    Japan headed Group 3 (8 points), while Singapore and Indonesia each had 2 points.

Group 4

China	9-0	Philippines
Philippines	0-10	China
Hong Kong	0-0	China
China	1-0	Hong Kong
Philippines	0-5	Hong Kong
Hong Kong	7-0	Philippines

China (7 points) progressed, ahead of Hong Kong (5) and Philippines (no points).

Round 2 (Final round)

China	8-0	Nepal
Nepal	0-12	China
China	0-1	Japan
Thailand	0-1	China
China	2-0	Thailand
Japan	0-2	China
Thailand	0-0	Japan
Japan	5-0	Nepal
Nepal	0-9	Japan
Japan	1-0	Thailand
Thailand	3-0	Nepal
Nepal	1-2	Thailand

China qualified for Seoul with 10 points. Japan had 9 points, Thailand 5, and Nepal no points.

Oceania

One team qualified.

Round 1

Group 1

Taiwan	0-3	Australia
Australia	3-0	Taiwan

Papua New Guinea withdrew.
   Australia progressed.

Group 2

Western Samoa	0-7	New Zealand
New Zealand	12-0	Western Samoa

Fiji withdrew.
   New Zealand progressed.
   Runners-up' play-off: Taiwan 5-0 Western Samoa.
   Taiwan progressed, as did Israel, with a bye.

Round 2 (Final round)

(Matches played in Australia)

Australia	2-0	Israel
Australia	3-2	Taiwan
Australia	3-1	New Zealand
New Zealand	1-0	Taiwan
New Zealand	0-2	Israel
Taiwan	1-5	Israel

(Matches played in New Zealand)

Australia	0-0	Israel
New Zealand	2-0	Taiwan
Australia	3-0	Taiwan
New Zealand	1-1	Australia
New Zealand	0-1	Israel
Israel	9-0	Taiwan

Australia qualified for Seoul with 10 points, ahead of Israel (9), New Zealand (5) and Taiwan (no points).

21. Barcelona, 1992

Gaudi weeks

Barcelona hosted the Olympics in 1992, 500 years after Columbus first sighted America on his Spanish-financed voyage. Its bid succeeded in the third round of voting, with 47 votes, ahead of Paris and Brisbane. This was the last Olympiad when both Winter and Summer Games took place in the same year.

King Juan Carlos, himself an Olympic competitor in the Spanish sailing team in 1972, opened the Games attended by representatives of 169 countries. Juan Antonio Samaranch, President of the IOC, returned to his home city to tell 'our vast Olympic family' that 'our founder, Baron Pierre de Coubertin, would have been proud of you'. ('The Olympic Review', October 1992)

Among nations returning to the Olympics were a unified Germany, and South Africa. The theme song 'Barcelona' became a world wide hit, and in a homage to Greece Agnes Baltsa, the mezzo soprano, sang music specially composed by her compatriot Mikis Theodorakis, at the lavish opening ceremony. The city of Gaudi's architecture became the centre of world attention.

Almost every football playing nation entered the tournament at its qualifying stages, and 16 countries were successful in reaching the Group Stages. Groups, once more, were decided on a mini-league basis, the winners of each group facing the second placed team from a different group, in the quarter-finals.

The 16 who qualified were:

Spain (as host country)

(4) Europe: Denmark, Sweden, Italy and Poland qualified through the UEFA under 21 Championships. Poland replaced Scotland, who did not take the Olympic place.
(1) Oceania: Australia, who won every match in their region and then defeated the Netherlands over two legs.
(2) South America: Paraguay and Colombia. (Brazil and Argentina were eliminated at an earlier stage)

(2) North and Central America: USA and Mexico.
(3) Africa: Ghana, Egypt, and Morocco, who replaced Cameroon.
(3) Asia: Qatar, South Korea, and Kuwait.

Matches were played in five stadia, the largest being Barcelona's Nou Camp and the smallest Nova Creu Alta in Sabadell. The host city also welcomed teams to Estadi de Sarria, with Valencia's Estadi de Luis Casanova and La Romareda in Zaragoza providing the other venues.

Group A

24 July	Italy 2-1 USA (2-0)	Nou Camp, Barcelona
	Melli 15 Moore 65	
	Albertini 22	

24 July	Poland 2-0 Kuwait (1-0)	La Romareda, Zaragoza
	Juskowiak 7, 80	

27 July	USA 3-1 Kuwait (0-1)	La Romareda, Zaragoza
	Brose 56 Al-Hadiyah 16	
	Lagos 79	
	Snow 85	

27 July	Poland 3-0 Italy (1-0)	Estadi de Sarria, Barcelona
	Juskowiak 5	
	Staniek 48	
	Mielcarski 90	

29 July	USA 2-2 Poland (1-2)	La Romareda, Zaragoza
	Imler 20 Kozminski 31	
	Snow 52 Juskowiak 40	

29 July   Italy 1-0 Kuwait (1-0)   Estadi de Sarria, Barcelona
Melli 10

		Points	Goals for v against	
1	Poland	5	7-2	Qualified
2	Italy	4	3-4	Qualified
3	USA	3	6-5	
4	Kuwait	0	1-6	

Group A

Poland and Italy were two of the favourites to win medals in 1992, while Kuwait made their debut, shortly after the first Gulf War had been fought over the land. The USA made another hopeful entry in the tournament, although they had not progressed beyond Round One since the fledgling days of St Louis in 1904.

Poland found the two outsiders difficult to master. Facing Kuwait in Zaragoza, they relied on the free-scoring Juskowiak to open his account in seven minutes, but did not extend that lead until the number 10 scored again in the 80th minute.

Against the USA, Poland had to work even harder, when they fell behind to Imler's early goal. Eventually, the right-sided defender Zokminski and Juskowiak gave Poland a 2-1 lead at half-time, but Snow equalised to share the points.

Surprisingly, the Polish side's most convincing result was their 3-0 victory over Italy. A swift goal by Juskowiak and another just after the interval by Staniek were the central moments of a game marred by a plethora of cards. Two Polish players were cautioned in the first eight minutes, but Italy's players later saw red, when both Luzardi and their substitute Corini were sent off.

Italy's most successful half-hour of the Group stage was on their introduction to the tournament in Barcelona's Nou Camp stadium. Against the USA, Melli and Albertini put Italy 2-0 up in 22 minutes. Then the Americans took off a midfielder, Dayak, and his substitute Moore repaid their confidence with a goal in 65 minutes. In the end, Italy held on for two points.

After two matches, Italy had an inferior goal difference to America's, both sides with two points. As it turned out, Italy did just enough to progress by defeating Kuwait 1-0, thanks to Melli's early goal.

The USA were unfortunate not to go into the quarter-finals, after beating Kuwait with three second half goals from Brose, Lagos and Snow, and holding the strong Polish team to a 2-2 draw. They finished third in Group A, primarily because they had started slowly against Italy in that very first match.

Kuwait showed their mettle in every game, restricting Italy and Poland to low scores and even taking the lead against the US, before the Americans found their form.

Group B

24 July		Spain	4-0	Colombia (3-0)	Luis Casanova, Valencia
	Guardiola 10				
	Quico 37				
	Berges 41				
	Luis Enrique 69				

24 July		Qatar	1-0	Egypt (0-0)	Nova Creu Alta, Sabadell
	Nooralla 74				

27 July		Spain	2-0	Egypt (0-0)	Luis Casanova, Valencia
	Solozabal 55				
	Soler 70				

27 July		Colombia	1-1	Qatar (0-0)	Nova Creu Alta, Sabadell
	Aristizabal 62		Souf 89		

29 July		Spain	2-0	Qatar (1-0)	Luis Casanova, Valencia
	Alfonso 40				
	Quico 60				

29 July   Egypt 4-3 Colombia (1-2)   Nova Creu Alta, Sabadell
Abdelrazik 27   Gaviria 9, 84
El-Masry 47   Pacheco 14
Khashba 91, 94

		Points		
1	Spain	6	8-0	Qualified
2	Qatar	3	2-3	Qualified
3	Egypt	2	4-6	
4	Colombia	1	4-9	

Group B

Spain played all their Group matches in Valencia and eased into the Quarter-Finals with a 100% record and without losing a goal – both feats unrivalled by any other team.

First, they defeated Colombia 4-0, with four scorers and an early goal from Guardiola. The match, however, also produced four red cards. Colombia's Valenciano and Cassiani had to go, as did Spaniards Martinez and Abelardo.

None of Spain's opponents finished their Group contests with a full team. Egypt's left back Hamid was dismissed after 17 minutes, while Qatar were depleted on the hour, losing both Al Kuwari and Noorallah within three minutes of each other.

Even with their numerical advantage, Spain found it hard to break down the defences of Egypt and Qatar. It took them almost an hour to take the lead against the 10 Egyptians, through their defender Solozabal, with Soler doubling the score in 70 minutes. Qatar proved an equally difficult side to attack, and Spain did not increase their 2-0 lead even against nine men.

Spain therefore qualified, and so did Qatar, with a draw against Colombia and a win over Egypt. The Middle Eastern team, whose country will host the World Cup in 2022, only scored two, late goals in the Group but their defence denied their opponents time and again.

Before their third match, Colombia could have qualified ahead of Qatar, but only by scoring freely against Egypt.

It was not to be. The South Americans got off to a fine start with goals from Gaviria and Pacheco, but Abdelrazik reduced the leeway. 2-1 at half-time, and soon afterwards El-Masry equalised. Gaviria made it 3-2 for Colombia, only for his opposite number in Egypt's forwards – Khashba – to win Egypt the points with two goals in added time.

Both Colombia and Egypt bowed out, but this was Group B's most exciting match.

Group C

26 July	Sweden 0-0 Paraguay	Estadi de Sarria, Barcelona

26 July	Morocco 1-1 South Korea (0-0)	Luis Casanova, Valencia
	Bahja 64 J. Kwang-Seok 73	

28 July	Sweden 4-0 Morocco (2-0)	Nova Creu Alta, Sabadell
	Brolin 14, 69	
	Mild 20	
	Rodlund 56	

28 July	Paraguay 0-0 South Korea	Luis Casanova, Valencia

30 July	Sweden 1-1 South Korea (0-1)	Estadi de Sarria, Barcelona
	Rodlund 52 S. Jung-Won 28	

30 July	Paraguay 3-1 Morocco (1-0)	Luis Casanova, Valencia
	Arce 43 Naybet 87	
	Caballero 57	
	Gamarra 70	

		Points		
1	Sweden	4	5-1	Qualified
2	Paraguay	4	3-1	Qualified
3	South Korea	3	2-2	
4	Morocco	1	2-8	

Group C

This group's outcome was especially difficult to predict, with four teams who had rarely faced each other. Sweden had the pedigree – an Olympic gold in 1948 and consistently fine performances in World Cups. Paraguay were surprise qualifiers from their continent, with neither Brazil nor Argentina reaching this tournament. South Korea, hosts in the 1988 Games, were Asia's representatives, while from Africa Morocco qualified as replacements for Cameroon.

Four of the six matches ended in draws, two of them goalless, including Sweden's game against Paraguay and South Korea v Paraguay.

Fortunately for neutrals and Swedish supporters, they swept into an early two goal lead over Morocco and added two more in the second half. Thomas Brolin, who was to have a distinguished career, scored in the 14th and 69th minute, six minutes after Morocco's striker El Badraoui was dismissed.

With one match to play, any two from four teams could still progress to the next stage. Sweden had three points, South Korea and Paraguay two, Morocco one.

In contrast to their goal spree against Morocco, Sweden struggled against South Korea, who took a first half lead, but Rodlund's equaliser was enough to see Sweden through. With them qualified Paraguay, also on four points, as runners-up with a poorer goal difference, after a convincing win over Morocco.

Group D

26 July	Denmark 1-1 Mexico (0-1)	La Romareda, Zaragoza
	Thomsen 87 Rotllan (p) 40	

26 July	Ghana 3-1 Australia (1-0)	Nova Creu Alta, Sabadell
	Gargo 12 Vidmar 90	
	Ayew 82, 89	

28 July	Denmark 0-0 Ghana	La Romareda, Zaragoza

28 July	Mexico 1-1 Australia (0-1)	Estadi de Sarria, Barcelona
	Castaneda 63 Arambasic 20	

30 July	Australia 3-0 Denmark (1-0)	La Romareda, Zaragoza
	Markovski 32	
	Mori 60	
	Vidmar 75	

30 July	Mexico 1-1 Ghana (1-0)	Nova Creu Alta, Sabadell
	Rotllan 30 Ayew 79	

		Points		
1	Ghana	4	4-2	Qualified
2	Australia	3	5-4	Qualified
3	Mexico	3	3-3	
4	Denmark	2	1-4	

Group D

This group also included a Scandinavian team in Denmark, whose players had recently won the European Nations Cup in a surprise triumph. They were to face Ghana, Australia and Mexico.

As in Group C, four matches were drawn and the two teams who managed to win games progressed to the Quarter-Finals.

Ghana won Group D by defeating Australia 3-1 in an extraordinary contest. The African side led for 70 minutes through Gargo's early goal, for Australia could not find an equaliser. Suddenly the game burst into life with eight minutes to go: Ayew scored two goals for Ghana, and Vidmar countered on the whistle.

Australia also qualified in second place by beating Denmark 3-0. The team from Oceania had changed their forward line, after earlier failures to produce goals, and Markovski, Mori and Vidmar hit the net. The match was beyond the Danes when Molnar was sent off with 27 minutes to go.

Mexico finished just behind Australia after drawing every game 1-1. The similarities go further – in the matches against Denmark and Ghana Rotllan scored in the first half, their opponents levelling in the last few minutes.

Denmark, with two points, ended fourth and only Thomsen registered on the score-sheet, against Mexico.

Quarter-Finals

1 August	Spain 1-0 Italy (1-0)	Luis Casanova, Valencia
	Quico 38	
1 August	Poland 2-0 Qatar (1-0)	Nou Camp, Barcelona
	Kowalczyk 43	
	Jalocha 73	
2 August	Ghana 4-2 Paraguay (1-0)	La Romareda, Zaragoza
	(after extra time)	
	Ayew 17, 55, 121 Achaempong o.g. 77	
	Rahman 113 Campos 81	

2 August   Australia 2-1 Sweden (1-0)   Nou Camp, Barcelona

Markovski 30   Andersson 60

Murphy 53

Quarter-Finals

The most eagerly awaited match was Spain v Italy, but the game provided only one goal, Quico's for the hosts in 38 minutes. Both teams added to the lists of yellow cards, while Italy lost Buso to a red card in the final minute.

Poland's prize for winning Group A was a match against Qatar, who continued to show the defensive qualities noticeable in their Group. Eventually two left-sided Polish players won the game – Kowalczyk just on half-time, and his midfield colleague Jalocha in 73 minutes.

Ghana had topped Group D and for an hour they showed Paraguay how they had done so. Ayew scored both goals, adding to those against Australia. However, Paraguay came back into the match when Achaempong, Ghana's right-back, turned the ball into his own net, and then the substitute Campos levelled the scores at 2-2.

In extra time, the African side proved stronger and won 4-2, Ayew the hat-trick star.

Sweden were favoured to beat Australia, although neither team had found their best form in Group matches. But it was Australia who took the lead in half an hour through Markovski, their centre-forward, and the defender Murphy added a second after 53 minutes. Sweden could only find the net through their right-back Andersson, on the hour, and Australia reached the semi-finals for the first time.

Semi-Finals

5 August   Spain 2-0 Ghana (1-0)   Luis Casanova, Valencia

Abelardo 25

Berges 55

5 August   Poland 6-1 Australia (2-1)   Nou Camp, Barcelona

Kowalczyk 27, 88   Veart 35

Juskowiak
43, 52, 78

Murphy o.g. 67

Bronze medal match

7 August   Ghana 1-0 Australia (1-0)   Nou Camp, Barcelona

Asare 19

Semi-Finals

In reaching this stage of an Olympic tournament, Ghana and Australia had achieved a great deal, but now came their biggest challenges.

Spain enjoyed a straightforward 2-0 victory over Ghana with a goal in each half, a result made simpler after Kuffour was sent off in 46 minutes. The 10 Ghanaians contained Spain's forwards to a Berges strike soon after, but Ayew could not find the net, even for a consolation goal.

Poland proved too strong for Australia, although they competed well in the first half. Juskowiak's goals for Poland, just before and after the interval, decided the game, and his hat-trick was the feature of 1992's biggest victory, 6-1.

Bronze medal match

Two days after the semi-finals, Ghana took full advantage of their first appearance at the Nou Camp. Only one goal, from their midfielder Asare's free-kick in 19 minutes, won the day; Australia were still recovering from that heavy defeat to Poland.

The first African medal winners in Olympic football, Ghana owed a lot to their keeper Dossey who saved a penalty and had to be substituted later in the match. Even the dismissal of Quaye, for two yellow cards, could not dampen their joy.

Final

8 August   Spain 3-2 Poland (0-1)   Nou Camp, Barcelona

Abelardo 65   Kowalczyk 44
Quico 72, 90   Staniek 76

By far the biggest crowd, 95,000, saw a splendid match to crown the tournament. Spain conceded their first goals but came back to win gold, the first host nation to achieve it since Belgium in 1920.

Just before the interval, Kowalczyk scored for Poland and it was still 1-0 until Abelardo headed in from Guardiola's free kick to equalise. Buoyed by their supporters, who now included King Juan Carlos, the Spanish forwards made chances and their left-sided striker Francisco 'Quico' Narvaez gave them a 2-1 lead. Back came Poland's Staniek to level the scores.

Extra time was seconds away when Enrique's shot, after a corner, was blocked, Quico collected the rebound and chipped over Poland's keeper to win the match.

There were many fine players in this Olympics. Some went on to become famous, such as Dino Baggio (Italy), Faustino Asprilla (Colombia), Thomas Brolin (Sweden), and Mark Bosnich (Australia), as well as Spain's Luis Enrique.

The medal winners

Gold: Spain

Toni	Guardiola	Goicoechea
Lopez	Luis Enrique	Manjarin
Solozabal	Berges	Pinilla
Abelardo	Alfonso	Soler
Lasa	Quico ('Kiko')	Vidal
Amavisca	Canizares	Villabona
Ferrer	Hernandez	Paqui Martinez

Silver: Poland

Klak	Adamczuk	Waligora
Jalocha	Mielcarski	Kosela
Lapinski	Brzeczek	Kowalczyk
Kozminski	Juskowiak	

Waldoch	Stanjek	
Gesior	Bajor	
Swierczewski	Kobylanski	

Bronze: Ghana

Mensah	Rahman	Kalilu
Dossey	Lamptey	Aryee
Amankwah	Ayew	Addo
Asare	Quaye	Konadu
Gargo	Kumah	Preko
Acheampong	Kuffour	Amadu
Nyarko	Adjel	

Goal scorers:

Juskowiak (Poland): 7
Ayew (Ghana): 6
Quico (Spain): 5
Kowalczyk (Poland): 5

Referees

M.D. Vega (Spain)	Italy v USA
	Sweden v South Korea
J.F. Escobar (Portugal)	Poland v Kuwait
	Denmark v Ghana
A.L.K. Chong (Mauritius)	USA v Kuwait
	Poland v USA
P. Don (Great Britain)	Poland v Italy
	Qatar v Egypt
A.B. Carter (Mexico)	Italy v Kuwait
	Colombia v Qatar
	Australia v Sweden
	Spain v Ghana (Semi-Final)
M. Merk (Germany)	Spain v Colombia
	Paraguay v Morocco
M.R. de Freitas (Brazil)	Spain v Egypt
	Spain v Italy
	Poland v Australia (Semi-Final)

A. Angeles (USA)	Spain v Qatar
	Morocco v South Korea
A.M. Bujsaim (UAE)	Egypt v Colombia
	Ghana v Australia
	(Bronze medal)
	Ghana v Paraguay
J.T. Cadena (Colombia)	Sweden v Morocco
	Mexico v Ghana
	Spain v Poland (Final)
M. Sendid (Algeria)	Paraguay v South Korea
	Poland v Qatar
F. Baldas (Italy)	Denmark v Mexico
	Australia v Denmark
K. Tachi (Japan)	Mexico v Australia

The qualifying tournament

The 16 teams in Barcelona would include:

Host country: Spain
Europe: Four teams (or five)
North and Central America: Two
South America: Two
Africa: Three
Asia: Three
Oceania: One team (or none)
    (There would be a play-off between the fifth team from Europe and the Oceania winner)

Europe

(UEFA Under 21 Championship)
    Extra round before the preliminary round.
    Austria 16-0 Liechtenstein (aggregate score over two legs)

Group 1

Iceland	0-0	Albania
Iceland	0-1	France
Czechoslovakia	7-0	Iceland

Spain	2-0	Iceland
France	1-2	Czechoslovakia
Czechoslovakia	3-1	Spain
Spain	1-0	Albania
Albania	0-0	France
France	0-1	Spain
France	3-0	Albania
Albania	1-5	Czechoslovakia
Albania	2-1	Iceland
Iceland	0-1	Czechoslovakia
Czechoslovakia	1-0	France
Iceland	1-0	Spain
Spain	0-0	France
Czechoslovakia	3-0	Albania
Spain	1-1	Czechoslovakia
France	2-1	Iceland
Albania	v	Spain – not played

Czechoslovakia went into the next round with 15 points. France and Spain had 8, Albania 4, Iceland 3

Group 2

Scotland	2-0	Romania
Switzerland	0-2	Bulgaria
Romania	0-1	Bulgaria
Scotland	4-2	Switzerland
Bulgaria	2-0	Scotland
Scotland	1-0	Bulgaria
Switzerland	0-2	Romania
Bulgaria	1-0	Switzerland
Switzerland	0-3	Scotland
Romania	1-3	Scotland

Romania	1-3	Switzerland
Bulgaria	0-1	Romania

Scotland (10 points) progressed. Bulgaria had 8, Romania 4, Switzerland two.

Group 3

USSR	2-2	Norway
Norway	3-1	Hungary
Italy	1-0	Hungary
Hungary	0-0	USSR
Hungary	0-1	Italy
Norway	6-0	Italy
Italy	1-0	USSR
Norway	0-1	USSR
USSR	2-0	Hungary
USSR	1-1	Italy
Italy	0-1	Norway
Italy	2-1	Norway

Italy, on 9 points, went through, ahead of Norway (7), USSR (7) and Hungary (one).

Group 4

San Marino	0-3	Denmark
Yugoslavia	1-0	Austria
Denmark	3-0	Yugoslavia
San Marino	0-2	Austria
Yugoslavia	5-0	San Marino
Austria	3-0	San Marino
Denmark	7-0	San Marino
Yugoslavia	2-6	Denmark

Denmark	1-1	Austria
Austria	1-1	Denmark
Austria	1-2	Yugoslavia
San Marino	0-1	Yugoslavia

Denmark (10 points) progressed. Yugoslavia had 8, Austria 6, and San Marino none.

Group 5

Luxembourg	0-3	Germany
Belgium	2-0	Luxembourg
Germany	3-1	Belgium
Luxembourg	0-2	Belgium
Belgium	0-3	Germany
Germany	3-0	Luxembourg

Germany (8 points) went through, ahead of Belgium (4) and Luxembourg (none).

Group 6

Finland	0-1	Portugal
Portugal	0-0	Netherlands
Malta	1-4	Netherlands
Malta	1-3	Portugal
Portugal	2-0	Malta
Netherlands	7-1	Malta
Netherlands	1-0	Finland
Finland	1-7	Netherlands
Finland	3-1	Malta
Portugal	2-0	Finland
Netherlands	1-1	Portugal
Malta	1-3	Finland

Netherlands (10 points) progressed with a better goal difference than Portugal (10). Finland had 4, Malta none.

Group 7

England	0-1	Poland
Ireland	3-2	Turkey
Ireland	0-3	England
Turkey	0-1	Poland
England	3-0	Ireland
Poland	2-0	Turkey
Ireland	1-2	Poland
Turkey	2-2	England
England	2-0	Turkey
Poland	2-0	Ireland
Poland	2-1	England
Turkey	2-1	Ireland

Poland went through with 12 points. England were second (7), Turkey had 3, Ireland 2.

Group 8

Sweden	5-0	Greece
Cyprus	1-1	Sweden
Greece	2-2	Israel
Israel	4-0	Cyprus
Cyprus	1-0	Greece
Sweden	6-0	Cyprus
Sweden	2-1	Israel
Israel	2-1	Greece
Israel	0-0	Sweden
Greece	1-3	Sweden
Cyprus	1-2	Israel
Greece	2-0	Cyprus

Sweden progressed (10 points), ahead of Israel (8), Greece (3), and Cyprus (3).

Final round

(aggregate scores over two legs)

Scotland	5-4	Germany
Sweden	2-2	Netherlands (Sweden won on away goals)
Denmark	6-1	Poland
Italy	4-1	Czechoslovakia

The four teams who qualified for Barcelona were **Sweden**, **Denmark**, **Italy** and – since Scotland did not take part in the Olympic tournament – **Poland**, because of their group results. The Netherlands were the best losing team, in the Final round, and went on to play off against the Oceania winner.

North and Central America

Caribbean zone

Round 1 (aggregate scores over two legs)

Haiti	3-3	Cuba (Haiti won on away goals)
Jamaica	5-0	Puerto Rico
St Lucia	9-0	Aruba
Barbados	5-0	Antigua
Surinam	1-0	Dutch Antilles

Bye: Trinidad and Tobago

Round 2 (aggregate scores over two legs)

Surinam	2-1	Barbados
Trinidad and Tobago	2-1	Jamaica (after a 1-1 aggregate, the teams played another match)
Haiti	3-2	St Lucia

Central American zone (aggregate scores over two legs)

Honduras	4-2	Guatemala
El Salvador	5-0	Belize
Panama walkover	v	Costa Rica

Semi-Final round (of 3 groups)

Group A

Surinam	1-1	Mexico
Honduras	1-1	Mexico
Mexico	0-1	Honduras
Mexico	6-0	Surinam
Honduras	2-0	Surinam
Surinam	0-2	Honduras

Honduras (7 points) and Mexico (4) progressed, while Surinam had one point.

Group B

Canada	3-0	Trinidad and Tobago
El Salvador	3-1	Canada
Trinidad and Tobago	1-3	Canada
El Salvador	v	Trinidad and Tobago (awarded 2-0 to El Salvador)
Trinidad and Tobago	2-0	El Salvador
Canada	4-0	El Salvador

Canada (6 points) went through. El Salvador had 4, Trinidad and Tobago two.

Group C

USA	8-0	Haiti
Panama	1-1	USA
USA	7-1	Panama
Haiti	0-2	USA
Panama	2-2	Haiti (Haiti v Panama was not played)

USA (7 points) progressed. Panama had 2, Haiti one.

Final round

USA	3-0	Mexico
USA	3-1	Canada
USA	4-3	Honduras
Mexico	1-2	USA
Mexico	4-1	Canada
Mexico	5-1	Honduras
Honduras	3-4	USA
Honduras	1-3	Mexico
Honduras	1-0	Canada
Canada	2-1	USA
Canada	1-1	Mexico
Canada	2-2	Honduras

USA (10 points) and **Mexico** (7) qualified for Barcelona. Canada had 4, Honduras 3.

South America

Round 1

Group A

Paraguay	1-0	Venezuela
Brazil	2-1	Peru
Peru	1-4	Colombia
Paraguay	0-1	Brazil
Peru	3-0	Venezuela
Brazil	0-2	Colombia
Colombia	4-0	Venezuela
Paraguay	7-1	Peru
Paraguay	0-0	Colombia
Brazil	1-1	Venezuela

Colombia (7 points) and Paraguay (5) went on to Round 2. Brazil also had 5 points, with a lesser goal difference. Peru had 2, Venezuela one.

Group B

Uruguay	0-2	Ecuador
Argentina	1-0	Bolivia
Uruguay	1-0	Chile
Argentina	1-0	Ecuador
Ecuador	4-1	Bolivia
Argentina	1-1	Chile
Uruguay	4-0	Bolivia
Chile	1-5	Ecuador
Chile	v	Bolivia – match cancelled
Argentina	1-2	Uruguay

Ecuador (6 points) and Uruguay (6) went on to Round 2. Argentina had 5, Chile one, Bolivia none.

Round 2

Paraguay	1-0	Ecuador
Colombia	3-0	Uruguay
Paraguay	1-0	Colombia
Uruguay	1-0	Ecuador
Paraguay	0-0	Uruguay
Colombia	1-1	Ecuador

Paraguay (5 points) and **Colombia** (3) qualified for Barcelona. Uruguay (3 points) had a lesser goal difference, Ecuador had one point.

Africa

Round 1

(aggregate scores over two legs in all African matches)

Mauritius	2-2	Somalia (Mauritius won on away goals)
Mozambique	1-0	Swaziland
Gabon	2-1	Botswana
Ethiopia walk-over	v	Libya
Burkina Faso walk-over	v	Senegal
Sierra Leone walk-over	v	Mali
Mauritania walk-over	v	Gambia
Togo walk-over	v	Congo

Round 2

Group 1

Egypt	4-1	Sudan
Uganda	4-1	Mozambique
Mauritius walk-over	v	Zambia
Ivory Coast walk-over	v	Angola
Malawi walk-over	v	Ethiopia
Cameroon walk-over	v	Gabon

Group 2

Tunisia	3-2	Senegal
Sierra Leone	1-0	Algeria
Morocco	6-0	Mauritania
Togo walk-over	v	Liberia
Ghana walk-over	v	Guinea
Zimbabwe walk-over	v	Zaire

Round 3

Group 1

Egypt	3-1	Malawi
Cameroon	4-1	Uganda
Mauritius walk-over	v	Ivory Coast

Group 2

Zimbabwe	6-5	Tunisia
Ghana	4-4	Sierra Leone (Ghana won on away goals)
Morocco walk-over	v	Togo

Round 4

Cameroon	2-0	Morocco
Ghana	10-1	Mauritius
Egypt	4-1	Zimbabwe

Cameroon, **Ghana** and **Egypt** qualified for Barcelona.

Asia

Round 1

Group A (West and Central Asia)

Yemen	1-0	Pakistan
Qatar	2-0	Iran
Iran	2-2	UAE
Yemen	1-1	Qatar
Pakistan	0-4	Qatar
UAE	2-1	Yemen
Yemen	1-1	Iran
Pakistan	0-1	UAE
Qatar	2-1	UAE
Iran	5-0	Pakistan
Pakistan	0-2	Yemen
Iran	2-0	Qatar
UAE	0-1	Iran
Qatar	3-0	Yemen
Qatar	2-0	Pakistan
Yemen	0-0	UAE
Iran	2-1	Yemen

UAE	2-0	Pakistan
UAE	0-2	Qatar
Pakistan	0-6	Iran

Qatar went through to Round 2 with 13 points. Iran had 12, both UAE and Yemen 7, Pakistan none.

Group B (West and Central Asia)

India	1-1	Oman
Lebanon	0-1	Syria
Kuwait	1-0	Oman
India	1-3	Lebanon
Syria	1-1	Kuwait
Oman	1-0	Lebanon
India	0-1	Syria
Lebanon	1-2	Kuwait
Oman	0-0	Syria
India	1-2	Kuwait

Kuwait (7 points) went through to Round 2. Syria had 6, Oman 4, Lebanon 2, and India one.

Group C (West and Central Asia)

Bahrain	6-0	Sri Lanka
Saudi Arabia	1-2	Jordan
Bahrain	4-0	Jordan
Sri Lanka	1-5	Saudi Arabia
Jordan	7-0	Sri Lanka
Bahrain	0-2	Saudi Arabia

Afghanistan withdrew

Bahrain (4 points) progressed, with a better goal difference than Saudi Arabia and Jordan, both on 4 points. Sri Lanka had none.

Group D (East Asia)

South Korea	10-0	Philippines
Bangladesh	2-3	Thailand
Philippines	0-5	Malaysia
South Korea	6-0	Bangladesh
Bangladesh	0-1	Malaysia
South Korea	2-1	Thailand
Thailand	4-1	Malaysia
Philippines	0-8	Bangladesh
Philippines	1-7	Thailand
South Korea	0-0	Malaysia
Malaysia	1-0	Thailand
Philippines	0-7	South Korea
Malaysia	0-2	South Korea
Thailand	4-0	Bangladesh
Bangladesh	0-1	South Korea
Malaysia	5-0	Philippines
Bangladesh	3-0	Philippines
Thailand	0-2	South Korea
Thailand	6-0	Philippines
Malaysia	0-1	Bangladesh

South Korea (15 points) went on to Round 2. Thailand had 10, Malaysia 9, Bangladesh 6, Philippines none.

Group E (East Asia)

North Korea	5-0	Nepal
Maldive Islands	0-12	China
North Korea	2-0	Singapore

Nepal	0-1	Maldive Islands
North Korea	4-0	Maldive Islands
Singapore	0-3	China
Nepal	0-4	China
Maldive Islands	1-1	Singapore
Nepal	1-4	Singapore
North Korea	1-1	China
Nepal	0-5	North Korea
China	17-0	Maldive Islands
Singapore	1-3	North Korea
Maldive Islands	1-2	Nepal
Maldive Islands	0-7	North Korea
China	3-0	Singapore
China	10-0	Nepal
Singapore	4-2	Maldive Islands
Singapore	4-1	Nepal
China	1-0	North Korea

China (15 points) went through. North Korea (13) were second, Singapore had 7, Maldive Islands 3 and Nepal 2.

Group F (East Asia)

Hong Kong	1-1	Taiwan
Indonesia	1-2	Japan
Indonesia	2-1	Taiwan
Hong Kong	3-1	Japan
Indonesia	0-0	Hong Kong
Taiwan	0-3	Japan
Japan	2-0	Taiwan
Hong Kong	1-1	Indonesia
Japan	3-0	Hong Kong

Taiwan	3-1	Indonesia
Japan	3-1	Indonesia
Taiwan	0-1	Hong Kong

Japan (10 points) progressed. Hong Kong had 7, Indonesia 4, Taiwan 3.

Round 2

Qatar	1-0	South Korea
Kuwait	3-0	Qatar
Qatar	1-0	China
Qatar	1-0	Japan
Qatar	1-0	Bahrain
Kuwait	1-1	South Korea
South Korea	3-1	China
China	1-0	Kuwait
South Korea	1-0	Bahrain
Japan	1-1	Kuwait
Kuwait	3-0	Bahrain
Japan	6-1	Bahrain
China	2-1	Japan
China	3-0	Bahrain
South Korea	1-0	Japan

Qatar (8 points), **South Korea** (7) and **Kuwait** (6) qualified for Barcelona. China had 6, Japan 3 and Bahrain none.

Oceania

Australia	4-0	Papua New Guinea
Australia	2-0	New Zealand
New Zealand	4-0	Fiji
Australia	7-0	Fiji

Papua New Guinea	0-2	Fiji
Papua New Guinea	0-5	Australia
New Zealand	1-2	Australia
Papua New Guinea	1-3	New Zealand
Fiji	0-3	Australia
New Zealand	4-2	Papua New Guinea
Fiji	0-0	New Zealand
Fiji	1-1	Papua New Guinea

Australia went through to the play-off with a European team, after gaining 12 points. New Zealand had 7, Fiji 4, Papua New Guinea one.

Play-off (aggregate score over two legs)

Australia 3-3 Netherlands (Australia won on away goals)

22. Atlanta, 1996

Georgia on my Mind

These games were the centenary of the first modern Olympics, in Athens, and the Greek capital led the IOC voting in 1990 until Round 4, when Atlanta established itself as the front runner. Other bids came from Toronto, Melbourne, Manchester and Belgrade. Ironically, after Atlanta were awarded the 1996 Games, they scheduled semi-finals and Final football matches at the Sanford Stadium in Athens, Georgia.

The principal legacy of 1996 was the Centennial Olympic Park in Atlanta's tourist area. Opening and closing ceremonies in the Stadium featured songs such as 'Summon the heroes', 'The power of the dream', 'Reach', and the official State song, 'Georgia on my mind' – composed by Hoagy Carmichael, a native of Indiana.

197 nations took part, 79 won medals, and both were new peaks. Bobby Jones, born in Atlanta and the supreme amateur golfer, would have applauded the sporting achievements and sportsmanship of that summer.

Donovan Bailey broke the 100 metres world record in winning Canada a gold in athletics, and Carl Lewis, veteran of Los Angeles, collected his fourth long jump gold. There were rare double golds at 200 and 400 metres for Michael Johnson, another American, and Marie-Jose Perec, of France.

The football tournament

Now that the champions no longer gained automatic entry to the last 16, only the hosts took part without qualifying. These teams arrived for the tournament.

Hosts: USA
Europe: Portugal, Spain, France, Italy, Hungary
North and Central America: Mexico
South America: Argentina, Brazil
Africa: Tunisia, Ghana, Nigeria
Asia: Saudi Arabia, South Korea, Japan
Oceania: Australia.

There were no signs of nations' interest in the tournament abating, especially among countries which had previously been part of the USSR.

Five stadia in the U.S. staged tournament matches –

The RFK Stadium in Washington DC, (6 matches)
Legion Field in Birmingham, Alabama, (8 matches)
The Citrus Bowl in Orlando, Florida, (6 matches)
The Orange Bowl in Miami, Florida, (8 matches)
and the Sanford Stadium in Athens, Georgia. (4 matches)

The Washington Stadium, built in 1961, was later named after Robert F. Kennedy, while the 1926 Legion Field was named in honour of U.S. Legion war veterans.

The Florida arenas dated from 1936 and 1937. The Citrus Bowl, previously called the Orlando Stadium and the Tangerine Bowl, hosted World Cup matches in 1994. So did the Orange Bowl, which was demolished in 2008.

Athens' Sanford Stadium, built in 1928, had the largest capacity (over 85,000) and finest surface of the tournament, ideal for the four top matches it housed. (It is near the small town of Fairplay, one of two so named in Georgia).

The 1996 tournament began the present system of 3 points for a win, one point for a draw.

Group A

| 20 July | Portugal 2-0 Tunisia (1-0) | RFK Stadium, Washington DC |

A. Martins 13, 68

| 20 July | Argentina 3-1 USA (1-1) | Legion Field, Birmingham |

G. Lopez 26   Reyna 1 (31 seconds)

Crespo 55

Simeone 90

| 22 July | Portugal 1-1 Argentina (0-1) | Washington |

N. Gomes 70   Ortega 45

22 July   USA 2-0 Tunisia (1-0)   Birmingham
Kirovski 38
Maisonneuve 90

24 July   Argentina 1-1 Tunisia (1-0)   Birmingham
Ortega 5   M'Kacher 74

24 July   USA 1-1 Portugal (0-1)   Washington
Maisonneuve 75   P. Alves 33

Qualified:	Argentina	5 points	(5 goals for – 3 against)
Qualified:	Portugal	5 points	(4-2)
	USA	4 points	(4-4)
	Tunisia	1 point	(1-5)

Group A

The USA were drawn in a difficult group with Portugal, Argentina and Tunisia as they made yet another attempt to reach the quarter-finals.

Argentina had won every qualifying game, except for their draw with Brazil, en route to this stage. Portugal had played well in the European under 21 Championships but arrived in the USA as losing quarter-finalists in that competition. Tunisia had been reinstated after their defeat by Togo, who had fielded too many over-age players and were disqualified.

Portugal controlled most of the play against **Tunisia** and Alfonso Martins gave them a fine start in 13 minutes. Midway through the second half, he doubled their lead. Tunisia's left-winger, Sellimi, missed a penalty, and both sides lost a player late in the match – Bouazizi and Andrade were dismissed from the African and European teams.

Argentina were favourites to win against the **USA** in the hosts' opener, but it was Claudio Reyna who scored first for the home team. His goal, in 31 seconds, was the fastest in any Olympic match, and he had several more chances he could not convert.

Gustavo Lopez levelled the score in 26 minutes as Argentina stepped up a gear, but there were no more goals until the 55th minute. Then a new star, River Plate's Hernan Crespo, put Argentina in front and his midfield colleague, Simeone, confirmed the victory right at the end.

In the seventh minute, Ortega had to go off, and the South American coach Daniel Passarella brought on Claudio Lopez, who was to retain his place in the other matches.

A draw between **Argentina** and **Portugal** did scant justice to the former. Claudio Lopez alone had nearly as many chances to score as the whole Portuguese team, who brought on all three substitutes during, or just after, the first half. Their captain, Peixe, remained only 12 minutes on the field before being replaced, although he did return five days later for the quarter-final.

Ortega put Argentina 1-0 up just on the interval, but Nuno Gomes, one of Portugal's two strikers, equalised with 20 minutes to go. Crespo could have put Argentina two ahead from the spot, but his penalty was stopped by Nuno Herlander, who replaced the unfortunate Costinha and remained Portugal's keeper in the tournament.

In defeating **Tunisia** 2-0, **USA** put on a much improved performance and, in Kirovski and Joseph, they had the most stylish forwards on the day. Tunisia, already one down at the interval to Kirovski's opener, were handicapped by two dismissals – Chouchane, after 68 minutes, and Chrouda, after 86. In the last minute, Maisonneuve added the second US goal.

With one game left to play, Argentina and Portugal had 4 points, USA 3 and Tunisia none. If the USA beat Portugal, they would qualify for the next stage; a draw would see the Europeans progress. Argentina required a point from their third match, against Tunisia.

As it turned out, both **USA** v **Portugal** and **Argentina** v **Tunisia** ended 1-1. The Americans' skills and tactics improved with each contest, but still they were denied goals by near-misses and fine goalkeepers. Reyna took 14 of his side's 16 corners while Portugal won five, an indicator of how the hosts dominated outfield play.

But goals count, and Paulo Alves scored first for the Portuguese in 33 minutes. Reyna and his strikers did create chances, but only Maisonneuve hit the target late in this tie.

Argentina were under less pressure against **Tunisia**. After Ortega's early goal, they were in charge, without adding to that lead. Instead, M'Kacher came out of Tunisian defensive duties to equalise with 16 minutes left. His team-mate Baccouche received a red card in the 83rd minute, but they gained their first point.

The South Americans rested both strikers, C. Lopez and Crespo, in the second half, saving them for the quarter-final, which they reached by winning Group A. Portugal qualified in second place, having scored one goal fewer..

Group B

20 July	Spain	1-0	Saudi Arabia (0-0)	The Citrus Bowl, Orlando
	Oscar 80			
20 July	France	2-0	Australia (1-0)	The Orange Bowl, Miami
	Pires 11			
	Maurice 74			
22 July	France	1-1	Spain (1-0)	Orlando
	Legwinski 38		Oscar 85	
22 July	Australia	2-1	Saudi Arabia (1-1)	Miami
	Tsekenis 11		Al-Kilaiwi 37	
	Viduka 63			
24 July	Spain	3-2	Australia (1-2)	Orlando
	Raul 40, 90		Vidmar 3, 12	
	Santi 86			
24 July	France	2-1	Saudi Arabia (1-0)	Miami
	Maurice 20 (p)		A. Amin 26	
	Sibierski 49			

Qualified:	France	7 points	(5-2)
Qualified:	Spain	7 points	(5-3)
	Australia	3 points	(4-6)
	Saudi Arabia	0 points	(2-5)

Group B

Spain and France had performed impressively in the demanding European qualifiers, finishing second and third. Saudi Arabia came third of the three Asian qualifiers, while Australia, winner of the Oceanic group, had the extra task of defeating Canada.

When **Spain** met **Saudi Arabia** the most famous participant was the Italian referee, Pierluigi Collina. A single goal came from evenly matched sides who created some excellent chances, notably the Saudi striker Falatah. However, it was a late substitute for Spain, Oscar, who found the net in 80 minutes, to give them three points as they began the defence of their championship.

France, with a star-studded team, had almost all the play as they defeated **Australia** 2-0. Robert Pires gave them an early lead, and the Australians were hampered by playing a man short for 68 minutes. Tiatto received a red card, and the midfield had to be reorganised. It took France 74 minutes to secure their advantage with Maurice's goal, but when Vairelles replaced him he had three clear shots in only 10 minutes.

The match between **France** and **Spain** was dominated by defences. Legwinski put France ahead in the 38th minute, and Spain committed all their substitutes around the hour mark. This refreshed their attack, as Barcelona's striker Lardin replaced a defender. Eventually Oscar levelled the score with five minutes to go, making amends for his penalty earlier in the half, which was saved by Letizi.

On the same day, **Australia** enjoyed their best performance, against **Saudi Arabia**. Deciding to play three forwards instead of two, as they had in the earlier match, they created chances galore for Viduka and Spiteri. There was a goal in 11 minutes for Tsekenis, and the promise of more, but Al-Kilaiwi equalised near the interval. The Asian team had already replaced two players after only 26 minutes.

In the second half Mark Viduka restored Australia's lead in 63 minutes, and they took the points. The 2-1 result did not reflect their many opportunities, and Anwar Amin's penalty, which he missed, could have changed the result to a draw.

Spain and France now had gained 4 points, Australia 3, Saudi Arabia none. Both European teams would go on to the quarter-finals, unless Australia defeated Spain. A less likely scenario would arise if France lost to Saudi Arabia, and the other teams drew; then goal difference would be significant.

Spain v **Australia** turned out to be an extraordinary encounter, with bursts of goals. First, Aurelio Vidmar scored twice for Australia inside 12 minutes. Gradually, Spain regrouped, brought on their reliable striker Lardin for a defender, and made openings. After 40 minutes, Raul reduced the deficit to one. Even before that goal, Australia had replaced a striker, Spiteri, with the midfielder Tiatto.

In the second half, Vidmar made way for another midfielder, Lozanovski, so that Australia eventually reduced three specialist strikers to one, Viduka. Four minutes to go, Spain were still 2-1 behind and heading home. Then Santi, a defender, levelled the match, and Raul scored the winner with seconds to go.

The Spanish just merited their 3-2 victory, but, after leading for the whole game until the 86th minute, fans Down Under were disappointed.

France won 2-1 over **Saudi Arabia** and were the more attacking team throughout. Maurice's early penalty eased any nerves, but Anwar Amin soon equalised, and the Saudi midfielder was a problem for Bonnissel's side on several occasions. Sibierski gave France back the lead in 49 minutes, and they headed Group B.

Spain finished just behind on goal difference, while Saudi Arabia took no points while conceding only five goals.

Group C

21 July	Mexico 1-0 Italy (0-0)	Birmingham
	Palencia 83	

21 July	South Korea 1-0 Ghana (1-0)	Washington
	Jong-Hwan 41 (p)	

23 July	Mexico 0-0 South Korea	Birmingham

23 July	Ghana 3-2 Italy (1-2)	Washington
	Saba 15, 74 Branca 8, 44 (p)	
	Ahinful 63 (p)	

25 July	Mexico 1-1 Ghana (0-1)	Washington
	Abundis 65 Ebenezer 44	

25 July   Italy 2-1 South Korea (1-0)   Birmingham
            Branca 24, 82   Ki-Hyung 62

Qualified: Mexico   5 points   (2-1)
Qualified: Ghana   4 points   (4-4)
              South Korea   4 points   (2-2)
              Italy   3 points   (4-5)

Group C

Italy had already won the prize of the Under 21 tournament in their continent, while South Korea qualified as the top team in Asia. Mexico won every qualifying match in their North and Central American competition, while Ghana had a lighter task in defeating two other teams.

Ghana's meeting with **South Korea**, a rare encounter between the teams, was largely one-way traffic towards the Korean penalty area. Ghana's Ahinful and the substitute Aboagye had eight goal opportunities between them. Yet just one chance was taken, a penalty close to half-time converted by South Korea's Jong-Hwah. Ghana lost three points they deserved to win on outfield play and possession.

On the other hand, **Mexico's** slim victory over **Italy** was merited. Despite great names in the Italian team – Cannavaro, Lucarelli, Delvecchio, Mexico dominated this match. After an hour the Central Americans brought on two substitutes, and Palencia proved his value with the only goal, after 83 minutes.

Yet **Mexico** could not take three points from **South Korea** who were once again outplayed over much of the park but held firm in defence. Villa, one of the Mexican back four, even had space to make four efforts on goal, but the match ended goalless.

Italy made a fine start against **Ghana**, Branca scoring after eight minutes. Ghana pushed men into attack, and their defender Saba – then a Bayern Munich player – levelled the score. Branca had the best opportunities, and right on the interval his penalty restored Italy's lead.

The African team equalised again, through Ahinful's penalty, and Saba won the match in 74 minutes. An exciting match was marred by 10 yellow cards and the dismissal of Galante after 62 minutes, in the incident leading to Ghana's penalty.

Italy, without a point, could not now reach the quarter-finals. Mexico and South Korea had 4 points, Ghana 3, and two of those teams would progress.

Mexico v **Ghana** was a more cautious encounter than earlier matches. There were no goals for 44 minutes, but then Ebenezer put Ghana ahead. Abundis made it 1-1 in the 65th minute, soon after Ghana's substitute Baidoo was dismissed. His involvement lasted only 11 minutes.

At the final whistle, Ghana's ten men were sure they had been eliminated, but the Mexican coach Carlos de los Cobos gave them good news. The 1-1 draw saw Mexico top Group C with 5 points. Ghana's 4 points would only give them a runners-up place if South Korea lost to Italy, in a low-scoring match.

So everything depended on events in Birmingham, where **Italy** faced **South Korea**. Branca, as before, gave Italy the lead in 24 minutes, but the Korean side were always dangerous and their midfielder Lee Ki-Hyong equalised just after an hour. One point would see them through, but Branca took another chance eight minutes from time and Italy won the points 2-1. Cannavaro was sent off in the last seconds.

Both sides' tournament ended in disappointment – Italy finished fourth in the Group, South Korea went out on goal difference. Only because they scored more goals did Ghana reach the quarter-finals ahead of the Asian team.

Group D

21 July	Japan 1-0 Brazil (0-0)	Miami
	Ito 72	

21 July	Nigeria 1-0 Hungary (1-0)	Orlando
	Kanu 44	

23 July	Brazil 3-1 Hungary (1-0)	Miami
	Ronaldo 35 Madar 58	
	Juninho 61	
	Bebeto 84	

23 July		Nigeria	2-0	Japan (0-0)		Orlando
	Babangida 82					
	Okocha 90 (p)					

25 July		Brazil	1-0	Nigeria (1-0)		Miami
	Ronaldo 30					

25 July		Japan	3-2	Hungary (1-1)		Orlando
	Maezono 39, 90		Sandor 2			
	Vemura 90		Madar 48			

Qualified:	Brazil	6 points	(4-2)
Qualified:	Nigeria	6 points	(3-1)
	Japan	6 points	(4-4)
	Hungary	0 points	(3-7)

Group D

Hungary, like Portugal, qualified as losing quarter-finalists in Europe's Under 21 matches. Brazil, on the other hand, had won every qualifier except two, and appeared to be the team in form once again. Nigeria had narrow victories over Egypt and Zimbabwe, while Japan were second only to South Korea in their games.

Brazil, with their stars Roberto Carlos, Juninho, Rivaldo and Ronaldo, created chances galore against **Japan**. So the result, 1-0 to Japan, was extraordinary as they converted not one opportunity. Japan played with a single striker and Ito – one of a packed midfield of five – scored the only goal in 72 minutes. Juninho and Roberto Carlos each had more scoring chances than the whole Japanese team.

Nigeria v **Hungary** produced fewer shots on goal, but the African team were the better side. Okocha regularly came forward from his midfield role to test Safar, but Hungary's keeper defied everyone except the Nigerian captain, Kanu, who later became a familiar player in England's top flight. He scored the only goal, just before the interval.

Brazil could afford no more mistakes when they met **Hungary**.

Ronaldo started this match, after coming on as a substitute two days earlier, and in 35 minutes he scored – his first goal in a world tournament. Once again, Brazil created a host of chances, but Madar, Hungary's substitute, equalised from a rare attack after almost an hour.

This time, however, Juninho responded with a quick goal to restore Brazil's lead. Rivaldo and Ronaldo then were replaced, and their captain Bebeto at last turned his outfield play into a goal to ensure a 3-1 victory.

Nigeria and **Japan** both won their opening game 1-0. Japan were the most defensive side in Group D, and there was stalemate until eight minutes from time, when Nigeria's striker Babangida hit the net. Okocha secured the points with a penalty in the final minute.

After their two matches, Nigeria (6 points) were almost certainly in the quarter-finals, unless they lost heavily to Brazil. Both Brazil and Japan had 3 points, the Asian team with a poorer goal difference. Statistically, Hungary (no points) could still finish above both those sides, if they beat Japan and Brazil lost to Nigeria – improbable as that appeared.

Brazil and **Nigeria** saw fine attacking teams delight 55,000 spectators in Miami. Okocha was once again Nigeria's player to watch, while Conceicao made clear chances for Brazil. The day was decided by the young prodigy Ronaldo, scoring the only goal after half an hour.

The teams were to meet again, in an even more exciting match six days later.

Hungary at last found their form against **Japan** when Sandor took only two minutes to score. Japan replied, led by Jo, who should have scored before his colleague Maezono's penalty goal in 39 minutes.

The second half had a similar pattern. Madar restored Hungary's lead at the start, Japan made chances and missed them. That was until an unexpected last minute. Vemura came on as a substitute and equalised in seconds. Almost from the restart, Maezono gained possession and won it for Japan 3-2.

Brazil therefore headed the group on goal difference from Nigeria, Japan narrowly finished third, again on goal difference. Hungary, winners of three Olympic championships, could not win a point on this occasion.

Quarter-Finals

27 July　　　　　　Portugal　2-1　France (1-0)　　　　Miami

　　　　　　　　　　Capucho 7　　　Maurice 49 (p)

　　　　　　　　　　Calado 105 (p)

(after extra time: Portugal scored first during extra time, winning on the 'golden goal' rule)

27 July	Argentina 4-0 Spain (0-0)		Birmingham
	Crespo 47, 88 (p)		
	Aranzabal (o.g.) 52		
	C. Lopez 66		

28 July	Nigeria 2-0 Mexico (1-0)		Birmingham
	Okocha 20		
	C. Babayaro 84		

28 July	Brazil 4-2 Ghana (1-1)		Miami
	Duodo (o.g.) 17	Akunnor 23	
	Ronaldo 56, 62	Aboagye 53	
	Bebeto 72		

Quarter-finals

Portugal's reward for finishing second in Group A was a contest with **France**, who held off Spain to lead Group B.

Yet again the team with most of the possession lost out. France were on top from the start in the chances they created, but Portugal took the lead in seven minutes through Capucho. However, soon after, their defence was rearranged when Litos was injured and replaced by Beto.

Nuno Herlander, in goal for Portugal, kept the French forwards at bay, with saves from Florian Maurice and Robert Pires. At last, four minutes after the interval, Maurice equalised with a penalty. Portugal responded by bringing on their two other substitutes, while France made one change. Still it remained 1-1, and into extra time.

Under the 'golden goal' rule, the first goal in extra time immediately ended the match. 15 minutes into the added period the French defender, Bonnissel, conceded a penalty and was sent off. Calado stepped up to the spot and won it for Portugal.

Argentina met **Spain**, the 1992 gold medallists, with only one victory in their group matches. Spain had won two games and drawn once. This was an even contest for the first 45 minutes, as might have been expected.

The second half was a different story. Crespo quickly opened the scoring for Argentina, and five minutes later Spain's right back, Aranzabal, deflected the ball past his own keeper. Claudio Lopez clinched the victory with a third goal in 66 minutes, Crespo added the icing on the cake with a late penalty.

Raul had chances to reduce the leeway and Spain introduced two fresh players when they went 2-0 down, but the defence of their championship ended there.

Nigeria met **Mexico** in what promised to be a match for connoisseurs of stylish forward play. The African team took the lead in 20 minutes, through the elusive Okocha, and Mexico quickly brought on Arellano, as they had when they went behind to Ghana. The Central Americans kept making but not taking chances, and near the interval their left back Davino was sent off.

After half-time Blanco, a striker, came on to replace a midfield colleague – a throw of the dice from Mexico's coach, with his 10 men already a goal down. However, Nigeria won the match 2-0 with a late strike by right back Babayaro. The only drawback for his team was that Oliseh was dismissed with seconds to go, and he sat out the semi-final.

Ghana then attempted to become the second team from their continent to reach the semis. A Nigeria v Ghana tie would confirm the remarkable achievement of African football.

Brazil, especially their captain Bebeto and Ronaldo, had to be beaten first, and they took the lead in 17 minutes after an own goal by Duodo. Ghana quickly levelled through Akunnor, and it stood at 1-1 after 45 minutes.

Another surprise, in a tournament of shocks, was likely when Aboagye gave Ghana a 2-1 advantage early in the second half. But now Ronaldo proved his mettle, turning two of his many opportunities into the net. Just over an hour gone, and Brazil 3-2 up. Bebeto soon increased Brazil's lead, and Ghana's task became impossible with Saba's red card near the end.

There would be two teams from one continent in the semi-finals; the continent of South America.

Semi-Finals

30 July   Argentina 2-0 Portugal (0-0)   Sanford Stadium, Athens, Georgia

Crespo 55, 61

31 July   Nigeria 4-3 Brazil (1-3)   Athens
R. Carlos (o.g.) 20   F. Conceicao 1, 38
Ikpeba 78   Bebeto 28
Kanu 90, 94

(Nigeria won in extra time on the 'golden goal' rule.)

Semi-Finals

Portugal had excelled themselves in reaching the last four and now they met **Argentina** for the second time. Since the teams' 1-1 draw in Group A, Argentina had come into scoring form and this would be a difficult task for the Europeans.

As in the quarter-final, Portugal suffered an injury early in the match and Beto was replaced by Nuno Afonso. Argentina's forwards, especially Claudio Lopez, came close several times, with Portuguese chances falling to Calado.

The result turned on a period of six minutes early in the second half. Crespo put Argentina ahead in 55 minutes and swiftly doubled the lead. 2-0 up, they were confident enough to rest the goal-scorer and replaced him with a River Plate colleague, Gallardo.

Next day, in Athens, another 78,000 crowd anticipated an equally fine contest, and they were not disappointed. **Nigeria** v **Brazil** had hardly started when Flavio Conceicao put Brazil ahead. Time – one minute. There followed goalmouth incidents at both ends before Roberto Carlos put through his own net.

Bebeto restored Brazil's lead, Conceicao made it 3-1 for them, all within 38 minutes. After half-time Victor Ikpeba, the Monaco striker, came on, and Nigeria made more opportunities, which usually fell to Okocha.

Even so, Ronaldo was always a threat, and 12 minutes from time, Brazil were two goals ahead and within touching distance of an all South American final, the first since Uruguay v Argentina in 1928. Okocha had a gilt-edged chance to revive Nigeria, but Dida saved his penalty.

Now came Ikpeba's moment. He had never started a match in the event, always coming on as a substitute. Just outside the penalty area, he was given the ball and hit it from 20 yards into the net. 3-2 to Brazil.

Nigeria's captain, Kanu, had nothing to lose, and led a goalmouth scramble in the 90th minute to equalise. Unbelievably, the match had ended level. Extra time, with Nigerian morale soaring, and it lasted a mere four minutes. Kanu took his second chance of the game and hit home from the edge of the area.

However greatness is judged in team sports, Nigeria 4 – Brazil 3 must rank as one of the finest football matches ever seen, and not only in the Olympics.

Bronze medal match

2 August   Brazil   5-0   Portugal (2-0)   Athens

                    Ronaldo 4

             F. Conceicao 10

         Bebeto 46, 53 (p), 74

Bronze medal match

Two days on, **Brazil** had to return to the same field in Athens and put such a blow to one side. The opening 10 minutes against **Portugal** helped dispel the clouds, as Ronaldo and Conceicao gave their side a two goal lead.

Portugal also made chances, but Dida was once again superb in saving Calado's late penalty. Bebeto made the best of the game, scoring the only hat-trick of 1996 with goals in 46, 53 and 74 minutes, the second a penalty. Although his Brazilians had to be content with bronze, Jose de Oliveira, 'Bebeto', captained the top scorers and was outstanding, not least for his six goals.

The Final

3 August   Nigeria   3-2   Argentina (1-1)   Athens

           C. Babayaro 28   C. Lopez 3

            Amokachi 74   Crespo 50 (p)

            Amuneke 90

Final

If Nigeria's dramatic win over Brazil could not be surpassed, the Final promised to equal its style and tension.

Nigeria and **Argentina** produced scoring chances every two minutes on average. On show were stars such as Kanu, Okocha, Lopez and Crespo, who had nine opportunities to score.

It was Claudio Lopez who took the plaudits with his third minute goal for Argentina. Nigeria's right-back Babayaro, who had scored in the quarter-final, equalised after 28 minutes. 1-1 at the interval on a pulsating night in Georgia.

Five minutes into the second half, Crespo scored Argentina's second, a penalty. Play swept from one penalty box to the other, and in 74 minutes the match was level once more, as Amokachi took his chance. 2-2 and that 'golden goal' beckoned.

Then Amuneke, a late substitute, evaded Argentina's offside claims and ran through to score in the last seconds.

Nigeria had won, the first African team to succeed in a world football championship. Led by their coach Johannes Bonfrere, they had fulfilled the promise of their outstanding youth teams of 1985-90, and come from behind to win a brilliant semi-final and Final, against South America's best teams.

Top Scorers

6: Crespo (Argentina)
   Bebeto (Brazil)
5: Ronaldo (Brazil)

Medal Winners

Gold: Nigeria

E. Babayaro	Amuneke	Kanu (captain)
Dosu	Babangida	Ikpeba
C. Babayaro	Oruma	Amokachi
West	Fatusi	
Uche	Okocha	
Obafemi	Lawal	
Obiekwu	Oliseh	
Oparaku		

Silver: Argentina

Bossio	Almeyda	C. Lopez
Cavallero	Simeone	Crespo
Ayala	Ortega	Delgado

Chamot
Zanetti
Sensini
Pineda
Paz

Morales
Bassedas (captain)
G. Lopez
Gallardo

Bronze: Brazil

Dida	F. Conceicao	Bebeto (Captain)
Danrlei	Amaral	Savio
Ze Maria	Juninho	Luizao
Aldair	Rivaldo	Ronaldo
R. Guiaro	Narciso	
Roberto Carlos	Ze Elias	
A. Luiz	M. Paulista	

Referees

A. Da Silva (Brazil)

Portugal v Tunisia
Mexico v Ghana

L. Bouchardeau (Nigeria)

Argentina v USA
Mexico v South Korea
Japan v Hungary

O. Al Muhanna (Saudi Arabia)

Argentina v Portugal
Nigeria v Mexico

H. Dallas (GB)

USA v Tunisia
Spain v Australia
Mexico v Italy

P. Un-Prasert (Thailand)

Argentina v Tunisia
France v Spain
Nigeria v Hungary
Brazil v Ghana

E. Lennie (Australia)

USA v Portugal
South Korea v Ghana

P. Collina (Italy)

Spain v Saudi Arabia
Nigeria v Japan
Portugal v France
Nigeria v Argentina (Final)

R. Ruscio (Argentina)

France v Australia
Italy v South Korea

E. Baharmast (USA)	Australia v Saudi Arabia
	Brazil v Nigeria
	Argentina v Portugal
	(Semi-final)
A. Archundia (Mexico)	France v Saudi Arabia
	Japan v Brazil
J. Aranda (Spain)	Ghana v Italy
	Nigeria v Brazil (Semi-final)
G. El-Ghandour (Egypt)	Brazil v Hungary
	Argentina v Spain
	Brazil v Portugal
	(Bronze medal match)

Qualifying tournament

There were 15 places as the prizes, as follows:

Europe: Five
North and Central America: One or two
South America: Two
Africa: Three
Asia: Three
Oceania: One or none

The winning team from North and Central America qualified for Atlanta; the second placed team played Oceania's winner for the last qualifying place at Atlanta.

Europe

The European Under-21 championships acted as qualifiers for Atlanta. Five European teams qualified – the four semi-finalists in these championships, and the best quarter-final losers. An added complexity was that, if Scotland, England or Wales reached the semi-finals, another quarter-final team would replace them, since the home countries did not enter separate football teams in the Olympics.

Group 1

(Group winners entered the quarter-finals)

(France, Poland, Romania, Slovakia, Israel, Azerbaijan)

Slovakia	0-3	France
France	0-0	Romania
Poland	0-4	France
Azerbaijan	0-5	France
Israel	1-1	France
France	0-1	Slovakia
France	4-1	Poland
France	5-0	Azerbaijan
Romania	0-0	France
France	3-0	Israel
Israel	2-2	Poland
Poland	5-0	Azerbaijan
Romania	1-2	Poland
Poland	1-0	Israel
Poland	1-0	Slovakia
Poland	3-3	Romania
Slovakia	3-1	Poland
Azerbaijan	1-2	Poland
Israel	2-0	Slovakia
Romania	0-0	Slovakia
Slovakia	3-0	Azerbaijan
Azerbaijan	1-0	Slovakia
Slovakia	1-1	Israel
Slovakia	3-1	Romania

Romania	5-2	Azerbaijan
Israel	0-1	Romania
Azerbaijan	0-5	Romania
Romania	1-0	Israel
Azerbaijan	1-2	Israel
Israel	4-0	Azerbaijan

France won Group 1 with 21 points, ahead of Poland (17), Romania (16), Slovakia (14), Israel (12) and Azerbaijan (3).

Group 2

(Spain, Belgium, Denmark, Macedonia, Cyprus, Armenia)

Cyprus	0-6	Spain
Macedonia	0-1	Spain
Spain	1-0	Denmark
Belgium	3-3	Spain
Spain	1-1	Belgium
Armenia	0-3	Spain
Spain	4-0	Armenia
Spain	3-1	Cyprus
Denmark	5-1	Spain
Spain	4-0	Macedonia
Belgium	7-0	Armenia
Denmark	0-1	Belgium
Belgium	7-0	Macedonia
Belgium	1-0	Cyprus
Macedonia	3-0	Belgium
Belgium	2-2	Denmark

Armenia	0-3	Belgium
Cyprus	1-1	Belgium
Macedonia	5-3	Denmark
Cyprus	1-5	Denmark
Denmark	5-2	Macedonia
Denmark	4-0	Cyprus
Armenia	2-3	Denmark
Denmark	4-0	Armenia
Macedonia	1-0	Cyprus
Armenia	2-0	Macedonia
Macedonia	3-2	Armenia
Cyprus	3-2	Macedonia
Armenia	1-2	Cyprus
Cyprus	3-2	Macedonia

Spain (23 points) won Group 2 ahead of Denmark (19), Belgium (19), Macedonia (12), Cyprus (10) and Armenia (3).

Group 3

(Hungary, Sweden, Turkey, Switzerland, Iceland)

Hungary	2-1	Turkey
Sweden	0-1	Hungary
Hungary	1-0	Switzerland
Hungary	2-1	Sweden
Iceland	1-1	Hungary
Turkey	2-1	Hungary
Switzerland	2-3	Hungary
Hungary	3-1	Iceland

Iceland	0-1	Sweden
Switzerland	0-5	Sweden
Turkey	0-0	Sweden
Sweden	1-0	Iceland
Sweden	1-0	Switzerland
Sweden	6-1	Turkey
Turkey	3-0	Iceland
Turkey	1-1	Switzerland
Switzerland	0-2	Turkey
Iceland	2-3	Turkey
Switzerland	2-1	Iceland
Iceland	2-4	Sweden

Hungary (19 points) won Group 3, ahead of Sweden (16), Turkey (14), Switzerland (7) and Iceland (1).

Group 4

(Italy, Ukraine, Slovenia, Croatia, Lithuania, Estonia)

Slovenia	1-1	Italy
Estonia	1-4	Italy
Italy	2-1	Croatia
Italy	7-0	Estonia
Ukraine	2-1	Italy
Lithuania	0-2	Italy
Italy	1-0	Slovenia
Croatia	2-2	Italy
Italy	2-1	Ukraine
Italy	0-0	Lithuania

Ukraine	3-2	Lithuania
Ukraine	1-0	Slovenia
Ukraine	3-0	Estonia
Croatia	1-0	Ukraine
Estonia	2-5	Ukraine
Ukraine	1-1	Croatia
Lithuania	3-3	Ukraine
Slovenia	0-5	Ukraine
Slovenia	3-0	Lithuania
Slovenia	5-0	Estonia
Croatia	0-2	Slovenia
Lithuania	1-2	Slovenia
Estonia	1-2	Slovenia
Slovenia	4-2	Croatia
Croatia	2-0	Lithuania
Lithuania	0-1	Croatia
Croatia	1-0	Estonia
Estonia	1-2	Croatia
Estonia	0-5	Lithuania
Lithuania	3-0	Estonia

Italy (21 points) won Group 4 ahead of Ukraine (20), Slovenia (19), Croatia (17), Lithuania (8) and Estonia (none).

Group 5

(Czech Republic, Norway, Netherlands, Belarus, Malta, Luxembourg)

Czech Republic	1-0	Malta
Malta	0-1	Czech Republic

Netherlands	2-3	Czech Republic
Czech Republic	2-0	Belarus
Czech Republic	2-2	Netherlands
Luxembourg	0-7	Czech Republic
Norway	3-4	Czech Republic
Czech Republic	1-2	Norway
Czech Republic	4-0	Luxembourg
Belarus	0-3	Czech Republic

Norway	4-0	Belarus
Norway	1-0	Netherlands
Malta	2-3	Norway
Luxembourg	0-8	Norway
Norway	5-0	Luxembourg
Belarus	4-2	Norway
Norway	3-0	Malta
Netherlands	2-1	Norway

Luxembourg	0-4	Netherlands
Netherlands	3-0	Luxembourg
Netherlands	4-0	Malta
Belarus	3-1	Netherlands
Netherlands	3-0	Belarus
Malta	0-2	Netherlands

Belarus	3-0	Luxembourg
Belarus	4-0	Malta
Luxembourg	0-5	Belarus
Malta	1-1	Belarus

Malta	1-0	Luxembourg
Luxembourg	0-0	Malta

Czech Republic (23 points) won Group 5 ahead of Norway (21), Netherlands (20), Belarus (16), Malta (5) and Luxembourg (1).

Group 6

(Portugal, England, Republic of Ireland, Austria, Latvia)

England	0-0	Portugal
Latvia	0-1	Portugal
Portugal	2-0	Austria
Ireland	1-1	Portugal
Portugal	4-0	Latvia
Portugal	2-0	England
Austria	0-1	Portugal
Portugal	3-1	Ireland
Austria	1-3	England
England	1-0	Ireland
Ireland	0-2	England
Latvia	0-1	England
England	4-0	Latvia
England	2-1	Austria
Latvia	1-1	Ireland
Ireland	3-0	Austria
Austria	1-0	Ireland
Ireland	1-0	Latvia
Austria	0-0	Latvia
Latvia	0-2	Austria

Portugal (20 points) won Group 6, ahead of England (19), Ireland (8), Austria (7) and Latvia (2).

Group 7

(Germany, Bulgaria, Wales, Moldova, Georgia)

Bulgaria	1-0	Germany
Moldova	1-1	Germany
Georgia	0-2	Germany
Germany	1-0	Wales
Bulgaria	2-0	Germany
Germany	3-0	Georgia
Germany	3-1	Moldova
Wales	1-5	Germany
Germany	7-0	Bulgaria
Bulgaria	2-0	Moldova
Wales	1-1	Bulgaria
Moldova	0-0	Bulgaria
Bulgaria	3-1	Wales
Bulgaria	1-0	Georgia
Georgia	1-2	Bulgaria
Moldova	1-0	Wales
Georgia	1-2	Wales
Wales	5-1	Georgia
Wales	1-0	Moldova
Georgia	3-0	Moldova
Moldova	2-1	Georgia

Germany (19 points) won Group 7 ahead of Bulgaria (17), Wales (10), Moldova (8) and Georgia (3).

Group 8

(Scotland, Finland, Russia, Greece, San Marino)

Finland	1-0	Scotland
Scotland	2-1	Russia
Greece	1-2	Scotland
San Marino	0-1	Scotland
Scotland	3-0	Greece
Scotland	5-0	Finland
Scotland	1-0	San Marino
Russia	1-2	Scotland
Greece	3-4	Finland
Finland	4-0	San Marino
San Marino	0-6	Finland
Finland	1-0	Greece
Finland	1-1	Russia
Russia	3-0	Finland
Russia	3-0	San Marino
Greece	0-1	Russia
San Marino	0-7	Russia
Russia	0-1	Greece
Greece	4-0	San Marino
San Marino	1-3	Greece

Scotland (21 points) won Group 8 ahead of Finland (16), Russia (13), Greece (9) and San Marino (none).

Quarter-finals

Hungary	3-4	Scotland	(2-1, 1-3)
Germany	1-4	France	(0-0, 1-4)
Portugal	1-2	Italy	(1-0, 0-2)
Spain	4-2	Czech Republic	(2-1, 2-1)

France, **Italy**, and **Spain** therefore qualified for Atlanta. Since Scotland did not take their place, two more teams qualified as the best quarter-final losers, by their record in the group matches and quarter-finals.

Hungary and **Portugal** qualified for Atlanta, under this complex system.

The Under-21 championships continued, and, in Barcelona, semi-final results were:

Italy	1-0	France
Spain	2-1	Scotland

Third place match: France 1-0 Scotland
Final: Italy 1-1 Spain (after extra time: Italy won 4-2 on penalties)

North and Central America

Preliminary Round

(North and Central America zone)

Guatemala	6-2	Belize	(4-0, 2-2)

Round One

El Salvador	2-1	Guatemala	(1-0, 1-1)
Costa Rica	7-0	Bermuda	(2-0, 5-0)
Mexico	9-0	Panama	(5-0, 4-0)

Canada: Bye, and El Salvador, Costa Rica, and Mexico went through to the next Round.

Round One

(Caribbean zone – Jamaica)

Four teams each played three games against each other.

Jamaica	6-0	Saint Lucia
Jamaica	6-1	Antigua and Barbuda
Jamaica	7-0	Cayman Islands
Cayman Islands	2-1	Antigua and Barbuda
Saint Lucia	4-0	Cayman Islands
Saint Lucia	4-0	Antigua and Barbuda

Jamaica (9 points) went into the next Round, ahead of Saint Lucia (6), Cayman Islands (3), and Antigua and Barbuda (0).

Round One

(Trinidad and Tobago)

When Surinam withdrew, three teams competed, playing two matches each.

Trinidad and Tobago	5-0	Guyana
Trinidad and Tobago	2-1	St Vincent and Grenadines
St Vincent and Grenadines	2-1	Guyana

Trinidad and Tobago (6 points) progressed, ahead of St Vincent and Grenadines (3) and Guyana (0).

Final Round

(Edmonton, Canada)

Six teams each played five games.

Mexico	3-0	El Salvador
Mexico	4-0	Costa Rica
Mexico	2-0	Trinidad and Tobago
Mexico	2-1	Jamaica
Canada	0-1	Mexico
Canada	3-0	Jamaica
Canada	0-0	Trinidad
Canada	4-2	El Salvador
Canada	0-0	Costa Rica
Costa Rica	4-2	Trinidad
Costa Rica	4-1	El Salvador
Costa Rica	1-2	Jamaica
Jamaica	1-3	El Salvador
Jamaica	3-2	Trinidad
Trinidad and Tobago	2-1	El Salvador

Mexico (15 points) qualified for Atlanta.

Canada (8 points) then played the winner of the Oceania Group, Australia, over two legs – Australia won 7-2 on aggregate.

Other teams scored 7 points (Costa Rica), 6 (Jamaica), 4 (Trinidad and Tobago), 3 (El Salvador).

South America

Group A

(Tandil, Argentina)

Brazil	4-1	Peru
Brazil	3-1	Paraguay
Brazil	4-1	Bolivia
Brazil	0-0	Uruguay
Uruguay	2-0	Bolivia
Uruguay	4-2	Peru
Uruguay	3-2	Paraguay
Paraguay	4-2	Peru
Paraguay	1-4	Bolivia
Peru	2-1	Bolivia

Brazil (10 points) and Uruguay (10) progressed, ahead of Bolivia (3), Peru (3) and Paraguay (3).

Group B

(Mar del Plata, Argentina)

Argentina	6-0	Ecuador
Argentina	2-1	Chile
Argentina	3-0	Venezuela
Argentina	4-0	Colombia
Venezuela	1-0	Colombia
Venezuela	5-2	Ecuador

Venezuela	0-0	Chile
Colombia	3-3	Ecuador
Colombia	3-3	Chile
Chile	4-0	Ecuador

Argentina (12 points) and Venezuela (7) progressed, ahead of Chile (4), Colombia (2) and Ecuador (one).

Final Stage

(Mar del Plata)

Brazil	5-0	Venezuela (in Tandil)
Argentina	2-0	Uruguay
Brazil	3-1	Uruguay
Argentina	2-0	Venezuela
Uruguay	3-1	Venezuela
Argentina	2-2	Brazil

Brazil (7 points) and **Argentina** (7) qualified for Atlanta, ahead of Uruguay (3) and Venezuela (no points).

Africa

Group One

Round One

Nigeria	3-0	Kenya	(0-0, 3-0)
Zimbabwe	4-0	Malawi	(4-0, 0-0)
Egypt	2-0	Mauritius	(1-0, 1-0)
Zambia	6-1	Botswania	(2-0, 4-1)

Round Two

| Nigeria | 4-3 | Egypt | (3-2, 1-1) |
| Zimbabwe | 3-2 | Zambia | (1-1, 2-1) |

Round Three

Nigeria 2-0 Zimbabwe (1-0, 1-0)

Nigeria qualified for Atlanta.

Group Two

Preliminary Round

Burkina Faso progressed – Guinea-Bissau withdrew.

Round One

Guinea	3-1	Algeria	(1-1, 2-0)
Senegal	1-0	Morocco	(0-0, 1-0)
Togo	3-1	Mali	(2-1, 1-0)
Tunisia	4-2	Burkina Faso	(4-1, 0-1)

Round Two

Guinea 5-2 Senegal (3-2, 2-0)

Tunisia v Togo: after Togo won 3-2 on aggregate, their team was suspended for fielding too many over-23 players: Tunisia were awarded the result.

Round Three

Tunisia 5-4 Guinea (5-2, 0-2)

Tunisia qualified for Atlanta.

Group Three

Preliminary Round

Namibia	3-1	Lesotho	(0-1, 3-0)
Burundi	v	Djibouti	- Djibouti withdrew

Round One

Burundi	5-2	South Africa	(1-1, 4-1)
Cameroon	1-0	Namibia	(0-0, 1-0)
Angola	5-1	Gabon	(3-1, 2-0)
Ghana	v	Congo	- Congo withdrew after the first leg (0-0)

Round Two

Ghana	3-2	Angola	(3-1, 0-1)
Cameroon	2-1	Burundi	(0-1, 2-0)

Round Three

Ghana	3-0	Cameroon	(3-0, 0-0)

Ghana qualified for Atlanta.

Asia

Eight Groups (A-H) produced one winner each. They progressed to a Final Round in Malaysia.

Group A

China	4-0	Singapore
China	2-1	Malaysia
Singapore	2-0	Malaysia

Singapore	1-3	China
Malaysia	0-0	Singapore
Malaysia	0-2	China

China progressed with 12 points, ahead of Singapore (4) and Malaysia (1).

Group B

Japan	6-0	Taiwan
Japan	1-0	Thailand
Thailand	0-5	Japan
Thailand	7-0	Taiwan
Taiwan	1-4	Japan
Taiwan	0-5	Thailand

Japan (12 points) progressed, ahead of Thailand (6) and Taiwan (0).

Group C

South Korea	7-0	Hong Kong
South Korea	1-0	Indonesia
Indonesia	1-2	South Korea
Indonesia	1-0	Hong Kong
Hong Kong	0-5	South Korea
Hong Kong	1-4	Indonesia

South Korea (12 points) progressed ahead of Indonesia (6) and Hong Kong (10).

Group D

Oman	3-2	India
Oman	6-0	Pakistan
India	3-1	Pakistan

India	1-2	Oman
Pakistan	0-2	Oman
Pakistan	1-2	India

Oman (12 points) progressed ahead of India (6) and Pakistan (0).

Group E

Kazakhstan	3-1	Tajikistan
Kazakhstan	6-0	Kyrgyzstan
Kazakhstan	3-1	Uzbekistan
Uzbekistan	2-0	Tajikistan
Uzbekistan	1-2	Kazakhstan
Uzbekistan	2-1	Kyrgyzstan
Kyrgyzstan	1-5	Uzbekistan
Kyrgyzstan	2-2	Kazakhstan
Kyrgyzstan	5-4	Tajikistan
Tajikistan	0-3	Kazakhstan
Tajikistan	3-0	Kyrgyzstan
Tajikistan	1-1	Uzbekistan

Kazakhstan (17 points) progressed ahead of Uzbekistan (10), Kyrgyzstan (4) and Tajikistan (4).

Group F

Saudi Arabia	2-0	Syria
Saudi Arabia	0-0	Kuwait
Kuwait	0-1	Saudi Arabia
Kuwait	2-2	Syria
Syria	0-1	Kuwait
Syria	0-1	Saudi Arabia

Saudi Arabia (10 points) progressed ahead of Kuwait (4) and Syria (one).

Group G

UAE (United Arab Emirates)	2-1	Turkmenistan
UAE	1-0	Iran
Iran	1-1	UAE
Iran	4-0	Turkmenistan
Turkmenistan	2-4	Iran
Turkmenistan	1-1	UAE

UAE (8 points) progressed ahead of Iran (7) and Turkmenistan (one).

Group H

Iraq	3-2	Qatar
Iraq	1-1	Jordan
Qatar	0-0	Iraq
Qatar	4-2	Jordan
Jordan	1-2	Qatar
Jordan	0-4	Iraq

Iraq (8 points) progressed ahead of Qatar (7) and Jordan (one).

Final Round

(In Shah Alam, Malaysia)

Group A: Winner to play Group B's runners-up in the Semi-Finals.
Group B: Winner to play Group A's runners-up in the Semi-Finals.

Group A

Japan	4-1	Oman
Japan	1-0	UAE
Iraq	1-1	Japan

Iraq	3-1	UAE
Iraq	1-0	Oman
Oman	3-1	UAE

Japan (7 points) won Group A, Iraq (7 points) were second, on goal difference. Oman had 3 points, UAE none.

Group B

South Korea	1-1	Saudi Arabia
South Korea	2-1	Kazakhstan
South Korea	3-0	China
Saudi Arabia	1-1	China
Saudi Arabia	4-0	Kazakhstan
China	4-2	Kazakhstan

South Korea (7 points) progressed, with Saudi Arabia second (5); China had 4, Kazakhstan no points.

Semi-finals

Japan	2-1	Saudi Arabia
South Korea	2-1	Iraq

Third place

Saudi Arabia	1-0	Iraq

Final

South Korea	2-1	Japan

South Korea, **Japan**, and **Saudi Arabia** qualified for Atlanta.

Oceania

Final Round

Australia	9-1	Vanuatu
Australia	10-0	Fiji
Australia	7-0	Solomon Islands
Australia	0-1	New Zealand
Australia	(4-0)	Solomon I. – Australia fielded an ineligible player; match awarded to Solomon Islands
Australia	5-0	New Zealand
Australia	12-0	Vanuatu
Australia	5-0	Fiji
New Zealand	3-1	Fiji
New Zealand	1-2	Fiji
New Zealand	10-0	Vanuatu
New Zealand	5-1	Vanuatu
New Zealand	2-0	Solomon Islands
New Zealand	6-0	Solomon Islands
Solomon Islands	0-4	Fiji
Solomon Islands	2-1	Vanuatu
Solomon Islands	1-1	Vanuatu
Solomon Islands	1-1	Fiji
Fiji	4-0	Vanuatu
Fiji	0-1	Vanuatu

Australia (18 points) won the Oceania tournament, with New Zealand (18 points), next on goal difference. Fiji had 10, Solomon Islands 8, and Vanuatu 4.

Australia qualified for Atlanta by defeating Canada (runners-up from North and Central America) 7-2 over two legs (5-0, 2-2).

23. Women's football, 1996-2008

Towards a level playing field

It took a century for women's football to appear at the Olympics, in 1996. Even before the first Athens Olympics, a British Ladies' Football Club was underway in North London in 1895. A few women Olympians competed in other sports in 1900, just as men's football began in Paris.

During the First World War, women's teams based on factories were organised, including the remarkable Dick, Kerr Ladies, in Preston. Charity matches were held and Dick, Kerr v St Helen's Ladies drew a record 53,000 to Everton's Goodison Park in 1920. The FA then declared football was 'suitable' only for men and barred clubs from staging women's matches. Dick, Kerr Ladies continued to play, and win, matches at rugby grounds and overseas till 1965, but most teams folded much earlier.

In 1971, the ban was removed, and 1993 saw the FA take over running football for women and men. That is the norm today in many lands where football is the most popular team sport for women. Every continent now has its own competitions, and a World Cup started in the 1970s, unofficially, before FIFA gave its blessing. (The Scottish player Rose Reilly won the World Cup with Italy in 1983, and her achievement is recognised at Hampden Park's Hall of Fame.)

FIFA rankings show the breadth of this sport's appeal – USA, Germany, Japan and Brazil are the top four countries – and over 50 nations tried to gain a place at London 2012.

In one respect, women's football at the Olympics is a step ahead of men's, for there are no age restrictions. Media coverage does not yet equal that for men's matches, but 2012 could help change even that for the better.

1996

The debut of women's Olympic football took place at the Atlanta Games, with 8 teams:

Hosts: USA
Europe: Sweden, Denmark, Germany, Norway

South America: Brazil
Asia: China, Japan.

There were two Groups, with the winner and runners-up going directly from each Group to semi-finals.

Groups were titled E and F, overtly linking this event to the men's tournament with Groups A-D, and that continues in 2012.

Group E

| 21 July | | USA 3-0 Denmark (2-0) | Orlando, Florida |

Venturini 37
Hamm 41
Milbrett 49

| 21 July | | China 2-0 Sweden (2-0) | Miami, Florida |

Shi Guihong 31
Zhao Lihong 32

| 23 July | | USA 2-1 Sweden (1-0) | Orlando |

Venturini 15   o.g. (player uncertain)
MacMillan 62

| 23 July | | China 5-1 Denmark (4-0) | Miami |

Shi Guihong 10   L. Madsen 55
Liu Ailing 15
Sun Qingmei 29, 59
Fan Yunjie 32

| 25 July | | USA 0-0 China | Miami |

25 July		Sweden 3-1 Denmark (0-0)		Orlando
	Swedberg 62, 68		Jensen 90	
	Videkull 76			

Q:	China	7 points	7 goals for – 1 against	
Q:	USA	7 points	5-1	
	Sweden	3 points	4-5	
	Denmark	0 points	2-11	

Q: Qualified for Semi-finals.

Group E brought the hosts together with China and two Scandinavian countries, Sweden and Denmark.

The **USA** took the lead against **Denmark** when Venturini scored after 37 minutes and Mia Hamm quickly added a second. Once they were 3-0 ahead, thanks to Tiffeny Milbrett four minutes after the interval, the Americans substituted both Hamm and Milbrett.

Meanwhile, **China** were establishing a two goal advantage over **Sweden** from strikes by Shi Guihong and Zhao Lihong after the 30 minute mark. **China** next produced a more emphatic win over **Denmark**. Four up at half-time, they benefited from four players' finding the net – Sun Qingmei scored twice.

Sweden lost out to the **USA** by the odd goal in three, the American goals from Venturini and MacMillan overcoming their loss of an own goal in the second half.

Since the **USA** and **China** had full points, they could already prepare for the semi-finals, and the match between them ended goalless – a rarity in women's football.

Sweden and **Denmark** crowded four goals into the last 28 minutes, and Swedberg took the honours with a double strike.

Group F

21 July		Brazil 2-2 Norway (0-1)		Washington D.C.
	Pretinha 57, 89		Medalen 32	
			Aarones 68	

21 July	Germany 3-2 Japan (2-2)	Birmingham, Alabama
	Wiegmann 5 — Kioka 18	
	Tomei o.g. 29 — Noda 33	
	Mohr 52	

23 July	Brazil 2-0 Japan (0-0)	Birmingham
	Katia 68	
	Pretinha 78	

23 July	Norway 3-2 Germany (2-1)	Washington
	Aarones 5 — Wiegmann 32	
	Medalen 34 — Prinz 62	
	Riise 65	

25 July	Brazil 1-1 Germany (0-1)	Birmingham
	Sissi 53 — Wunderlich 4	

25 July	Norway 4-0 Japan (1-0)	Washington
	Pettersen 25, 60	
	Medalen 74	
	Tangeraas 86	

Q:	Norway	7 points	9-4
Q:	Brazil	5 points	5-3
	Germany	4 points	6-6
	Japan	0 points	2-9

Q: Qualified for Semi-finals.

Group F included Norway and Germany from Europe; Brazil; and Japan, so that four continents were represented by the eight nations.

Germany got off to a winning start against **Japan**, Wiegmann opening their account in only five minutes and Kioka equalising soon after. In an end-to-end contest, Japan's Tomei scored an own goal, but Noda levelled the score at 2-2. Germany's midfielder Mohr won the points after 52 minutes.

Brazil v **Norway** saw the Europeans go ahead in the 32nd minute through Medalen, but early in the second half Pretinha equalised. Midway through the half, Aarones put Norway back in front, only for Pretinha to make it 2-2 on the final whistle.

Brazil then found **Japan** difficult to overcome until Katia came on as a substitute. She made the breakthrough in 68 minutes, and the prolific Pretinha ensured a Brazilian victory 10 minutes later.

Germany matched **Norway** in everything but goals. Aarones opened for the Norwegians in the fifth minute, and Wiegmann levelled the game after half an hour. Almost immediately, Medalen gave Norway a 2-1 lead, and so it stood at the interval. The German substitute Prinz equalised just past the hour, only for Riise to restore Norwegian hopes yet again. Their 3-2 win was to prove decisive in Group F.

Both Brazil and Norway had 4 points, Germany 3 and Japan, already out of the reckoning, with none. To reach the semi-finals, Germany had to defeat Brazil, while Norway could not afford to lose to Japan.

Germany's Wunderlich scored the fastest goal of 1996 in four minutes, but **Brazil's** defenders then stood firm. Soon after the interval, their midfielder Sissi levelled the match, and that second draw was sufficient for the South Americans to progress.

Norway won the group with a 4-0 victory over **Japan**. Pettersen scored early and late, while Medalen and her substitute Tangeraas added two more in the second half.

Semi-finals

28 July		China	3-2	Brazil (1-0)	Athens, Georgia
	Sun Qingmei 5			Roseli 67	
	We Haiying 83, 90			Pretinha 72	

28 July		USA	2-1	Norway (0-1)	Athens, Georgia
	Akers 76 (p.)			Medalen 18	
	MacMillan 100				

China, Group E winners, took the lead with Sun Qingmei's early shot against Brazil, but this contest was always close. **Brazil** levelled after an hour, through Roseli, and Pretinha put her team in front. China's substitute, We Haiying, then turned the tide and won the match with two late goals.

Norway, top scorers in the event so far, went ahead of the **USA** in 18 minutes via Medalen's goal. With under a quarter-of-an-hour to go, Akers's penalty brought parity and extra time. Shannon MacMillan, the one US substitute, hit the winning 'golden goal' after an hour and 40 minutes.

Bronze medal match

1 August   Norway 2-0 Brazil (2-0)   Athens
           Aarones 21, 25

Norway had the consolation of bronze medals in defeating a skilful Brazilian team, before one of the largest attendances for any third place football match – 62,000.

The Final

1 August   USA 2-1 China (1-1)   Athens
           MacMillan 19   Sun Wen 32
           Milbrett 68

76,000 spectators came to watch the home team play China in Athens, part of the host city of Atlanta. The Americans made one change from the semi-final team, including MacMillan from the start, and she repaid that confidence with a 19th minute opener. Sun Wen equalised, but Tiffeny Milbrett won the gold after 68 minutes.

This inaugural Olympics for women's football was a success all round for the hosts. The US team won (a distinction their men have still to achieve) and big crowds attended – up to 44,000 in Birmingham, 46,000 in Miami and Washington, and an average 64,000 in Athens.

Top goal-scorers

4 – Aarones, Medalen (both Norway), Pretinha (Brazil)

The medal winners

Gold: USA

Scurry	Venturini	Roberts
Overbeck	Lilly	Harvey
Chastain	Akers	Parlow
Fawcett	Hamm	Wilson
MacMillan	Milbrett	
Foudy	Gabarra	

Silver: China

G. Hong	Z. Lihong	W. Haiying
W. Lipang	S. Qingxia	C. Yufeng
Y. Hongqti	L. Ailing	Z. Honglian
F. Yunjie	S. Qingmei	
X. Huilin	L. Ying	
S. Wen	S. Guihong	

Bronze: Norway

Nordby	A. Nymark Andersen	Aarones
Espeseth	Pettersen	Frustol
N. Nymark Andersen	Haugenes	Carlsen
Svensson	Medalen	Stoere
Myklebust	Sandaune	Thun
Riise	Tangeraas	Sternhoff

Referees

C. Guedes (Brazil)

G. El-Ghandour (Egypt)
B. Skogvang (Norway)

A. Archunda (Mexico)
P. Collina (Italy)
J. Garcia-Aranda (Spain)
S. Denoncourt (Canada)

USA v Denmark
Sweden v Denmark
China v Sweden
USA v Sweden
USA v China (Final)
China v Denmark
USA v China
Brazil v Norway
Germany v Japan
Brazil v Germany
USA v Norway (semi-final)

I. Jonsson (Sweden)				Brazil v Japan
						China v Brazil (semi-final)
						Norway v Brazil
						(Bronze medal match)
E. Lennie (Australia)				Norway v Germany
O. Al-Muhanna (Saudi Arabia)		Norway v Japan

2000

The second tournament, in Sydney, again included eight teams – from Europe, Germany, Sweden and Norway; from North America, the reigning champions USA; from South America, Brazil; from Asia, China; and new continents represented – Africa, with Nigeria, and the hosts, Australia.

Round One

Group E

13 September		Germany 3-0 Australia (1-0)		Canberra
			Grings 35
			Wiegmann 70
			Lingor 90

13 September		Brazil 2-0 Sweden (1-0)		Melbourne
			Pretinha 21
			Katia 70

16 September		Australia 1-1 Sweden (0-0)		Sydney
			Salisbury 57	Andersson 66 (p)

16 September		Germany 2-1 Brazil (2-0)		Canberra
			Prinz 33, 41	Raquel 72

19 September		Brazil	2-1	Australia (0-1)	Sydney
	Raquel 56			Hughes 33	
	Katia 64				

19 September		Germany	1-0	Sweden (0-0)	Melbourne
	Hingst 88				

Qualified:	Germany	9 points	(6-1)
Qualified:	Brazil	6 points	(5-3)
	Sweden	1 point	(1-4)
	Australia	1 point	(2-6)

Group E

Australia made their debut in the tournament in Group E. Germany, Brazil and Sweden had all played in 1996.

The hosts' most disappointing match was their first, when **Germany** were too strong for them. **Australia** kept the German attackers at bay until Inka Grings scored in 35 minutes; Bettina Wiegmann doubled their lead after 70 minutes, before Renate Lingor made it 3-0 in the final seconds.

At the same time, **Brazil** were being frustrated by a series of saves from **Sweden's** keeper Jonsson. Even she could not stop Pretinha's goal in 21 minutes, and Katia scored the second in the later stages. The closest Sweden came to a goal was Ljungberg's shot which hit the post.

Germany now met **Brazil**, recalling those teams' drawn match four years earlier. This time Birgit Prinz established a 2-0 lead for the Germans before half-time, hitting home a 20 yarder after 33 minutes, and converting Meinert's accurate cross eight minutes later. Brazil introduced substitutes, including Raquel, who scored in the 72nd minute.

Sweden were the better team against **Australia**, but fell behind in 57 minutes when Cheryl Salisbury headed home Black's free kick. Malin Andersson's penalty equaliser was poor recompense for the chances Sweden missed.

Both teams' tasks became even more difficult after their draw. Germany (6 points) were already sure of a semi-final place, Brazil (3 points) needed one point against Australia. Sweden (1 point) and their hosts (1) each had to win their third game.

To their credit, **Australia** went ahead after 33 minutes through Sunni Hughes, but **Brazil's** Raquel and Katia scored early in the second half to guarantee their semi-final place.

Germany's victory over **Sweden** came by a single, very late goal from Ariane Hingst, but the match was notable for the German midfielder, Steffi Jones, who controlled much of the play and helped her side win all three fixtures.

Group F

14 September	USA	2-0	Norway (2-0)	Melbourne
	Milbrett 18			
	Hamm 24			

14 September	China	3-1	Nigeria (1-0)	Canberra
	Z. Lihong 12		Nkwocha 85 (p)	
	Sun Wen 57, 83			

17 September	USA	1-1	China (1-0)	Melbourne
	Foudy 38		Sun Wen 67	

17 September	Norway	3-1	Nigeria (1-0)	Canberra
	Mellgren 22		Akide 78	
	Riise 62 (p)			
	Pettersen 90			

20 September	USA	3-1	Nigeria (2-0)	Melbourne
	Chastain 26		Akide 48	
	Lilly 35			
	MacMillan 56			

20 September   Norway 2-1 China (0-0)   Canberra
                    Pettersen 55   Sun Wen 75 (p)
                    Haugenes 78

Qualified: USA   7 points   6-2
Qualified: Norway 6 points   5-4
            China   4 points   5-4
            Nigeria 0 points   3-9

Group F

USA, the reigning gold medallists, were drawn with Atlanta's other medal winners, China and Norway, as well as Nigeria.

Against **Norway**, the **USA** were soon in command. Tiffeny Milbrett's shot in 18 minutes was saved, but she followed up to score. Six minutes later, Mia Hamm beat the offside trap to hit a fine goal – and also hit the bar before half-time.

China's win over **Nigeria** was founded on an early strike from Zhao Lihong when she chipped over the defence and collected her own pass. Sun Wen's double made it three – in 57 minutes, she controlled another chip, from Jin Yan, to score, and after 83 minutes her 20 yard free kick hit the net. Nigeria's consolation was Perpetua Nkwocha's penalty near the end.

USA v **China** was their third Olympic contest. Gao, the Chinese keeper, had a superb game, preventing American forwards from adding to Julie Foudy's goal, especially when she blocked a penalty taken by Kristine Lilly. Sun Wen levelled the match from a prodigious free kick, 30 yards out.

Nigeria lost each game 3-1, and **Norway** opened their account in 22 minutes from Dagny Mellgren. After the hour, Hege Riise made it 2-0 from the penalty spot. Although Mercy Akide reduced the lead, Marianne Pettersen ensured the points went to Norway in stoppage time.

After two games each, USA and China had 4 points, Norway 3. Any team could still reach the next stage, except for Nigeria, with no points.

Nigeria created more goal chances than **USA**, but Brandi Chastain and Lilly scored for a 2-0 interval advantage to the Americans. The first was a textbook goal – Hamm's cross found Foudy, who headed it on to Chastain – while the second was a solo effort from Lilly. Soon after half-time, Akide beat two defenders and brought Nigeria back into the match with a goal. However, Shannon MacMillan's free-kick sealed the US victory after 56 minutes.

Norway needed a victory, **China** a draw at least, to reach the semi-finals. Pettersen put the Norwegians in front in 55 minutes, a goal equalised by Sun Wen's penalty. Almost immediately, Margunn Haugenes regained the lead for Norway and their 2-1 win took them through, along with the USA.

Semi-Finals

24 September　　　　　　Norway 1-0 Germany (0-0)　Sydney
　　　　　Wunderlich 80 o.g.

24 September　　　　　　USA 1-0 Brazil (0-0)　Canberra
　　　　　Hamm 60

Germany had scored maximum points in Group E, while **Norway** had lost to the Americans in the more demanding Group F. One goal decided the match – and it was Tina Wunderlich's own goal after 80 minutes that gave Norway their victory.

The **USA** v **Brazil** semi-final produced few clear chances, although the Brazilians won a large number of corners without scoring. It was Mia Hamm's goal on the hour that won the day, as she ran on to a pass from Fair to score the decider for the USA.

Bronze medal match

28 September　　　　　Germany 2-0 Brazil (0-0)　Sydney
　　　　　Lingor 64
　　　　　Prinz 79

Germany won bronze, thanks to second half goals from Renate Lingor and Birgit Prinz.

The Final

28 September   Norway 3-2 USA (1-1)   Sydney

                  Espeseth 44   Milbrett 5, 90
            R. Gulbrandssen 78
            Mellgren 102

In their Group F match a fortnight earlier, the **USA** had defeated **Norway** with two early goals. In the Final, the US team went straight into attack, with Milbrett scoring the fastest goal of the tournament, after five minutes.

But Norway weathered the storm against the faster Americans, and Gro Espeseth equalised just before the interval. Buoyed by that strike, they began to create more attacks and even took the lead through Ragnhild Gulbrandssen in 78 minutes. With seconds left, Milbrett made it 2-2.

On to extra time, and Dagny Mellgren hit the golden goal after 12 minutes. Norway had won their first Olympic football gold, the USA had to be content with silver this time.

Top goal scorers

3: Prinz (Germany)
    Sun Wen (China)
    Milbrett (USA)

The medal winners

Gold: Norway

Nordby	S Gulbrandssen	Mellgren
Espeseth	Houland	Kringen
Riise	Jensen	Tonnessen
Bekkevold	Jorgensen	Lehn
Pettersen	Haugenes	Rapp
R. Gulbrandssen	Knudsen	

Silver: USA

Scurry	Lilly	Mullinix
Overbeck	Hamm	Pearce

Chastain	Milbrett	Serlenga
Fawcett	Parlow	Slaton
MacMillan	French	Sobrero
Foudy	Fair	Whalen

Bronze: Germany

Rottenberg	T. Wunderlich	Lingor
Stegemann	Gotte	Brandebusemeyer
Hoffmann	Gottschlich	Fitschen
Muller	Meinert	Grings
Minnert	Prinz	Grings
Jones	Weigemann	Hingst

Referees

B. Abidoye (Nigeria)	Australia v Germany
S. Hunt (USA)	Brazil v Sweden
S. Denoncourt (Canada)	Australia v Sweden
	Norway v China
	Norway v USA (Final)
M. Toro (Colombia)	Germany v Brazil
	China v Nigeria
V. Karlsen (Norway)	Brazil v Australia
W. Toms (Great Britain)	Germany v Sweden
I.E. Ju (South Korea)	USA v Norway
	USA v Nigeria
	Norway v Germany (semi-final)
	Germany v Brazil (bronze medal match)
N. Petignat (Switzerland)	USA v China
	USA v Brazil (semi-final)
T. Ogston (Australia)	Norway v Nigeria

2004

Athens in 2004 extended the participants from eight teams to ten, who came through the first ever qualifying tournament. The awkward number of ten produced three Groups, two of three teams and one of four. On the other hand, eight would now progress to quarter-finals.

The teams taking part were:

Hosts: Greece
Europe: Sweden, Germany
North and Central America: USA, Mexico
South America: Brazil
Africa: Nigeria
Asia: China, Japan
Oceania: Australia

Round One

Group E

11 August	Japan 1-0 Sweden (1-0)	Volos
	Arakawa 26	

14 August	Nigeria 1-0 Japan (0-0)	Athens
	Okolo 55	

17 August	Sweden 2-1 Nigeria (0-1)	Volos
	Marklund 67 Akide 25	
	Mostrom 73	

Qualified:	Sweden	3 points	2-2
Qualified:	Nigeria	3 points	2-2
Qualified:	Japan	3 points	1-1

Group E

Sweden's 1-0 defeat by **Japan** got the 2004 tournament underway. In a match of few scoring opportunities, Eriko Arakawa scored the decider after 26 minutes.

Japan lost that momentum against a skilful **Nigerian** side, who won by the only goal, from Vera Okolo early in the second half.

With only three matches in Group E, **Sweden** had to defeat **Nigeria** to go through to the quarter-finals. At first, the African team were in charge and Mercy Akide gave them the lead in the 25th minute, but the match turned round after an hour. Hanna Marklund equalised, and Malin Mostrom won Sweden the three points.

Sweden and Nigeria progressed, in the top two positions, and so did Japan, who performed better than China and Greece in the other groups.

Group F

11 August		Germany	8-0	China (2-0)	Patra
	Prinz 12, 21, 73, 88				
	Wunderlich 65				
	Lingor 76 (p)				
	Pohlers 82				
	Muller 90				

14 August		China	1-1	Mexico (1-1)	Patra
		J. Ting 34		Dominguez 11	

17 August		Germany	2-0	Mexico (1-0)	Athens
	Wimbersky 19				
	Prinz 79				

Qualified:	Germany	6 points	10-0
Qualified:	Mexico	1 point	1-3
Qualified:	China	1 point	1-9

Group F

This group saw the first of three one-sided results in the tournament, when **Germany** defeated **China** 8-0. Remarkably, China had almost as many shots on target, but could turn none of them into goals.

Birgit Prinz gave the German team an ideal start with two goals in 12 and 21 minutes, but there were no more for the next 44 minutes as China had their best spell of the match. In the last 25 minutes, however, Germany added six more. Pia Wunderlich made it 3-0, Prinz collected her third and fourth, and three colleagues scored one each – Renate Lingor, with a penalty, Conny Pohlers, and Martina Muller.

China restored their form against **Mexico**, although they lost an early goal to Maribel Dominguez. This time they did convert a chance, through Ji Ting in the 34th minute, as the game ended 1-1.

Germany were assured of a place in the last eight when they met **Mexico**. Yet another scorer, Petra Wimbersky, found the net as the Europeans went ahead in 19 minutes. Prinz doubled the lead, and Germany won both matches without losing a goal.

Mexico also progressed in second place, ahead of China on goal difference.

Group G

11 August   USA 3-0 Greece (2-0)   Iraklion
                   Boxx 15
                Wambach 30
                  Hamm 77

11 August   Brazil 1-0 Australia (1-0)   Thessaloniki
                  Marta 35

14 August   Australia 1-0 Greece (1-0)   Iraklion
                Garriock 27

14 August   USA 2-0 Brazil (0-0)   Thessaloniki
                  Hamm 57
                Wambach 78

17 August   Brazil 7-0 Greece (2-0)   Patra
                  Pretinha 21
                Cristiane 45, 57, 77
                   Grazielle 49
                    Marta 70
                    Alves 72

17 August   USA 1-1 Australia (1-0)   Thessaloniki
                    Lilly 23   Peters 83

Qualified: USA   7 points   6-1
Qualified: Brazil   6 points   8-2
Qualified: Australia 6 points   2-2
             Greece   0 points   0-11

Group G

This group required all the teams to play three matches in three days, and USA, Australia and Greece had to travel to Crete as well as to mainland stadia.

The **USA** began with a 3-0 win over **Greece**. In the first half-hour they were two up through Shannon Boxx and Abbey Wambach, and Mia Hamm's late goal made the points certain. Greece's keeper Giatrakis made several fine saves when a packed defence in front of her goal was breached.

Australia also played defensively, with one forward, against **Brazil**, who converted only one of many chances, taken by Marta in the 35th minute. It was sufficient to win three points.

Greece v **Australia** was a vital match for both teams, who were still playing with caution and creating few attacks. Australia's Heather Garriock scored the only goal after 27 minutes.

At the same time, **Brazil** met the **USA** in a match likely to decide who won Group G. Brazilian midfielders controlled the first half, upsetting the Americans' customary pattern of play, but when Wambach was fouled in the 57th minute, Hamm took the penalty and scored. Now it was all America, and Wambach scored a second in 78 minutes to take the points.

The third **USA** match, against **Australia**, was played at a slower tempo. Kristine Lilly gave the Americans an early lead, and it was a surprise when Joanne Peters earned Australia a point in 83 minutes.

Greece needed to win against **Brazil**, but the South Americans were 2-0 up by half-time, after goals from Pretinha and Cristiane. Cristiane's hat-trick was the highlight, but Grazielle, Marta, and Daniela Alves also contributed to a 7-0 victory.

While the USA, Brazil and Australia went ahead, Greece dropped out at this stage of their first tournament, along with China.

Quarter-finals

20 August	Germany 2-1 Nigeria (0-0)	Patra
	Jones 75 Akide 50	
	Pohlers 81	

20 August	USA 2-1 Japan (1-0)	Thessaloniki
	Lilly 43 Yamamoto 48	
	Wambach 59	

20 August	Brazil 5-0 Mexico (2-0)	Iraklion
	Cristiane 25, 49	
	Formiga 29, 54	
	Marta 60	

20 August	Sweden 2-1 Australia (2-0)	Volos
	Ljungberg 25 De Vanna 79	
	Larsson 30	

Quarter-finals

Germany won their match against **Nigeria**, who made a strong start and outpaced their opponents, taking the lead through Mercy Akide in 50 minutes. But steadily the Germans came back, and Steffi Jones equalised with 15 minutes to go, before Conny Pohlers hit the winning goal.

USA v **Japan** also ended 2-1. Kristine Lilly gave the USA a 43rd minute lead, but Emi Yamamoto equalised just after the interval. The winner came before the hour mark, as Hamm's free kick put Boxx through, and her pass gave Wambach a simple chance.

Brazil took five of their many chances to score against **Mexico**. Cristiane hit the opener in 25 minutes, Formiga scored four minutes later, and their tally was complete by the 60th minute, with goals from Cristiane again, Formiga and Marta.

Sweden's victory over **Australia** was the third quarter-final to end 2-1. Hanna Ljungberg and Sara Larsson scored in 25 and 30 minutes to give Sweden a comfortable advantage. Australia now had to attack in numbers and they put the Europeans under pressure, especially late on, when Lisa DeVanna scored in the 79th minute.

Semi-finals

23 August USA 2-1 Germany (1-0) Iraklion
Lilly 33   Bachor 90
O'Reilly 99

23 August Brazil 1-0 Sweden (0-0) Patra
Pretinha 64

In the first semi-final, the **USA** went ahead through Kristine Lilly, who had put them in front in two other matches. **Germany** had few chances to score, but Isabell Bachor found the net in the last seconds of the game. Although the Americans won the match in extra time, thanks to Heather O'Reilly, and had more shots on goal, the quality of play of both sides was probably the highest of the whole tournament.

Brazil's victory over **Sweden**, with Pretinha's the only goal, showed their ability to mop up Sweden's long ball attacks, and to create a host of chances.

Bronze medal match

26 August Germany 1-0 Sweden (1-0) Athens
Lingor 17

Renate Lingor's strike won **Germany** the bronze for the second Olympics in a row, and once more Steffi Jones was the outstanding player, preventing **Sweden's** attacks from bearing fruit.

The Final

26 August   USA 2-1 Brazil (1-0)   Athens
                  Tarpley 39   Pretinha 73
                  Wambach 112

The Final was influenced by a total of 51 fouls – and Brazilian chances not converted. The **USA** created fewer opportunities but caught **Brazil's** forwards offside several times. Lindsay Tarpley gave America a first-half lead, with Pretinha taking the match to extra time.

Before the added half-hour began, a new referee was required, as the official was affected by humidity and heat.

Abby Wambach again proved a match-winner, as the USA regained the gold.

Top goal-scorers

5: Prinz (Germany), Cristiane (Brazil)
4: Wambach (USA)

The medal winners

Gold: USA

Scurry	Boxx	Lilly
Mitts	Hucles	Fawcett
Rampone	Hamm	Markgraf
Reddick	Wagner	Wambach
Tarpley	Foudy	O'Reilly
Chastain	Parlow	Luckenbill

Silver: Brazil

Andreia	Rosana	Pretinha
Maravilha	R. Costa	Marta
Monica	Aline	Cristiane

Tania	Formiga	Roseli
Juliana	Elaine	Dayane
Daniela	Maycon	Grazielle

Bronze: Germany

Rottenberg	P. Wunderlich	Minnert
Stegemann	Wimbersky	Bachor
Garefrekes	Prinz	Fuss
Jones	Lingor	Pohlers
Gunther	Muller	Hingst
Odebrecht	Omilade	Angerer

Referees

F. Gaye (Senegal)	Japan v Sweden
	Brazil v Mexico
D. Ferreira-James (Guyana)	Nigeria v Japan
	Brazil v Sweden (semi-final)
S. de Oliveira (Brazil)	Sweden v Nigeria
	USA v Japan
	Sweden v Australia
K. Seitz (USA)	Germany v China
	Germany v Sweden (bronze medal match)
C. Ionescu (Romania)	China v Mexico
	USA v Australia
	Germany v Mexico
J. Palmquist (Sweden)	USA v Greece
	USA v Brazil
D. Damkova (Czech Republic)	Brazil v Australia
	USA v Brazil (Final)
B. D'Coth (India)	Australia v Greece
	Germany v Nigeria
C. Frai (Germany)	Brazil v Greece
K. Szokolai (Australia)	USA v Germany (semi-final)

2008

Beijing included 12 teams, who had qualified through their World Cup placing (for European sides) or success in their own continent's tournaments.

The participants were:

Hosts: China
Europe: Sweden, Germany, Norway
North and Central America: Canada, USA
South America: Brazil, Argentina
Africa: Nigeria
Asia: North Korea, Japan
Oceania: New Zealand

Round One

Group E

6 August	Canada 2-1	Argentina (1-0)	Tianjin
	Chapman 27	Manicler 85	
	Lang 72		

6 August	China 2-1	Sweden (1-1)	Tianjin
	Xu Yuan 6	Schelin 38	
	Han Duan 72		

| 9 August | Sweden 1-0 | Argentina (0-0) | Tianjin |
| | Fischer 57 | | |

| 9 August | Canada 1-1 | China (1-1) | Tianjin |
| | Sinclair 34 | Xu Yuan 36 | |

12 August	China 2-0	Argentina (0-0)	Qinhuangdao
	Han Duan 52		
	Gu Yasha 90		

| 12 August | Sweden 2-1 | Canada (1-0) | Beijing |
| | Schelin 19, 51 | Tancredi 63 | |

Qualified:	China	7 points	(5-2)
Qualified:	Sweden	6 points	(4-3)
Qualified:	Canada	4 points	(4-4)
	Argentina	0 points	(1-5)

Group E

China, Sweden, Canada and Argentina contested this group, and attendances were up to 52,000 – not only for the home team, but also to see Sweden v Canada.

Canada's opening victory over **Argentina** by 2-1 was a fair reflection of play, as the Canadians had three times as many shots on target. Candace Chapman gave them the lead in 27 minutes, with Kara Lang scoring another in the second half. With five minutes to go, Ludmila Manicler reduced the deficit for Argentina.

Later the same evening, **China** got off to a flying start with Xu Yuan's strike in six minutes. But **Sweden** came back strongly, equalising through Schelin after 38 minutes. Eventually, Han Duan won the game for China with 18 minutes left, an ideal beginning for their supporters.

Sweden now faced **Argentina**, with neither side having points on the board. The Europeans saw most of the ball and created more attacks without hitting the net before the interval. Just one goal separated these teams, as Nilla Fischer won it for Sweden early in the second half.

Canada took the lead against **China** with Christine Sinclair's goal in the 34th minute, but Xu Yuan levelled the scores two minutes later. A 1-1 draw satisfied neither side, and Canada again missed a series of good chances.

China and Canada now had 4 points, Sweden 3, Argentina none.

Against **Argentina**, **China** were in command without scoring until Han Duan's vital goal in 52 minutes. Gu Yasha sealed the points with seconds to go.

Sweden defeated **Canada**, thanks to Lotta Schelin's double in 19 and 51 minutes. Melissa Tancredi's response after an hour ensured that an even contest remained uncertain till the whistle. China and Sweden went on to the quarter-final stage – Canada also reached the last eight, as one of the best third placed teams in group matches.

Group F

6 August	Germany	0-0	Brazil	Shenyang

6 August	North Korea	1-0	Nigeria (1-0)	Shenyang

Kim Kyong-Hwa 27

9 August	Germany	1-0	Nigeria (0-0)	Shenyang

Stegemann 65

9 August	Brazil	2-1	North Korea (2-0)	Shenyang

Daniela 14 Ri Kum-Suk 90
Marta 23

12 August	Germany	1-0	North Korea (0-0)	Tianjin

Mittag 86

12 August	Brazil	3-1	Nigeria (3-1)	Beijing

Cristiane 34, 35, 45 Nkwocha 19 (p)

Qualified: Brazil   7 points   (5-2)
Qualified: Germany   7 points   (2-0)
           North Korea 3 points   (2-3)
           Nigeria   0 points   (1-5)

Group F

Brazil and **Germany** produced few chances and no goals in their first group match, though Brazil's passing skill ensured they kept possession for most of the 90 minutes. That was also a feature of all their contests.

North Korea's Kim Kyong-Hwa won the game against **Nigeria** with her goal midway through the first half, although the result could have gone to either side.

Germany v **Nigeria** was another even game, decided by one strike from the German player Kerstin Stegemann in 65 minutes. **Brazil's** Daniela and Marta put them 2-0 ahead within 23 minutes against **North Korea**, who converted only one of their chances, with Ri Kum-Suk's goal in 90 minutes.

Brazil and Germany (both 4 points) were in a strong position to progress to the next stage, while North Korea (3) also had a good chance if they won their last group match.

Both the remaining games were finely balanced, and **Germany's** Anja Mittag only secured three points from **North Korea** in the 86th minute. **Brazil** fell behind to **Nigeria** when Perpetua Nkwocha netted a penalty after 19 minutes, and it needed an outstanding hat-trick from Brazil's Cristiane between 34 and 45 minutes to win the match.

Both Brazil and Germany reached the quarter-finals, while North Korea finished just outside the top eight sides.

Group G

6 August	New Zealand 2-2	Japan (1-0)	Qinhuangdao
	Yallop 37	Miyama 72 (p)	
	Hearn 56 (p)	Sawa 86	
6 August	Norway 2-0	USA (2-0)	Qinhuangdao
	Kavrin 2		
	Wiik 4		
9 August	USA 1-0	Japan (1-0)	Qinhuangdao
	Lloyd 27		
9 August	Norway 1-0	New Zealand (1-0)	Qinhuangdao
	Wiik 8		

12 August	Japan 5-1 Norway (1-1)	Shanghai
	Kinga 31 Knutsen 27	
	Folstad 51 (o.g.)	
	Ohno 52	
	Sawa 71	
	Hara 83	

12 August	USA 4-0 New Zealand (2-0)	Shenyang
	O'Reilly 1	
	Rodriguez 43	
	Tarpley 56	
	Hucles 60	

Qualified:	USA	6 points	(5-2)
Qualified:	Norway	6 points	(4-5)
Qualified:	Japan	4 points	(7-4)
	New Zealand	1 point	(2-7)

Group G

In the opening match, **Japan** found themselves 2-0 down to **New Zealand** through goals from Kirsty Yallop, in 37 minutes, and an Amber Hearn penalty after 56 minutes. The Japanese forwards made more chances than the Kiwis but only found the net in the last 18 minutes, through Aya Miyama's spot kick and a late equaliser from Homare Sawa.

Norway took a remarkable two goal lead, within four minutes, over the **USA**, with goals from Leni Larsen Kavrin and Melissa Wiik. Though the Americans made several chances, the Norwegians held firm, to show their status as gold medallists in 2000 was well earned.

Carli Lloyd's goal after 27 minutes gave the **USA** a narrow victory over **Japan**, but it was a concern that they still did not convert more of their scoring opportunities. While 16,000 watched that contest, fewer than half stayed on to see **Norway** defeat **New Zealand** by Wiik's strike, another early goal in eight minutes.

The Norwegians, with three goals all scored before the tenth minute of their games, had 6 points, the USA 3, and Japan and New Zealand one point each. While Norway were already sure of a quarter-final place, any of the other teams could join them.

At last, the **USA** began to take their chances, scoring four against **New Zealand** without reply. Heather O'Reilly opened their account within 60 seconds, Amy Rodriguez scored another before the interval, and near the hour mark Lindsay Tarpley and Angela Hucles added two more.

Surely the most unexpected result of 2008 was **Japan's** 5-1 victory over **Norway**. There was no inkling of that in the first half, with Guro Knutsen opening for Norway and Yukari Kinga equalising. 1-1 at the interval, but a Folstad own goal (the only one of the tournament) turned the match. Shinobu Ohno immediately made it 3-1 for Japan, with late goals from Sawa and Hara completing the extraordinary total.

Japan benefited from that result to finish in the top eight and move into the next stage. The USA topped Group G just ahead of Norway.

Quarter-finals

15 August	USA 2-1 Canada (1-1)	Shanghai
	Hucles 12 Sinclair 30	
	Kai 101	

15 August	Brazil 2-1 Norway (1-0)	Tianjin
	Daniela 43 Nordby 83 (p)	
	Marta 57	

15 August	Germany 2-0 Sweden (0-0)	Shenyang
	Garefrekes 104	
	Laudehr 115	

15 August	Japan 2-0 China (1-0)	Qinhuangdao
	Sawa 15	
	Nagasato 80	

Quarter-finals

Based on shots attempted, the **USA** should have eased past **Canada** but after 90 minutes it remained 1-1. Hucles gave the Americans a lead in the 12th minute, but Christine Sinclair equalised on the half-hour. It took Natasha Kai's extra-time goal to see the USA through to the semi-finals.

Brazil also defeated **Norway** 2-1. Daniela put Brazil ahead just before the interval, with Marta doubling their lead in 57 minutes. Siri Nordby reduced the leeway with a late penalty, almost the only clear chance Norway had.

Later the same evening, **Germany** v **Sweden** was an even contest, which ended without a goal in 90 minutes. The result went to Germany, with extra-time strikes from Kerstin Garefrekes and Simone Laudehr.

China's match with **Japan** ended 2-0 to the Japanese, who scored early and late, throuth Sawa and Yuki Nagasato.

Semi-finals

18 August	Brazil 4-1 Germany (1-1)	Shanghai
	Formiga 43	Prinz 10
	Cristiane 49, 76	
	Marta 53	

18 August	USA 4-2 Japan (2-1)	Beijing
	Hucles 41, 80	Ohno 16
	Chalupny 44	Arakawa 90
	O'Reilly 70	

Brazil had already met **Germany** in their goalless Group F match, but now Birgit Prinz gave Germany the advantage in 10 minutes. Brazil levelled with Formiga's goal in the 43rd minute. The game was virtually decided within eight minutes of restarting, as Cristiane and Marta gave Brazil a 3-1 lead. Cristiane then scored her fifth goal of 2008 with 14 minutes left. Germany had created as many chances, but Brazil converted theirs.

The **USA** and **Japan** provided an exciting contest before 51,000 in Beijing, with Japan going ahead through Ohno in 16 minutes. American pressure paid off before the interval with goals from Hucles and Lori Chalupny. In the last 20 minutes O'Reilly and Hucles increased the Americans' tally to four, with a very late consolation from Eriko Arakawa completing a 4-2 score.

Bronze Medal Match

21 August   Germany 2-0 Japan (0-0)   Beijing
               Bajramaj 68, 87

In this third place match, defences were usually in control, and it required something special to break the deadlock. A new scorer, Fatmire Bajramaj, provided it, eluding her markers twice in the second half to ensure a German victory.

The Final

21 August   USA 1-0 Brazil (0-0)   Beijing
                  (after extra time)
                  Lloyd 96

Two attacking teams, USA and Brazil, could not muster a goal in 90 minutes, though Brazil forced 14 corners. As in their quarter-final, the Americans came through in extra-time as Carli Lloyd struck the essential goal.

Top Goal-scorers

5: Cristiane (Brazil)
4: Hucles (USA)

The Medal Winners

Gold: **USA**

Solo	Markgraf	Lloyd
Barnhart	Chalupny	Heath
Mitts	Tarpley	Hydes

Rampone	Boxx	Kai
Buehler	O'Reilly	Rodriguez
Cox	Wagner	Cheney

Silver: **Brazil**

Andreia	Erika	Francielle
Barbara	Rosana	Maurine
Simone	Maycon	Marta
Rosa	Daniela	Cristiane
Tania	Formiga	Pretinha
R. Costa	Ester	Fabiana

Bronze: **Germany**

Angerer	Hingst	Bajramaj
Holl	Bresonik	Garefrekes
Stegemann	Behringer	Smisek
Bartosiak	Lingor	Prinz
Peter	da Mbabi	Mittag
Krahn	Laudehr	Pohlers

Referees

C. Beck (Germany)	Canada v Argentina
	Japan v China
H. Eun-Ah (South Korea)	China v Sweden
	Brazil v Nigeria
	Brazil v Germany (semi-final)
D. Ferreira-James (Guyana)	Sweden v Argentina
	Germany v North Korea
D. Damkova (Czech Republic)	Canada v China
	USA v New Zealand
	Germany v Sweden
	USA v Brazil (Final)
N. Petignat (Switzerland)	China v Argentina
	Norway v USA
	USA v Japan (semi-final)
P. Kamnveng (Thailand)	Sweden v Canada
	USA v Japan
K. Seitz (USA)	Germany v Brazil
	Brazil v Norway

S. de Silva (Trinidad and Tobago)

N. Huijin (China)
D. Mitchell (South Africa)
J. Palmquist (Sweden)

E. Alvarez (Argentina)

North Korea v Nigeria
Japan v Norway
Brazil v North Korea
New Zealand v Japan
Germany v Nigeria
USA v Canada
Norway v New Zealand
Germany v Japan
(bronze medal match)

24. Sydney, 2000

Tropic of Capricorn

The 2000 Olympics were awarded to Sydney in 1994, ahead of Beijing – which had more support until round four of IOC voting – Manchester, Berlin, Istanbul and Brasilia.

It is claimed that 3.7 billion people watched the opening ceremony, which marked a century of women's taking part at the Olympics. The oath was taken by Rechelle Hawkes, who went on to win her third hockey gold, and six women champions carried the torch to Cathy Freeman, who lit the flame.

In swimming, Ian Thorpe, of Australia, and Inge de Bruijn, from the Netherlands, each won three golds and a silver. On the track, a record 112,000 crowd cheered on Cathy Freeman to win the 400 metres.

Thorpe was the youngest winner, Haig Prieste (born 1897) the oldest medallist present – he won bronze in 1920, for diving. A different kind of record was set by Eric Moussambani, from Equatorial Guinea: when other competitors were disqualified for false starts, he won his 100 metres freestyle heat in the slowest time at any Olympics.

Great Britain won 28 medals, including 11 golds, their best since 1920. Australia's successes featured 16 golds, fourth behind the USA, Russia, and China.

Football was staged in six stadia. Melbourne Cricket Ground, the oldest and biggest in Australia, hosted seven matches. The new Sydney Olympic Stadium could seat a few thousand more spectators than MCG, and 104,000 came to the final match. Sydney Football Stadium, Bruce Stadium in Canberra, Hindmarsh Stadium (Adelaide), and The Gabba-Brisbane Cricket Ground – all presented Olympic football.

Once again the sport was central to disseminating the Olympic experience beyond the one host city. Melbourne, Adelaide, and Brisbane each saw seven matches, Canberra five, Sydney six – all but the Final in the Football Stadium.

The 16 participants were:

Hosts: Australia
Europe: Italy, Spain, Czech Republic, Slovakia

North and Central America: Honduras, USA
South America: Chile, Brazil
Africa: Nigeria, Morocco, Cameroon, South Africa
Asia: South Korea, Kuwait, Japan

Group A

13 September	Italy 1-0	Australia (0-0)	Melbourne
	Pirlo 81		

13 September	Nigeria 3-3	Honduras (0-1)	Adelaide
	Igbinadolor 50	D Suazo 35, 76 (p)	
	Agali 78	Leon 60	
	Yakubu 90		

16 September	Nigeria 3-2	Australia (2-2)	Sydney
	Ikedia 16	Foxe 41	
	Aghahowa 22	Wehrman 44	
	Agali 64		

16 September	Italy 3-1	Honduras (3-1)	Adelaide
	Comandini 12, 22	Comandini 29 (o.g.)	
	Ambrosini 18		

19 September	Honduras 2-1	Australia (1-0)	Sydney
	D. Suazo 3, 60	Rosales 51 (o.g.)	

19 September	Italy 1-1	Nigeria (0-1)	Adelaide
	Baronio 65	Lawal 40 (p)	

Qualified: Italy   7 points   (5 goals for – 2 against)
Qualified: Nigeria   5 points   (7-6)
           Honduras 4 points   (6-7)
           Australia 0 points   (3-6)

Group A

Australia were drawn against Italy, Nigeria and Honduras in their group. Italy impressed by winning the UEFA Under-21 Championships, beating the Czech Republic in the Final.

Nigeria, the reigning gold medallists, qualified from a section which included Angola, Zimbabwe, and Uganda. In the North and Central America zone, Honduras overcame Mexico in a penalty decider, and also defeated the USA, who came to Australia in the second qualifying place.

Australia began their home tournament against **Italy** before a huge 93,000 crowd in Melbourne. The hosts, captained by Brett Emerton of Feyenoord, lined up 5-3-2, while Italy were more attacking with 3-5-2. Mark Viduka, a 1996 veteran and then with Leeds United, formed Australia's strike force with Michael Curcija.

The Italians created most opportunities but, as often in the past, found goals hard to come by: only Inter Milan's midfielder, Andrea Pirlo, found the net here with just nine minutes to go.

Nigeria started against **Honduras**, with Yakubu and Aghahowa leading their attacks, but it was the underdogs who took the initiative.

David Suazo, one of Cagliari's strikers, gave Honduras the interval lead with a goal in 35 minutes. In an end-to-end contest, Igbinadolor equalised soon after half-time, only for De Leon to restore Honduras' lead on the hour. Suazo then made it 3-1, with 14 minutes to go. However, the substitute Agali brought hope to Nigeria within two minutes, and in the final seconds Yakubu salvaged a point, in a 3-3 draw.

Italy's game against **Honduras** was all about the opening half-hour. In the 12th minute the AC Milan striker Gianni Comandini gave Italy the lead, and his club colleague Ambrosini doubled the score in 18 minutes. Comandini quickly made it 3-0, but ironically he gave Honduras a way back when he put the ball into his own net in 29 minutes.

Now Italy, with six points, were already sure of a quarter-final place.

Australia's match with **Nigeria** was key for both – the winners were likely to join Italy in the next stage. At first Nigeria made all the running as Ajax's Pius Ikedia and Julius Aghahowa opened up a two goal lead in 22 minutes. But the hosts were not out of it, and just before half-time Hayden

Foxe, one of West Ham's squad, and Kasey Wehrman scored two precious goals. 2-2, and all to play for.

This game was affected by a clash in 56 minutes which saw both captains – Brett Emerton and Chelsea's Celestine Babayaro – dismissed. Australia quickly brought on a substitute; Nigeria kept their players and adjusted better. Victor Agali made it 3-2 for the African team, and won the match with that 64th minute strike.

With one match left for the four teams, Australia (on no points) could not progress, while Nigeria (4 points) had an easier task than Honduras (one point) to join Italy in the next round.

Nigeria required a point against **Italy** and their replacement captain, Lawal, hit the net from a penalty in 40 minutes. Once again, they lost a player to a red card, as Oliseh was sent off. Six minutes later, the match was level – Lazio's midfielder Baronio hit a powerful shot that was deflected in, after hitting Okunowo, Nigeria's full-back. The 1-1 result saw both teams through.

Honduras took the honours against **Australia**, as David Suazo scored his third and fourth goals in the Group. The opener silenced Sydney's crowd in three minutes and, on the hour, he hit another. Australian attacks briefly produced an equaliser in 51 minutes from Rosales's own goal.

Italy topped Group A with 7 points, Nigeria came second on 5. Honduras (4) could well have gone further, but for that late concession to Nigeria in their opening match. Australia felt an even keener disappointment, losing all three games.

Group B

14 September   Spain 3-0 South Korea   Adelaide
(3-0)
T. Velamazan 10
Jose Mari 26
Xavi 37

14 September   Chile 4-1 Morocco (2-0) Melbourne
Zamorano 36, 45 (p), 55   Ouchla 79
Navia 72 (p)

17 September	South Korea	1-0	Morocco (0-0)	Adelaide
	Lee Chun-soo 53			

17 September	Chile	3-1	Spain (2-0)	Melbourne
	Olarra 24		Lacruz 54	
	Navia 41, 90			

20 September	South Korea	1-0	Chile (1-0)	Adelaide
	Lee Dong-gook 28			

20 September	Spain	2-0	Morocco (1-0)	Melbourne
	Jose Mari 33			
	Gabri 90			

Qualified:	Chile	6 points	(7-3)	
Qualified:	Spain	6 points	(6-3)	
	South Korea	6 points	(2-3)	
	Morocco	0 points	(1-7)	

Group B

Group B combined Spain, gold medallists in 1992, with Chile, Morocco, and South Korea. The Spanish came through a qualifying group where their strongest opponents were the Netherlands, and took third place in the UEFA Under-21 event by defeating Slovakia.

Chile qualified with Brazil from their continent; Morocco overcame Egypt, Ivory Coast and Tunisia. South Korea's challenge in their Asian section came from China and Bahrain.

In Adelaide **Spain** began in confident style with a 3-0 win over **South Korea**. Their captain, Toni Velamazan, showed them the way after 10 minutes, and Jose Mari doubled the Spanish lead in 26 minutes. Xavi's strike soon after meant there was no way back for the Korean side.

Chile, making a rare appearance in the last 16, took most of the first half to come to terms with **Morocco** and the MCG setting. But once their captain, Ivan Zamorano of Inter Milan, found his range, he went on to collect the second hat-trick of the event. His first goal came in 36 minutes, the second from a penalty just on the interval. His third hit the net in the 55th minute.

When Chile were awarded another penalty, Zamorano chose his fellow striker Navia to take it, and he was then rested, with all three substitutes coming on. Morocco's only goal came in 79 minutes from their substitute Ouchla; their task was more difficult once the defender Chbouki received a red card in only six minutes.

Morocco's next match produced a better performance but **South Korea** still won by a single goal from Lee Chun-soo. Morocco conceded their third penalty – in 53 minutes – and, though El-Jarmouni saved the kick, Lee was first to the ball and scored.

Chile v **Spain** brought together teams fresh from three goal victories, and Chile took the early lead in 24 minutes from Olarra, with Navia giving them a 2-0 advantage before half-time. Spain kept faith with their starting eleven and Lacruz, the Bilbao full-back, made it 2-1 after 54 minutes.

With no equaliser, Spain brought on Ferron, of Real Zaragoza, to replace their captain Velamazan, and an extra striker, Luque from Mallorca. All to no avail, as Navia's second goal clinched an unexpected victory for Chile in the last minute.

It seemed Chile, with 6 points, had booked a quarter-final place, while Spain or Morocco (both on 3) would join them. In theory, Morocco (no points) could finish second in the Group – but only if they beat Spain and South Korea defeated Chile.

Spain's 2-0 win over **Morocco** was just enough to see them progress. Jose Mari, AC Milan's striker, scored for Spain in 33 minutes, and their substitute Gabri added a second in the 90th minute – a goal that was essential for his side. The last few seconds saw two men sent off – El Brazi, of Morocco, and Felip, Spain's substitute keeper who was still on the bench when he received a red card.

South Korea defeated **Chile** 1-0, thanks to Lee Dong-gook's strike in 28 minutes. This was a victory against the odds – the Koreans played almost the whole match without their midfielder Lee Chun-soo, sent off after 12 minutes. Another feature was that Chile's Zamorano was rested, with Pizarro, from Udinese, taking the captaincy.

Chile won the group, Spain came second, and South Korea third, but only on goal difference, since all three had 6 points.

Group C

13 September   USA 2-2 Czech Republic (2-1)   Canberra
                     Albright 21   Jankulovski 28
                     Wolff 44   Lukas Dosek 52 (p)

13 September   Cameroon 3-2 Kuwait (1-0)   Brisbane
                     Alnoudji 37   Al-Mutairi 63
                     M'Boma 76   Mubarak 88
                     Lauren 86

16 September   Cameroon 1-1 USA (1-0)   Canberra
                     M'Boma 16 (p)   Vagenas 64 (p)

16 September   Kuwait 3-2 Czech Republic (0-1)   Brisbane
                     Al-Mutairi 56   Heinz 2
                     Saeed 64, 73   Lengyel 90

19 September   USA 3-1 Kuwait (1-0)   Melbourne
                     Califf 40   Najem 83
                     Albright 63
                     Donovan 88

19 September   Cameroon 1-1 Czech Republic (1-0)   Brisbane
                     Lauren 24   Lukas Dosek 74

Qualified: USA   5 points   (6-4)
Qualified: Cameroon   5 points   (5-4)
             Kuwait   3 points   (6-8)
             Czech Republic   2 points   (5-6)

Group C

The Group C teams were new to each other – the Czech Republic, USA, Cameroon and Kuwait.

The Czechs did not win their initial qualifying section, but reached the next stage as strong runners-up; eventually they qualified for Sydney in second place to Italy.

The USA qualified by defeating Guatemala; Cameroon beat Ghana and Guinea, while Kuwait's opponents were Saudi Arabia and Qatar.

Cameroon v **Kuwait** attracted the largest attendance in this Group – over 26,000 – to Brisbane Cricket Ground. The teams were slow to start, and the main excitement came in the last quarter of an hour. Alnoudji put Cameroon in front after 37 minutes, and Kuwait took over an hour to equalise through Al-Mutairi, who came on after the interval.

Eventually, the African pressure told and two of their stars, Patrick M'Boma, of Parma, and Arsenal's Lauren, scored in 76 and 86 minutes. Kuwait's defenders came forward at that point, and Mubarak scored a late consolation in their 3-2 defeat.

The **USA** have often struggled to win Olympic matches, but they got off to a fine start in Canberra against the **Czech Republic**, Chris Albright scoring in 21 minutes. His counterpart in left midfield, Marek Jankulovski from the Napoli squad, made it 1-1 seven minutes later. Josh Wolff restored the Americans' lead near the half-time whistle but Lukas Dosek, of Slavia Prague, levelled the game with a penalty in 52 minutes. 2-2 it finished.

The **Czech Republic** lined up 3-4-3 against **Kuwait's** 3-5-2, and their extra striker paid off early on – Hamburg's Marek Heinz scored the fastest goal of the Olympics, in two minutes. But the second half was different. Al-Mutairi equalised in the 56th minute, and within a short period Kuwait were 3-1 ahead through two goals from Saeed in 64 and 73 minutes. All-out attack by the Czechs came too late, although their right-back Lengyel scored in the last seconds.

Against the **USA**, **Cameroon** benefited from M'Boma's penalty in only 16 minutes. The Americans salvaged a point, through another penalty scored by Pete Vagenas, of LA Galaxy, in the 64th minute. Cameroon played three strikers in that match, reverting to two in the others.

Cameroon now led Group C, with 4 points; Kuwait (3), USA (2), and the Czech Republic (one) were close enough to ensure any two teams could reach the quarter-finals.

Cameroon, requiring one point at least, drew with the **Czech Republic**, scoring in 24 minutes, thanks to Lauren. The Czechs could find only a single goal, 50 minutes later, from Lukas Dosek.

USA and **Kuwait** had different targets – the Americans needed three points, Kuwait one, to progress. Danny Califf, of LA Galaxy, broke the deadlock in 40 minutes, Albright made it 2-0 after 63.

Kuwait soon introduced two substitutes, one of whom, Najem, scored with seven minutes to go. The USA won 3-1 with an even later strike by Landon Donovan, of Bayer Leverkusen.

The Americans' victory edged them ahead of Cameroon to win Group C on goal difference, while Kuwait and the Czech Republic missed out.

Group D

14 September	Brazil 3-1 Slovakia (1-1)	Brisbane
	Edu 30 — Porazik 26	
	Cisovsky 68 (o.g.)	
	Alex 90	

14 September	Japan 2-1 South Africa (1-1)	Canberra
	Takahara 45, 79 — Nomvethe 31	

17 September	South Africa 3-1 Brazil (1-1)	Brisbane
	Fortune 10 — Edu 11	
	Nomvethe 74	
	Lekoelea 90	

17 September	Japan 2-1 Slovakia (0-0)	Canberra
	H. Nakata 67 — Porazik 83	
	Inamoto 74	

20 September	Brazil 1-0 Japan (1-0)	Brisbane
	Alex 5	

20 September	Slovakia 2-1 South Africa (0-0)	Canberra
	Czinege 47 — B. McCarthy 75	
	Slahor 72	

Qualified:	Brazil	6 points	(5-4)
Qualified:	Japan	6 points	(4-3)
	South Africa	3 points	(5-5)
	Slovakia	3 points	(4-6)

Group D

Brazil were strong favourites to win Group D, which set them alongside Slovakia, South Africa and Japan.

Slovakia performed strongly as a new team in the European qualifiers, topping a section which included Portugal.

South Africa, second in their zone behind Cameroon, still qualified by defeating New Zealand, Oceania's winner, and Japan played Kazakhstan and Thailand.

Brazil found themselves one down to **Slovakia** when Porazik scored in the 26th minute. Edu, the Sao Paulo midfielder, soon levelled the match, and 1-1 it remained until 22 minutes from the end. Then Cisovsky, the Slovakian right-back, hit an own goal, and Brazil's victory was complete when their captain Alex made it 3-1 right on the final whistle.

South Africa made a good start against **Japan**, with Nomvethe's goal after 31 minutes. The Asian team had a match-winner, however, in Takahara, who scored seconds before half-time and again in 79 minutes.

The least expected result came from **Brazil's** match with **South Africa**. Quinton Fortune, one of Manchester United's centre-backs, scored for the African side in 10 minutes, but Edu immediately restored parity. Brazil's attacks did not bring the goals they merited, and instead Nomvethe, a first-half substitute, restored their lead with 16 minutes to go. Lekoelea then made it 3-1 in the last minute, throwing the Group table into uncertainty.

Japan v **Slovakia**, their first meeting, saw Japan outnumber the Europeans 5 to 4 in midfield, a tactic which paid off late in the game. Goals came from Roma's Hidetoshi Nakata and Junichi Inamoto, both midfielders, while Porazik's was only a consolation.

At this point Japan topped the Group with 6 points, and both Brazil (3) and South Africa (3) still aspired to reach the next stage. Slovakia (no points) needed considerable luck to go through.

Brazil's third match, against **Japan**, promised several goals but perhaps too much was at stake. Certainly Japan packed their midfield again, although the only goal came from the Brazilian captain, Alex, in the fifth minute. Both teams then had 6 points, with Brazil ahead on goals scored, as they headed for the quarter-finals.

At last **Slovakia** gained a victory against **South Africa** in the second half from their captain Czinege and Slahor, the striker. Benni McCarthy's goal did not change the result.

So Brazil won Group D on goal difference from Japan.

Quarter-finals

23 September USA 2-2 Japan (0-1) Adelaide

(after extra time: USA won 5-4 on penalties)
Wolff 68   Yanagisawa 30
Vagenas 90 (p)   Takahara 72

23 September Cameroon 2-1 Brazil (1-0) Brisbane

(after extra time: Cameroon won by a 'golden goal')
M'Boma 17   Ronaldinho 90
M'Bami 113

23 September Spain 1-0 Italy (0-0) Sydney

Gabri 86

23 September Chile 4-1 Nigeria (3-0) Melbourne

Contreras 17   Agali 76
Zamorano 18
Navia 42
Tello 65

Quarter-finals

In the first quarter-final the **USA** played **Japan**. After Yanagisawa gave Japan the lead after 30 minutes, there were no more goals until the three American strikers took one of their chances, with Wolff's shot in the 68th minute. Takahara quickly restored the Japanese lead, but in the last minute Vagenas scored with a penalty.

Extra-time came and without a 'golden goal' – then on to penalties. All five players scored for the USA, while everyone except Nakata hit the net for Japan, who lost 5-4 on spot-kicks. The Americans reached the semi-finals for the first time, at least since the different format of 1904.

Cameroon had impressed so far, while **Brazil** lost to South Africa. M'Boma's strike in 17 minutes showed Cameroon were not overawed, while Brazil introduced two substitutes in the 46th minute. Their opponents' problems were those of discipline. With 15 minutes left, Cameroon's captain and Real Madrid midfielder, Geremi, was sent off. Then, just as Ronaldinho equalised for Brazil in the last seconds of normal time, Nguimbat also received a red card.

Extra time set nine men against eleven, yet it was the depleted Cameroon who scored a golden goal in 113 minutes from M'Bami – still a hero to this day.

The only European contest of these Olympics, between **Spain** and **Italy**, promised flowing forward play but produced just one goal. Spain's Gabri, from Barcelona, was only on the field 16 minutes when he scored the late winner. This was the only time his captain, Velamazan, played a full 90 minutes.

Chile, after their surprise victory over Spain, now met the reigning champions, **Nigeria**. Any doubts about the South Americans' abilities did not last – Contreras, from Monaco, gave them the lead in 17 minutes, and Zamorano hit a second, almost straight from the restart. Nigeria's problems grew as Navia made it 3-0 before half-time. Even bringing on two substitutes after the much needed break did not help, as Tello completed a fourth goal for Chile.

Nigeria's left back, Agali, did score in 76 minutes, but his captain Lawal had the double disappointment of the result and his last-minute red card.

Semi-finals

26 September	Spain 3-1 USA (2-1)	Sydney
	Tamudo 16 Vagenas 42 (p)	
	Angulo 25	
	J. Mari 87	

26 September	Cameroon 2-1 Chile (0-0)	Melbourne
	M'Boma 84 Abanda 78 (o.g.)	
	Lauren 89 (p)	

Semi-finals

In **Spain's** match with the **USA**, which drew 39,000 to Sydney, each side had a player booked before the 10th minute. Spain began to take control, and their striker Tamudo, from Valencia's squad, and Barcelona's midfielder Angulo scored in 16 and 25 minutes.

Before half-time the Americans fielded two substitutes, Donovan and Victorine, and quickly Vagenas brought them back into the game with his third penalty of the tournament.

Only 2-1 ahead, Spain could not find a decisive goal and themselves replaced two players in 76 minutes. At last Jose Mari scored with three minutes to go, and was immediately substituted as the US challenge faded. The Spanish could now prepare for their chance to repeat 1992's gold medals.

Cameroon v **Chile**, before 64,000 in Melbourne, seemed likely to be a close contest, and so it proved. There were no goals, despite chances at both ends, until Chilean pressure forced a mistake by Abanda and his own goal in the 78th minute. Neither side would give up, and M'Boma equalised six minutes later.

Extra time looked certain until Cameroon were awarded a penalty with a minute to go, and Lauren made no mistake. In a frenetic last few seconds, Suffo replaced his captain, Eto'o, and N'Gom Kome received a yellow card.

Bronze medal match

29 September   Chile 2-0 USA (0-0)   Sydney
              Zamorano 69 (p), 84

The Bronze medal match

Third place matches have sometimes attracted small audiences, but 26,000 saw **Chile** defeat **USA** with two second-half goals. There was no lack of effort from these teams, as seven yellow cards were dispensed. Zamorano was the match-winner, with a penalty in 69 minutes and a second strike six minutes from the end. The medals won by Chile were, in large part, due to his goals and his captaincy during the whole event.

The Final

30 September   Cameroon 2-2 Spain (0-2)   Sydney

(after extra time. Cameroon won 5-3 on penalties).
Amaya 53 (o.g.)   Xavi 2
Eto'o 58   Gabri 45

The Final

An enormous crowd of 104,000 flocked to see Spain play **Cameroon**, and **Spain** quickly imposed themselves on the Final. Xavi's powerful free-kick put them ahead in two minutes, and Angulo soon stepped up to take a penalty. But Cameroon's Kameni dived to stop a disastrous beginning for his team.

Spain's captain had to go off after just 27 minutes, but his replacement Gabri sent the team in at half-time with a second goal in 45 minutes. Yet the match had a long way to go, and Cameroon, including a substitute defender in N'Gom Kome, pushed into the Spanish penalty area – Amaya's own goal, after 53 minutes, was an early reward. Cameroon's captain Geremi was back after missing the semi-final, so that Eto'o could concentrate on scoring goals after taking the captaincy against Chile. That freedom helped him in the second half, when he hit the equaliser in 58 minutes.

In a mirror image of Cameroon's discipline problems against Brazil, Spain now lost two players – Gabri, to a red card, and Jose Mari, to a second yellow, for diving, in the final minute.

In extra time, Spain held out with nine men to Cameroon's eleven. Eto'o's disallowed goal after two hours was called offside, though he seemed to collect the ball in his own half.

Penalties now decided the championships. M'Boma scored the first, and everyone scored, except Amaya for Spain, who hit the post. Another extraordinary finale had produced another African gold.

Top goal-scorers

6: Zamorano (Chile)
4: D. Suazo (Honduras)

The medal winners

Gold (Cameroon)

Kameni	Lauren	Meyong
Bekono	Alnoudji	Beaud
Nguimbat	Wome	Suffo
Mimpo	Eto'o	
Abanda	M'Boma	
Branco	Kome	
Geremi (captain)	Epalle	
M'Bami		

Silver (Spain)

Aranzubia	Albelda	Unai
Felip	Xavi	Albeida
Lacruz	Angulo	Ismael
Marchena	Tamudo	Luque
Amaya	Jose Mari	Capdevila
Puyol	Ferron	Garcia
Toni Velamazan (captain)		Gabri

Bronze (Chile)

N. Tapia	Tello	Rojas
di Gregorio	Maldonado	Nunez
Alvarez	Pizarro	Gonzalez
Contreras	Ormazabal	Henriquez
Reyes	Navia	Ibarra
Olarra	Zamorano (captain)	Arrue
H. Tapia		

Referees

L. Michel (Slovakia)

P. Prendergast (Jamaica)
L. Jun (China)

Nigeria v Honduras
South Korea v Chile
Italy v Australia
Italy v Honduras
Spain v Morocco

C. Simon (Brazil)	Nigeria v Australia
	USA v Czech Republic
	Spain v Italy
F. Ramos (Mexico)	Italy v Nigeria
	Spain v South Korea
	Cameroon v Spain (Final)
M. Daami (Tunisia)	Honduras v Australia
	Kuwait v Czech Republic
	Spain v USA (Semi-final)
S. Mane (Kuwait)	Chile v Morocco
	Chile v Nigeria
H. Fandel (Germany)	South Korea v Morocco
	USA v Kuwait
	Cameroon v Brazil
F. Tangawarima (Zimbabwe)	Chile v Spain
	USA v Japan
B. Grimshaw (New Zealand)	Cameroon v Kuwait
	South Africa v Brazil
M. Sanchez Yanten (Chile)	USA v Cameroon
	Slovakia v South Africa
S. Micallef (Australia)	Czech Republic v Cameroon
	Brazil v Slovakia
	Chile v USA
	(Bronze medal match)
S. Bre (France)	Japan v South Africa
	Brazil v Japan
	Cameroon v Chile
	(Semi-final)
F. N'Doye (Senegal)	Japan v Slovakia

The qualifying tournament

16 teams would participate in the 2000 tournament.

Hosts: Australia
Europe: four teams
North and Central America: two teams
South America: two teams
Africa: three teams or four
Asia: three teams
Oceania: one or none, depending on the Oceania v Africa play-off.

Europe

(The UEFA Under-21 Championship):

Round 1

Group 1

Belarus	0-2	Denmark
Wales	1-2	Italy
Denmark	2-2	Wales
Italy	1-0	Switzerland
Switzerland	2-0	Denmark
Wales	0-0	Belarus
Denmark	1-2	Italy
Switzerland	1-0	Wales
Italy	4-1	Belarus
Denmark	2-0	Belarus
Italy	6-2	Wales
Wales	1-2	Denmark
Switzerland	0-0	Italy
Belarus	1-0	Switzerland
Belarus	1-0	Wales
Denmark	1-3	Switzerland
Switzerland	2-1	Belarus
Italy	3-1	Denmark
Belarus	1-2	Italy
Wales	0-0	Switzerland

Italy (22 points) progressed. Switzerland (14) were second, with Denmark on 10, Belarus 7, and Wales 3.

Group 2

Georgia	0-1	Albania
Norway	2-0	Latvia
Greece	2-2	Slovenia
Latvia	1-2	Georgia
Slovenia	1-3	Norway
Greece	3-2	Georgia
Norway	4-1	Albania
Slovenia	0-1	Latvia
Albania	0-5	Greece
Greece	2-1	Norway
Georgia	0-0	Slovenia
Latvia	0-2	Greece
Latvia	0-0	Albania
Georgia	0-3	Norway
Norway	0-0	Georgia
Albania	1-2	Norway
Georgia	1-1	Greece
Latvia	1-1	Slovenia
Greece	6-0	Latvia
Albania	1-1	Slovenia
Slovenia	3-1	Albania
Norway	2-1	Greece
Albania	1-1	Latvia
Slovenia	2-2	Georgia
Georgia	4-2	Latvia

Norway	3-0	Slovenia
Greece	5-2	Albania
Albania	0-0	Georgia
Latvia	2-1	Norway
Slovenia	0-5	Greece

Greece (23 points) won Group 2, ahead of Norway (22), Georgia (11), Latvia (9), Slovenia (8), Albania (7).

Group 3

Finland	1-0	Moldova
Turkey	2-0	Northern Ireland
Turkey	2-0	Germany
N. Ireland	1-1	Finland
Moldova	0-2	Germany

Turkey	1-1	Finland
N. Ireland	1-1	Moldova
N. Ireland	1-0	Germany
Turkey	2-0	Moldova
Germany	2-0	Finland

Moldova	0-0	N. Ireland
Germany	2-0	Moldova
Finland	0-0	Turkey
Moldova	1-1	Finland
Finland	3-1	Germany

N. Ireland	1-2	Turkey
Germany	1-0	N. Ireland
Moldova	1-1	Turkey
Finland	2-1	N. Ireland
Germany	1-1	Turkey

Turkey won the group (16 points) from Germany (13), Finland (13), Northern Ireland (6) and Moldova (4).

Group 4

Ukraine	1-0	Russia
Iceland	0-2	France
Armenia	3-1	Iceland
Russia	2-1	France
Iceland	8-0	Armenia

Iceland	1-2	Russia
France	4-0	Ukraine
Armenia	0-2	Russia
Ukraine	5-1	Iceland
France	3-1	Armenia

France	2-0	Russia
Iceland	2-0	Armenia
Armenia	1-1	Ukraine
Russia	3-0	Iceland
Ukraine	0-0	France

Russia	6-0	Armenia
Iceland	4-1	Ukraine
Armenia	1-4	France
Russia	2-0	Ukraine
France	2-0	Iceland

France won the group with 19 points, Russia (18 points) were second, Ukraine had 11, Iceland 6 and Armenia 4.

Group 5

Sweden	0-2	England
Bulgaria	2-2	Poland
Poland	5-0	Luxembourg
England	1-0	Bulgaria
Bulgaria	2-1	Sweden
Luxembourg	0-5	England
England	5-0	Poland
Sweden	3-0	Luxembourg
Luxembourg	0-3	Bulgaria
Poland	2-0	Sweden
England	3-0	Sweden
Poland	3-3	Bulgaria
Bulgaria	0-1	England
Luxembourg	0-4	Poland
England	5-0	Luxembourg

Sweden	1-4	Bulgaria
Luxembourg	0-1	Sweden
Poland	3-1	England
Sweden	1-2	Poland
Bulgaria	3-0	Luxembourg

England headed the group on 21 points, Poland had 17, Bulgaria 14, Sweden 6 and Luxembourg no points.

Group 6

Austria	0-1	Israel
Cyprus	1-3	Spain
Cyprus	2-1	Austria
Netherlands	3-0	Israel
Israel	0-4	Spain
Netherlands	3-2	Austria
Cyprus	0-3	Netherlands
Spain	4-0	Austria
Israel	1-1	Cyprus
Netherlands	0-1	Spain
Austria	0-1	Netherlands
Spain	4-1	Netherlands
Israel	2-1	Austria
Netherlands	5-1	Cyprus
Austria	1-2	Spain

Cyprus	1-1	Israel
Israel	0-1	Netherlands
Spain	1-1	Cyprus
Austria	3-0	Cyprus
Spain	2-1	Israel

Spain were top of the group (22 points), Netherlands had 18, Israel 8, Cyprus 6, and Austria 3.

Group 7

Slovakia	2-1	Azerbaijan
Hungary	0-3	Portugal
Azerbaijan	2-1	Hungary
Portugal	1-1	Romania
Slovakia	1-0	Portugal
Hungary	1-2	Romania
Portugal	5-0	Azerbaijan
Romania	0-1	Slovakia
Azerbaijan	0-2	Romania
Slovakia	4-1	Hungary
Portugal	1-1	Slovakia
Romania	2-1	Hungary
Hungary	3-0	Slovakia
Romania	1-1	Azerbaijan
Azerbaijan	0-2	Portugal

Slovakia	0-0	Romania
Hungary	4-1	Azerbaijan
Romania	2-3	Portugal
Azerbaijan	0-3	Slovakia
Portugal	2-1	Hungary

Slovakia won the group with 17 points, ahead of Portugal (also on 17) on results between the two teams. Romania came third (12), with Hungary on 6, Azerbaijan 4.

Group 8

Ireland	2-2	Croatia
Macedonia	1-0	Malta
Malta	0-3	Croatia
Ireland	2-1	Malta
Croatia	4-0	Macedonia
Malta	5-1	Macedonia
Yugoslavia	1-1	Ireland
Malta	1-5	Yugoslavia
Macedonia	0-2	Croatia
Ireland	3-0	Macedonia (0-0 on the day, but Macedonia fielded an ineligible player, and the result was changed by UEFA rules)
Yugoslavia	7-0	Malta
Croatia	1-0	Malta
Ireland	0-2	Yugoslavia
Croatia	5-1	Ireland
Yugoslavia	2-0	Macedonia

Macedonia	0-8	Yugoslavia
Malta	1-3	Ireland
Croatia	2-2	Yugoslavia
Macedonia	0-1	Ireland
Yugoslavia	2-6	Croatia

Croatia (20 points) won the group, Yugoslavia had 17 points, Ireland 14, Malta 3, Macedonia 3.

Group 9

Lithuania	0-0	Scotland
Bosnia-Herzegovina	3-2	Estonia
Belgium	0-2	Czech Republic
Lithuania	0-1	Belgium
Bosnia-Herzegovina	0-0	Czech Republic

Scotland	2-0	Estonia
Lithuania	4-0	Bosnia-Herzegovina
Czech Republic	3-0	Estonia
Belgium	2-0	Scotland
Scotland	2-2	Belgium

Czech Republic	1-0	Lithuania
Lithuania	4-1	Estonia
Scotland	0-1	Czech Republic
Belgium	4-0	Bosnia-Herzegovina
Bosnia-Herzegovina	1-2	Lithuania

Estonia	0-3	Czech Republic
Czech Republic	3-2	Scotland
Estonia	0-2	Lithuania
Estonia	1-7	Belgium
Belgium	5-0	Estonia

Lithuania	0-2	Czech Republic
Bosnia-Herzegovina	2-5	Scotland
Belgium	3-0	Lithuania
Czech Republic	1-0	Bosnia-Herzegovina
Estonia	0-4	Scotland

Bosnia-Herzegovina	3-4	Belgium
Scotland	2-0	Bosnia-Herzegovina
Czech Republic	1-3	Belgium
Estonia	0-2	Bosnia-Herzegovina
Scotland	1-2	Lithuania

Belgium's 25 points won the group from the Czech Republic (on 25) on away goals in the matches betwen the two teams: Lithuania had 16, Scotland 14, Bosnia-Herzegovina 7, Estonia no points.

Round 2

16 teams – 9 group winners and the best 7 runners-up, based on their results against teams in their group who finished top, third and fourth.

Group winners: Italy, Greece, Turkey, France, England, Spain, Slovakia, Croatia, Belgium.

Runners-up: Czech Republic, Netherlands, Russia, Yugoslavia, Portugal, Poland, Norway.

(Aggregate scores over 2 legs)

Croatia	3-2	Portugal
Czech Republic	3-1	Greece
Turkey	2-2	Poland

Netherlands	4-2	Belgium
Spain	7-1	Norway
England	3-0	Yugoslavia
Slovakia	4-1	Russia
Italy	3-2	France

Round 3

Group A

Spain	1-1	Czech Republic
Netherlands	2-1	Croatia
Spain	0-0	Croatia
Czech Republic	3-1	Netherlands
Spain	1-0	Netherlands
Czech Republic	4-3	Croatia

Czech Republic (7 points) progressed to the Final of the UEFA tournament. Spain (5) reached the third place match. The Netherlands had 3 points, Croatia one.

Group B

Italy	2-0	England
Slovakia	2-1	Turkey
Italy	1-1	Slovakia
England	6-0	Turkey
Italy	3-1	Turkey
Slovakia	2-0	England

Italy (7 points) reached the UEFA Final. Slovakia (7) were second on goal difference and played in the third place match. England had 3 points, Turkey no points.

Spain   1-0   Slovakia (Third place match)
Italy   2-1   Czech Republic (Final)

Those four teams reached the Sydney tournament.

North and Central America

Preliminary round

(aggregate scores over two legs)

Panama   3-2   El Salvador
Honduras   10-2   Nicaragua
Guatemala   9-2   Belize

Caribbean: Preliminary round 1

Trinidad and Tobago   9-1   St Vincent/Grenadines
Domenica   1-3   St Kitts and Nevis
Dutch Antilles   13-1   Aruba
Cuba   walk-over   Bahamas
Dominican Republic   3-3   Haiti (Dominican Republic won on away goals)
Barbados   5-3   St Lucia
Guyana   8-4   Surinam

Jamaica – bye

Preliminary round 2

Jamaica   5-2   St Kitts and Nevis
Cuba   8-0   Dominican Republic
Dutch Antilles   1-1   Guyana (Dutch Antilles won on away goals rule)
Trinidad and Tobago 6-3   Barbados

Jamaica progressed to Group B, Cuba to Group C, with Dutch Antilles and Trinidad and Tobago in Group A.

Group A

(matches played in Trinidad)

Canada	0-0	Guatemala
Trinidad and Tobago	6-0	Dutch Antilles
Canada	1-0	Dutch Antilles
Trinidad and Tobago	0-0	Guatemala
Guatemala	9-1	Dutch Antilles
Canada	2-0	Trinidad and Tobago

Canada progressed to Group D with 7 points, Guatemala into Group E with 5. Trinidad and Tobago had 4, Dutch Antilles none.

Group B

(in Mexico)

Mexico	2-2	Honduras
Mexico	5-0	Jamaica
Mexico	5-1	Costa Rica
Honduras	1-1	Costa Rica
Honduras	2-0	Jamaica
Costa Rica	2-1	Jamaica

Mexico went through to Group E on 7 points, Honduras to Group D with 5. Costa Rica came third on 4, Jamaica had none.

Group C

(in Panama)

Panama	1-0	Bermuda

Panama	1-1	Cuba
Cuba	0-0	Bermuda

Panama joined Group E (with 4 points). Cuba had 2, Bermuda one.

Final round

(held in USA. USA had a bye to this round)

Group D

USA	3-0	Honduras
Honduras	2-0	Canada
USA	0-0	Canada

USA had 4 points, Honduras 3, and Canada one.
USA and Honduras progressed.

Group E

Guatemala	2-1	Panama
Guatemala	1-1	Mexico
Mexico	3-0	Panama

Mexico had 4 points, Guatemala 4, Panama no points.

Mexico and Guatemala progressed.

Semi-finals

USA	4-0	Guatemala
Honduras	0-0	Mexico

(Honduras won 5-4 on penalties)

USA and **Honduras** qualified for the Sydney tournament.

North and Central America:

Third place: Mexico   5-0   Guatemala

Final: Honduras   2-1   USA

South America
(matches played in Brazil)

Round 1

Group A

Brazil	1-1	Chile
Brazil	2-0	Ecuador
Brazil	3-0	Venezuela
Brazil	9-0	Colombia
Chile	2-1	Ecuador
Chile	3-0	Venezuela
Colombia	5-1	Chile
Colombia	4-2	Ecuador
Colombia	1-1	Venezuela
Venezuela	4-2	Ecuador

Brazil (10 points) progressed, as did Chile (7), on goal difference from Colombia. Venezuela had 4 points, Ecuador none.

Group B

Uruguay	2-0	Peru
Uruguay	2-1	Bolivia
Uruguay	1-0	Paraguay
Uruguay	2-1	Argentina

Argentina	3-1	Paraguay
Argentina	1-1	Peru
Argentina	2-0	Bolivia
Peru	4-3	Paraguay
Peru	5-2	Bolivia
Paraguay	3-1	Bolivia

Uruguay (12 points) progressed, as well as Argentina (7) on goal difference from Peru (7). Paraguay had 3 points, Bolivia none.

Final Round

Brazil	4-2	Argentina
Brazil	3-1	Chile
Brazil	2-2	Uruguay
Chile	4-1	Uruguay
Chile	1-0	Argentina
Argentina	3-0	Uruguay

Brazil (7 points) and **Chile** (6) qualified for Sydney. Argentina had 3 points, Uruguay one.

Africa

(matches' scores are aggregates over two legs)

Preliminary round

Mauritius	6-0	Seychelles
Tanzania	2-1	Kenya
Uganda	2-1	Sudan
Botswana	5-2	Swaziland
Namibia	3-3	Mozambique

(Namibia won on away goals)

Congo-Brazzaville	2-1	Equatorial Guinea
Gabon	walk-over	Sierra Leone
Mali	walk-over	Guinea-Bissau
Congo-Kinshasa	walk-over	Libya

Round 1

Group 1

Uganda	2-2	Zambia
(Uganda won on away goals)		
Nigeria	6-3	Namibia
Angola	8-2	Botswana
Zimbabwe	4-1	Mauritius
		(who withdrew after the first leg)

Group 2

Cameroon	5-0	Congo-Brazzaville
Guinea	5-1	Gabon
Ghana	4-2	Tanzania
South Africa	3-2	Togo

Group 3

Ivory Coast	4-2	Algeria
Tunisia	3-2	Senegal
Egypt	4-2	Mali
Morocco	1-2	Congo-Kinshasa
		(who withdrew after the first leg)

Round 2

Group 1

Nigeria	2-0	Angola

Zimbabwe	2-1	Nigeria
Nigeria	1-0	Uganda
Uganda	2-3	Nigeria
Angola	3-1	Nigeria
Nigeria	4-0	Zimbabwe
Angola	3-1	Uganda
Zimbabwe	3-2	Angola
Angola	4-2	Zimbabwe
Uganda	0-1	Angola
Uganda	0-3	Zimbabwe
Zimbabwe	1-0	Uganda

Nigeria won on goal difference from Angola and Zimbabwe – all three had 12 points – while Uganda had no points. Nigeria qualified for Sydney.

Group 2

| Guinea | 0-3 | Cameroon |
| Cameroon | 2-1 | Ghana |

(This match followed an earlier fixture between the teams, abandoned because of visibility problems)

South Africa	2-0	Cameroon
Cameroon	2-0	South Africa
Cameroon	2-1	Guinea
Ghana	0-3	Cameroon
Ghana	2-2	South Africa
South Africa	3-1	Guinea
South Africa	1-0	Ghana
Guinea	1-4	South Africa
Ghana	2-0	Guinea
Guinea	1-2	Ghana

Cameroon (15 points) qualified for Sydney.
South Africa (13) were the best runners-up in the African groups and went on to play Oceania's winner, New Zealand, for a place in Sydney.
 Ghana had 7 points, Guinea none.

Group 3

Morocco	1-0	Egypt
Ivory Coast	4-1	Morocco
Tunisia	2-4	Morocco
Morocco	2-0	Tunisia
Egypt	1-1	Morocco
Morocco	2-1	Ivory Coast
Egypt	2-1	Tunisia
Ivory Coast	3-3	Egypt
Egypt	2-1	Ivory Coast
Tunisia	0-3	Egypt
Tunisia	1-1	Ivory Coast
Ivory Coast	3-1	Tunisia

Morocco (13 points) qualified for Sydney, ahead of Egypt (11), Ivory Coast (8), and Tunisia (one).

Asia

Round 1

Group 1

Qatar	3-0	Yemen
UAE	6-1	Yemen
UAE	0-1	Qatar
Qatar	3-1	Yemen
UAE	0-5	Yemen
Qatar	2-2	UAE

Qatar went on to Round 2.

Group 2

Oman	2-2	Kuwait
Syria	1-2	Kuwait
Kuwait	3-2	Syria
Syria	0-1	Oman
Kuwait	3-1	Oman
Oman	1-5	Syria

Kuwait progressed to Round 2.

Group 3

Jordan	1-3	Saudi Arabia
Jordan	2-4	Iraq
Jordan	0-2	Saudi Arabia
Jordan	5-0	Iraq
Saudi Arabia	1-1	Iraq
Saudi Arabia	2-2	Iraq

Saudi Arabia reached Round 2.

Group 4

Iran	2-1	Bahrain
Bahrain	2-1	Lebanon
Lebanon	2-0	Iran
Bahrain	2-0	Iran
Lebanon	0-2	Bahrain
Iran	1-1	Lebanon

Bahrain went on to Round 2.

Group 5

Uzbekistan	3-1	Kyrgyzstan
Tajikistan	1-2	Turkmenistan
Uzbekistan	3-0	Tajikistan
Tajikistan	0-0	Kazakhstan
Turkmenistan	1-1	Uzbekistan
Kazakhstan	4-1	Turkmenistan
Kyrgyzstan	1-0	Tajikistan
Turkmenistan	3-0	Kyrgyzstan
Uzbekistan	0-2	Kazakhstan
Kyrgyzstan	2-1	Turkmenistan
Kazakhstan	3-1	Uzbekistan

Turkmenistan	3-2	Kazakhstan
Tajikistan	1-2	Kyrgyzstan
Kazakhstan	5-1	Tajikistan
Uzbekistan	3-0	Turkmenistan
Kazakhstan	1-1	Kyrgyzstan
Tajikistan	0-2	Uzbekistan
Kyrgyzstan	2-3	Kazakhstan
Kyrgyzstan	0-2	Uzbekistan
Turkmenistan	6-1	Tajikistan

Kazakhstan reached Round 2.

Group 6

Japan	13-0	Philippines
Hong Kong	1-2	Nepal
Japan	5-0	Nepal
Hong Kong	2-2	Malaysia
Nepal	1-0	Philippines
Japan	4-0	Malaysia
Malaysia	6-1	Philippines
Hong Kong	1-4	Japan
Nepal	1-1	Malaysia (match abandoned)
Hong Kong	4-1	Philippines
Japan	9-0	Nepal
Hong Kong	4-1	Philippines
Philippines	0-1	Hong Kong
Hong Kong	2-1	Nepal
Japan	4-0	Malaysia
Nepal	2-2	Philippines
Hong Kong	3-0	Malaysia
Malaysia	5-0	Philippines
Japan	2-0	Hong Kong
Malaysia	3-2	Nepal

| Japan | 11-0 | Philippines |

Japan (who won every match they played) reached Round 2.

Group 7

North Korea	1-0	Myanmar
Vietnam	0-4	China
Vietnam	1-2	North Korea
Myanmar	0-4	China
Vietnam	1-2	Myanmar
China	1-0	North Korea
North Korea	6-0	Myanmar
China	3-0	Vietnam
North Korea	1-1	Vietnam
China	6-0	Myanmar
Myanmar	0-0	Vietnam
China	2-0	North Korea

China went into Round 2, having won all their games.

Group 8

Indonesia	2-1	Taiwan
South Korea	5-0	Sri Lanka
Indonesia	2-1	Sri Lanka
South Korea	7-0	Taiwan
Taiwan	4-1	Sri Lanka
South Korea	7-0	Indonesia

South Korea reached Round 2 with full points.

Group 9

| Thailand | 2-0 | India |
| India | 0-0 | Thailand |

Singapore, Brunei and Laos withdrew.
Thailand reached Round 2.

Round 2

Group A

Qatar	4-1	Saudi Arabia
Saudi Arabia	2-1	Kuwait
Kuwait	4-0	Qatar
Kuwait	3-0	Saudi Arabia
Saudi Arabia	2-0	Qatar
Qatar	1-2	Kuwait

Kuwait (9 points) qualified for Sydney. Saudi Arabia had 6 points, Qatar 3.

Group B

South Korea	1-0	China
China	2-1	Bahrain
Bahrain	0-1	South Korea
China	1-1	South Korea
Bahrain	1-0	China
South Korea	2-1	Bahrain

South Korea qualified for Sydney with 10 points – China had 4, Bahrain 3.

Group C

Kazakhstan	0-0	Thailand
Kazakhstan	0-2	Japan
Japan	3-1	Thailand
Thailand	1-4	Kazakhstan
Japan	3-1	Kazakhstan
Thailand	0-6	Japan

Japan (12 points) qualified for Sydney, Kazakhstan had 4, Thailand one.

Oceania

(matches played in New Zealand)

Group A

Solomon Islands	7-0	Tonga
Solomon Islands	2-1	Western Samoa
Solomon Islands	2-0	Fiji
Fiji	4-0	Western Samoa
Fiji	9-0	Tonga
Western Samoa	4-1	Tonga

Solomon Islands (9 points) progressed, ahead of Fiji (6), Western Samoa (3) and Tonga (no points).

Group B

New Zealand	4-0	Vanuatu
New Zealand	5-0	Papua New Guinea
Papua New Guinea	2-0	Vanuatu

New Zealand (6 points) progressed, ahead of Papua New Guinea (3) and Vanuatu (no points).

Semi-finals

Solomon Islands	3-1	Papua New Guinea
New Zealand	5-2	Fiji

Final

New Zealand	4-1	Solomon Islands

Oceania winner v best African runners-up (two legs)

New Zealand	2-4	South Africa

South Africa qualified for Sydney.

25. Athens, 2004

Back home to Greece

Athens finally staged the Olympics for the first time since the inaugural event of 1896 and the 'Intercalated' Games of 1906. 14 cities presented bids, and in 1997 Athens won, ahead of Rome, Stockholm, Cape Town and Buenos Aires.

The torch was carried from Sydney across five continents, travelling over 48,000 miles in 78 days. At Olympia, the American shot-putter Kristin Heaston was the first woman ever to compete at the ancient site.

201 countries took part, entering the stadium in the opening parade according to their names in Greek. So St Lucia were first, Hong Kong last before the hosts.

Once again, swimming caught the world's attention as Michael Phelps, of the USA, swam 17 races to win six golds and two bronzes. Remarkable, too, that Merlene Ottey reached the 200 metres semi-final on the track at the age of 44, in her seventh Games.

The football tournament

The 16 participants were:

Hosts: Greece
Europe: Italy, Serbia-Montenegro, Portugal
North and Central America: Mexico, Costa Rica
South America: Paraguay, Argentina
Africa: Mali, Ghana, Tunisia, Morocco
Asia: South Korea, Japan, Iraq
Oceania: Australia

Football was now the most important sport for spreading the Olympic experience across a nation as well as within the host city.

Greece's second city, Thessaloniki, staged eight matches in its Kaftantzoglio Stadium. Patra upgraded their Pampeloponnisiako Stadium to present seven fixtures, and Volos hosted five in the Panthessaliko Stadium.

In Crete, the Pankritio Stadium at Iraklion welcomed teams for six matches, while Athens presented another six.

Two arenas in the Greek capital were involved. The Karaiskaki Stadium held five games – in 1896 cyclists competed there – and the new Olympic Stadium hosted the Final.

Group A

11 August	Greece 2-2 South Korea (0-1)	Thessaloniki
	Taralidis 78 Kim Dong-jin 43	
	Papadopoulos 82 (p) Vyntra 64 (o.g.)	

11 August   Mali 0-0 Mexico   Volos

14 August   South Korea 1-0 Mexico (1-0)   Athens (Karaiskaki Stadium)

Kim Jung-woo 16

14 August   Mali 2-0 Greece (2-0)   Thessaloniki

Berthe 2
N'Diaye 45

17 August   Mali 3-3 South Korea (2-0)   Thessaloniki

N'Diaye 7, 24, 55   Cho Jae-jin 57, 59
                   Tamboura 64 (o.g.)

17 August   Mexico 3-2 Greece (0-0)   Volos

Marquez 47   Taralidis 82 (p)
Bravo 70, 86   Stoltidis 90

Qualified:	Mali	5 points	(5 goals for – 3 against)
Qualified:	South Korea	5 points	(6-5)
	Mexico	4 points	(3-3)
	Greece	1 point	(4-7)

Group A

Greece were drawn with Mexico, Mali, and South Korea in the first Group.

Mexico qualified by defeating the USA and Honduras, as well as Costa Rica, who also joined the tournament in Group D. Mali emerged from a section that included Ivory Coast, Congo-Kinshasa, and the 2000 gold medallists, Cameroon, whom they defeated in their last home fixture. South Korea were again qualifiers, ahead of Iran, China and Malaysia.

Greece got the event underway in Thessaloniki against **South Korea**. The hosts lined up 3-5-2 against a Korean formation which soon had to change from its initial 3-4-3. After 31 minutes, South Korea lost left-back Kim Chi-gon, whose red card put Greece a man up for almost an hour.

Yet it was South Korea who scored just before half-time, through Kim Dong-jin, and went 2-0 up when Vyntra scored an own goal in the 64th minute.

Greece had introduced two substitutes after the interval, and Vyntra was later replaced by Tarolidis, who scored in 78 minutes. The match was drawn 2-2 after Papadopoulos's penalty with only eight minutes left.

Mali, newcomers to the tournament, played **Mexico** in a cautious goalless draw at Volos. Both teams replaced their forwards in the second half, but there was no tangible result, and the original choices returned in later matches.

Greece now faced **Mali**. The hosts' late surge against South Korea had earned them a point, but 8,000 fewer turned up to watch their second match. The fastest goal of 2004 took only two minutes to arrive, as Berthe scored for Mali, and N'Diaye doubled their lead right on the interval.

The perennial substitute, Taralidis, came on in 30 minutes, but could not produce a goal this time. Nor could Papadopoulos, who missed from the spot in the last seconds.

South Korea's victory over **Mexico** came from a 16th minute goal by Kim Jung-woo, and they now had 4 points and were favourites to reach the quarter-finals with Mali (4). Greece and Mexico both had one point and had to depend on a convincing victory in their third match, forging ahead of the others on goal difference.

Mali's striker N'Diaye was the star against **South Korea**, collecting a hat-trick with goals in seven, 24 and 55 minutes. Even then, the result was not settled. Cho Jae-Jin quickly responded with two goals before the hour, and the Korean revival led to an own goal by Tamboura of Mali. Three goal comebacks are rare, even rarer are those that take only nine minutes.

At the same time, **Mexico** and **Greece** still had a chance of progress, as long as the other match was not drawn. Mexico took 47 minutes to gain the advantage, when Marquez scored, followed by his colleague Bravo in the 70th minute. But Greece were then awarded a penalty, from which Taralidis scored. As the match came to a close, Bravo made it 3-1 to Mexico, with the Greek captain Stoltidis scoring just before the whistle.

Both teams, however, went out, as Mali headed Group A with 5 points, South Korea second on goal difference.

Group B

12 August	Paraguay 4-3 Japan (3-1)	Thessaloniki
	Gimenez 5 — Ono 22 (p), 53 (p)	
	Cardozo 26, 37 — Okubo 81	
	Torres 62	

12 August	Italy 2-2 Ghana (0-2)	Volos
	Pinzi 49 — Pappoe 36	
	Gilardino 83 — Appiah 45	

15 August	Ghana 2-1 Paraguay (0-0)	Thessaloniki
	Tiero 81 — Gamarra 76	
	Appiah 84	

15 August	Italy 3-2 Japan (3-1)	Volos
	De Rossi 3 — Abe 21	
	Gilardino 8, 36 — Takamatsu 90	

18 August	Paraguay 1-0 Italy (1-0)	Athens
	Bareiro 14	

18 August	Japan 1-0 Ghana (1-0)	Volos
	Okubo 37	

Qualified: Paraguay   6 points   (6-5)
Qualified: Italy   4 points   (5-5)
           Ghana   4 points   (4-4)
           Japan   3 points   (6-7)

Group B

Italy, Paraguay, Ghana and Japan made up Group B, with the Italians favoured to win their matches.

They had become the best young side in Europe, winning the UEFA Under-21 championship, defeating Serbia-Montenegro and Denmark en route.

Paraguay qualified with Argentina, ahead of Brazil and Chile, bronze medallists in 2000. Ghana's main rivals in their section were Zambia, South Africa, and Algeria. In their Asian zone, Japan returned to the tournament with points gained from Bahrain, United Arab Emirates, and Lebanon.

Paraguay began with an outstanding first half against **Japan**. Gimenez opened their account in five minutes, and, despite Ono's equaliser from a penalty, Cardozo hit a double before half-time to establish Paraguay's 3-1 lead.

In 53 minutes, Ono scored another from the spot, but Torres came out of defence to claim a fourth goal in 62 minutes for the South Americans. The match was the highest scoring game of 2004, ending 4-3 as Okubo added a third for Japan.

Ghana faced **Italy** with a defensive 5-4-1 formation, while 4-4-2 was Italy's set-up. Remarkably, it was Ghana who scored twice late in the first half, from their defender Pappoe and midfielder Appiah. Italy's reply through Pinzi in 49 minutes halted their decline, and Gilardino equalised seven minutes from time.

Ghana v **Paraguay** drew only 1,000 spectators, one of the smallest crowds of the football event, and they waited 76 minutes for a goal. At last Paraguay's captain Gamarra scored, five minutes later Tiero levelled the score, and Appiah quickly won the game in 84 minutes. Not even two substitutions helped Paraguay, who lost 2-1.

Italy and **Japan** were both disappointed by their first matches. Now the match had hardly begun before Italy's De Rossi and Gilardino created a 2-0 lead, in three and eight minutes. Japan made the fastest substitution of 2004, with Nasu arriving in 19 minutes, and Abe scored almost immediately. Gilardino, however, restored Italy's two goal advantage. The match finished 3-2, with Takamatsu's strike in 90 minutes.

After two matches, Italy had 4 points, Ghana also had 4, Paraguay 3. Japan were already eliminated, with no points, but any of the other teams could win the Group.

Both of the final Round B games ended with a single, first half goal, from the winner's right-sided striker. **Paraguay**'s Bareiro won their match against **Italy** with a shot in 14 minutes. Italian attacks could not produce a goal, and every substitution was made by both sides after the interval. Even Italy's captain, Pirlo, was replaced, by Donadel, although he returned for subsequent fixtures.

The result from **Japan** v **Ghana**, a 1-0 victory for the Japanese after Okubo's strike in 37 minutes, meant that neither reached the next stage.

Paraguay won Group B, and, while Italy and Ghana both had 4 points and equal goal difference, Italy went through by scoring one more goal. Without Gilardino's three goals, they would have struggled.

Group C

11 August	Australia 1-1 Tunisia (1-0)	Iraklion
	Aloisi 45 Zitouni 69	

11 August	Argentina 6-0 Serbia-Montenegro (4-0)	Patra
	Delgado 11	
	K. Gonzalez 17	
	Tevez 42, 43	
	Heinze 74	
	Rosales 77	

14 August	Australia 5-1 Serbia-Montenegro (2-0)	Iraklion
	Cahill 11 Radonjic 72	
	Aloisi 45, 57	
	Elrich 60, 86	

14 August Argentina 2-0 Tunisia (1-0) Patra
Tevez 39
Saviola 72

17 August Argentina 1-0 Australia (1-0) Athens
D'Alessandro 9

17 August Tunisia 3-2 Serbia-Montenegro Patra
 (1-0)
Clayton 41   Krasic 70
Jedidi 83 (p) Vukcevic 87
Zitouni 89

Qualified:	Argentina	9 points	(9-0)
Qualified:	Australia	4 points	(6-3)
	Tunisia	4 points	(4-5)
	Serbia-Montenegro	0 points	(3-14)

Group C

Serbia-Montenegro, Argentina, Tunisia, and Australia were drawn together in Group C. After missing the previous tournament, Argentina qualified as the best team in their zone.

Serbia-Montenegro finished second to Italy in their UEFA Under-21 section, but then progressed to the final, where they were runners-up and took a place in the Athens event.

Tunisia's qualification came from an African zone that included Nigeria, Senegal, and Egypt. As usual, Australia won the Oceania group, with New Zealand second.

Australia v **Tunisia** drew over 15,000 to the Pankritio Stadium in Iraklion. Both sides started cautiously, and it was not until the 45th minute that Aloisi, Australia's striker, found the net. Tunisia brought on their defender Ayari when the teams restarted, and he kept his place in all three matches. The African side equalised in 69 minutes from their forward Zitouni, and it finished 1-1.

Argentina's match against **Serbia-Montenegro** was 2004's most one-sided. Argentina played four forwards, one of whom, Delgado, took just eleven minutes to score. His midfield colleague Kily Gonzalez quickly added a second, and Carlos Tevez scored two in 60 seconds before the interval.

The South Americans substituted two forwards later in the game, but the procession continued to Milojevic's goal. Heinze, Argentinian left-back, came up to score a fifth in the 74th minute, and Rosales made it 6-0 soon after.

Argentina next played **Tunisia**, whose defence made scoring more difficult. Tevez did find his range in 39 minutes and scored the opener. Saviola doubled the Argentine lead in the 72nd minute after coming on as a substitute – he did not start a match in Group C. 2-0 was sufficient for Argentina to win, and qualify for the semi-final after two games.

Australia's performance against **Serbia-Montenegro** was perhaps their most convincing at the Olympics. Tim Cahill opened the scoring for Australia in 11 minutes, and Serbia had a chance to equalise from the spot, midway through the half. Vukcevic's shot was blocked by Galekovic in goal. Instead of 1-1, the score was 2-0 when Aloisi scored for Australia right on half-time.

The goals continued to flow from Australian right-sided players – Aloisi in 57 minutes, and Elrich, in 60 and 86. Radonjic, a Serbian substitute, got one back in the 72nd minute, but the 5-1 score added up to 11 goals lost in two matches for the new team.

With 4 points, Australia were likely to join Argentina in the next stage, and a draw in their third game would ensure that they did. Tunisia, on one point, needed a win to have any chance of passing Australia on goal difference.

There was less pressure on **Argentina**, especially when they led **Australia** after nine minutes, through D'Alessandro's strike. The captaincy of Craig Moore, Rangers' defender, helped his team, playing in 4-4-2 structure, restrict the 3-4-3 of Argentina to only one goal.

Serbia-Montenegro's best match was against **Tunisia**. Clayton put Tunisia in front just before half-time, but Krasic levelled in the 70th minute. The African team regained the lead as Jedidi scored the Group's only penalty goal, but Vukcevic equalised with three minutes to go. A last seconds decider went to Zitouni for Tunisia, who won 3-2 in a match which could hardly have been tighter.

However, Australia took second place to Argentina in Group C, with Tunisia third on goal difference, both teams on 4 points. Argentina (9 points) had not conceded a goal.

Group D

12 August	Morocco 0-0 Costa Rica		Iraklion

12 August   Iraq 4-2 Portugal (2-2)   Patra
                      E. Mohammed 16   Jabbar 13 (o.g.)
                      M. Mohammed 29   Bosingwa 45
                      Mahmoud 56
                      Sadir 90

15 August   Iraq 2-0 Costa Rica (0-0)   Athens
                      M. Mohammed 67
                      Karim 72

15 August   Portugal 2-1 Morocco (1-0)   Iraklion
                      C. Ronaldo 40   Bouden 85
                      R. Costa 73

18 August   Costa Rica 4-2 Portugal (0-1)   Iraklion
                      Villalobos 50   H. Almeida 29
                      F. Meira 68 (o.g.)   J. Ribeiro 54
                      Saborio 71
                      Brenes 90

18 August   Morocco 2-1 Iraq (0-0)   Patra
                      Bouden 69   Sadir 63
                      Aqqal 77

Qualified:	Iraq	6 points	(7-4)
Qualified:	Costa Rica	4 points	(4-4)
	Morocco	4 points	(3-3)
	Portugal	3 points	(6-9)

Group D

Portugal, Costa Rica, Morocco, and Iraq formed Group D. Portugal had one of the best European under-21 teams, and narrowly defeated France and Sweden to gain a place in the Olympic sixteen.

Costa Rica enjoyed a rare qualification, ahead of USA, Honduras, Panama, and Canada. Morocco's rivals were Angola, Ethiopia, and Uganda, while Iraq came through in front of Oman, Kuwait and Saudi Arabia.

Costa Rica and **Morocco** could not muster a goal in their opening match, like Mali v Mexico in Group A. The advantage lay with Costa Rica in the last half-hour, once Morocco's captain and centre-back Alioui received a red card after 59 minutes. Yet Costa Rica's 5-3-2 formation was tuned to defence rather than attack, and only when they pushed men forward in their third match did goals arrive.

Portugal benefited early in their game with **Iraq** when Jabbar, the Iraqi centre-back, scored an own goal in 13 minutes. E. Mohammed quickly equalised, however, and M. Mohammed put Iraq 2-1 ahead before half an hour had passed. The action ebbed and flowed and Bosingwa restored Portugal's hopes to make it 2-2 right on the interval.

Their striker Boa Morte was sent off after 51 minutes, and Mahmoud's goal in the 56th minute gave Iraq a 3-2 lead. Soon after, Portugal replaced both linkmen in their 5-2-3 line-up, but to no avail. Sadir scored a fourth goal for Iraq in the 90th minute.

Iraq next faced **Costa Rica**, and this match seemed to be heading for another goalless draw until M. Mohammed gave Iraq the lead after 67 minutes. Karim, who had just come on as substitute, scored a second and decisive goal five minutes later. Costa Rica introduced three substitutes in the final quarter of an hour without success.

Portugal's win over **Morocco** depended on goals by the young Christiano Ronaldo, in 40 minutes, and his captain Ricardo Costa after 73. Morocco eventually found the net through Bouden five minutes from the end in a 2-1 defeat.

Iraq (6 points) were already sure of a quarter-final place, while Portugal (3), Costa Rica (1), and Morocco (1) could still join them.

Costa Rica v **Portugal** was the most eventful fixture of the group, as

Portugal, switching to 5-3-2, took the lead through Hugo Almeida in 29 minutes. Neither Ronaldo nor Boa Morte played in this match. Just before the referee blew for half-time, Portugal's defender Joao Paulo was sent off.

The second half was Costa Rica's. Villalobos came out of defence to equalise in the 50th minute. Portugal briefly reclaimed the lead through Jorge Ribeiro; but the Central Americans, who introduced two fresh players after the interval, increased their attacks. Fernando Meira, Portugal's centre-back, put through his own net in 68 minutes: 2-2. Then the substitute Saborio quickly gave Costa Rica a lead for the first time in any group match. In the last seconds, Brenes made victory certain with a fourth goal. Portugal ended their tournament with nine men, as Hugo Viana was dismissed.

Morocco and **Iraq** produced no goals for over an hour, until Sadir put Iraq ahead. Then Bouden took his chance to equalise with a penalty in 69 minutes, and Aqqal celebrated his appearance as a late substitute with a goal inside two minutes. Iraq, playing an unfamiliar 3-5-2 arrangement, could not recover.

The second place in Group D went to Costa Rica. Both they and Morocco had a goal difference of zero, but Costa Rica scored one goal more – that late strike by Brenes was the key.

Quarter-finals

21 August	Italy 1-0 Mali (0-0)	Athens
	(after extra-time)	
	Bovo 116	

21 August	Paraguay 3-2 South Korea (1-0)	Thessaloniki
	Bareiro 19, 71 Lee Chun-soo 74, 79 (p)	
	Cardozo 61	

21 August	Argentina 4-0 Costa Rica (2-0)	Patra
	Delgado 24	
	Tevez 43, 82, 83	

21 August	Iraq 1-0 Australia (0-0)	Iraklion
	E. Mohammed 64	

Quarter-finals

Mali's first contest with **Italy** produced nine yellow cards – six for Italy – but no goals for almost two hours. That would have been different if Sissoko's penalty had gone in after 34 minutes, but Pelizzoli, Italy's keeper, saved it. Neither side risked more than one substitute before extra time began, but after 116 minutes Italian centre-back Bovo joined a late attack and scored the winner.

Iraq, one of the unexpected successes of these Olympics, also won their quarter-final by a single goal against **Australia**. It came in the 64th minute from Emad Mohammed. With 10 minutes left, Iraq chose to leave one striker upfield and defend their lead against Australia's three forwards.

Paraguay met **South Korea** in a match which ran in the South Americans' favour until the last 16 minutes. Bareiro gave them an early lead, and they trebled that in the second half through Cardozo and Bareiro. But in the 74th minute Lee Chun-soo scored for South Korea, and quickly added another from the penalty spot. As in their draw with Mali, the Korean side showed they could come back from three goals down. This time, it was too late, and the semi-final tie would be between Paraguay and Iraq.

Costa Rica had defeated Portugal, but **Argentina** offered a stern test of their five man defence. There was an initial scare for Argentina, as Heinze had to be replaced in defence by Rodriguez in the 18th minute, but Delgado soon put them ahead.

Afterwards, this became the Carlos Tevez show with the tournament's second hat-trick. Late in the first half, and in the second, he hit the net in 43, 82 and 83 minutes.

Semi-finals

24 August	Argentina	3-0	Italy (1-0)	Athens
	Tevez 16			
	L. Gonzalez 69			
	M. Gonzalez 84			
24 August	Paraguay	3-1	Iraq (2-0)	Thessaloniki
	Cardozo 17, 34		Farhan 83	
	Bareiro 68			

Semi-finals

Argentina v **Italy** drew 31,000 to watch what many regarded as the best teams of their continents. Pirlo, the Italian captain, was booked after six minutes, one of five cautions in the game, and Tevez continued his form by scoring 10 minutes later. Argentina had the better chances, but it remained 1-0 at the interval.

Italy's concern about the left side of their team led to substitutes Donadel and Del Nero arriving in 46 minutes, but the South Americans went further ahead. In a team which fielded three players named Gonzalez, Lucho made it 2-0 in the 69th minute, and then Mariano scored a third within seconds of coming off the bench. Only Kily Gonzalez did not add to the total, though he scored in a Group C match.

Later that evening, **Paraguay** met **Iraq** and Cardozo was the key striker with goals in 17 and 34 minutes. Like Italy, Iraq introduced two substitutes at the start of the second half, and later even their captain al-Hail was replaced. Bareiro's goal after 68 minutes gave Paraguay a 3-0 lead, and their two strikers were then rested. Farhan did reduce the leeway with seven minutes to go, but Paraguay were through to the Final.

Bronze medal match

27 August   Italy   1-0   Iraq (1-0)   Thessaloniki

Gilardino 8

The bronze medal match

Italy vied with **Iraq** for third place before just over 5,000 spectators in Thessaloniki. Gilardino's opening strike in eight minutes did not herald a feast of goals, but was enough to give Italy their first football medal since 1936. Iraq's fourth place was the highest for any team from the Middle East.

Final

28 August   Argentina   1-0   Paraguay (1-0)   Athens (Olympic Stadium)

Tevez 18

The Final

In the first all South American final since Uruguay v Argentina in 1928, **Argentina** and **Paraguay** drew easily the biggest crowd of the event, 41,000, to Athens. The starting time, 10am, on a late August morning, was hardly conducive to cool brows or temperaments.

Tevez was again the match winner with the only goal in 18 minutes. His total of eight in the tournament was the highest since Bebeto's tally for Brazil in 1988.

Unfortunately, the Final's statistics concerned red and yellow cards. After an hour most of the Paraguayan team, except for their keeper and two forwards, were in the referee's book. Martinez was sent off in 66 minutes, Figueredo followed him with a second yellow in 82. The team's substitutions meant that they replaced an entire midfield by the end of this match.

Argentina won the gold they had sought for 76 years, with 17 goals to nil – a record to match that of the previous South American champions, in the 1920's.

Top goal-scorers

8: Tevez (Argentina)
5: Cardozo (Paraguay)
4: N'Diaye (Mali)
    Bareiro (Paraguay)

The medal winners

Gold (Argentina)

Lux	K. Gonzalez	M. Gonzalez
Coloccini	Rosales	Burdisso
Ayala (captain)	Tevez	
Heinze	Delgado	
L. Gonzalez	C. Rodriguez	
Mascherano	Saviola	
D'Alessandro	Medina	

Silver (Paraguay)

D. Barreto	Esquivel	Cardozo
Martinez	Figueredo	Gonzalez

Gamarra (captain) Bareiro   Benitez
Manzur   Gimenez
Torres   Cristaldo
E. Barreto   Diaz
Enciso   Devaca

Bronze (Italy)

Pelizzoli   Pirlo (captain)   De Rossi
Ferrari   Donadel   Sculli
Bovo   Gilardino   Gasbarroni
Barzagli   Del Nero
Moretti   Chiellini
Pinzi   Mesto
Palombo   Bonera

Referees

J. Larrionda (Uruguay)   Greece v South Korea
                                    Italy v Iraq
                                    (Bronze medal match)
                                    Italy v Japan
S. Salleh (Malaysia)   Mali v Mexico
                                    Australia v
                                    Serbia-Montenegro
C. Larsen (Denmark)   South Korea v Mexico
                                    Paraguay v Italy
C. Torres (Paraguay)   Mali v Greece
                                    Costa Rica v Portugal
                                    Italy v Mali
E. Poulat (France)   South Korea v Mali
                                    Argentina v Tunisia
                                    Paraguay v Iraq (Semi-final)
R. Divine (Cameroon)   Mexico v Greece
                                    Iraq v Portugal
E. Abdel–Fattah (Egypt)   Paraguay v Japan
                                    Argentina v Australia
H. Elizondo (Argentina)   Ghana v Italy
                                    Morocco v Iraq
B. Archundia (Mexico)   Ghana v Paraguay
                                    Argentina v Italy (Semi-final)

K. Vassaras (Greece)	Japan v Ghana
	Tunisia v Australia
	Argentina v Costa Rica
	Argentina v Paraguay (Final)
C. Batres (Guatemala)	Argentina v Serbia-Montenegro
	Portugal v Morocco
	Iraq v Australia
C. Ariiotima (Tahiti)	Tunisia v Serbia-Montenegro
	Iraq v Costa Rica
M. de Santis (Italy)	Costa Rica v Morocco
	Paraguay v South Korea

The qualifying tournament

The 16 teams taking part in Athens comprised:

Hosts: Greece
Europe: three teams
North and Central America: two teams
South America: two teams
Africa: four teams
Asia: three teams
Oceania: one team

Europe

(The European Under-21 Championship was also the Olympic qualifying event)

Group 1

Slovenia	1-0	Malta
Cyprus	0-1	France
France	1-0	Slovenia
Malta	0-1	Israel
Malta	0-3	France

Cyprus	2-0	Malta
Cyprus	2-0	Israel
France	2-0	Malta
Israel	0-3	France
Slovenia	2-0	Cyprus
Malta	0-0	Slovenia
Israel	0-3	Cyprus
Israel	0-0	Slovenia
Malta	0-1	Cyprus
France	2-0	Cyprus
Slovenia	1-2	Israel
Israel	3-0	Malta
Slovenia	0-0	France
France	2-0	Israel
Cyprus	4-0	Slovenia

France won Group 1 with 22 points. Cyprus came second (15), with Israel on 10, Slovenia 9, Malta one.

Group 2

Norway	3-0	Denmark
Bosnia-Herzegovina	2-1	Romania
Denmark	9-0	Luxembourg
Romania	0-1	Norway
Norway	0-0	Bosnia-Herzegovina
Luxembourg	0-2	Romania
Bosnia-Herzegovina	1-0	Luxembourg
Romania	0-1	Denmark
Luxembourg	0-5	Norway
Denmark	3-0	Bosnia-Herzegovina

Denmark	2-0	Norway
Romania	0-1	Bosnia-Herzegovina
Luxembourg	0-6	Denmark
Norway	2-1	Romania
Bosnia-Herzegovina	1-3	Norway
Romania	2-0	Luxembourg
Luxembourg	0-1	Bosnia-Herzegovina
Denmark	0-0	Romania
Norway	5-0	Luxembourg
Bosnia-Herzegovina	0-3	Denmark

Norway topped Group 2 with 19 points ahead of Denmark (19) because their results were slightly better over the two matches between the teams. Bosnia-Herzegovina had 13, Romania 7, Luxembourg none.

Group 3

Netherlands	0-1	Belarus
Austria	1-0	Moldova
Belarus	0-1	Austria
Moldova	0-2	Czech Republic
Austria	1-1	Netherlands
Czech Republic	3-0	Belarus
Netherlands	0-3	Czech Republic
Belarus	3-1	Moldova
Czech Republic	3-1	Austria
Moldova	2-2	Netherlands
Belarus	2-1	Netherlands
Moldova	0-1	Austria
Czech Republic	3-0	Moldova
Austria	0-2	Belarus
Netherlands	0-0	Austria

Belarus	1-0	Czech Republic
Czech Republic	1-2	Netherlands
Moldova	0-2	Belarus
Austria	0-2	Czech Republic
Netherlands	0-0	Moldova

The Czech Republic (18 points) won the Group from Belarus (18) because of better results in the matches between those sides. Austria came third (11), Netherlands gained 7 points, Moldova 2.

Group 4

San Marino	1-5	Poland
Latvia	0-4	Sweden
Sweden	1-0	Hungary
Poland	3-0	Latvia
Hungary	4-1	San Marino
San Marino	0-2	Latvia
Poland	3-2	Hungary
Poland	7-0	San Marino
Hungary	5-2	Sweden
Latvia	4-1	San Marino
Hungary	3-1	Latvia
San Marino	1-5	Sweden
Sweden	1-1	Poland
San Marino	1-2	Hungary
Latvia	0-2	Poland
† Sweden v	San Marino (awarded 3-0 to San Marino)	
Poland	1-1	Sweden
Latvia	2-0	Hungary
San Marino	3-2	Latvia
Hungary	1-2	Poland

Poland (20 points) won the group from Sweden (14), Hungary (12), Latvia (9) and San Marino (3).

† Sweden defeated San Marino 6-0, but fielded a suspended player – UEFA then awarded the tie to San Marino.

Group 5

Lithuania	1-4	Germany
Iceland	0-2	Scotland
Iceland	1-2	Lithuania
Scotland	1-0	Iceland
Germany	1-0	Lithuania
Lithuania	2-1	Scotland
Scotland	2-2	Germany
Lithuania	3-0	Iceland
Iceland	1-3	Germany
Germany	0-1	Scotland
Scotland	3-2	Lithuania
Germany	1-0	Iceland

Scotland won the group with 13 points from Germany (13), by winning one, and drawing the other, match between the two teams. Lithuania had 9 points, Iceland none.

Group 6

Greece	1-0	Spain
Armenia	1-1	Ukraine
Spain	1-0	Northern Ireland
Ukraine	1-1	Greece
Greece	2-1	Armenia

Northern Ireland	1-1	Ukraine
Armenia	2-0	Northern Ireland
Ukraine	0-0	Spain
Northern Ireland	2-6	Greece
Spain	5-0	Armenia
Spain	2-0	Greece
Ukraine	4-0	Armenia
Northern Ireland	1-4	Spain
Greece	0-0	Ukraine
Armenia	0-0	Greece
Ukraine	1-0	Northern Ireland
Northern Ireland	3-1	Armenia
Spain	2-0	Ukraine
Greece	0-1	Northern Ireland
Armenia	0-2	Spain

Spain headed Group 6 with 19 points. Greece had 12, Ukraine 11, Northern Ireland 7, Armenia 5.

Group 7

Turkey	2-1	Slovakia
Portugal	1-0	Macedonia
Slovakia	0-4	England
Macedonia	0-4	Turkey
Turkey	4-2	Portugal
England	3-1	Macedonia
Portugal	4-2	England
Macedonia	0-2	Slovakia
England	1-1	Turkey
Slovakia	0-2	Portugal

Slovakia	0-1	Turkey
Macedonia	1-4	Portugal
England	2-0	Slovakia
Turkey	3-0	Macedonia
Portugal	1-2	Turkey
Macedonia	1-1	England
England	1-2	Portugal
Slovakia	5-1	Macedonia
Turkey	1-0	England
Portugal	4-1	Slovakia

Turkey won the group on 22 points, Portugal came second with 18, England third on 11, Slovakia had 6, Macedonia one.

Group 8

Belgium	3-1	Bulgaria
Croatia	3-1	Estonia
Bulgaria	1-3	Croatia
Estonia	0-1	Belgium
Croatia	1-1	Belgium
Estonia	1-1	Bulgaria
Bulgaria	2-1	Belgium
Estonia	0-0	Croatia
Bulgaria	1-0	Estonia
Belgium	0-2	Croatia
Croatia	0-1	Bulgaria
Belgium	4-2	Estonia

Croatia headed the group with 11 points. Belgium and Bulgaria had 10, Estonia two.

Group 9

Azerbaijan	0-3	Italy
Finland	2-1	Wales
Finland	3-0	Azerbaijan
Italy	4-1	Serbia-Montenegro
Wales	1-2	Italy
Serbia-Montenegro	3-3	Finland
Azerbaijan	0-1	Wales
Serbia-Montenegro	3-0	Azerbaijan
Italy	1-0	Finland
Wales	1-0	Azerbaijan
Finland	1-2	Serbia-Montenegro
Finland	1-2	Italy
Azerbaijan	0-2	Serbia-Montenegro
Serbia-Montenegro	3-0	Wales
Italy	8-1	Wales
Azerbaijan	0-1	Finland
Wales	0-0	Finland
Serbia-Montenegro	1-0	Italy
Italy	6-0	Azerbaijan
Wales	0-1	Serbia-Montenegro

Italy won the group with 21 points, Serbia-Montenegro were second (19), Finland had 11, Wales 7, Azerbaijan none.

Group 10

Russia	2-0	Ireland
Switzerland	2-0	Georgia
Albania	0-0	Switzerland
Georgia	0-3	Russia
Ireland	2-3	Switzerland

Russia	1-0	Albania
Georgia	1-1	Ireland
Albania	1-4	Russia
Albania	1-0	Ireland
Georgia	0-2	Switzerland
Ireland	v	Albania – awarded to Albania, since Ireland fielded a suspended player.
Switzerland	1-0	Russia
Ireland	1-1	Georgia
Switzerland	2-1	Albania
Ireland	2-0	Russia
Georgia	3-1	Albania
Albania	3-0	Georgia
Russia	1-2	Switzerland
Russia	3-2	Georgia
Switzerland	0-2	Ireland

Switzerland (19 points) headed the group, Russia had 15, Albania 10, Ireland 8, and Georgia 5.

Round 2

16 teams played two legs at this stage.

The 16 were the winners of the ten groups – France, Norway, Czech Republic, Poland, Scotland, Spain, Turkey, Croatia, Italy, and Switzerland – and the six best runners-up. They were Denmark (Group 2), Belarus (3), Sweden (4), Germany (5), Portugal (7), and Serbia-Montenegro (Group 9).

(Aggregate scores over two legs)

Germany	2-1	Turkey
Portugal	3-3	France (Portugal won on penalty kicks)
Serbia-Montenegro	5-4	Norway
Italy	1-1	Denmark (Italy won on away goals rule)

Belarus	5-1	Poland
Sweden	3-1	Spain
Switzerland	3-3	Czech Republic (Switzerland won on away goals rule)
Croatia	2-1	Scotland

Those 8 winners went on to play in a final stage in two groups.

Final group stage

Group A

Italy	1-2	Belarus
Italy	2-1	Serbia-Montenegro
Italy	1-0	Croatia
Serbia-Montenegro	3-2	Croatia
Serbia-Montenegro	2-1	Belarus
Belarus	1-1	Croatia

Italy (6 points) and Serbia-Montenegro (6) went into the semi-finals, Italy heading this group because they beat Serbia-Montenegro. Belarus had 4 points, Croatia one.

Group B

Sweden	3-1	Portugal
Sweden	2-1	Germany
Sweden	3-1	Switzerland
Germany	2-1	Switzerland
Switzerland	2-2	Portugal
Portugal	2-1	Germany

Sweden (9 points) and Portugal (4) progressed. Germany had 3, Switzerland one.

Semi-finals

| Serbia-Montenegro | 1-1 | Sweden (Serbia won on penalties) |
| Italy | 3-1 | Portugal |

Third place match

| Portugal | 3-2 | Sweden (after extra time) |

Final

| Italy | 3-0 | Serbia-Montenegro |

Italy, **Serbia-Montenegro**, and **Portugal** qualified for Athens.

North and Central America

(CONCACAF Under-23 Tournament)

Preliminary Round

(aggregate scores over two legs)

Round 1

Trinidad and Tobago	6-1	Bahamas
El Salvador walk-over	v	Puerto Rico
St Lucia walk-over	v	Antigua and Barbuda
Panama	6-3	Nicaragua
Grenada	10-1	Cayman Islands
Canada	24-0	US Virgin Islands
St Kitts and Nevis	4-1	Dominica
Haiti	2-0	Dominican Republic
Jamaica	2-1	Cuba
Guatemala	8-0	Surinam
Guyana	5-3	Barbados
Costa Rica	23-0	Belize

Round 2

Panama	13-1	St Lucia
Canada	1-1	El Salvador (Canada won on penalty kicks)
USA	10-0	St Kitts and Nevis
Trinidad and Tobago	4-1	Grenada
Costa Rica	10-1	Guyana
Honduras	3-2	Haiti
Jamaica	3-2	Guatemala

Final Round

(played in Mexico)

Group A

Honduras	1-0	Canada
USA	4-3	Panama
Honduras	3-1	Panama
USA	2-0	Canada
Panama	2-1	Canada
USA	4-3	Honduras

USA (9 points) won Group A and went into the semi-finals. Honduras (6 points) finished second and also reached the next stage. Panama had 3 points, Canada none.

Group B

Costa Rica	3-0	Jamaica
Mexico	3-1	Trinidad and Tobago
Costa Rica	4-0	Trinidad and Tobago
Mexico	4-0	Jamaica
Trinidad and Tobago	2-1	Jamaica
Mexico	1-1	Costa Rica

Costa Rica (7 points) won Group B to reach the semi-finals, as did Mexico

(7), second on goal difference. Trinidad and Tobago had 3 points, Jamaica none.

Final Stage

Semi-finals

Costa Rica	2-0	Honduras
Mexico	4-0	USA

Final

Mexico	1-0	Costa Rica

Mexico and **Costa Rica** qualified for Athens.

(Third place match: Honduras 1-1 USA, won by Honduras on penalty kicks)

South America

(matches played in Chile)

Final Round

Group A

Chile	3-0	Uruguay
Chile	3-0	Venezuela
Chile	3-2	Paraguay
Chile	1-1	Brazil
Brazil	4-0	Venezuela
Brazil	3-0	Paraguay
Brazil	1-1	Uruguay
Paraguay	3-1	Venezuela
Paraguay	2-1	Uruguay
Uruguay	1-1	Venezuela

Chile won Group A with 10 points to reach the final stage. Brazil (8 points) were second, Paraguay third on 6 points to go into a play-off. Uruguay had 2 points, Venezuela 1.

Group B

Argentina	0-0	Peru
Argentina	2-1	Bolivia
Argentina	5-2	Ecuador
Argentina	4-2	Colombia
Ecuador	1-0	Colombia
Ecuador	4-2	Peru
Ecuador	3-2	Bolivia
Colombia	3-1	Peru
Colombia	2-0	Bolivia
Peru	3-2	Bolivia

Argentina won Group B with 10 points. Ecuador (9) and Colombia (6) finished second and third to reach the play-offs. Peru had 4 points, Bolivia none.

Play-offs

| Brazil | 3-0 | Colombia |
| Paraguay | 0-0 | Ecuador (Paraguay progressed after penalty kicks) |

Final Stage

Argentina	1-0	Brazil
Argentina	2-1	Paraguay
Argentina	2-2	Chile
Paraguay	1-0	Brazil
Paraguay	2-1	Chile

Brazil 3-1 Chile

Argentina (7 points) and **Paraguay** (6) qualified for Athens. Brazil had 3 points, Chile one.

Africa

Group A

Preliminary Round

Mauritania walk-over v Cape Verde

Benin and Equatorial Guinea both withdrew.

Round 1

Nigeria	3-1	Namibia (over two legs)
Egypt walk-over	v	Tanzania
Senegal walk-over	v	Mauritania

Bye: Tunisia

Round 2

Tunisia	0-0	Senegal
Tunisia	2-0	Egypt
Tunisia	2-0	Nigeria
Nigeria	1-1	Tunisia
Egypt	1-3	Tunisia
Senegal	0-0	Tunisia
Egypt	0-2	Nigeria
Senegal	4-3	Nigeria
Nigeria	2-0	Senegal
Nigeria	3-0	Egypt
Senegal	2-0	Egypt
Egypt	0-1	Senegal

Tunisia (12 points) qualified for Athens. Senegal had 11 points, Nigeria 10, and Egypt none.

Group B

Preliminary Round (over two legs)

Rwanda	3-1	Malawi
Congo walk-over	v	Central African Republic

Round 1 (over two legs)

Cameroon	3-2	Congo
D.R. Congo	3-0	Rwanda
Mali	1-0	Guinea
Ivory Coast walk-over	v	Burkina Faso

Round 2

Mali	3-0	Ivory Coast
Cameroon	2-0	Mali
D.R. Congo	0-2	Mali
Mali	3-1	D.R. Congo
Ivory Coast	2-1	Mali
Mali	1-0	Cameroon
D.R. Congo	1-4	Cameroon
Ivory Coast	1-1	Cameroon
Cameroon	2-0	Ivory Coast
Cameroon	1-1	D.R. Congo
Ivory Coast	4-1	D.R. Congo
D.R. Congo	1-0	Ivory Coast

Mali qualified for Athens with 12 points. Cameroon had 11, Ivory Coast 7, and D.R. Congo 7.

Group C

Preliminary Round (over two legs)

Seychelles	2-1	Mauritius
Ethiopia	2-1	Sudan
Gambia walk-over	v	Guinea-Bissau
Lesotho	1-0	Mozambique

Round 1 (over two legs)

Uganda	5-4	Seychelles
Ethiopia	3-2	Zimbabwe
Angola	5-2	Lesotho
Morocco	5-3	Gambia

Round 2

Morocco	4-0	Ethiopia
Angola	0-0	Morocco
Uganda	1-1	Morocco
Morocco	5-0	Uganda
Ethiopia	1-0	Morocco
Morocco	2-1	Angola
Uganda	1-2	Angola
Angola	4-0	Ethiopia
Angola	1-0	Uganda
Ethiopia	1-0	Angola
Ethiopia	1-0	Uganda
Uganda	2-1	Ethiopia

Morocco qualified for Athens with 11 points. Angola had 10, Ethiopia 9, Uganda 4.

Group D

Preliminary Round (over 2 legs)

Kenya	15-0	Somalia
Botswana	5-3	Swaziland
Chad	6-1	Libya

Round 1 (over 2 legs)

South Africa	2-1	Kenya
Algeria	5-0	Chad (only first leg was played – Chad then withdrew)
Zambia	3-2	Botswana
Ghana	6-0	Liberia

Round 2

Ghana	1-0	South Africa
Zambia	0-0	Ghana
Algeria	1-0	Ghana
Ghana	2-0	Algeria
South Africa	1-2	Ghana
Ghana	2-0	Zambia
South Africa	4-1	Algeria
South Africa	0-1	Zambia
Zambia	2-1	South Africa
Algeria	0-1	South Africa
Algeria	1-0	Zambia
Zambia	4-2	Algeria

Ghana qualified for Athens with 13 points; Zambia had 10, South Africa 6, Algeria 6.

Asia

Preliminary Round (aggregate scores over 2 legs)

Round 1

Oman	17-0	Cambodia
Turkmenistan	2-1	India
Lebanon	1-1	Jordan (Lebanon won on away goals rule)
Palestine	3-1	Nepal
Myanmar	3-0	Bangladesh
Iran walk-over	v	Maldives
Syria	8-1	Pakistan
UAE	4-0	Tajikistan
Singapore	5-3	Taiwan
Iraq	4-2	Vietnam
Hong Kong	3-0	Sri Lanka
Kyrgyzstan walk-over	v	Yemen

12 other teams received byes to Round 2.

Round 2

Japan	8-0	Myanmar
Bahrain	7-2	Kyrgyzstan
Iran	9-2	Uzbekistan
Oman	2-1	Qatar
Lebanon	5-2	Indonesia
Kuwait	3-2	Palestine
Malaysia walk-over	v	Turkmenistan
UAE	5-2	Thailand
China	4-3	Syria
Iraq	4-3	North Korea
South Korea	3-0	Hong Kong
Saudi Arabia	10-0	Singapore

Those 12 winners then played in three groups A, B and C.

Final Round

Group A

South Korea	1-0	China
Iran	0-1	South Korea
Malaysia	0-1	South Korea
South Korea	3-0	Malaysia
China	0-2	South Korea
South Korea	1-0	Iran
Malaysia	1-4	Iran
China	3-1	Iran
Iran	2-1	China
Iran	6-0	Malaysia
China	1-1	Malaysia
Malaysia	1-2	China

South Korea (18 points) qualified for Athens. Iran had 9 points, China 7, Malaysia one.

Group B

Japan	0-0	Bahrain
Lebanon	0-4	Japan
Japan	2-0	UAE
Bahrain	1-0	Japan
Japan	2-1	Lebanon
UAE	0-3	Japan
Bahrain	0-3	UAE
Bahrain	5-3	Lebanon
UAE	0-2	Bahrain
Lebanon	1-1	Bahrain

| UAE | 4-2 | Lebanon |
| Lebanon | 2-2 | UAE |

Japan (13 points) qualified for Athens. Bahrain had 11 points, UAE 7, Lebanon 2.

Group C

Iraq	4-0	Oman
Saudi Arabia	1-0	Iraq
Iraq	2-1	Kuwait
Kuwait	2-0	Iraq
Oman	2-0	Iraq
Iraq	3-1	Saudi Arabia
Oman	1-0	Kuwait
Saudi Arabia	1-1	Oman
Oman	0-0	Saudi Arabia
Kuwait	0-0	Oman
Kuwait	0-0	Saudi Arabia
Saudi Arabia	0-1	Kuwait

Iraq qualified for Athens with 9 points. Oman, also on 9, had a poorer goal difference, with Kuwait on 7 points, Saudi Arabia 6.

Oceania

Final Round

Group A

(matches played in Australia)

Australia	6-0	Samoa
Australia	9-0	Papua New Guinea
Australia	5-0	Solomon Islands
Australia	6-0	Fiji

Fiji	4-1	Solomon Islands
Fiji	4-1	Papua New Guinea
Fiji	4-0	Samoa
Solomon Islands	4-2	Papua New Guinea
Samoa	4-4	Papua New Guinea
Samoa	1-0	Solomon Islands

Australia progressed to the next stage with 12 points, while Fiji had 9. Samoa were on 4 points, Solomon Islands 3, Papua New Guinea one.

Group B

(matches played in New Zealand)

New Zealand	9-0	Cook Islands
New Zealand	11-0	American Samoa
New Zealand	3-2	Vanuatu
New Zealand	2-0	Tonga
Vanuatu	6-0	Tonga
Vanuatu	11-0	Cook Islands
Vanuatu	8-0	American Samoa
Tonga	1-0	Cook Islands
Cook Islands	3-2	American Samoa
Tonga	3-0	American Samoa

New Zealand went through to the next stage with 12 points. Vanuatu had 9, Tonga 6, Cook Islands 3, American Samoa none.

Final

Australia	3-1	New Zealand (over two legs)

Australia qualified for Athens.

26. Beijing, 2008

Blue and white tango

In 2001 Beijing was awarded the 2008 Games ahead of Toronto, Paris, Istanbul and Osaka, and its opening ceremony featured 15,000 performers over four hours. At the other end of the time spectrum, Usain 'lightning' Bolt became the fastest runner with 100, 200 and 4 × 100 metres relay golds, as he detained huge crowds for only a few seconds.

86 countries won medals, with China leading the golden table with 51, while USA won 36, Russia 23 and Great Britain 19. Eight of Britain's were for cycling, including three for Sir Chris Hoy. The American swimmer Michael Phelps set a new record for the number of victories, amassing eight golds in five individual and three team races.

After an extended closing ceremony, Beijing's Mayor handed the Olympic flag to the Mayor of London, Boris Johnson, to signal a new Olympiad that would culminate in London 2012.

The football tournament

The teams in Beijing were:

Hosts: China
Europe: Serbia, Netherlands, Belgium, Italy
North and Central America: USA, Honduras
South America: Argentina, Brazil
Africa: Ivory Coast, Nigeria, Cameroon
Asia: Japan, South Korea, Australia
Oceania: New Zealand

Six stadia presented matches. In Beijing the new National Stadium, nicknamed 'The Bird's Nest', hosted the Final and the 1959 Workers' Stadium four matches. Shanghai Stadium, opened in 1997, was the venue for nine fixtures, Qinhuangdao Sports Centre six, Tianjin Olympic Centre six, and Shenyang Olympic Sports Centre six more. Those regional stadia were built in 2004 (Qinhuangdao) and 2007.

The field of 16 countries included the 2004 winners, Argentina, in their traditional blue and white colours, and Brazil. Of the two, Brazil had a more comfortable qualifying event, losing none of their nine matches. Argentina lost to Colombia, drew with Chile and Ecuador, and narrow wins over Paraguay and Uruguay were essential.

Of the four European qualifiers, The Netherlands were most impressive, winning the UEFA Under 21 championship, admittedly in their own country. Serbia came second after wins against Italy and the Czech Republic. Italy defeated a strong Spanish side as well as Portugal en route to the last 16. Belgium's most significant result was a draw with the Dutch.

Out of all the North and Central American entrants, Honduras played most matches and defeated their fellow qualifiers, the USA, 1-0.

From Africa, Ivory Coast won matches against Egypt, Senegal, Mali and Zambia. Nigeria's key result was a narrow win over Ghana, while Cameroon defeated Guinea, Morocco and Botswana.

Japan qualified just ahead of Qatar, despite two goalless draws with Saudi Arabia. South Korea's principal rivals proved to be Bahrain, whom they beat by a single goal, and Australia came through after playing matches in Iran, Jordan, Saudi Arabia, Lebanon, Iraq and North Korea.

Oceania's representatives (who used to be Australia) were New Zealand, who won all five fixtures, their narrowest victory against Fiji.

Group A

7 August	Australia 1-1 Serbia (0-0)	Shanghai
	Zadkovich 69 Rajkovic 78	

7 August	Argentina 2-1 Ivory Coast (1-0)	Shanghai
	Messi 43 Cisse 53	
	Acosta 86	

10 August	Argentina 1-0 Australia (0-0)	Shanghai
	Lavezzi 76	

10 August	Ivory Coast 4-2 Serbia (2-1)	Shanghai
	Cisse 3 Mrdakovic 16	
	Rajkovic o.g. 24 Rakic 90	
	Kalou 70	
	Gervinho 90	

13 August   Ivory Coast 1-0 Australia (0-0)   Tianjin
                    Kalou 81

13 August   Argentina 2-0 Serbia (1-0)   Beijing
                    Lavezzi 13 (p)
                    Buonanotte 84

Qualified: Argentina   9 points   (5 goals for – 1 against)
Qualified: Ivory Coast 6 points   (6-4)
            Australia   1 point   (1-3)
            Serbia   1 point   (3-7)

Group A brought together the reigning champions, Argentina, with Australia, Serbia and Ivory Coast, a country making their debut.

Serbia were on top for most of the first match, with **Australia**, but there were no goals till the last 21 minutes. Tosic alone had seven shots saved by Australia's keeper Federici or the woodwork. Australia had one corner and conceded 14. Their plan was to counter-attack, and this succeeded when Ruben Zadkovich put them ahead from David Carney's cross. Nikita Rukavytsja then hit the post for Australia, but it ended 1-1 as Rajkovic headed Serbia's equaliser.

Argentina were pleased to have Lionel Messi in their squad, despite his club Barcelona's reluctance, and the young midfielder scored after 43 minutes, against **Ivory Coast**.

Ivory Coast, however, were just as ready to attack, and Cisse levelled the match early in the second half, heading past Ustari in goal. The African team's captain Gervinho was proving difficult for Argentine defenders, marshalled by Riquelme, but the South Americans found a late winner. Acosta, only on the field six minutes, benefited from a Messi-Riquelme move to score in 86 minutes.

Argentina controlled play against **Australia** but Messi could not score from five good chances. Monzon and Riquelme were also denied by a resolute defence, in which Federici shone in goal. At last Di Maria's cross eluded Australia's back four and Lavezzi struck home a powerful drive in 76 minutes, for all three points.

Against **Serbia**, **Ivory Coast** took a third minute lead through Cisse, but the match was soon level as Mrdakovic chipped over Angban, the Ivory

Coast keeper. Serbia's Rajkovic then headed into his own net and the African side regained the advantage, creating but missing chances. Solomon Kalou made it 3-1 for Ivory Coast in the 70th minute, and in a hectic last 60 seconds Rakic of Serbia and Gervinho both scored, for a 4-2 result.

Ivory Coast (3 points), Serbia and Australia (both 1 point) all still cherished hopes of a quarter-final place; Argentina (6) were already there.

Argentina rested Riquelme, Ustari and Messi against **Serbia** and Mascherano took over the captaincy. Lavezzi's penalty gave the South Americans an early lead, but Serbia prevented further goals at that point. Rajkovic was in the right place to clear Lavezzi's shot off the goal line, while at the other end Romero denied Serbia's Kacar.

Argentina could not benefit from a second penalty – Di Maria's shots were saved by Stojkovic (it had to be taken twice). Then Buonanotte did make it 2-0 with an unstoppable free kick, six minutes from time. In the last seconds, two Serbian players received red cards.

Australia had to win against **Ivory Coast**, and their best attempts, from Carney and Musialik, were both saved by Angban. Kalou was the most effective striker for Ivory Coast and he hit the winning goal in 81 minutes. Despite five substitutions after that, there was no more scoring.

Ivory Coast (6 points) progressed along with Argentina (9); with Australia and Serbia missing out after one draw.

Group B

7 August	USA 1-0 Japan (0-0)		Tianjin
	Holden 47		
7 August	Netherlands 0-0 Nigeria		Tianjin
10 August	Nigeria 2-1 Japan (0-0)		Tianjin
	Obinna 58	Toyoda 79	
	Anichebe 74		
10 August	USA 2-2 Netherlands (0-1)		Tianjin
	Babel 16	Kljestan 64	
	Altidore 72	Sibon 90	

13 August   Netherlands 1-0 Japan (0-0)   Shenyang
                 Sibon 73 (p)

13 August   Nigeria 2-1 USA (1-0)   Beijing
                 Isaac 39   Kljestan 88 (p)
                 Obinna 79

Qualified: Nigeria   6 points   (4-2)
Qualified: Netherlands   5 points   (3-2)
             USA   4 points   (4-4)
             Japan   0 points   (1-4)

Group B included the 1996 champions Nigeria with two regular qualifiers, the USA and Japan, and the Netherlands.

The **USA** survived early scares from **Japan**, especially when Morishige had a great chance. The Americans' Adu then hit a 20 yard shot over the bar. Stuart Holden won the match for the USA with a piledriver just after half-time. Japan's claims for a penalty, when Lee seemed to be fouled, were turned down.

Only one goal in that match, and none between **Nigeria** and the **Netherlands** – cautious beginnings are not unknown in major tournaments. In fact both teams made good opportunities, notably the Dutch midfielder Jonathan De Guzman, who tested Nigeria's keeper Vanzekin with a 30 yard free kick. The Dutch captain Roy Makaay also hit the bar. Nigeria's striker Victor Obinna had three near-misses, heading or shooting just wide, and forcing Vermeer in goal to deflect a shot round the post.

Although Makaay had to go off after an injury, his team continued to attack, while Odemwingie and Isaac for Nigeria were denied by Vermeer's saves, in an entertaining match. Only Evander Sno's red card in the last minute was a blot on the Dutch landscape.

Nigeria began slowly against **Japan** but in the 30th minute tempo quickened as Odemwingie missed from close range, and Taniguchi drew a fine save from Vanzekin at the other end. After nearly an hour, Obinna and Odemwingie made the breakthrough with a move that let Obinna score. During one Japanese attack, Anichebe intercepted and doubled Nigeria's lead in the 74th minute. Although Toyoda scored with a low drive, the African side held on to win.

The **USA** faced a **Netherlands** team captained by Maduro, with Makaay on the bench. The Dutch attack included Babel, of Liverpool, Beerens, and Drenthe from Real Madrid; for the Americans captain Brian McBride was making his third appearance in the Olympics.

The Dutch winger Babel scored in 16 minutes, despite Guzan saving his initial header. Freddy Adu gave the USA hope when he beat three defenders but shot over, Holden tested the Dutch keeper from 18 yards, and McBride's header was tipped over the bar.

At last Sacha Kljestan found that elusive American equaliser in 64 minutes, and Altidore put them 2-1 up soon after. But the most important goal in Group B was Gerald Sibon's when he drove in a free kick after 90 minutes, to gain the Netherlands a point.

Nigeria now had 4 points, as had the USA, the Netherlands two, Japan none.

The **Netherlands** welcomed their captain back against **Japan**, whose single goal in Group B scarcely did their attacking play justice. The Dutch keeper, Vermeer, was in brilliant form to prevent Babel's own goal and stop Toyoda's 20 yarder. His crossbar then came to the rescue when Monshige hit the target.

Gradually the Netherlands won more possession, and the only goal was a Sibon penalty in 73 minutes after Babel was fouled. Both keepers were busy near the end, especially when Nishikawa kept Makaay's shot out.

Nigeria and **USA** were playing for a quarter-final place, and the Americans lost their left back, Michael Orozco, to a red card after only three minutes. Nigeria controlled first-half play, and Ogbuke strikes were saved by the US keeper Guzan. In the 39th minute he created an easier chance for Isaac, who scored.

The Americans also missed Adu, suspended for this match, but McBride, Kljestan and Szetela all missed chances. Obinna took his for Nigeria after running through the defence in 79 minutes. Kljestan did reduce the deficit with a penalty, and the closing stages were hectic. The USA abandoned defence and Davies headed Feilhaber's cross against a post.

Nigeria won Group B with 6 points, with the Netherlands second on 5. Once again, the USA were unfortunate to finish third (with 4 points) – Japan had none.

Group C

7 August	Brazil	1-0	Belgium (0-0)	Shenyang
	Hernanes 79			

7 August	China	1-1	New Zealand (0-0)	Shenyang
	D. Fangzhuo 78		Brockie 53	

10 August	Brazil	5-0	New Zealand (2-0)	Shenyang
	Anderson 3			
	A. Pato 34			
	Ronaldinho 55, 61 (p)			
	R. Sobis 90			

10 August	Belgium	2-0	China (1-0)	Shenyang
	Dembele 8			
	Mirallas 80			

13 August	Brazil	3-0	China (1-0)	Qinuangdao
	Diego 18			
	T. Neves 69, 73			

13 August	Belgium	1-0	New Zealand	Shanghai
	Haroun 35			

Qualified: Brazil 9 points (9-0)
Qualified: Belgium 6 points (3-1)
China 1 point (1-6)
New Zealand 1 point (1-7)

Brazil were favourites to win Group C, but Belgium had been champions (in 1920). The hosts, China, were assured of home crowds' support, and New Zealand were Oceania's representative.

Brazil v **Belgium** was the first of two matches between the sides, who met later in the bronze medal fixture. Brazilian attackers faced a well organised Belgian defence, led by Martens, and three players were booked in the first two minutes.

Ronaldinho's team created chances without scoring until the 79th minute, through Hernanes. Late in this match two Belgians were sent off for a second yellow card – Vincent Kompany and Marouane Fellaini. Against nine opponents, Jo's late 'goal' for Brazil was disallowed for offside.

China v **New Zealand** drew 41,000 to Shenyang, slightly more than for the afternoon match. Early play was marred by too many fouls, and the Kiwis' centre-back Steven Old was dismissed in 39 minutes for two yellow cards. Against 10 men, China were in charge, but after 53 minutes Craig Henderson's pass found Jeremy Brockie, who ran through to score.

New Zealand then blocked Chinese attacks, with their keeper Jacob Spoonley and captain Ryan Nelsen outstanding. At last China's substitute Dong Fangzhuo headed an equaliser in 88 minutes.

New Zealand's good performance raised hopes, which **Brazil** soon dispelled. Anderson put the South Americans ahead after three minutes – Spoonley saved his fine drive, but the Brazilian headed back into the net. Alexandre Pato, from AC Milan, headed a second from Marcello's cross. 2-0 and Brazil in control by half-time.

New Zealand brought on two substitutes after half-time, but there was no respite. Ronaldinho scored twice, from a free-kick and a penalty. The last word went to Rafael Sobis who scored in the 90th minute.

Brazil's six points ensured their quarter-final place, but who would join them? **Belgium** made a fine start against **China**, as Moussa Dembele went past defenders and drove the ball past Qiu Shengjiong in goal. China responded, and Gao Lin had only to beat Belgium's keeper Bailly – instead he passed to a colleague.

China were reduced to nine men by the 64th minute as Tan Wangsong and his captain Zheng Zhi were shown red cards. With 10 minutes left, Belgium's Kevin Mirallas ensured a 2-0 victory with an 18 yard strike.

Although the Belgians had 3 points, New Zealand and China (each with one point) could still claim second place in this group.

Brazil ended **China**'s hopes with a comfortable 3-0 win. China missed several first choice defenders, and in 18 minutes Diego ran on to Ronaldinho's through ball to score. Thiago Silva then blocked a good drive from Jiang Ning to stop the equaliser. Thiago Neves, the Brazilian midfielder, scored twice late in the match with powerful shots, the first from a free kick.

Belgium reached the next stage with a narrow victory over **New Zealand**. Faris Haroun's header after a corner made the difference in the 35th minute, and New Zealand's attack was blunted when Ellensohn was sent off just after the second half got underway.

Although Belgium had the better chances – Tom De Mul hit the bar – Chris Killen almost equalised against the run of play, only to be denied by keeper Logan Bailly.

Belgium's two wins brought them second place in Group C, in which Brazil had not conceded a goal while scoring nine.

Group D

7 August	Italy 3-0 Honduras (2-0)	Qinhuangdao
	Giovinco 41	
	Rossi 45 (p)	
	Acquafresca 52 (p)	

7 August	Cameroon 1-1 South Korea (0-0)	Qinhuangdao
	Mandjeck 81 Park J.Y. 68	

10 August	Cameroon 1-0 Honduras (0-0)	Qinhuangdao
	M'Bia 74	

10 August	Italy 3-0 South Korea (2-0)	Qinhuangdao
	Rossi 15	
	Rocchi 31	
	Montolivo 90	

13 August	South Korea 1-0 Honduras (1-0)	Shanghai
	Kim D.J. 23	

| 13 August | Italy 0-0 Cameroon | Tianjin |

Qualified:	Italy	7 points	(6-0)
Qualified:	Cameroon	5 points	(2-1)
	South Korea	4 points	(2-4)
	Honduras	0 points	(0-5)

Italy's 3-0 win over **Honduras** was a fair reflection of the match as a whole, but the Italians took almost all the first half to find the net. Then Sebastian Giovinco, from Juventus, hit a superb goal from the edge of the box. Four minutes later, Arzu, Honduras' centre-back, handled and Giuseppe Rossi scored from the penalty.

Early in the second half, Robert Acquafresca ran through the Honduran defence but was fouled by their keeper Hernandez. Acquafresca took the spot-kick to make it 3-0. Honduras then had chances – Jorge Caballero forced Italy's keeper Viviano into a fine save, and Carlos Pavon hit a late penalty over the bar.

South Korea and **Cameroon** produced an exhilarating match. The Koreans' Park Joo-Yong opened the scoring in 68 minutes with a free-kick over the defensive wall. Cameroon equalised 13 minutes later when Mandjeck hit the bar and saw his shot fall into the net. The African side had more of the chances and possession, but lost two points as well as their midfielder Baning, to a very late red card.

Cameroon's narrow victory over **Honduras** meant the losing team could not progress. Honduras almost made a perfect start, but their midfielder Ramon Nunez shot wide. Cameroon had most of the chances without taking any, until Stephane M'Bia scored the only goal with 16 minutes left.

Italy had a clear-cut win over **South Korea**, who found the Italian strikers Rossi, Rocchi and Giovinco too skilful to be marked out of the game. Rossi scored after 15 minutes, collecting the rebound when Tomasso Rocchi's strike was blocked. Then Marco Motta, Italy's right back, beat the defence and passed to Rocchi, who hit the net. Riccardo Montolivo got a third goal in the last minute. In the last half-hour, Italy replaced all three forwards.

With 6 points, Italy could already plan for the quarter-finals. Cameroon (4), would join them unless South Korea (1 point) defeated Honduras, and Italy scored an emphatic victory over Cameroon.

Honduras had their best performance against **South Korea**. Emil Martinez had good opportunities, based on fast-moving attacks built on their short passing game. But the Koreans won the match through Kim Dong-jin's early goal and they finished the stronger.

Cameroon's draw with **Italy** lacked goals but not incident. Giovinco drew a fine save from the Cameroon keeper and captain, Tignyemb, before Bocchetti's handling offence led to a Cameroon penalty: Chedjou's kick was well saved by Viviano. Once Mandjeck was sent off in 32 minutes, the advantage switched to Italy, but no goals resulted.

Italy (7 points) won Group D, ahead of Cameroon (5), who also progressed. South Korea had 4 points, Honduras none.

Quarter-finals

16 August　　　　　Brazil 2-0 Cameroon (0-0)　　Shenyang
(after extra time)
R. Sobis 101
Marcelo 105

16 August　　　　　Belgium 3-2 Italy (2-1)　　Beijing
Dembele 23, 79　　Rossi 18 (p), 74 (p)
Mirallas 45

16 August　　　　　Argentina 2-1 Netherlands (1-1)　　Shanghai
(after extra time)
Messi 14　　　　Bakkal 36
Di Maria 105

16 August　　　　　Nigeria 2-0 Ivory Coast (1-0)　　Qinhuangdao
Odemwingie 44
Obinna 82 (p)

Quarter-finals

Both **Cameroon** and **Brazil** began cautiously. The African side missed Kingue and Mandjeck, both suspended, and their right-back M'Bia was quickly substituted after being injured. Despite both teams' undoubted skills, they produced few chances and no goals for 90 minutes. Ronaldinho's powerful free kick and Bebbe's long-range shot were rare highlights.

Indeed, the referee worked as hard as anyone, booking five Brazilians and eight from Cameroon.

Cameroon's Albert Baning, sent off against South Korea, was again dismissed for a second yellow card, leaving his team a man short for almost an hour.

On to extra-time, when Bebbe hit a 20 yarder just over. But it was Brazil who scored twice – Rafael Sobis pouncing on Diego's through pass, and Marcelo coming out of defence to convert Thiago Neves's cross. Brazil quickly substituted Sobis and Diego as they prepared for a semi-final against Argentina.

Belgium v **Italy** produced a more enthralling contest. In only 18 minutes Belgium went a man and a goal down, as their centre-back Thomas Vermaelen was sent off after fouling Acquafresca; Giuseppe Rossi scored with the penalty. But the Belgians soon equalised, even if Moussa Dembele's header may have been cleared off the line. They even went ahead, through Mirallas, just before half-time.

Italy attacked constantly and received a second penalty award when Paolo De Ceglie, up helping his forwards, was tripped. Rossi calmly levelled the match on 2-2.

But Belgium never settled for extra time, and in 79 minutes Dembele's drive gave them victory. Italy's keeper Viviano was then sent off, and their team rearranged with two substitutes, to no avail.

Argentina had won all three Group A matches, the **Netherlands** just once in Group B. Lionel Messi gave Argentina an early lead, intercepting a Dutch attack before beating two defenders and the keeper. Netherlands came back to level the game in 36 minutes – Evander Sno's free kick hit an opponent to allow Otman Bakkal a simple chance.

There were no more goals in the 90 minutes, despite clear opportunities for Aguero of Argentina, and Babel and Drenthe for the Dutch. One strike decided this match in extra time, when Angel Di Maria controlled Messi's pass to shoot past Thomas Vermeer in the Dutch goal.

Nigeria and **Ivory Coast** met to ensure that at least one African team would progress. Defences were usually in charge, and individual forwards tended to rely on their own skills rather than passing. A rare exception was Victor Obinna's pass to Peter Odemwingie, which gave him space to score in the 44th minute.

For Ivory Coast, Solomon Kalou and Gervinho had good chances to equalise, but Nigeria extended their lead with a late penalty. Obinna took full advantage, after Ogbuke was fouled.

Semi-finals

19 August	Nigeria 4-1 Belgium (1-0)	Shanghai
	Adefemi 17 Ciman 88	
	Ogbuke 59, 72	
	Okonkwo 78	

19 August	Argentina 3-0 Brazil (0-0)	Beijing
	Aguero 52, 58	
	Riquelme 76 (p)	

Semi-finals

The first semi-final was surprisingly one-sided, especially in the second half, with **Nigeria** winning 4-1 over **Belgium**. Nigerian forwards, especially Okonkwo and Odemwingie, constantly tested the Belgian back three, and Adefemi capitalised with the first goal in 17 minutes. Vincent Kompany, now with Manchester City, was missed by the Belgian defenders – he only played in their first match, received a red card and was called back for club duties by Hamburg.

Belgium did make chances, notably Faris Haroun's drive which hit the bar, but just before an hour had gone Ogbuke doubled Nigeria's lead. He then made it 3-0 with a prodigious 40 yard strike. Only then did Belgium replace two forwards, too late. Okonkwo hit a fourth goal, before Laurent Ciman proved his value with an accurate free kick into the net. His Olympic experience lasted those 15 minutes as a substitute – he did not even make the bronze medal match.

Argentina v **Brazil** was a battle of South American giants, the reigning gold medallists against World Cup specialists who have yet to win the Olympic crown.

At first neither side could break the deadlock, but Brazil's captain Ronaldinho was less visible than his young opponent, Messi. The result hinged on 15 minutes of play after half-time. Aguero deflected home a shot by Di Maria to give Argentina the lead. Suddenly the game burst into life, and Rafael Sobis was inches from an equaliser with his 25 yard strike. Then Messi ran across the penalty area, Garay took his pass, sending it on to Aguero for his second goal.

With 14 minutes to go, Argentina's captain Riquelme converted a penalty for 3-0. Brazil now had every substitute on the field. Ronaldinho grazed a post with his free-kick, Alexandre Pato netted the rebound, only for an offside flag to rule it out. As they became frustrated, Brazil lost both Lucas and Thiago Neves to red cards in the last 10 minutes.

Bronze medal match

22 August   Brazil 3-0 Belgium (2-0)   Shanghai
                 Diego 27
                 Jo 45, 90

After **Belgium's** fine start, **Brazil** seemed to put their disappointment over the semi-final behind them. Diego shot Rafinha's cross into the net, and Jo, making a rare start upfront, headed a second on half-time. Brazil's defence then kept the ball away from Belgium's young forwards, and 50,000 spectators voiced their disapproval of defensive tactics.

Jo at least enhanced his reputation, scoring another goal right on the whistle. Brazil had once again won medals, and Belgium achieved their best performance since Antwerp in 1920.

The Final

23 August   Argentina 1-0 Nigeria (0-0)   Beijing
                 Di Maria 58

A huge crowd of 89,000 came to Beijing National Stadium, despite the noonday heat of 100°F plus. Players had to take breaks for a drink, an up to date version of the waterbuckets provided for 1912 matches at Stockholm, when it was almost as hot.

Nigeria marked Messi and Aguero closely, but **Argentina's** Di Maria, from Benfica's squad, took up the challenge. After 58 minutes, Messi ran between two defenders, Di Maria collected the ball and chipped over Ambrose Venzekin as the keeper ran off his line.

With half an hour left, Argentina began to defend in depth, which allowed Nigeria to push up and create more chances. Sergio Romero, the South Americans' keeper, did well to stop Obinna's shot, and neither Odemwingie nor Ekpo could control the ball after a fine right-wing move. Then Ajilore almost benefited as Argentina hesitated in defence, but he shot wide, before Kaita hit over the bar.

Messi almost had the last word, running, dribbling and shooting, but Apam blocked his drive. Both teams were going for a second gold, and Argentina won a close run match.

Top goal-scorers

4: Rossi (Italy)
3: Obinna (Nigeria)

The medal winners

Gold: Argentina

Ustari	Mascherano	Lavezzi
Romero	Gago	Banega
Zabaleta	Riquelme (captain)	Acosta
Garay	Aguero	Buonanotte
Pareja	Sosa	Fazio
Monzon	Di Maria	Navarro
Messi		

Silver: Nigeria

Vanzekin	Kaita	James
Adefemi	Ajilore	Obasi
Apam	Obinna	Ambrose
Adeleye	Isaac (captain)	Ezenwa
Okonkwo	Ekpo	Olufemi
Okoronkwo	Odemwingie	Anichebe

Bronze: Brazil

Renan	Hernanes	Thiago Neves
Rafinha	Ramires	Lucas
Alex Silva	Diego	Anderson
Breno	Jo	Rafael Sobis
Thiego Silva	Ronaldinho (captain)	Alexandre Pato
Marcelo	Isinho	

Referees

J. Damon (South Africa)	Australia v Serbia
	Brazil v China
W. Stark (Germany)	Argentina v Ivory Coast
	Nigeria v USA
V. Kassai (Hungary)	Argentina v Australia
	Argentina v Nigeria (Final)
R. Moreno (Panama)	Ivory Coast v Serbia
J. Marrufo (USA)	Ivory Coast v Australia
	Cameroon v South Korea
	Argentina v Netherlands
A. al-Hilali (Oman)	Argentina v Serbia
	Cameroon v Honduras
B. Diatta (Senegal)	USA v Japan
P. Pozo (Chile)	Netherlands v Nigeria
	Belgium v New Zealand
	Nigeria v Belgium (semi-final)
D. Skomina (Slovenia)	Italy v Honduras
	Brazil v Cameroon
M. Moradi (Iran)	Nigeria v Japan
	Nigeria v Ivory Coast
M. Hester (New Zealand)	USA v Netherlands
	South Korea v Honduras
H. Baldassi (Argentina)	Netherlands v Japan
	Belgium v China
	Belgium v Italy
K. al-Ghamdi (Saudi Arabia)	Brazil v Belgium
M. Vazquez (Uruguay)	China v New Zealand
	Cameroon v Italy
	Argentina v Brazil (semi-final)
S. Lannoy (France)	Brazil v New Zealand
T. Einwaller (Australia)	Italy v South Korea
	Brazil v Belgium (Bronze medal match)

The qualifying tournament

The 16 participants would be:

Hosts: China
Europe: four teams

North and Central America: two teams
South America: two teams
Africa: three teams
Asia: three teams
Oceania: one team

Once more, the popularity of the tournament was clear. 170 countries entered, and only 9 withdrew at some point.

Europe

(Under 21 Championship)

Preliminary Round

(Aggregate scores over two legs)

Northern Ireland	8-1	Liechtenstein
Macedonia FYR	5-0	Luxembourg
Georgia	4-2	Malta
Ireland	6-0	Azerbaijan
Wales	7-1	Estonia
Iceland	2-0	Andorra
Armenia	4-3	San Marino
Moldova	1-0	Kazakhstan

Round 1

(consisting of 14 groups of three teams, who played each other once).

Group 1

Bosnia-Herzegovina	3-2	Armenia
Armenia	1-0	Norway
Norway	1-1	Bosnia-Herzegovina

Bosnia-Herzegovina (4 points) progressed to Round 2.

Group 2

Slovakia	0-0	Albania
Albania	0-3	Spain
Spain	4-2	Slovakia

Spain (6 points) reached Round 2.

Group 3

Lithuania	1-0	Georgia
Georgia	1-3	Serbia
Serbia	2-0	Lithuania

Serbia (6 points) went on to Round 2.

Group 4

Greece	0-2	Ireland
Ireland	0-1	Belgium
Belgium	2-1	Greece

Belgium reached Round 2 with 6 points.

Group 5

Austria	0-0	Iceland
Iceland	0-1	Italy
Italy	1-0	Austria

Italy (6 points) went on to Round 2.

Group 6

Hungary	5-0	Finland
Finland	1-5	Russia
Russia	3-1	Hungary

Russia (6 points) reached Round 2.

Group 7

Poland	3-1	Latvia
Latvia	0-2	Portugal
Portugal	2-0	Poland

Portugal (6 points) progressed to Round 2.

Group 8

England	2-2	Moldova
Moldova	1-3	Switzerland
Switzerland	2-3	England

England (4 points) reached Round 2.

Group 9

Belarus	1-0	Cyprus
Cyprus	0-2	Czech Republic
Czech Republic	2-1	Belarus

Czech Republic, with 6 points, went on to Round 2.

Group 10

Romania	3-0	Northern Ireland
Northern Ireland	2-3	Germany
Germany	5-1	Romania

Germany (6 points) progressed to Round 2.

Group 11

Sweden	3-1	Macedonia FYR
Macedonia FYR	0-3	Denmark
Denmark	0-2	Sweden

Sweden (6 points) reached Round 2.

Group 12

Ukraine	0-3	Bulgaria
Bulgaria	2-1	Croatia
Croatia	1-2	Ukraine

Bulgaria (6 points) went through to Round 2.

Group 13

Israel	3-2	Wales
Wales	2-0	Turkey
Turkey	0-0	Israel

Israel (4 points) progressed to Round 2.

Group 14

Slovenia	1-0	Scotland
Scotland	1-3	France
France	2-0	Slovenia

France (6 points) reached Round 2.

Round 2

(aggregate scores over two legs)

Czech Republic	3-2	Bosnia-Herzegovina
England	3-0	Germany
Italy	2-1	Spain
Portugal	4-4	Russia (on away goals, Portugal went through)
Serbia	8-3	Sweden
Belgium	5-2	Bulgaria
Israel	2-1	France

Bye: Netherlands

Final Stage

(matches played in The Netherlands)

Group A

Netherlands	1-0	Israel
Portugal	0-0	Belgium
Belgium	1-0	Israel
Netherlands	2-1	Portugal
Netherlands	2-2	Belgium
Portugal	4-0	Israel

The Netherlands (7 points) and Belgium (5) reached the semi-finals, ahead of Portugal (4) and Israel (none).

Group B

England	0-0	Czech Republic
Serbia	1-0	Italy
Serbia	1-0	Czech Republic
England	2-2	Italy
Italy	3-1	Czech Republic
England	2-0	Serbia

Serbia (6 points) and England (5) went on to the semi-finals. Italy had 4 points, the Czech Republic one.

For Olympic qualification, England did not put themselves forward, and their place was taken by Italy, who defeated Portugal on penalties in the Fifth place match. (The game ended 0-0 after extra time).

Semi-finals

Netherlands	1-1	England (after extra time) The Netherlands won on penalties
Serbia	2-0	Belgium

Final

Netherlands 4-1 Serbia

Netherlands, **Serbia**, **Belgium** and **Italy** qualified for Beijing.

North and Central America

Preliminary Round

Caribbean Zone

Stage 1 (with six groups A-F)

Group A

Surinam	1-0	Dutch Antilles
Trinidad and Tobago	4-0	Guyana
Trinidad and Tobago	3-0	Dutch Antilles
Surinam	0-0	Trinidad and Tobago
Guyana	2-2	Dutch Antilles
Surinam	1-2	Guyana

Trinidad and Tobago progressed to Stage 2 with 7 points, ahead of Guyana (4), Surinam (4) and Dutch Antilles (one).

Group B

Aruba	0-2	Barbados
Jamaica	6-1	Antigua and Barbuda
Aruba	0-2	Antigua and Barbuda
Jamaica	1-0	Barbados
Antigua and Barbuda	2-1	Barbados
Aruba	0-5	Jamaica

Jamaica (9 points) went through to the next stage, ahead of Antigua and Barbuda (6 points), Barbados (3) and Aruba (none).

Group C

Puerto Rico	4-1	Cayman Islands
Cuba	6-0	Bermuda
Cuba	8-0	Puerto Rico
Cuba	6-0	Cayman Islands
Puerto Rico	2-0	Bermuda
Bermuda	0-0	Cayman Islands

Cuba (9 points) reached Stage 2, while Puerto Rico had 6, Bermuda and Cayman Islands one each.

Group D

St Kitts and Nevis	1-1	Dominican Republic
St Kitts and Nevis	0-1	Haiti
Haiti	0-0	Dominican Republic

Haiti (4 points) went through. The Dominican Republic had 2 points, St Kitts and Nevis one.

Group E

St Vincent and Grenadines	4-1	Dominica
Grenada	3-3	Saint Lucia
St Vincent and Grenadines	0-0	Saint Lucia
St Vincent and Grenadines	3-3	Grenada
Dominica	2-1	Saint Lucia
Grenada	3-0	Dominica

Grenada (5 points) progressed, ahead of St Vincent and Grenadines (also 5) on goals scored. Dominica had 3 points, St Lucia two.

Group F

| Bahamas | 6-1 | US Virgin Islands |

(British Virgin Islands withdrew)
Bahamas reached Stage 2.

Stage 2

Group G

Trinidad and Tobago	0-3	Cuba
Cuba	2-1	Grenada
Trinidad and Tobago	2-3	Grenada

Cuba (6 points) went on to the Final Round, while Grenada had 3 points, Trinidad and Tobago none.

Group H

Haiti	6-0	Bahamas
Bahamas	1-0	Jamaica
Haiti	2-1	Jamaica

Haiti (6 points) progressed, ahead of Bahamas (3) and Jamaica (none).

North and Central American Zone

Group 1 (Triangular)

Panama	2-1	El Salvador
Honduras	3-0	El Salvador
Panama	1-1	Honduras

Honduras reached the Final Round with 4 points, ahead of Panama (4) on goal difference, and El Salvador (none).

Group 2 (Triangular)

Guatemala	3-0	Nicaragua
Costa Rica	9-1	Nicaragua
Guatemala	2-1	Costa Rica

Guatemala (6 points) progressed, with Costa Rica on 3, Nicaragua none.

Play off (between Groups 1 and 2 runners-up)

Panama   1-1   Costa Rica (over 2 legs)

Panama reached the Final Round on penalty kicks.

North and Central America: Final Round

Byes to this stage: USA, Mexico, Canada

Group Stage

Group A

Honduras	1-0	Panama
Honduras	2-0	Cuba
USA	1-1	Cuba
USA	1-0	Panama
Panama	4-1	Cuba
USA	1-0	Honduras

USA (7 points) and Honduras (6) reached the Final Stage, while Panama had 3, Cuba one.

Group B

Guatemala	1-0	Haiti
Guatemala	2-1	Mexico
Canada	1-1	Mexico
Haiti	2-1	Canada
Canada	5-0	Guatemala
Mexico	5-1	Haiti

Guatemala (6 points) and Canada (4) reached the Final Stage. Mexico (4) were third on goal difference, Haiti had 3 points.

Final Stage

Semi-finals:

USA	3-0	Canada
Honduras	0-0	Guatemala (Honduras won on penalty kicks)

Final:

Honduras 1-0 USA

Honduras and **USA** qualified for Beijing.

(Canada beat Guatemala in the third place match on penalties, after a goalless draw).

South America

Round 1

Group A

Brazil	4-2	Chile
Brazil	2-1	Peru
Brazil	2-0	Bolivia
Brazil	1-1	Paraguay
Paraguay	0-0	Bolivia
Paraguay	1-0	Chile
Paraguay	1-0	Peru
Chile	4-0	Bolivia
Chile	4-2	Peru
Bolivia	4-1	Peru

Brazil (10 points), Paraguay (8) and Chile (6) went on to the Final Round. Bolivia had 4 points, Peru none.

Group B

Colombia	2-1	Argentina
Colombia	0-1	Uruguay
Colombia	1-0	Ecuador
Colombia	2-1	Venezuela
Uruguay	0-1	Venezuela
Uruguay	2-1	Ecuador
Uruguay	3-3	Argentina
Argentina	1-1	Ecuador
Argentina	6-0	Venezuela
Ecuador	3-1	Venezuela

Colombia (9 points), Uruguay (7) and Argentina (5) reached the Final Round. Ecuador had 4 points, Venezuela 3.

Final Round

Brazil	2-2	Argentina
Brazil	2-2	Chile
Brazil	3-1	Uruguay
Brazil	1-0	Paraguay
Brazil	2-0	Colombia
Argentina	1-0	Paraguay
Argentina	0-0	Chile
Argentina	0-0	Colombia
Argentina	1-0	Uruguay
Uruguay	3-1	Paraguay
Uruguay	2-0	Colombia
Uruguay	1-1	Chile

Chile	5-0	Colombia
Chile	2-3	Paraguay
Paraguay	3-2	Colombia

Brazil (11 points) and **Argentina** (9) qualified for Beijing. Uruguay had 7 points, Chile 6, Paraguay 6, and Colombia one.

Africa

Group A (aggregate scores over two legs in Rounds One and Two)

Round 1

South Africa	2-1	Namibia
Equatorial Guinea	5-2	Sudan
Uganda walk-over	v	Chad
Burkina Faso walk-over	v	Mauritius
Ethiopia walk-over	v	Liberia
Algeria walk-over	v	Central African Republic

Byes – Nigeria, Ghana

Round 2

Nigeria	5-2	Equatorial Guinea
South Africa	2-0	Uganda
Ghana	5-0	Burkina Faso
Ethiopia	4-2	Algeria

Round 3

Ethiopia	2-2	South Africa

(FIFA suspended Ethiopia from internationals over a dispute within its football federation. This result was then cancelled, and Ethiopia played no other matches in this Round)

Nigeria	3-2	Ghana
South Africa	1-1	Nigeria

South Africa	1-3	Ghana
Ghana	3-1	South Africa
Ghana	0-0	Nigeria
Nigeria	3-0	South Africa

Nigeria (8 points) qualified for Beijing. Ghana had 7, South Africa one.

Group B (aggregate scores over two legs)

Round 1

Egypt	4-0	Gambia
Mozambique	5-3	Libya
Malawi	2-0	Somalia (only one leg played)
Zambia	10-0	Djibouti (only one leg played)
Senegal walk-over	v	Comoros
Ivory Coast walk-over	v	Lesotho
D.R. Congo walk-over	v	Benin

Bye: Mali

Round 2

Zambia	4-3	Malawi
Ivory Coast	4-2	Egypt
Mali	3-3	Mozambique (Mali won on away goals rule)
Senegal walk-over	v	D.R. Congo

Round 3 (Round robin matches in this group)

Senegal	0-0	Mali
Zambia	2-0	Ivory Coast
Ivory Coast	2-0	Senegal
Mali	1-2	Zambia
Zambia	1-1	Senegal
Ivory Coast	3-1	Mali
Senegal	2-1	Zambia
Mali	1-2	Ivory Coast

Mali	1-0	Senegal
Ivory Coast	4-1	Zambia
Zambia	4-1	Mali
Senegal	1-2	Ivory Coast

Ivory Coast qualified for Beijing with 15 points. Zambia had 10, Senegal 5 and Mali 4.

Group C (Aggregate scores over two legs in Rounds One and Two)

Round 1

Rwanda	4-2	Sierra Leone
Guinea	2-0	Guinea-Bissau
Zimbabwe walk-over	v	Tanzania
Botswana walk-over	v	Mauritania

Byes – Tunisia, Morocco, Angola, Cameroon

Round 2

Botswana	1-0	Tunisia
Morocco	4-0	Rwanda
Guinea	2-0	Angola
Cameroon	4-2	Zimbabwe

Round 3

Morocco	1-0	Botswana
Cameroon	6-1	Guinea
Guinea	0-3	Morocco
Botswana	0-0	Cameroon
Guinea	2-0	Botswana
Cameroon	2-1	Morocco
Botswana	2-1	Guinea
Morocco	2-2	Cameroon
Botswana	2-0	Morocco
Guinea	1-3	Cameroon

Morocco	1-0	Guinea
Cameroon	1-0	Botswana

Cameroon qualified for Beijing with 14 points; Morocco had 10, Botswana 7, and Guinea 3.

Asia

Preliminary Round

Thailand	6-1	Turkmenistan
Indonesia	1-0	Maldives
India	2-2	Myanmar (India won on penalties)
Uzbekistan	6-1	Tajikistan
Yemen	3-2	Palestine
Hong Kong	3-1	Bangladesh
Australia	12-0	Taiwan
Pakistan	5-3	Singapore
Vietnam	2-0	Afghanistan (one leg only)
Jordan walk-over	v	Kyrgyzstan

Qualification Round

(In this round, there were six groups. The top two sides in each group went on to a Final Round.)

Group A

Qatar	2-2	Kuwait
Bahrain	8-0	Pakistan
Kuwait	3-0	Bahrain
Pakistan	0-2	Qatar
Bahrain	4-2	Qatar
Pakistan	0-3	Kuwait
Qatar	4-0	Bahrain
Kuwait	4-0	Pakistan
Pakistan	1-3	Bahrain
Kuwait	1-1	Qatar

Qatar	7-0	Pakistan
Bahrain	2-1	Kuwait

Bahrain (12 points) and Qatar (11) progressed. Kuwait also had 11, Pakistan none. Qatar had a better goal difference than Kuwait.

Group B

Syria	3-1	Malaysia
Japan	3-0	Hong Kong
Hong Kong	0-2	Syria
Malaysia	1-2	Japan
Japan	3-0	Syria
Hong Kong	0-1	Malaysia
Syria	0-2	Japan
Malaysia	0-1	Hong Kong
Hong Kong	0-4	Japan
Malaysia	0-0	Syria
Syria	4-1	Hong Kong
Japan	3-1	Malaysia

Japan (18 points) and Syria (10) went through. Malaysia had 4 points, Hong Kong 3.

Group C

Vietnam	2-0	Lebanon
Oman	3-0	Indonesia
Lebanon	1-0	Oman
Indonesia	0-1	Vietnam
Indonesia	1-2	Lebanon
Oman	3-1	Vietnam
Vietnam	2-0	Oman
Lebanon	2-1	Indonesia
Lebanon	1-0	Vietnam
Indonesia	2-1	Oman
Vietnam	2-0	Indonesia

Oman v Lebanon was not played

Vietnam (12 points) and Lebanon (12) progressed. Oman had 6, Indonesia 3.

Group D

Iran	0-0	Australia
Jordan	0-1	Saudi Arabia
Australia	1-1	Jordan
Saudi Arabia	1-0	Iran
Iran	0-0	Jordan
Australia	2-0	Saudi Arabia
Jordan	0-3	Iran
Saudi Arabia	2-1	Australia
Australia	3-1	Iran
Saudi Arabia	4-1	Jordan
Jordan	0-4	Australia
Iran	2-3	Saudi Arabia

Saudi Arabia (15 points) and Australia (11) went through. Iran had 5 points, Jordan 2.

Group E

Iraq	3-0	India
Thailand	0-1	North Korea
North Korea	2-2	Iraq
India	3-0	Thailand
Iraq	1-1	Thailand
India	0-2	North Korea
North Korea	2-1	India
Thailand	0-1	Iraq
North Korea	0-0	Thailand
India	1-1	Iraq
Thailand	2-0	India
Iraq	1-0	North Korea

Iraq (12 points) and North Korea (11) progressed. Thailand had 5, India 4.

Group F

Uzbekistan	2-1	United Arab Emirates (UAE)
South Korea	1-0	Yemen
Yemen	0-1	Uzbekistan
UAE	1-3	South Korea
Yemen	1-2	UAE
South Korea	2-0	Uzbekistan
Uzbekistan	0-1	South Korea
UAE	2-0	Yemen
Yemen	1-0	South Korea
UAE	0-2	Uzbekistan
Uzbekistan	3-0	Yemen
South Korea	3-1	UAE

South Korea (15 points) and Uzbekistan (12) went through. UAE had 6 points, Yemen 3.

Final Round Groups (A, B and C)

(Group A comprised Iraq, winners of group E, and the runner-up from C, D, and E. Group B included Bahrain and South Korea, winners of A and F, and runners-up from B and F. The most competitive group seemed to be Group C, with Japan, Vietnam, and Saudi Arabia, all winners from B, C and D, with Qatar, second in A.)

Group A (Final Round)

Iraq	0-0	Australia
North Korea	0-1	Lebanon
Australia	1-0	North Korea
Lebanon	0-5	Iraq
Australia	3-0	Lebanon
Iraq	2-0	North Korea
North Korea	0-0	Iraq
Lebanon	0-0	Australia

Lebanon	1-2	North Korea
Australia	2-0	Iraq
North Korea	1-1	Australia
Iraq	5-2	Lebanon

Australia (12 points) qualified for Beijing. Iraq had 11, North Korea 5, and Lebanon 4.

Group B (Final Round)

Syria	1-2	Bahrain
South Korea	2-1	Uzbekistan
Uzbekistan	0-0	Syria
Bahrain	0-1	South Korea
Uzbekistan	1-2	Bahrain
South Korea	1-0	Syria
Syria	0-0	South Korea
Bahrain	2-0	Uzbekistan
Uzbekistan	0-0	South Korea
Bahrain	1-1	Syria
Syria	3-3	Uzbekistan
South Korea	0-0	Bahrain

South Korea (12 points) qualified for Beijing. Bahrain had 11, Syria 4, Uzbekistan 3.

Group C (Final Round)

Qatar	1-0	Saudi Arabia
Japan	1-0	Vietnam
Vietnam	1-1	Qatar
Saudi Arabia	0-0	Japan
Vietnam	1-1	Saudi Arabia
Japan	1-0	Qatar
Qatar	2-1	Japan
Saudi Arabia	2-0	Vietnam
Vietnam	0-4	Japan

Saudi Arabia	2-1	Qatar
Qatar	3-1	Vietnam
Japan	0-0	Saudi Arabia

Japan (11 points) qualified for Beijing. Qatar had 10, Saudi Arabia 9, Vietnam 2.

Oceania

(Final Stage)

Fiji	1-2	New Zealand
New Zealand	2-0	Vanuatu
New Zealand	5-2	Papua New Guinea
New Zealand	2-0	Solomon Islands
New Zealand	8-0	Cook Islands
Fiji	7-1	Papua New Guinea
Fiji	9-0	Cook Islands
Fiji	2-0	Vanuatu
Fiji	2-3	Solomon Islands
Vanuatu	4-0	Cook Islands
Solomon Islands	11-0	Cook Islands
Solomon Islands	5-0	Vanuatu
Solomon Islands	6-1	Papua New Guinea
Papua New Guinea	7-0	Cook Islands
Papua New Guinea	7-2	Vanuatu

New Zealand qualified for Beijing with 15 points. Solomon Islands had 12, Fiji 9, Papua New Guinea 6, Vanuatu 3.

27. Paralympic football, 1984-2012

The Paralympics feature two kinds of football, 7-a-side, since 1984, and 5-a-side since 2004.

7-a-side, played by athletes with cerebral palsy, is similar to the familiar 11-a-side, with a smaller playing area, goals' size, and playing time (60 minutes). There is no offside, and throw-ins can be one-handed.

5-a-side teams must include four outfielders with visual impairments, and a sighted goalkeeper guides his colleagues as they play the ball, which has a noise-making device inside it. Every player except keepers wears an eyeshade to ensure there is equality between participants.

The central figure in Paralympic history was Dr (later Sir) Ludwig Guttman, director of Stoke Mandeville's Spinal Injuries Unit, where sport was central to patients' rehabilitation. He organised an archery contest for wheelchair athletes in 1948, as the London Olympics got underway. Only a year later, he foresaw sporting events for athletes with disabilities, that would be equivalent to the Olympics.

Although the term 'Paralympics' was not officially used until 1988, at Seoul, the Rome events in 1960 ran 'parallel' to the Olympic Games. Tokyo, Tel Aviv, Heidelberg, Toronto, Arnhem and New York hosted the contests between 1964 and 1984, when football joined the Paralympics.

Medal winners have been:

	Gold	**Silver**	**Bronze**
(7-a-side)			
1984	Belgium	Ireland	Great Britain
1988	Netherlands	Belgium	Ireland
1992	Netherlands	Portugal	Ireland
1996	Netherlands	Russia	Spain
2000	Russia	Ukraine	Brazil
2004	Ukraine	Brazil	Russia
2008	Ukraine	Russia	Iran

	Gold	**Silver**	**Bronze**
(5-a-side)			
2004	Brazil	Argentina	Spain
2008	Brazil	China	Argentina

In 1984 only, there was a wheelchair 7-a-side football event, with medals won by USA, Canada, and Great Britain.

The 2008 Summer Paralympics (7-a-side)

The 2008 Summer Paralympics (7-a-side) included eight teams: China, Ukraine, Russia, Netherlands, Great Britain, Ireland, Brazil, and Iran. Every match took place at the Olympic Green Hockey Field, Beijing.

Group A

8 September	Russia	6-0	China
8 September	Brazil	1-0	Netherlands
10 September	Russia	12-1	Netherlands
10 September	Brazil	8-0	China
12 September	Russia	3-0	Brazil
12 September	Netherlands	8-1	China

Q: Russia	9 points	21 goals for – 1 against
Q: Brazil	6 points	9-3
Netherlands	3 points	9-14
China	0 points	1-22

Q: Qualified for the semi-finals.

Group B

8 September	Iran	4-2	Ireland
8 September	Ukraine	8-1	Great Britain
10 September	Iran	3-0	Great Britain
10 September	Ukraine	7-0	Ireland
12 September	Ukraine	4-0	Iran

12 September		Great Britain	1-1	Ireland

Q: Ukraine	9 points	19-1
Q: Iran	6 points	7-6
Ireland	1 point	3-12
Great Britain	0 points	2-12

Q: Qualified for the semi-finals.

Matches to decide the 5th to 8th places

14 September	Netherlands	4-2	Great Britain
14 September	Ireland	4-1	China
16 September	Great Britain	10-2	China
16 September	Netherlands	4-2	Ireland

5th place:	Netherlands
6th place:	Great Britain
7th place:	Ireland
8th place:	China

Semi-finals

14 September	Ukraine	6-0	Brazil
14 September	Russia	5-0	Iran

Bronze medal match

16 September	Iran	4-0	Brazil

The Final

16 September	Ukraine	2-1	Russia (after extra time)

Medal winners

Gold: Ukraine

Antonyuk (captain)	Dutko	Mikhovych

Symashko	Shevchyk	Kosenko
Trushev	Devlysh	
Vakulenko	Shkvarlo	
Tsukanov		
Ponomaryov		

Silver: Russia

Potekhin (captain)	Kuvaev
Lekov	Smirnov
Murvanadze	Lozhechnikov
Borisov	Nadzharyan
Tumakov	Dzimistarishvili
Chesmin	Kolykhalov

Bronze: Iran

Mahini (captain)	Karimzadeh
Malekzadeh	Heidari-Mehr
Ansari	Najafi
Heidari	Safari
Gholam-Hosseinpour	Atash-Afrouz
Akbari	

At London 2012 the medals will be contested by Great Britain, Ukraine, Russia, Netherlands, USA, Brazil, Argentina and Iran.

The British team won bronze at the 2011 World Cup, and the squad of 12 for 2012 include:

Craig Connell	Blair Glynn	James Richmond
Billy Thompson	Josh Beacham	Alistair Patrick-Heselton
George Fletcher	Martin Sinclair	Ibrahim Diallo
Matt Dimbylow	Jonathan Paterson	Michael Barker

5-a-side football at the 2008 Paralympics

5-a-side football at the 2008 Paralympics took place in Beijing, at the Olympic Green Hockey Field. Six teams were there – China, Great Britain, Spain, Brazil, Argentina and South Korea.

Group stage

7 September	Argentina	2-0	Spain
7 September	China	3-0	Great Britain
7 September	Brazil	3-0	South Korea
9 September	Great Britain	2-1	South Korea
9 September	Brazil	1-0	Spain
9 September	China	1-0	Argentina
11 September	Brazil	0-0	Argentina
11 September	China	1-0	South Korea
11 September	Spain	3-1	Great Britain
13 September	China	1-0	Spain
13 September	Brazil	5-0	Great Britain
13 September	Argentina	2-0	South Korea
15 September	Argentina	3-1	Great Britain
15 September	South Korea	2-2	Spain
15 September	China	1-1	Brazil

1. China	13 points	7 goals for – 1 against	
2. Brazil	11 points	10-1	
3. Argentina	10 points	7-2	
4. Spain	4 points	5-7	
5. Great Britain	3 points	4-15	
6. South Korea	1 point	3-10	

17 September: Great Britain 1-1 South Korea (Great Britain won on penalty decider)
    Great Britain finished 5th, South Korea 6th.

Bronze medal match

17 September	Argentina	1-1	Spain (Argentina won on penalty decider)

The Final

17 September   Brazil   2-1   China

The medal winners

Gold: Brazil

Vasconcelos (captain)	Felipe
Soares	Oliveira
Ramos	J. Silva
S. Silva	Goncalves
Alves	Rego

Silver: China

Xiaoqiang (captain)	Zheng
Zheng	Qiang
Zhoubin	Yutan
Shanyong	Xinqiang
Yafeng	Wenfa

Bronze: Argentina

Velo (captain)	Lencina
Hachache	Mendoza
Diaz	Maidana
Cerega	Figueroa
Rodriguez	Jimenez

For the first time, eight teams will compete in London 2012.

The British squad are: Dan James, Lewis Skyers, Dave Clarke, Dan English, Darren Harris, Robin Williams, Keryn Seal, Lee Brunton, Will Norman, Roy Turnham.

Britain won bronze at the 2011 European Championships, and include Dave Clarke, who has received the Golden Boot at three World Cups. In April 2012 he summed up what the event means to him, and to many other Paralympic footballers.

'This is the realisation of a lifetime dream, to compete at the pinnacle of my sport and on home soil in front of our own fans.'

28. London, 2012

London pride

For a record third time, London was awarded the Olympics in 2005, ahead of bids from Paris, Madrid, New York and Moscow.

The 2012 Games are big, with 10,500 athletes from 205 countries in 26 sports, over 19 days. There are 29 venues – 8 in the Olympic Park, 12 elsewhere in London, 9 in other parts of the UK. 'Co-host city venues' include 5 football stadia as well as Wembley Stadium. Aquatic events also take place in Hertfordshire, Buckinghamshire, and Dorset, while mountain bikers head for Essex.

2012 is also a year of fine detail. The new Olympic Park Velodrome has banking angled at 42 degrees at its steepest; badminton shuttlecocks can move up to 400 kilometres an hour.

The official ticket guides for Olympics and Paralympics are not shy, referring to 'The greatest tickets on Earth' and 'Sport like never before'. 2012 mascots appear – 'Wenlock' recalls Dr William Penny Brookes's Much Wenlock Olympic Games from 1850, and 'Mandeville' the Paralympic origins at Stoke Mandeville.

The guides' forewords by Lord Coe are emotional, speaking of 'passion', 'drama', 'this once-in-a-lifetime experience' which is 'exciting', 'fantastic'. Pierre de Coubertin wrote hundreds of essays and speeches with comparable enthusiasm for his Olympic dream, and would approve the emphasis on how this 30th Olympiad enlivens and benefits everyone concerned.

Six football stadia host matches, and each has a story of its own. St James's Park, Newcastle, is the veteran from 1892, while Hampden Park in Glasgow was the biggest venue in the world when it opened in 1903, and Old Trafford, Manchester dates from 1910. All three were considerably renovated and expanded about a century later.

The Millennium Stadium in Cardiff opened in 1999, The City of Coventry Stadium six years later, and Wembley Stadium is the newest, from 2007, built on the site of its famous predecessor.

As is now standard, 16 teams take part in the men's football tournament, 12 in the women's.

The men's participants are:

Hosts: Great Britain
Europe: Switzerland, Belarus, Spain
North and Central America: Mexico, Honduras
South America: Uruguay, Brazil
Africa: Senegal, Gabon, Egypt, Morocco
Asia: UAE (United Arab Emirates), South Korea, Japan
Oceania: New Zealand

Group matches take place between 26 July and 1 August. The winners and runners-up from each group progress to quarter-finals (4 August). Semi-finals follow on 7 August, the bronze medal match on 10 August and Final on 11 August. As the official Guide states, this 'intense schedule' requires football matches to begin before the Opening Ceremony (27 July).

Group A

The hosts join Uruguay, Senegal and UAE in this group. Uruguay came second in the South American qualifying event (The Under-20 Campeonato Sudamericano). After early defeats, they recovered to beat Argentina, so that the 2008 gold medallists did not qualify. Uruguay, like Argentina, have won this tournament twice, in 1924 and 1928.

Senegal took their place by defeating Angola, Tunisia, Nigeria and then Oman in an April 2012 play-off. The UAE beat Sri Lanka, North Korea and Australia to reach the last 16.

But the most singular route was taken by Great Britain, without playing a match. The British football team last contested qualifiers for the 1972 Olympics, and Rome 1960 was the most recent tournament they were part of.

The re-forming of a British side was a key element of the London bid, backed by Lord Coe, the British Olympic Association and the FA in England. However the Football Associations in Scotland, Wales and Northern Ireland opposed the move.

To use an equestrian analogy, supporters of a GB football entry, with automatic qualification as hosts, saw a unique opportunity – a 'gift horse' to welcome. Opponents presented the move as a 'Trojan horse', a precedent which FIFA might later use to dilute the four home nations' privileges and separate teams.

The controversy was at its height in 2009, when MPs spent 90 minutes debating whether there should be a British team. Later that year, a compromise enabled English players to represent Great Britain, although individuals from all four countries expressed interest in playing at the 2012 tournament. The GB football managers, Stuart Pearce and Hope Powell, selected the men's and women's teams entirely on merit.

The men's squad is Joe Allen, Craig Bellamy, Ryan Bertrand, Jack Butland, Steven Caulker, Tom Cleverley, Jack Cork, Craig Dawson, Ryan Giggs, Aaron Ramsey, Micah Richards, Danny Rose, Scott Sinclair, Marvin Sordell, Jason Steele, Daniel Sturridge, Neil Taylor, James Tomkins.

Group B

Switzerland, Mexico, Gabon and South Korea meet in this Group. The Swiss, silver medallists in 1924, have rarely appeared in this event, but in UEFA's Under-21 championship (2011), they finished second to Spain. Teams they overcame included Iceland, Denmark, Belarus and the Czech Republic. Outstanding players were their keeper Sommer, defenders Klose and Rossini, and forwards Mehmedi and Shaqiri.

In qualifying, Mexico won every match against Trinidad and Tobago, Panama, Honduras and Canada. The surprise was that the USA, playing in Nashville, missed out.

Gabon's victories over Swaziland, Mali and Morocco – another qualifying team – were the key to their first tournament. South Korea gained more points than Oman, Saudi Arabia and Qatar, who were their closest rivals.

Group C

Belarus, Brazil, Egypt and New Zealand are the Group C teams. Belarus reached their first tournament, despite early defeats by Denmark and Switzerland, after a win over the Czech Republic.

Brazil were the most successful Under-20 team in their continent, with a series of victories including an emphatic 6-0 result against Uruguay. Egypt won against Botswana, Sudan, Senegal and Gabon in their qualifying campaign.

New Zealand are Oceania's representatives, after narrow victories over Papua New Guinea, Vanuato and Fiji.

Group D

Spain are the current Under-21 champions of Europe, following Euro 2008 and 2010 World Cup successes. When UEFA judges chose their Under-21 'team of the tournament' in 2011, they included seven Spanish players – De Gea, in goal, Vila in defence, midfielders Herrera, Martinez and Alcantara, forwards Lopez and Mata. Their Group D rivals are Honduras, Morocco and Japan, but the Euro 2012 champion nation are favourites.

Honduras qualified with successes against Panama, Trinidad and Tobago, and El Salvador. Morocco defeated Mozambique, the Democratic Republic of Congo, and Nigeria, while Japan came through matches against Bahrain, Malaysia, Syria and Kuwait.

The women's teams are:

Hosts: Great Britain
Europe: Sweden, France
North and Central America: Canada, USA,
South America: Brazil, Colombia
Africa: Cameroon, South Africa
Asia: Japan, North Korea
Oceania: New Zealand

There are three Groups, with the top two teams in each Group going on to quarter-finals alongside the two best performing third placed teams.

Group matches are played between 25 and 31 July, the quarter-finals on 3 August. Semi-finals take place on 6 August, the bronze medal game and the Final both on 9 August.

Group E

Great Britain, Brazil, Cameroon and New Zealand play in this Group. While a British men's team last played over 40 years ago, this is the first appearance in any football event by the British women's team, which includes Eniola Aluko, Anita Asante, Karen Bardsley, Sophie Bradley, Rachel Brown, Karen Carney, Ifeoma Dieke, Steph Houghton, Kim Little, Claire Rafferty, Alex Scott, Jill Scott, Kelly Smith, Casey Stoney, Fara Williams, Rachel Williams, Ellen White, Rachel Yankey. The four reserves are Jess Clarke, Emma Higgins, Jane Ross, Dunia Susi.

Brazil, silver medal winners in 2004 and 2008, have in Marta a player regularly chosen as FIFA's best in the world.

New Zealand will look to stars such as Hayley Moorwood, the Chelsea midfielder, while Cameroon hope to build on recent success at the African Games.

Group F

Sweden, Canada, South Africa and Japan form this Group. Japan are the current World Cup champions, losing only to England and defeating Germany, Sweden and the USA on penalties. Their outstanding players are Kaihon, in goal, and midfielders Miyama, Ohno and Sawa.

Sweden lost only to Japan in the World Cup semi-final, and will look to Almgren, Schelin and Seger to build on recent improvements. Canada qualified by winning every match in their zone (CONCACAF) of North and Central America, except for the final match against USA.

South Africa came through fixtures with Zambia, Tunisia and Ethiopia to their first Olympic event.

Group G

The USA join France, Colombia and North Korea at this stage. The Americans' record of three golds and a silver is unrivalled, and team members like Solo, in goal, and forwards Boxx, Cheney and Wambach are experienced Olympians.

France reached the 2011 World Cup semi-finals, defeating Canada and Nigeria but losing to the USA. This is their first Olympics, but Bussaglia, only 26, already has 99 caps.

Colombia, also at their first Games, lost only to Brazil in qualification, where they had several goals in hand against Uruguay and Venezuela. North Korea return for their second event with a team whose average age is only 19.

Looking at the three London tournaments reveals intriguing contrasts. In 1908 six teams played in October, months after track and field athletes had gone home. Every match was held at 'The great stadium', usually called White City, and medals went to Great Britain, Denmark, and the Netherlands.

1948 brought together 18 teams and 11 venues, so for men's football this was a bigger event than 2012, but there were no women's football teams. The successful sides were Sweden (fourth in 1908), Yugoslavia and Denmark, with Britain fourth.

Martin Polley's book, 'The British Olympics' (2011), illustrates some fascinating links between the three London Games. Henry Taylor, 'a swimming legend', won three gold medals in 1908, a British record now equalled by Sir Chris Hoy. A plaque at his local Chadderton Baths, near Oldham, pays tribute to a swimmer who competed in four Olympics, broke world records and won eight medals, four gold, in an illustrious career.

Just one venue hosts events in 1948 and 2012. Wembley Arena (formerly called The Empire Pool and Sports Arena) presented swimming and diving in 1948, now badminton will be the featured sport.

A short distance away, inside the new Wembley Stadium, is a substantial link between the generations. This is the 1948 Olympic Roll of Honour, listing every winner on a series of ceramic tiles which weigh 18 tons.

Another important, if intangible, connection between the three London Olympics is Pierre de Coubertin's dictum, highlighted at every Games since 1932. 'The important thing in the Olympic Games is not winning but taking part'. He first made those comments while attending the 1908 events.

In his remarks, he consciously echoed words spoken a few days earlier. Research by Ture Widlund discovered that Ethelbert Talbot, Bishop of Central Pennsylvania, preached at St Paul's Cathedral to Olympic athletes and officials on 19 July 1908. Appropriately, he drew upon St Paul's letters in his sermon, and said 'The Games themselves are better than the race and the prize ... Though only one may wear the laurel wreath, all may share the equal joy of the contest.' (quoted in T. Widlund, 1994).

Joy and pride in the Olympics are not reserved for winners, for every participant, volunteer, torch bearer, official, organiser, spectator can be moved by those positive emotions.

'London pride' is also a flower, known formally as 'Saxifraga x urbium', a hardy, tolerant perennial. Resilient rather than ostentatious, it has small petals shaped like stars, and enhances gardens in cities like its namesake.

There an interesting coincidence arises.

Each flower has its own special day, and London pride's happens to be 27 July. How appropriate that on that day, the 2012 Games officially begin.

29. Olympic footballers and lifelong memories

Everyone at the Olympics has a personal story of the honour of being present, as well as expectation, disappointment or success. Playing your part for team and nation in a global setting is unique, as Pierre de Coubertin recognised when he set the ball rolling.

Three footballers who played their part can look back on lifelong memories. Bill Slater, Peter Buchanan and Millar Hay were members of the British team in 1952, 1964 and 1968.

Bill Slater has known a career as one of the great half backs of the 1950s and 60s. He was still an amateur when he played for Blackpool in the 1951 Cup Final against Newcastle United. After a short stay at Brentford, he helped make Wolverhampton Wanderers the outstanding club of the decade – League Champions three times, Cup winners in 1960.

12 England caps meant he often played beside his club captain, Billy Wright, and went to the 1958 World Cup in Sweden. His award as Footballer of the Year recognised a rare combination of skills and sportsmanship; he never received a caution.

1952 was a significant year – just before joining Wolves, he was selected for the British Olympic team.

In July the players flew to Lahti, in Finland, for their match against Luxembourg. Instead of a simple victory, the score remained 1-1 after 90 minutes. Extra time produced many more opportunities and goals, one scored by Bill Slater, but Britain encountered an inspired keeper and lost the match.

Despite that, Bill was determined to learn all he could from the Helsinki Olympics. He watched the Hungarians and wrote a report on their tactics and performance, as Puskas's team swept on to gold. Possibly the greatest Olympic side of all time, their preparation was professional in every sense.

He realised that amateur teams could not compete with them, and neither could most full international elevens. That experience gave him insight into how sport was changing, and in 1961 he predicted a Premier League in England, over 30 years before it began.

Today, he looks forward to London 2012, with hopes that a Great Britain team can achieve success in the country which gave the world, and the Olympics, the sport he has enhanced.

★ ★ ★

Peter Buchanan is the third generation of his family to play for Queen's Park, Scotland's original club. Between 1959 and 1969, he was their centre-forward with over 150 goals, scoring from half-chances and any distance. In one season he hit 32, and could have moved to several top English clubs.

Instead, he remained with Queen's Park and became a member of Scotland's amateur squad. In 1963 they won an International Tournament to celebrate the FA's Centenary, defeating Italy and West Germany. A year earlier, his club had won 1-0 against Eintracht Frankfurt, with his the only goal.

He was selected for Great Britain at the Olympic qualifying event in 1963-4. Although injury prevented his appearing against Iceland in the first Round, he did play in both matches against Greece.

'We had get-togethers at Chelsea Barracks', he recalls. 'We played friendlies against Chelsea, Manchester United, Coventry City, and the squad also included Queen's Parkers Billy Neil, Bert Cromar, and John Pollatchek as reserve.'

There was elation at scoring in Britain's 2-1 win over Greece at Stamford Bridge, and of equalising in Athens, albeit in a defeat which gave Greece the aggregate result they wanted.

Just 48 hours later came the news that Greece's players were professionals, and the Greek Olympic Committee withdrew them from the next round of the tournament.

Nevertheless, for Peter Buchanan, nothing can equal the honour of being recognised as an outstanding goal-scorer and one of the best British amateurs of his time.

★ ★ ★

During the next Olympiad, Millar Hay was also at Queen's Park and then moved to Clyde in 1968. He was a midfielder in a 4-4-2 formation, as football moved irrevocably away from a fixed 2-3-5 line-up.

When he was chosen for the British Olympic team, he was eager to take that unique opportunity. The team coach, Charles Hughes, was 'dogmatic' but he ran the squad of amateurs in a professional manner. And that meant professional in the best sense, 'in training, preparation and organisation. We would train at Bisham Abbey, play matches against Chelsea, Arsenal, Watford, and international friendlies'.

Because Mexico were hosting the Olympics and World Cup in 1968 and 1970, the FA hoped to learn from those Olympic footballers' experience – if they reached the last 16 – when preparing the England squad for extreme height and heat. 'We would have undergone altitude training to prepare for Mexican conditions' in October 1968, and Millar was looking forward to the challenge.

However, GB still had to defeat Spain, whose amateurs came from clubs such as Real Madrid, Espanol and Atletico Bilbao.

In March 1968, the teams met in Sabadell, where Spain scored the only goal after seven minutes. Millar remembers that one tackle caused a stress fracture to his leg, though he only realised that weeks later.

Britain, one goal down, had high hopes for the return at London's White City. (Charles Hughes wanted the match to take place at Wembley to inspire his team, but did not get his wish). Still, a reasonable crowd of 23,000 cheered the home team that April night, and the official programme described Millar as a 'tireless worker, with a flair for the unexpected 25 yarder' shot at goal.

His side had most of the possession and the chances, but crosses would not produce even one goal. The conspicuous White City clocks made players and spectators all too aware that time was running out. Late in the match, Hendon's Roddy Haider came off the bench, ran clear through with the best chance to score and take the game into extra time. Instead, his shot went over the bar.

Like other British Olympians, Millar Hay still recalls those months as a unique facet of his career, representing the whole country and being part of what is now called Team GB.

★ ★ ★

This book began with 'the problem' of Olympic football – it ends by considering how many fine teams and individuals have graced the competitions. The following would comprise a remarkable squad, with a few reserves of note.

Vivian Woodward	(Great Britain, 1908-12)
Nils Middelboe	(Denmark, 1908-20)
Pedro Petrone	(Uruguay, 1924-8)
Nils Liedholm	(Sweden, 1948)
Gunnar Nordahl	(Sweden, 1948)
Ferenc Puskas	(Hungary, 1952)
Gyula Grosics	(Hungary, 1952)
Sandor Kocsis	(Hungary, 1952)
Nandor Hidegkuti	(Hungary, 1952)

Lev Yashin	(USSR, 1956)
Gianni Rivera	(Italy, 1960)
Antal Dunai	(Hungary, 1964–72)
Ferenc Bene	(Hungary, 1964)
Kunishige Kamamoto	(Japan, 1964–8)
Kazmierz Deyna	(Poland, 1972)
Michel Platini	(France, 1976)
Jurgen Klinsmann	(West Germany, 1988)
Romario	(Brazil, 1988)
Bebeto	(Brazil, 1988–96)
Ronaldo	(Brazil, 1996)
Hernan Crespo	(Argentina, 1996)
Nwankwo Kanu	(Nigeria, 1996–2000)
Patrick M'Boma	(Cameroon, 2000)
Lionel Messi	(Argentina, 2008)

Those players and thousands more contested qualifying matches, final tournaments and medal deciders.

All played their own, irreplaceable roles.

Footballers, at the Olympics.

Bibliography

J. Arlott (1975) 'The Oxford companion to sports and games' (OUP)
K. Baker (2008) 'The 1908 Olympics: the first London Games' (SportsBooks)
T. Bijkerk (1998) 'The football tournament at the Games of the IXth Olympiad, Amsterdam 1928' (Journal of Olympic History, 1998)
British Olympic Association (various dates) Reports from each Olympic Games, Handbooks, Books of instructions to competitors (In The British Olympic Library, University of East London)
M. Busby with D. Jack (1957) 'My Story' (Souvenir Press)
R.W. Cox (1994) 'History of sport – a guide to the literature and sources of information' (British Society of Sport Historians)
R. Crampsey (1967) 'The game for the game's sake' (Queen's Park FC)
H. Davies (2007) 'The bumper book of football' (Quercus)
J. Findling and K. Pelle (eds) (2004) 'Encyclopaedia of the modern Olympic movement' (Greenwood Press)
D. Goldblatt (2006) 'The ball is round' (Viking)
D. Goldblatt and J. Acton (2011) 'How to watch the Olympics' (Profile)
S. Greenberg (2012) 'The Olympic almanack' (SportsBooks) (8th edition)
J. Hampton (2008) 'The austerity Olympics: when the Games came to London' (Aurum)
C. Hilton (2006) 'Hitler's Olympics – the 1936 Berlin Olympic Games' (Sutton Publishing)
C. Hunt (2006) 'World Cup stories: the history of the World Cup' (Interact)
N. Jacobs (2005) 'Vivian Woodward, football's gentleman' (Tempus)
B. James (2007) 'Queen's Park Football Club' (Stadia)
R. Jenkins (2008) 'The first London Olympics of 1908' (Piatkus)
C. Jose (2004) 'Complete results and line-ups of the Olympic Football tournaments, 1900-2004' (Soccer Books)
C. Jose (n.d.) 'Galt FC, Olympic Champions 1904' (canadiansoccerhistory.com)
S. Kent (2008) 'Olympic follies: the madness and mayhem of the 1908 London Games' (JR Books)

Bill Mallon and his co-authors wrote a series of books about the early Olympics, all published by McFarland and Company. They have identical titles, except for the year of the Games.

B. Mallon (1997) 'The 1896 Olympic Games: Results for all competitors in all events with commentary'
B. Mallon (1997) 'The 1900 Olympic Games: Results for all competitors in all events with commentary'
B. Mallon (1999) 'The 1904 Olympic Games: Results for all competitors in all events with commentary'
B. Mallon (1999) 'The 1906 Olympic Games: Results for all competitors in all events with commentary'
B. Mallon and I. Buchanan (2000) 'The 1908 Olympic Games: Results for all competitors in all events with commentary'
B. Mallon and T. Widlund (2001) 'The 1912 Olympic Games: Results for all competitors in all events with commentary'
B. Mallon and A. Bijkerk (2003) 'The 1920 Olympic Games: Results for all competitors in all events with commentary'
J. MacAloon (1981) 'This great symbol: Pierre de Coubertin and the origins of the modern Olympic Games' (University of Chicago Press)
S. Menary (2010) 'GB United? British Olympic football' (Pitch)
D. Miller (2008) 'The official history of the Olympic Games and the IOC' (Mainstream)

Olympic Reports have been issued for every Games, and their authors or editors are listed here, with their publishing committees and dates of publication. These official reports are accessible through the website la84foundation.org.

1896 Olympics: P. de Coubertin, T. Philemon, N.G. Politis and C. Anninos, Central Olympic Committee, Athens, 1896
1900: F. Peck (summary in English of the French Ministry's Report) 'Programme of the international contests of physical exercises and sports' New York, 1900
1904: J.E. Sullivan (ed.) New York, Spalding, 1905
1908: T.A. Cook. British Olympic Council, 1908
1912: E. Bergvall (ed.), translated by E. Adams, Stockholm Organising Committee of the Olympic Games, 1912
1920: A. Verdyck (ed.) Belgian Olympic Committee, 1920
1924: French Olympic Committee, 1925
1928: G. Van Rossem, Netherlands Olympic Committee, 1930
1932: G. Browne (ed.) Los Angeles Organising Committee, 1933
1936: Berlin Olympic Organising Committee, 1936
1948: Lord Burghley (ed.) London Olympic Organising Committee, 1951

1952: S. Kolkka (ed.) Organising Committee for the Helsinki Olympic Games, 1955

1956: Melbourne Olympic Games Organising Committee, 1958

1960: R. Giacomini, translated by E. Byatt, Organising Committee of the Rome Olympic Games, 1960

1964: Tokyo Olympic Organising Committee, 1964

1968: B. Trueblood (ed.) Mexico City Olympic Games Organising Committee, 1968

1972: L. Diem and E. Knoesel, Munich Olympic Games Organising Committee, 1972

1976: R. Rousseau (ed.) Montreal Olympic Games Organising Committee, 1978

1980: Moscow Olympic Games Organising Committee, 1981

1984: Los Angeles Olympic Organising Committee, 1984

1988: S-K. Roh, K-H. Lee and B-J. Lee (eds) Seoul, Korean Textbook Co. Ltd, 1989

1992: R. Coyas (ed.) Barcelona Olympic Organising Committee, 1992

1996: G.T. Watkins (1997) Atlanta Committee for the Olympic Games (Peachtree Publishers)

2000: K. Toohey (ed.) (2000) Sydney Organising Committee for the Olympic Games

2004: Athens Olympic Organising Committee (2004)

2008: Beijing Organising Committee for the Games of the 29th Olympiad (2008)

B. Phillips (2007) 'The 1948 Olympics – how London rescued the Games' (SportsBooks)

M. Polley (2011) 'The British Olympics' (English Heritage)

F. Puskas (1955, reissued 2007) 'Captain of Hungary' (Tempus)

J. Rookwood and C. Buckley (2007) 'The significance of the Olympic soccer tournament, 1908-1928' (Journal of Olympic History, vol. 15, no. 1)

S. Rous (1948) 'Great Britain and the Olympic Games' (Olympic Review, May 1948)

M.L. Smith (2004) 'Olympics in Athens, 1896' (Profile Books)

A.J. Veal (2011) 'The Olympic Games: a bibliography' Australian Centre for Olympic Studies, University of Technology, Sydney

D. Wallechinsky (2008) 'The complete book of the Olympics' (Aurum)

T. Widlund (1994) 'Ethelbert Talbot, his life and place in Olympic history' ('Citius, Altius, Fortius', May 1994)

D.C. Young (1996) 'The modern Olympics: a struggle for revival' (Johns Hopkins)

Websites

boa.org.uk
fifa.com
la84foundation.org
linguasport.com (Olympic football information, maintained by Santiago Velasco)
london2012.com
olympic.org
paralympic.org
rsssf.com (website of Rec. Sport. Soccer Statistics Foundation) and its authors: Lars Aarhus, Macario Reyes, Soren Elbech, Karel Stokkermans, Mikael Jonsson, Russell Gerrard, Miran Goihman, Heiki Pietarinen, Thomas Esamie, Hans van Haren, Josef Bobrowsky, Antonio Zea, Hamden Saaid, Juan Pablo Andres, and Osvaldo Jose Gorgazzi.
womensoccer.com

A note on the 1906 tournament

Athens hosted 'Intercalated' Olympics in April and May 1906, between the 1904 and 1908 Games. (These 'inserted' Olympics were planned as the first of regular Athens Olympics in 1910, 1914 etc, which did not ensue.) At first the IOC regarded these as official, with their 'Olympic Review' issuing a souvenir edition for 'The Olympic Games of Athens' in April 1906.

Much later, however, the IOC removed that official status, and 1906 no longer features in the roll-call of Games and medals, despite historians' arguments that this was a genuine, well organised Olympic event.

Four football teams took part in 23-25 April 1906, with Denmark easily the strongest side. The results of four matches at the Neo Phaliron Velodrome were:

23 April	Greece	5-0	Thessaloniki
23 April	Denmark	5-1	Smyrna
24 April	Denmark	9-0	Greece (Greece withdrew at half-time)
25 April	Smyrna	3-0	Thessaloniki (Second place match)

Denmark's winning squad were: V. Andersen, P. Pedersen, von Buchwald, Ferslev, Rasmussen, A. Andersen, Nielsen-Norland, C. Pedersen, Frederiksen, Lindgren, Rambusch, Herup.

Smyrna were an international team, including a British forward line, all named Whittal. Donald and Harold were brothers, and their cousins, Albert, Edward and Godfrey, were siblings.